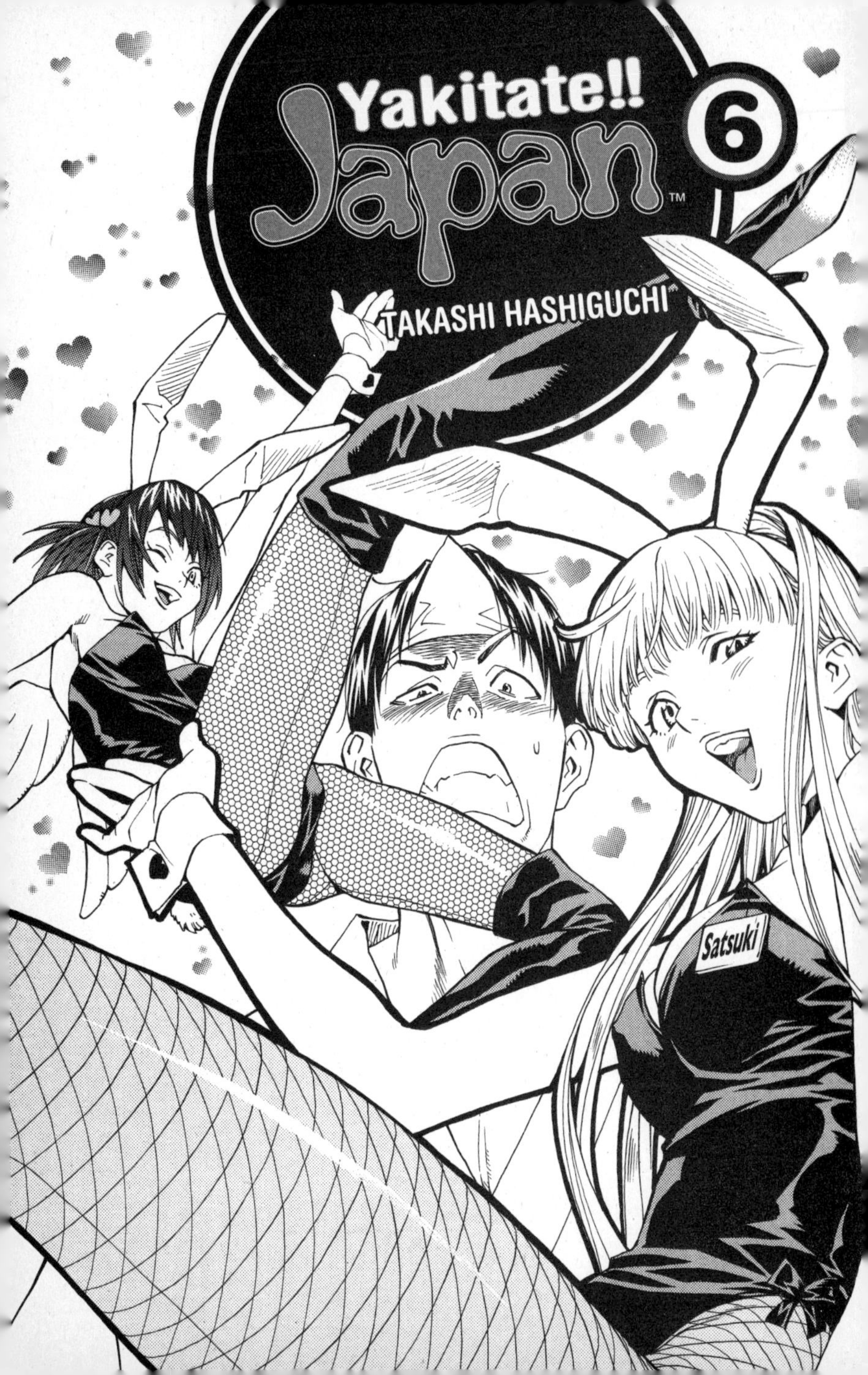
Yakitate!! Japan™ 6
TAKASHI HASHIGUCHI
Satsuki

YAKITATE!! JAPAN
6
VIZ Media Edition

★The Story Thus Far★

English bread, German bread, and French bread are well known to the world... but there is no national bread of Japan—no "Ja-pan"! A boy named Kazuma Azuma has decided to change that fact.

Tsukino Azusagawa—scion of the family that owns the popular bakery chain Pantasia—recognized Kazuma's talent and hired him, along with a knowledgeable baker named Kyosuke Kawachi, to work at Pantasia's South Tokyo Branch.

Now the two young bakers are participating in Pantasia Group's annual Rookie Tournament. Both of them advanced through the preliminaries and the early stages of the tournament, but Kawachi lost in the semifinals after Tsukino's half-sister, Yukino, sabotaged his ingredients.

Meanwhile, Azuma has unveiled Ja-pan Number 44 in his semifinal match against Suwabara—who is considered the greatest rookie ever. Then the competition took a tragic turn when the examiner, Kuroyanagi, died after taking a bite of Azuma's bread...

CONTENTS

Research Assistance/Bakery Consultant:
Koichi Uchimura.

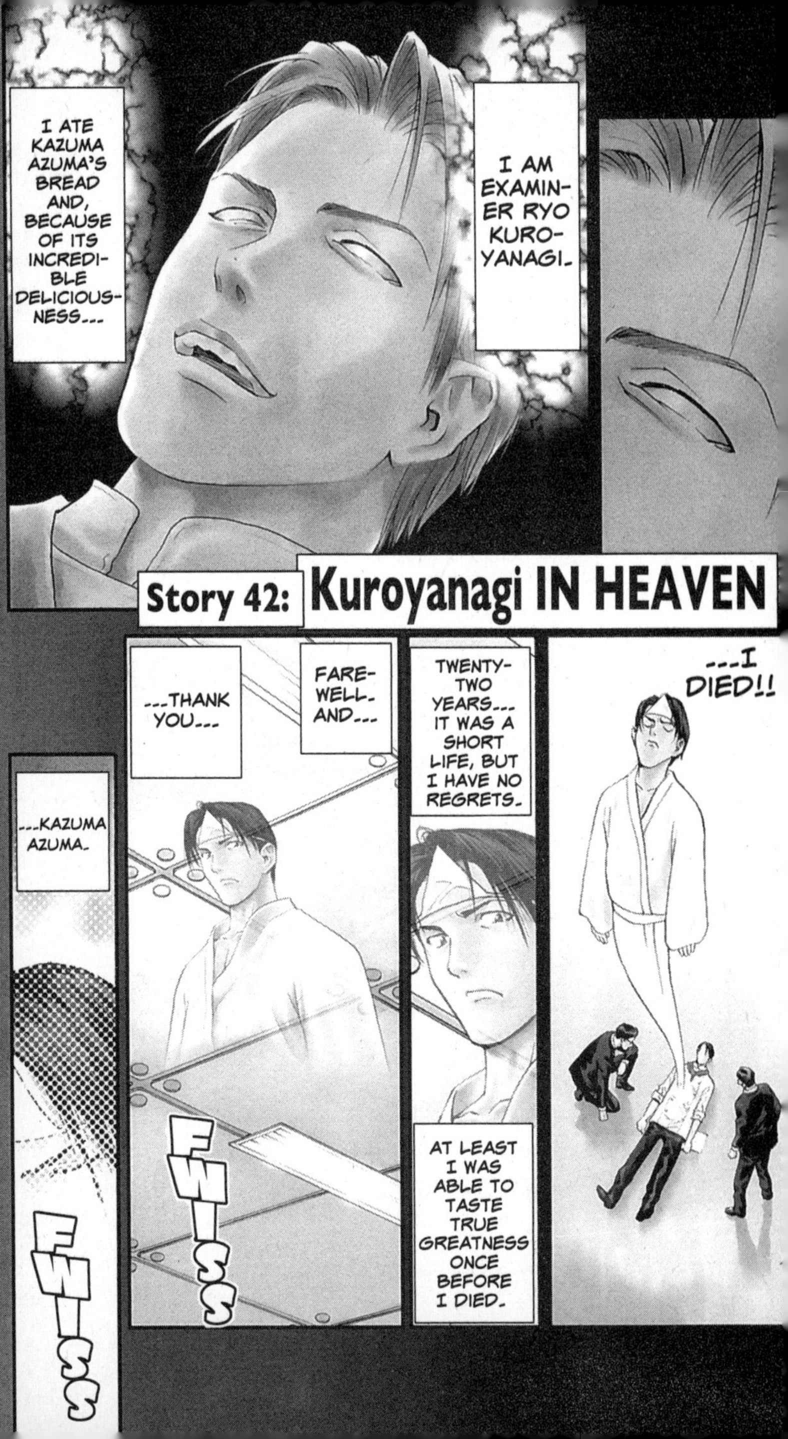
I AM EXAMINER RYO KUROYANAGI.
I ATE KAZUMA AZUMA'S BREAD AND, BECAUSE OF ITS INCREDIBLE DELICIOUSNESS...
Story 42: Kuroyanagi IN HEAVEN
...I DIED!!
TWENTY-TWO YEARS... IT WAS A SHORT LIFE, BUT I HAVE NO REGRETS.
AT LEAST I WAS ABLE TO TASTE TRUE GREATNESS ONCE BEFORE I DIED.
FAREWELL AND...
...THANK YOU...
FWISS
...KAZUMA AZUMA.
FWISS

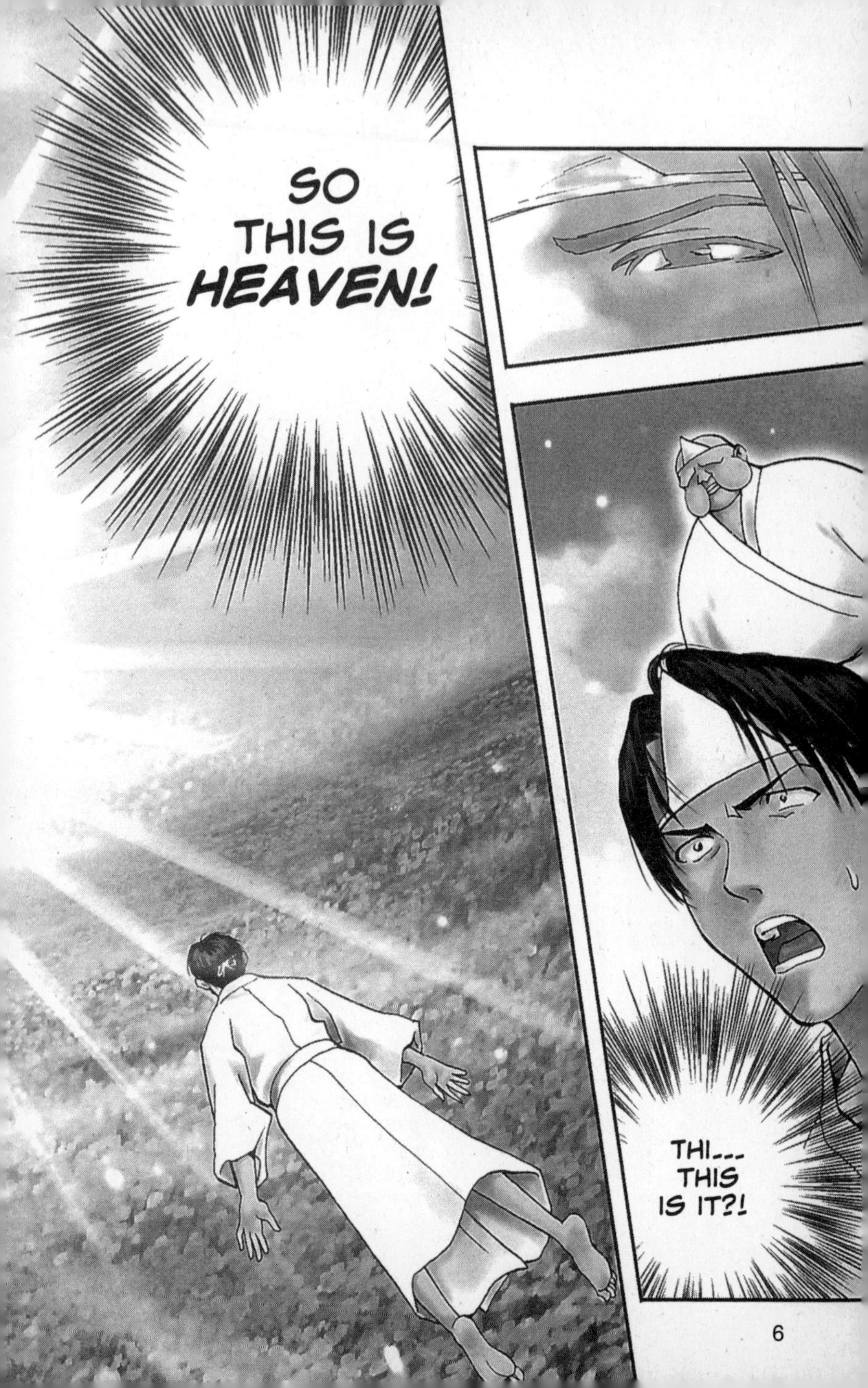
THI--- THIS IS IT?!
SO THIS IS HEAVEN!

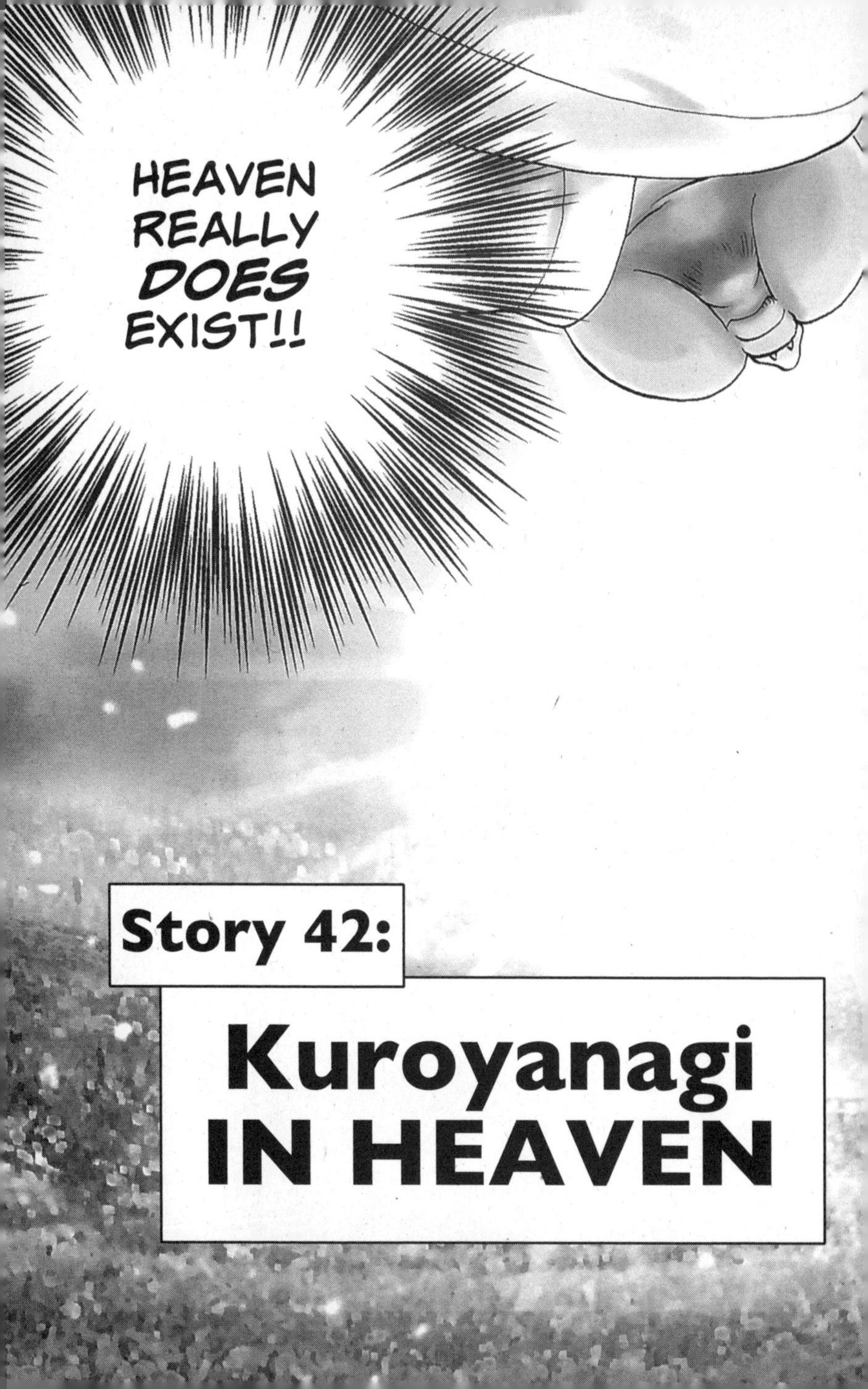
HEAVEN REALLY DOES EXIST!!

Story 42: Kuroyanagi IN HEAVEN

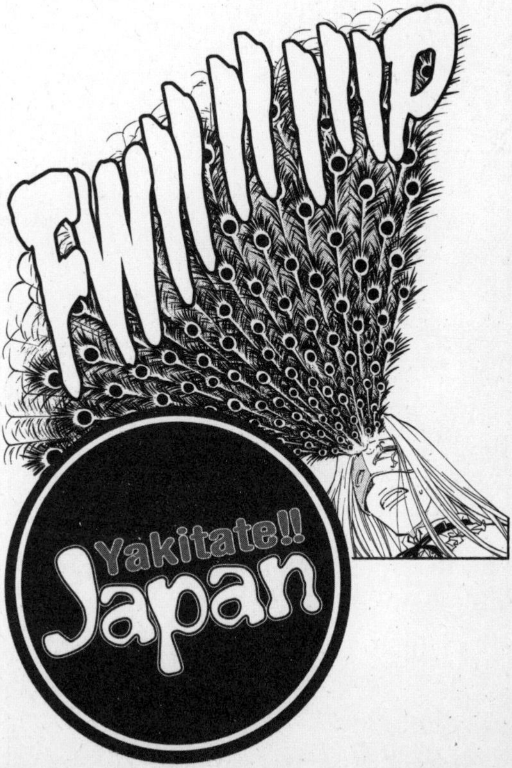
FWIIIIIIP
Yakitate!!
Japan

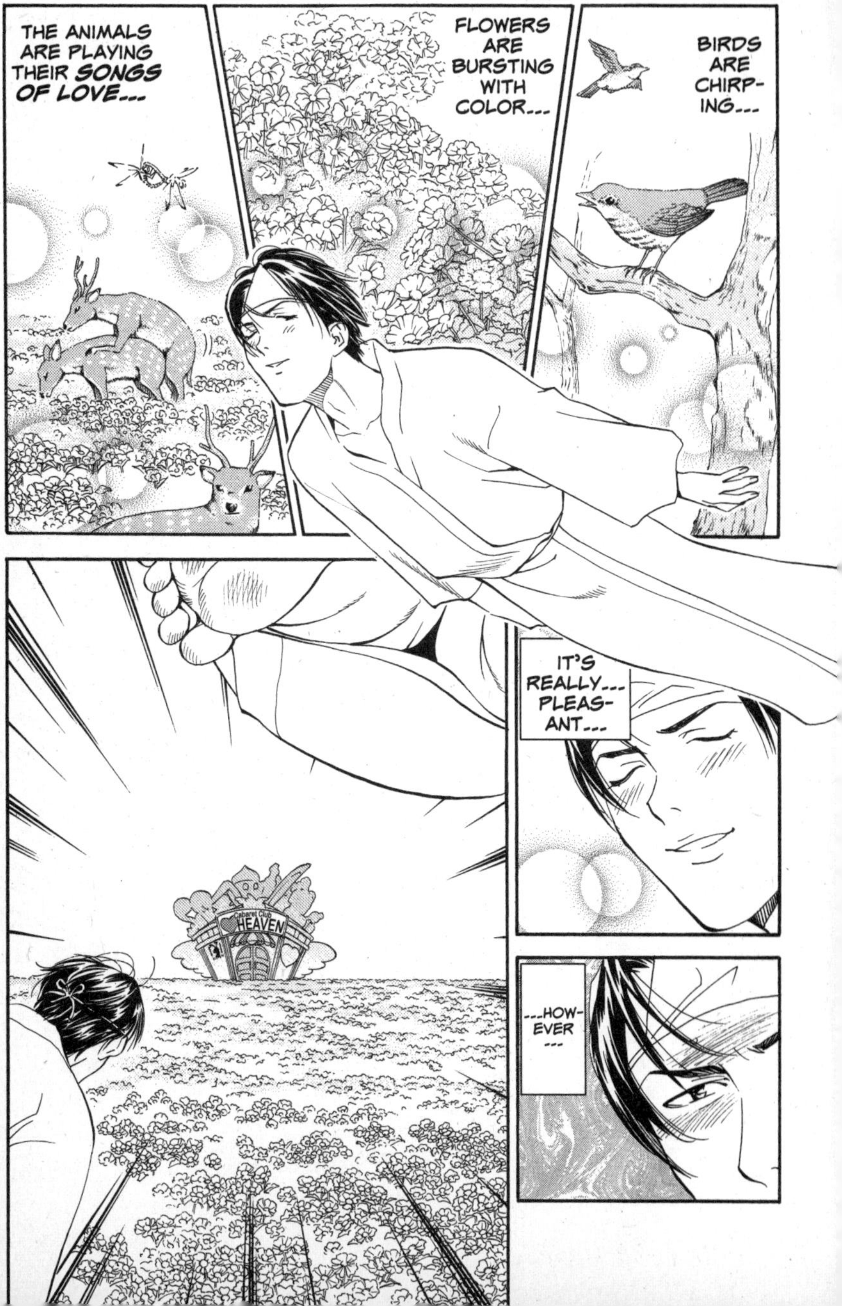
BIRDS ARE CHIRP-ING...
FLOWERS ARE BURSTING WITH COLOR...
THE ANIMALS ARE PLAYING THEIR SONGS OF LOVE...
IT'S REALLY... PLEAS-ANT...
...HOW-EVER...
Cabaret Club HEAVEN

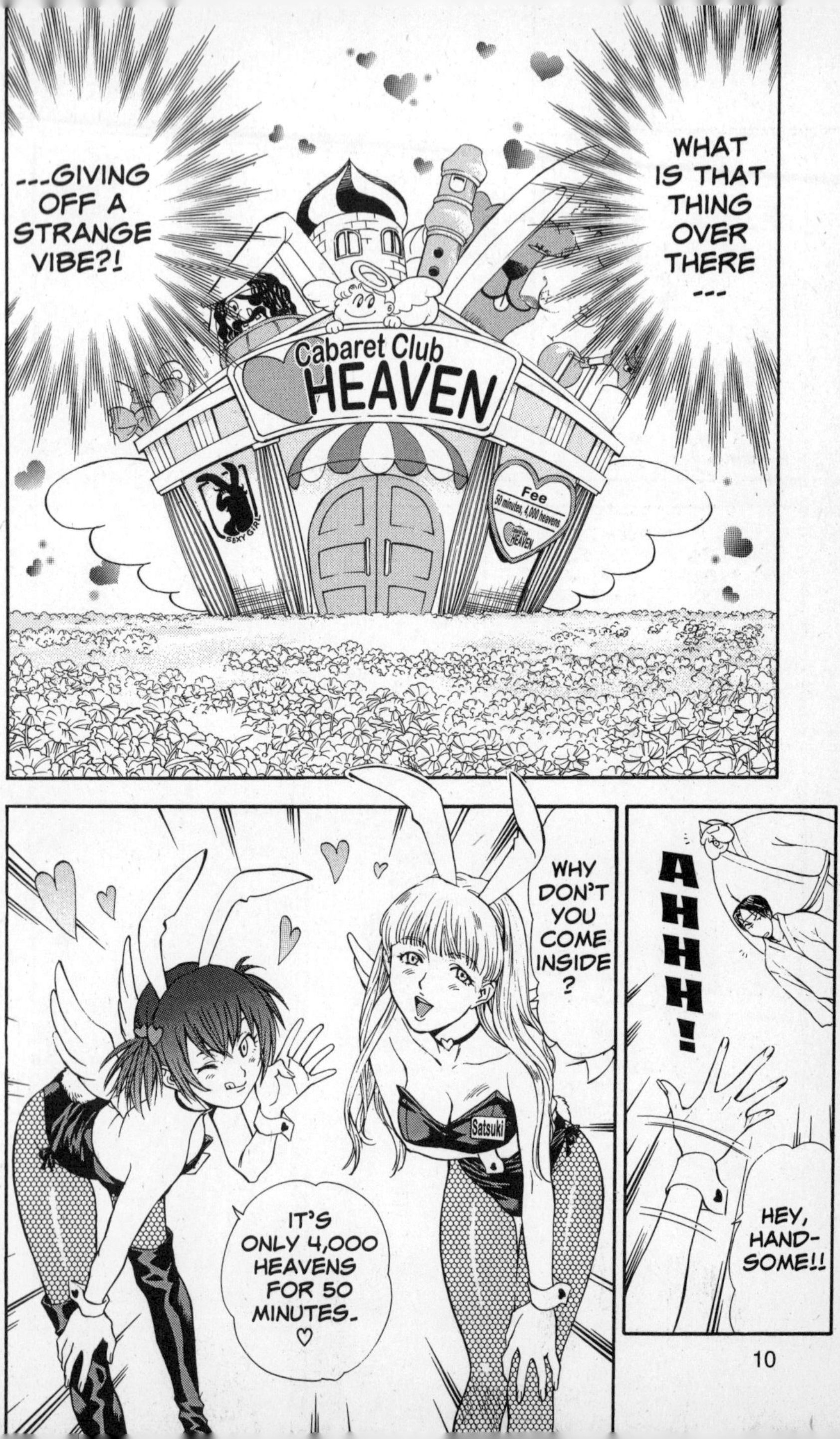
WHAT IS THAT THING OVER THERE ---
---GIVING OFF A STRANGE VIBE?!
Cabaret Club HEAVEN
Fee
50 minutes, 4,000 heavens
SEXY GIRL
AHHH!
HEY, HANDSOME!!
WHY DON'T YOU COME INSIDE?
Satsuki
IT'S ONLY 4,000 HEAVENS FOR 50 MINUTES. ♡

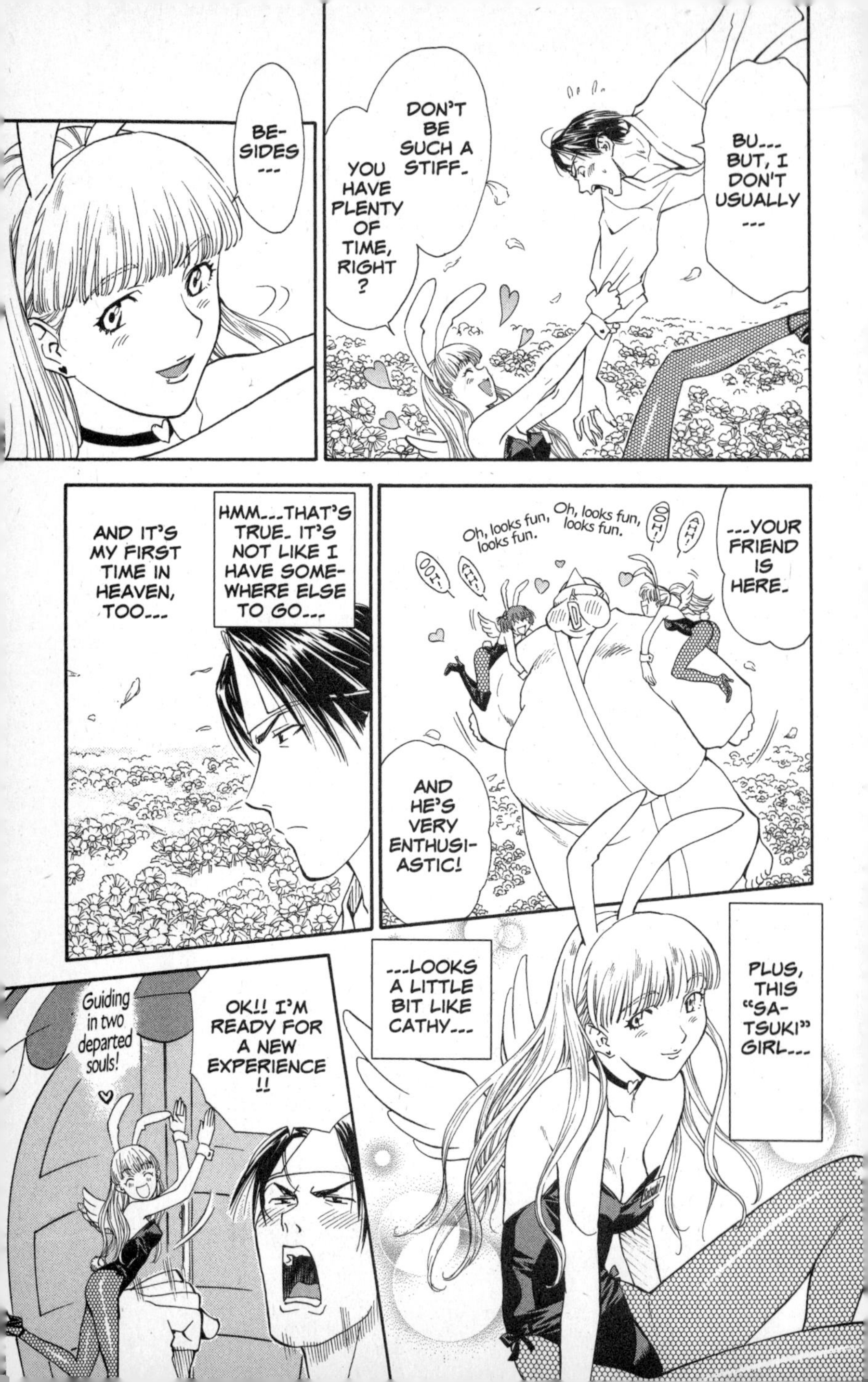
BU... BUT, I DON'T USUALLY...
DON'T BE SUCH A STIFF.
YOU HAVE PLENTY OF TIME, RIGHT?
BE-SIDES...
...YOUR FRIEND IS HERE.
AH!
OOH!
Oh, looks fun, looks fun.
Oh, looks fun, looks fun.
AH!
OOH!
AND HE'S VERY ENTHUSI-ASTIC!
HMM...THAT'S TRUE. IT'S NOT LIKE I HAVE SOME-WHERE ELSE TO GO...
AND IT'S MY FIRST TIME IN HEAVEN, TOO...
PLUS, THIS "SA-TSUKI" GIRL...
...LOOKS A LITTLE BIT LIKE CATHY...
OK!! I'M READY FOR A NEW EXPERIENCE!!
Guiding in two departed souls!

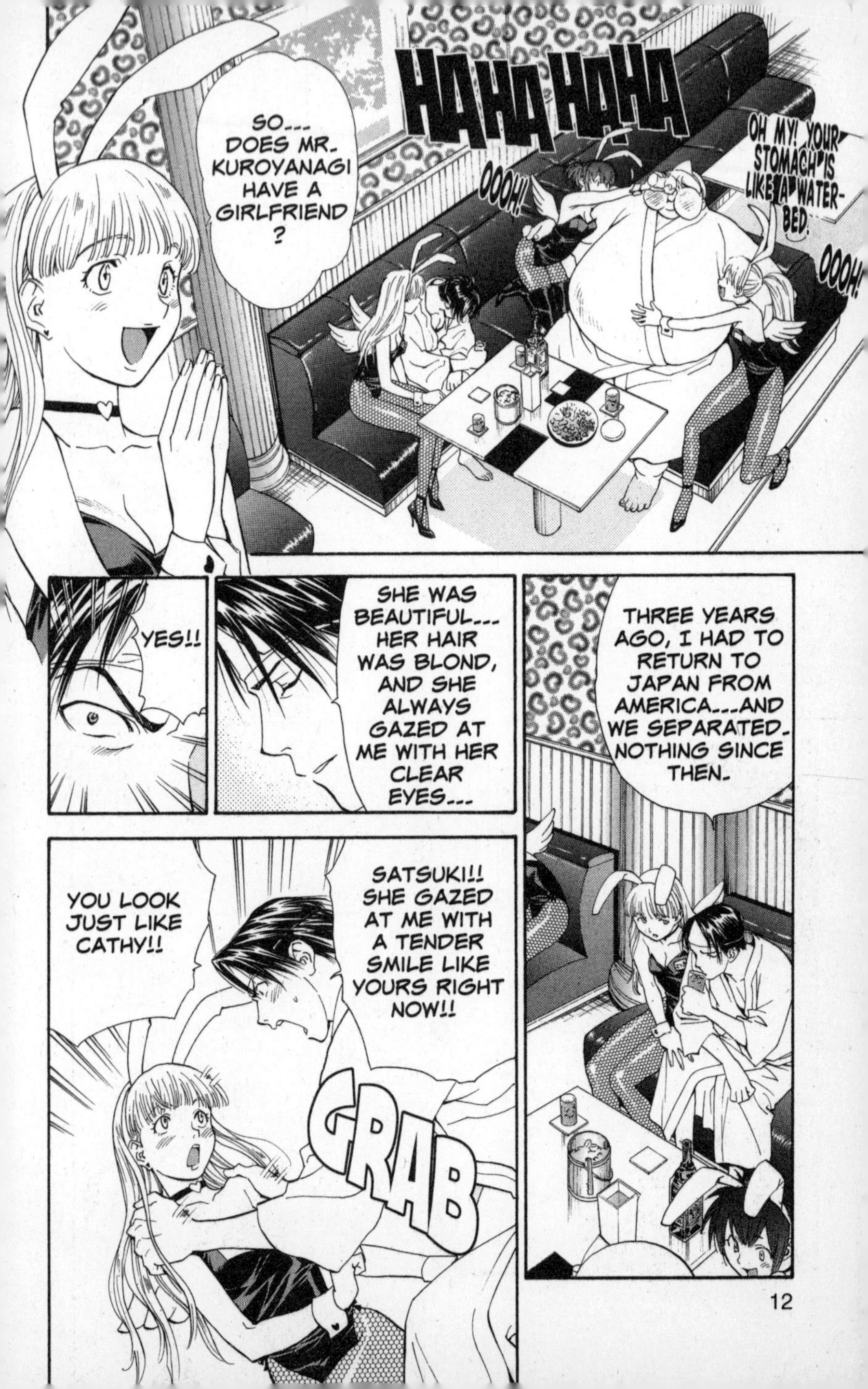
HAHAHAHA
OH MY! YOUR STOMACH IS LIKE A WATER-BED!
OOOH!
OOOH!
SO... DOES MR. KUROYANAGI HAVE A GIRLFRIEND?
THREE YEARS AGO, I HAD TO RETURN TO JAPAN FROM AMERICA...AND WE SEPARATED. NOTHING SINCE THEN.
SHE WAS BEAUTIFUL... HER HAIR WAS BLOND, AND SHE ALWAYS GAZED AT ME WITH HER CLEAR EYES...
YES!!
SATSUKI!!! SHE GAZED AT ME WITH A TENDER SMILE LIKE YOURS RIGHT NOW!!
YOU LOOK JUST LIKE CATHY!!
GRAB

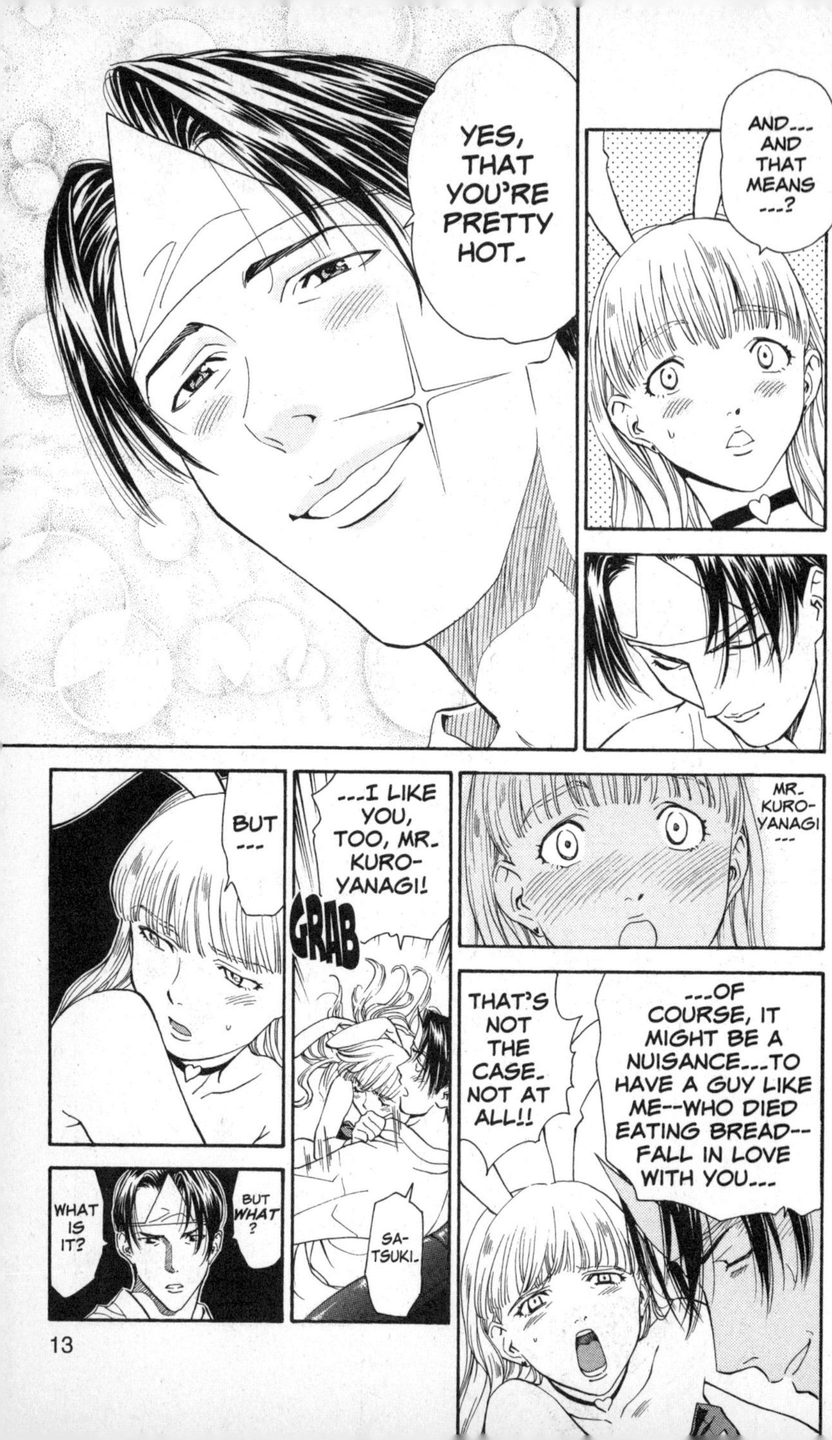
AND... AND THAT MEANS ...?
YES, THAT YOU'RE PRETTY HOT.
MR. KURO-YANAGI ...
---OF COURSE, IT MIGHT BE A NUISANCE...TO HAVE A GUY LIKE ME--WHO DIED EATING BREAD--FALL IN LOVE WITH YOU...
THAT'S NOT THE CASE. NOT AT ALL!!
---I LIKE YOU, TOO, MR. KURO-YANAGI!
GRAB
SA-TSUKI.
BUT ---
BUT *WHAT*?
WHAT IS IT?

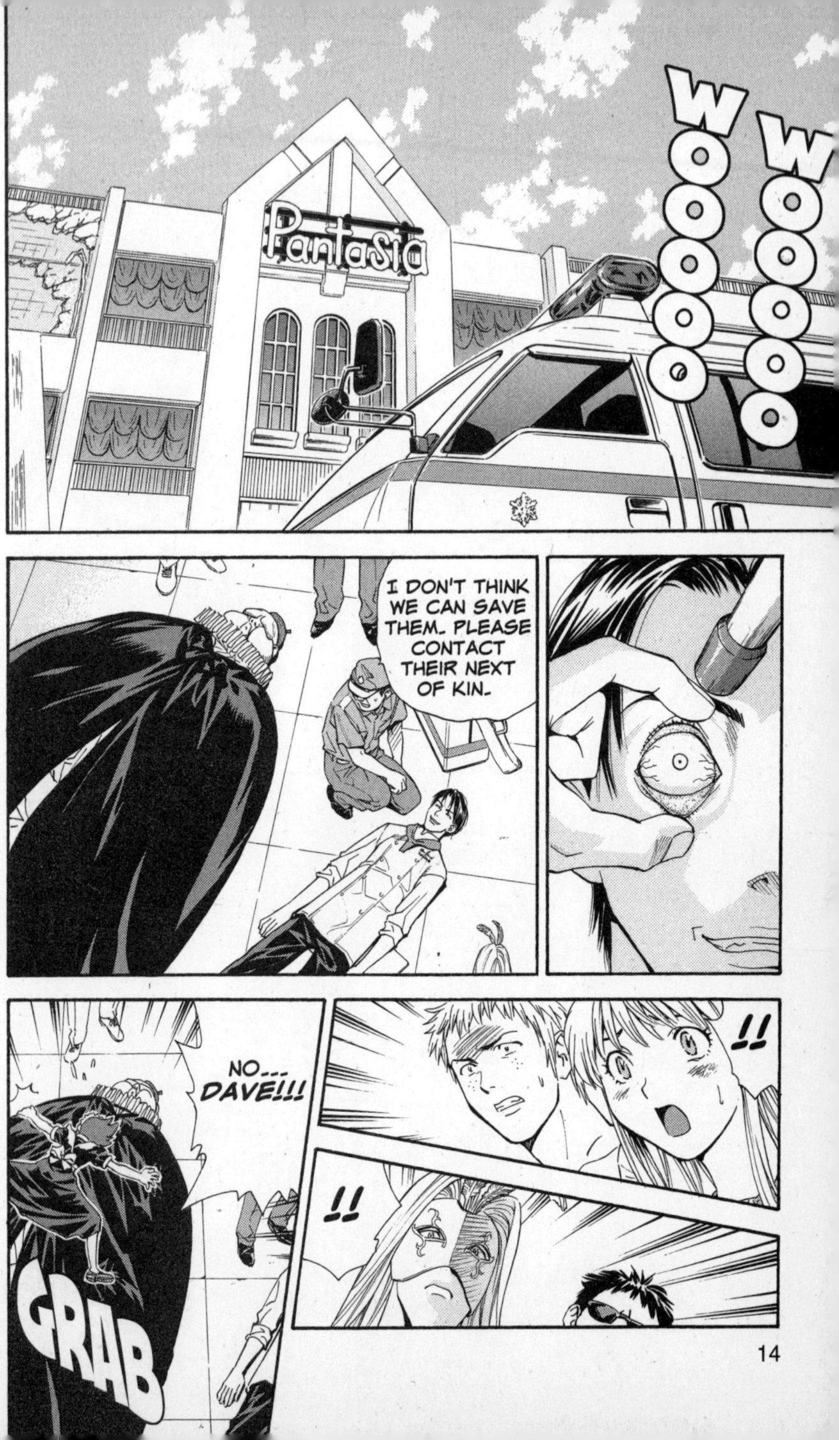
Pantasia
WOOOOOO
WOOOOOO
I DON'T THINK WE CAN SAVE THEM. PLEASE CONTACT THEIR NEXT OF KIN.
!!
!!
NO... DAVE!!!
GRAB

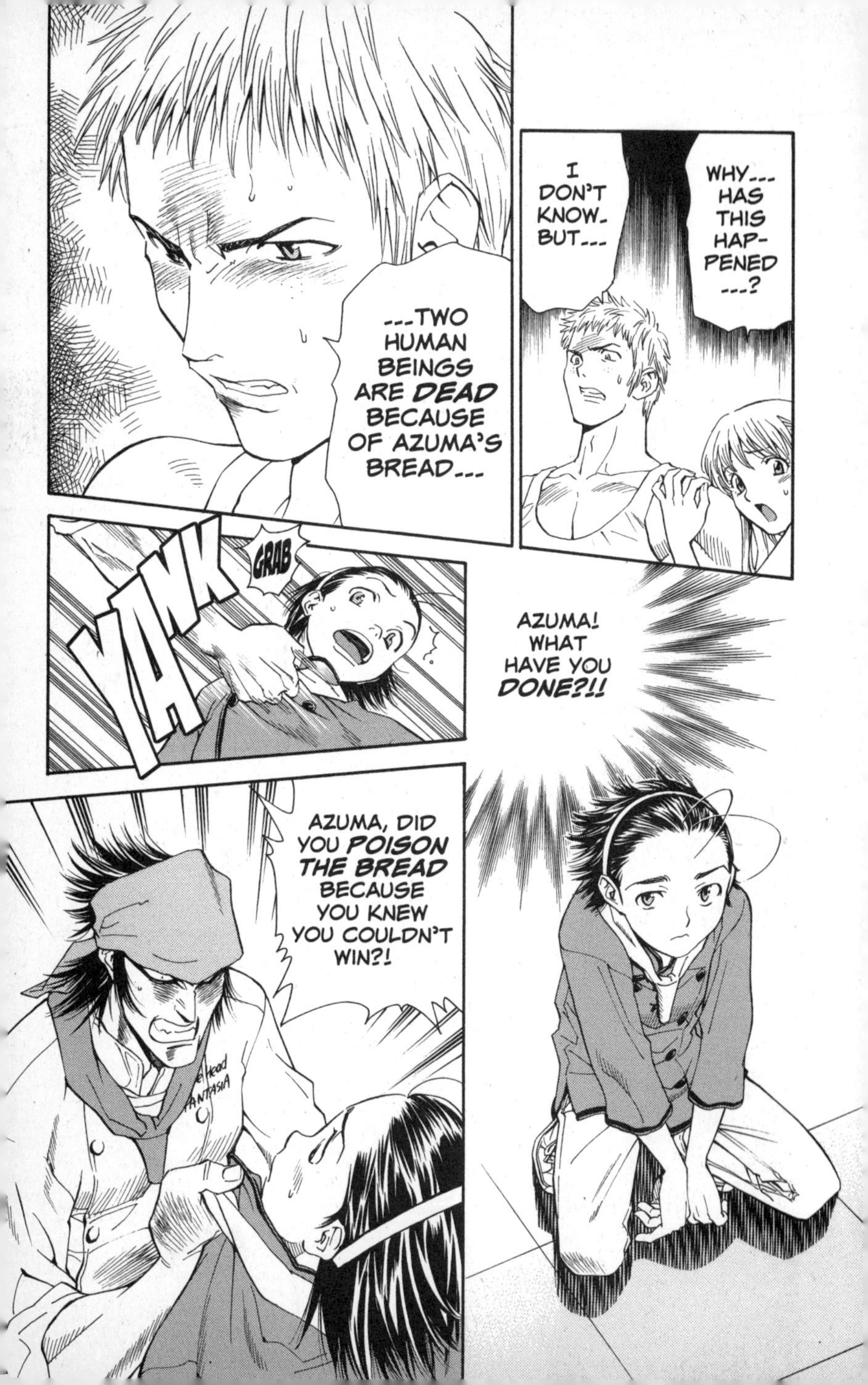
WHY... HAS THIS HAPPENED...?
I DON'T KNOW. BUT...
...TWO HUMAN BEINGS ARE DEAD BECAUSE OF AZUMA'S BREAD...
AZUMA! WHAT HAVE YOU DONE?!!
YANK
GRAB
AZUMA, DID YOU POISON THE BREAD BECAUSE YOU KNEW YOU COULDN'T WIN?!

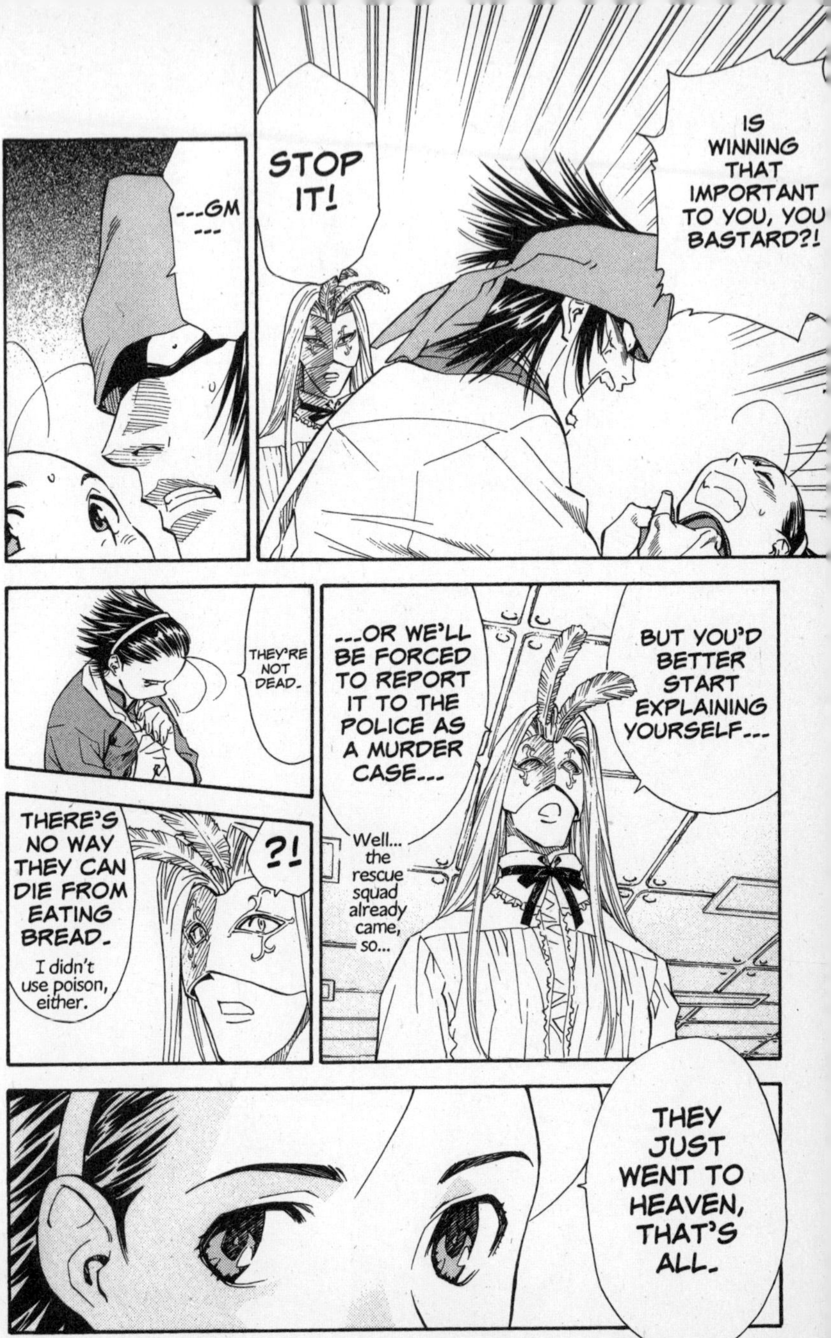
IS WINNING THAT IMPORTANT TO YOU, YOU BASTARD?!
STOP IT!
---GM ---
BUT YOU'D BETTER START EXPLAINING YOURSELF---
---OR WE'LL BE FORCED TO REPORT IT TO THE POLICE AS A MURDER CASE---
Well... the rescue squad already came, so...
THEY'RE NOT DEAD.
?!
THERE'S NO WAY THEY CAN DIE FROM EATING BREAD.
I didn't use poison, either.
THEY JUST WENT TO HEAVEN, THAT'S ALL.

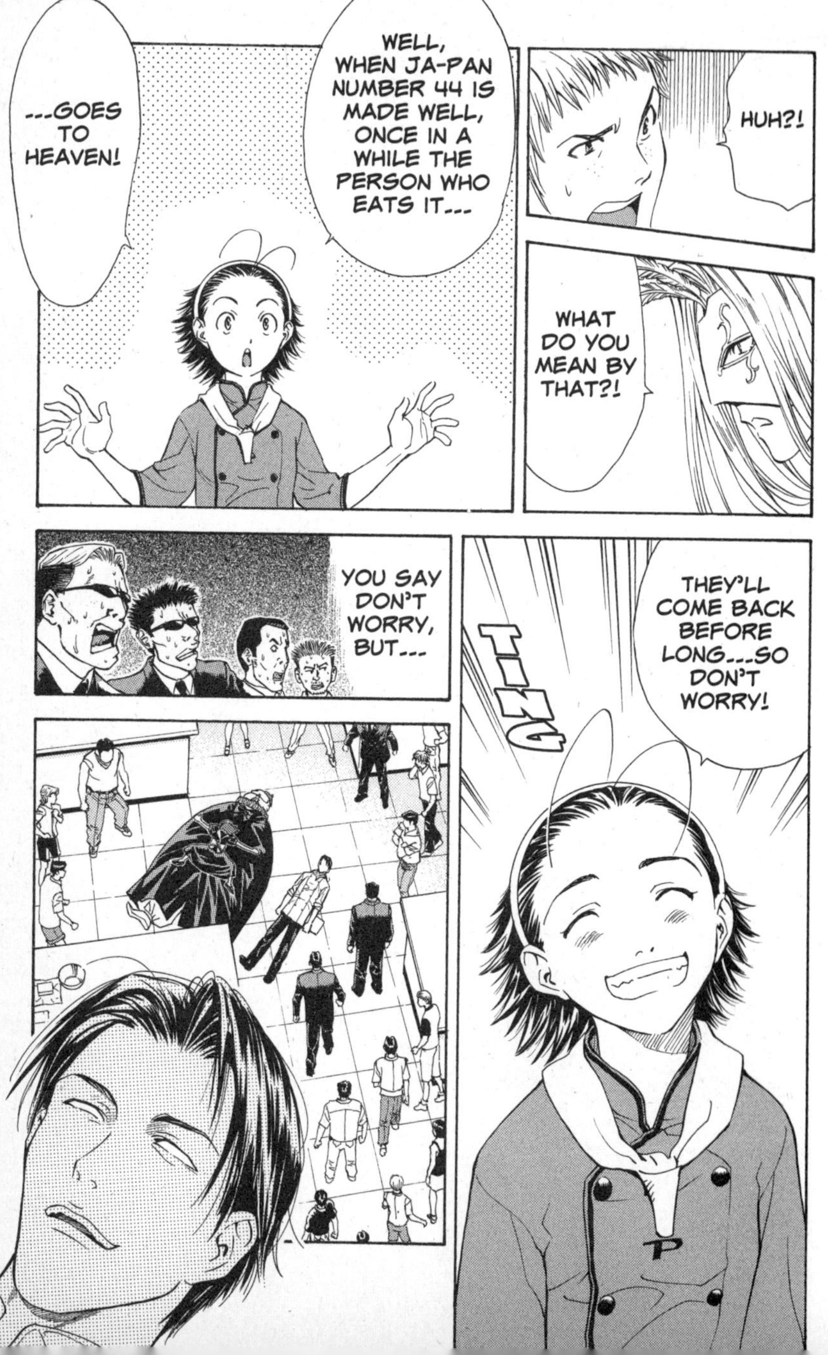
HUH?!
WHAT DO YOU MEAN BY THAT?!
WELL, WHEN JA-PAN NUMBER 44 IS MADE WELL, ONCE IN A WHILE THE PERSON WHO EATS IT...
...GOES TO HEAVEN!
THEY'LL COME BACK BEFORE LONG...SO DON'T WORRY!
TING
YOU SAY DON'T WORRY, BUT...

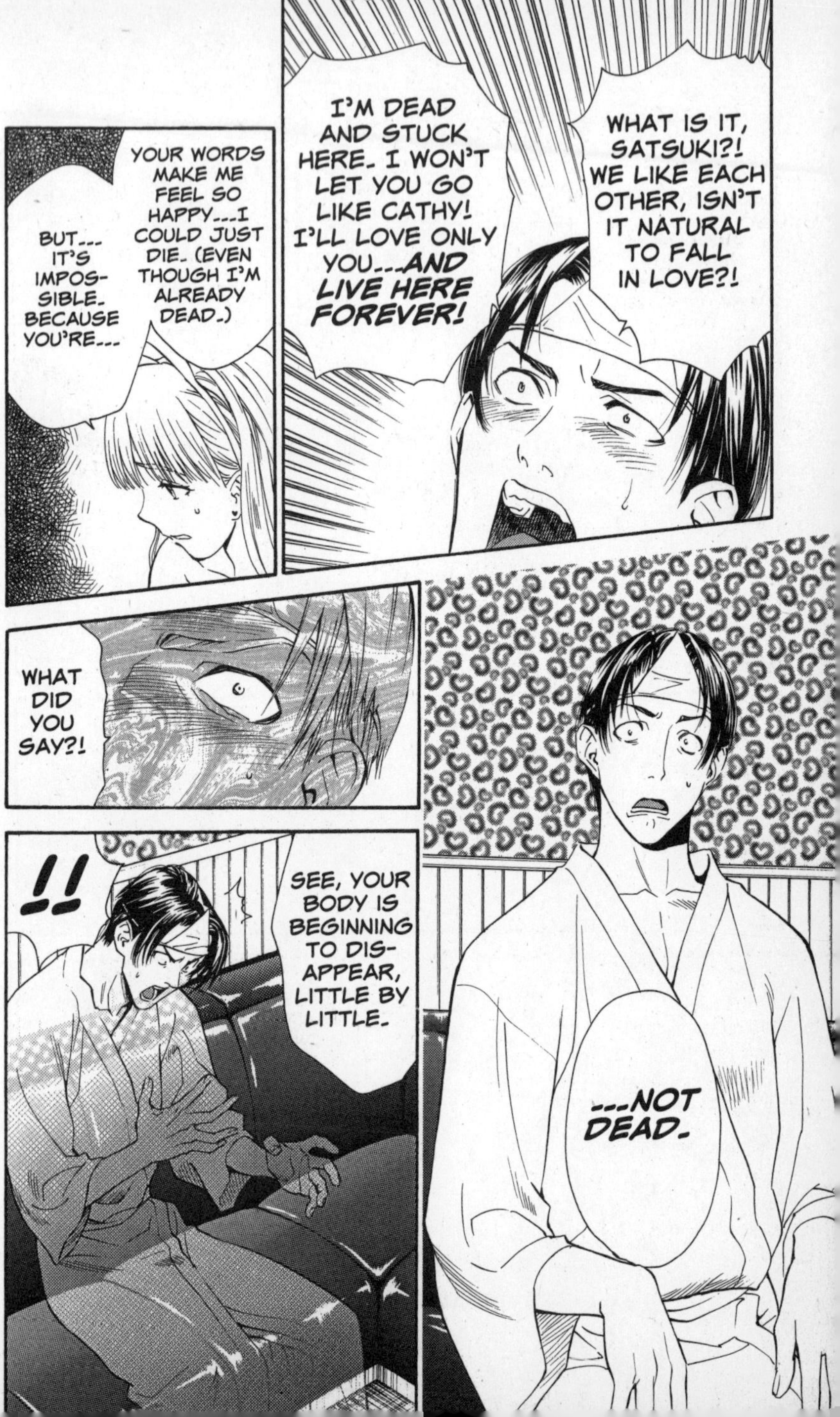
WHAT IS IT, SATSUKI?! WE LIKE EACH OTHER, ISN'T IT NATURAL TO FALL IN LOVE?!
I'M DEAD AND STUCK HERE. I WON'T LET YOU GO LIKE CATHY! I'LL LOVE ONLY YOU...AND LIVE HERE FOREVER!
YOUR WORDS MAKE ME FEEL SO HAPPY...I COULD JUST DIE. (EVEN THOUGH I'M ALREADY DEAD.)
BUT... IT'S IMPOSSIBLE. BECAUSE YOU'RE...
...NOT DEAD.
WHAT DID YOU SAY?!
!!
SEE, YOUR BODY IS BEGINNING TO DISAPPEAR, LITTLE BY LITTLE.

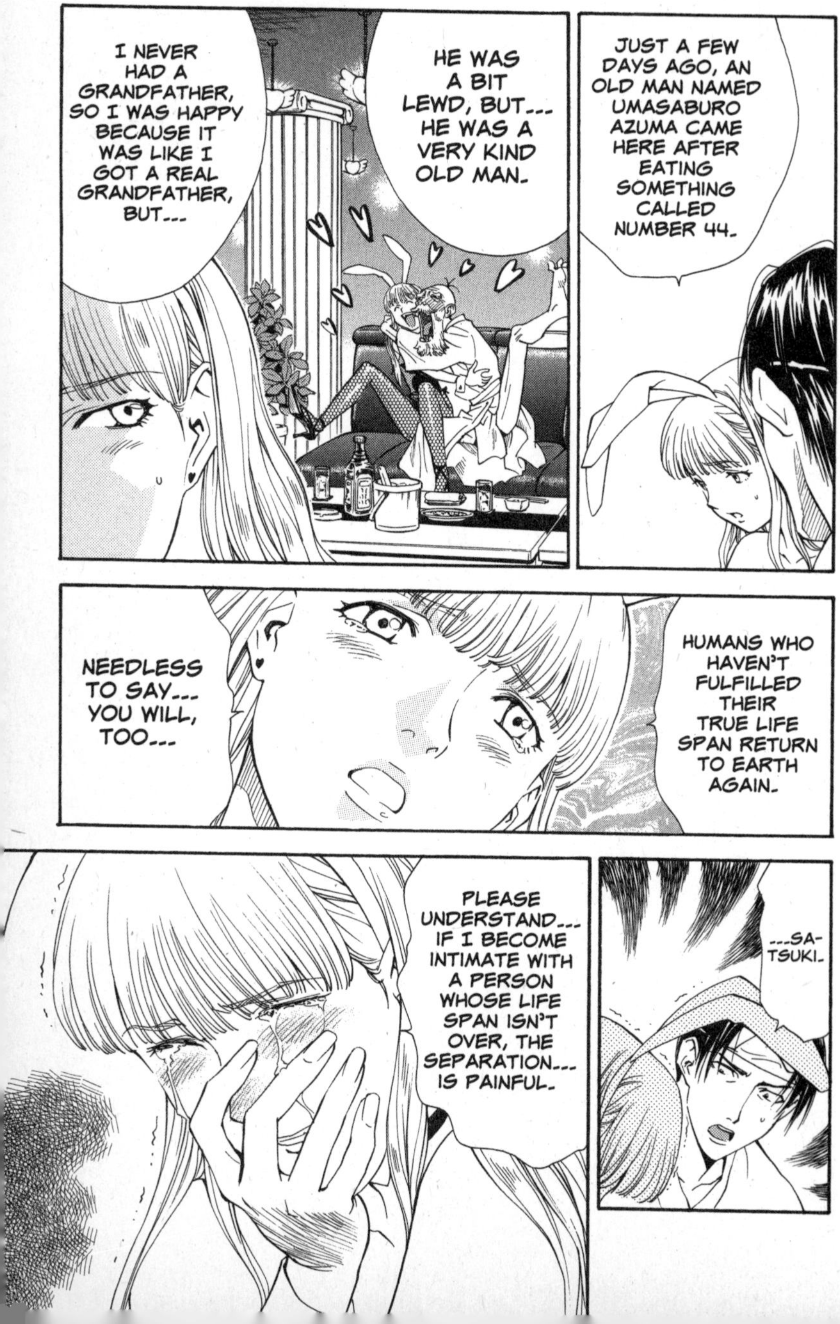
JUST A FEW DAYS AGO, AN OLD MAN NAMED UMASABURO AZUMA CAME HERE AFTER EATING SOMETHING CALLED NUMBER 44.
HE WAS A BIT LEWD, BUT... HE WAS A VERY KIND OLD MAN.
I NEVER HAD A GRANDFATHER, SO I WAS HAPPY BECAUSE IT WAS LIKE I GOT A REAL GRANDFATHER, BUT...
HUMANS WHO HAVEN'T FULFILLED THEIR TRUE LIFE SPAN RETURN TO EARTH AGAIN.
NEEDLESS TO SAY... YOU WILL, TOO...
...SA-TSUKI.
PLEASE UNDERSTAND... IF I BECOME INTIMATE WITH A PERSON WHOSE LIFE SPAN ISN'T OVER, THE SEPARATION... IS PAINFUL.

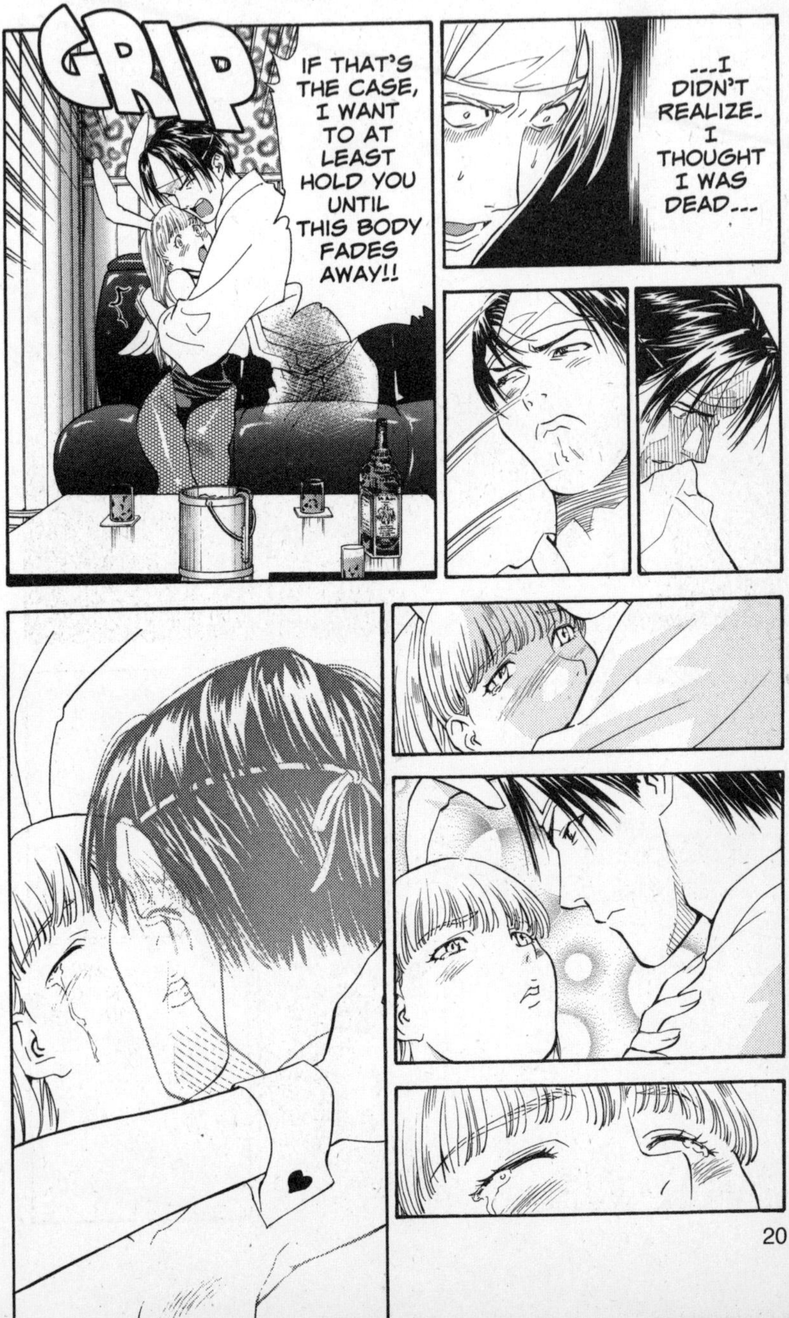
...I DIDN'T REALIZE. I THOUGHT I WAS DEAD...
GRIP
IF THAT'S THE CASE, I WANT TO AT LEAST HOLD YOU UNTIL THIS BODY FADES AWAY!!

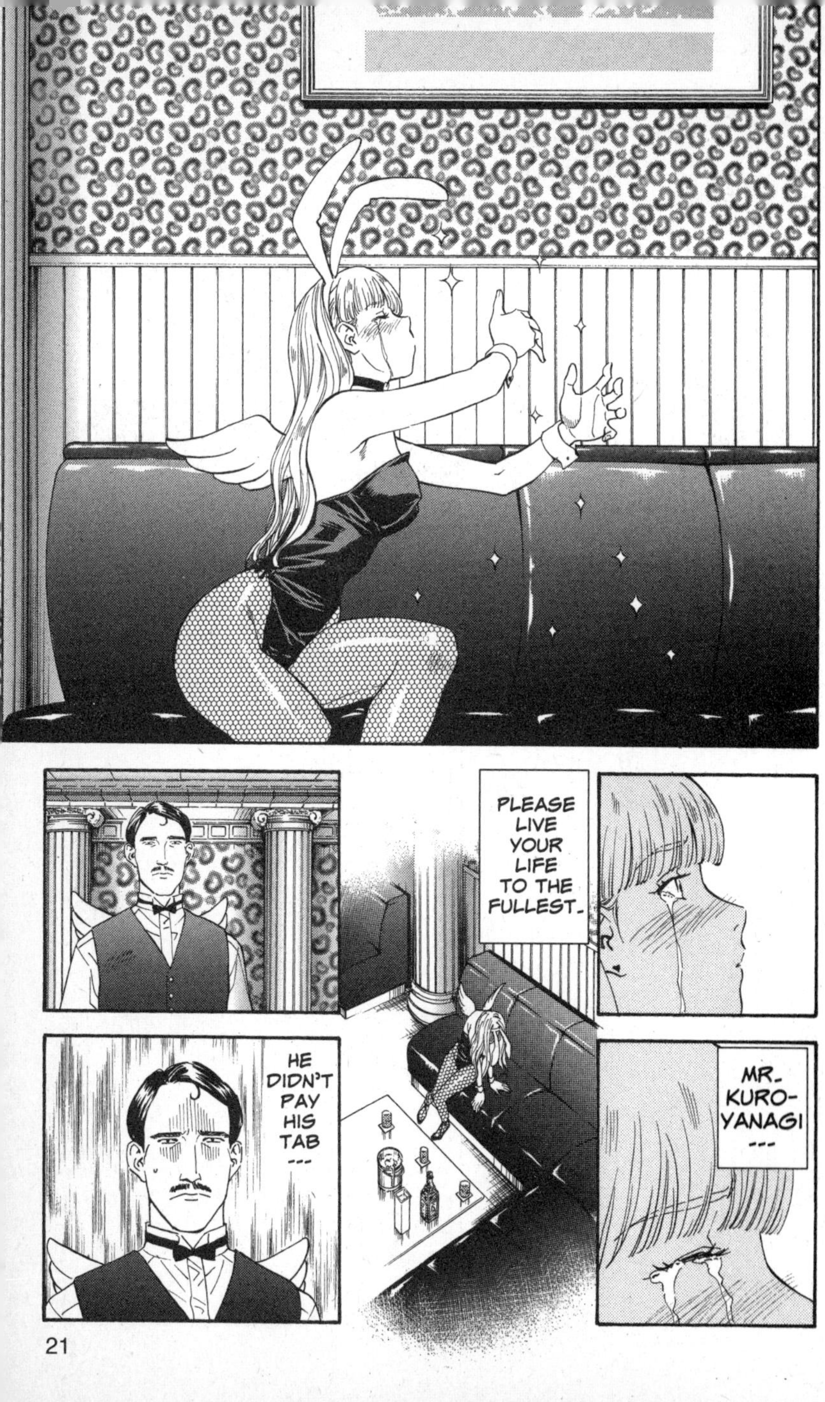
PLEASE LIVE YOUR LIFE TO THE FULLEST.
MR. KURO-YANAGI...
HE DIDN'T PAY HIS TAB...

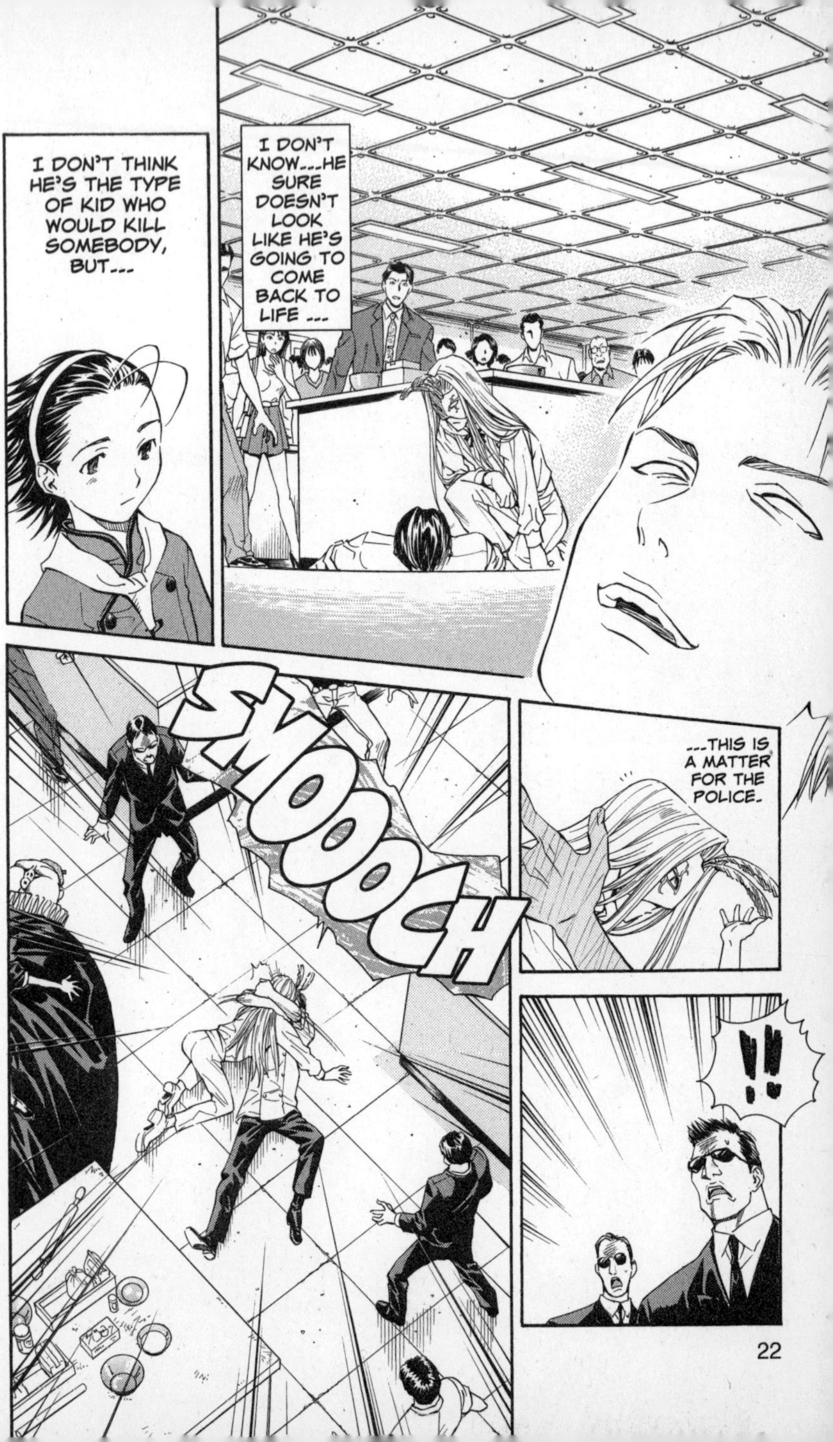
I DON'T KNOW...HE SURE DOESN'T LOOK LIKE HE'S GOING TO COME BACK TO LIFE ...
I DON'T THINK HE'S THE TYPE OF KID WHO WOULD KILL SOMEBODY, BUT...
...THIS IS A MATTER FOR THE POLICE.
!!
SMOOOCH

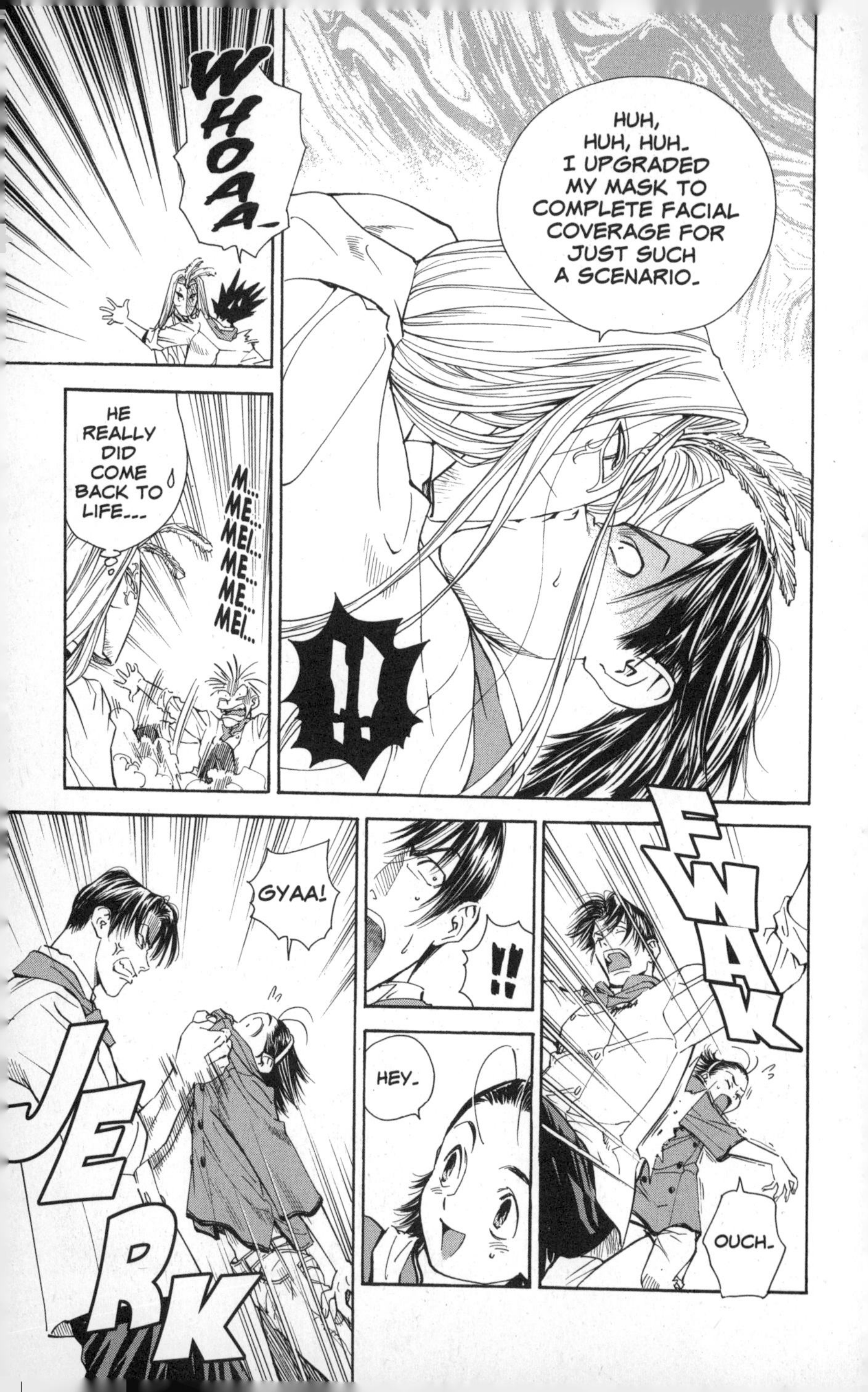
HUH, HUH, HUH. I UPGRADED MY MASK TO COMPLETE FACIAL COVERAGE FOR JUST SUCH A SCENARIO.
!!
WHOAA.
HE REALLY DID COME BACK TO LIFE...
M... ME... MEI... ME... ME... MEI...
FWAK
OUCH.
!!
HEY.
GYAA!
JERK

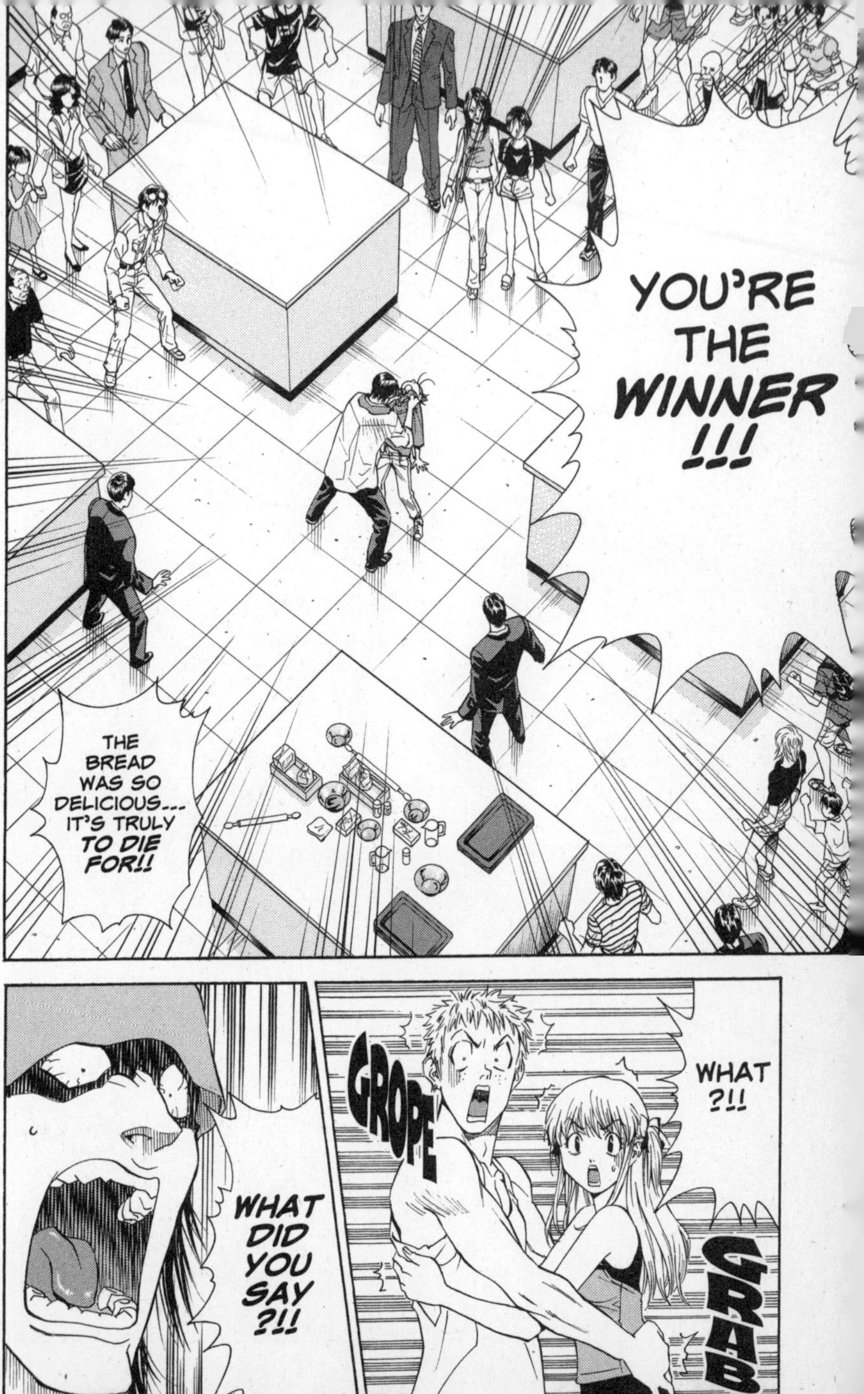
YOU'RE THE WINNER!!!
THE BREAD WAS SO DELICIOUS... IT'S TRULY TO DIE FOR!!
WHAT?!!
GROPE
GRAB
WHAT DID YOU SAY?!!

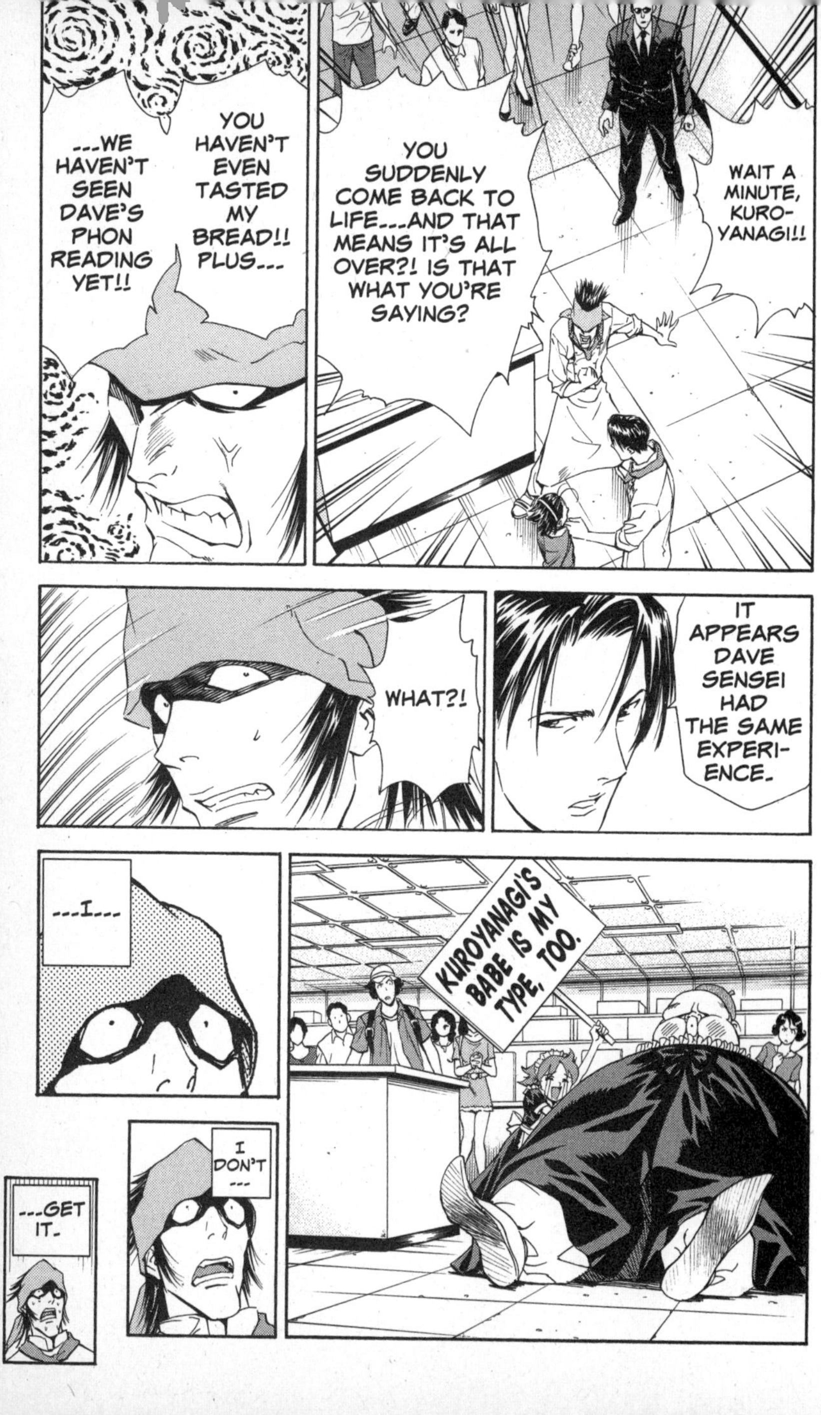
WAIT A MINUTE, KUROYANAGI!!
YOU SUDDENLY COME BACK TO LIFE...AND THAT MEANS IT'S ALL OVER?! IS THAT WHAT YOU'RE SAYING?
YOU HAVEN'T EVEN TASTED MY BREAD!! PLUS...
...WE HAVEN'T SEEN DAVE'S PHON READING YET!!
IT APPEARS DAVE SENSEI HAD THE SAME EXPERIENCE.
WHAT?!
KUROYANAGI'S BABE IS MY TYPE, TOO.
...I...
I DON'T ...
...GET IT.

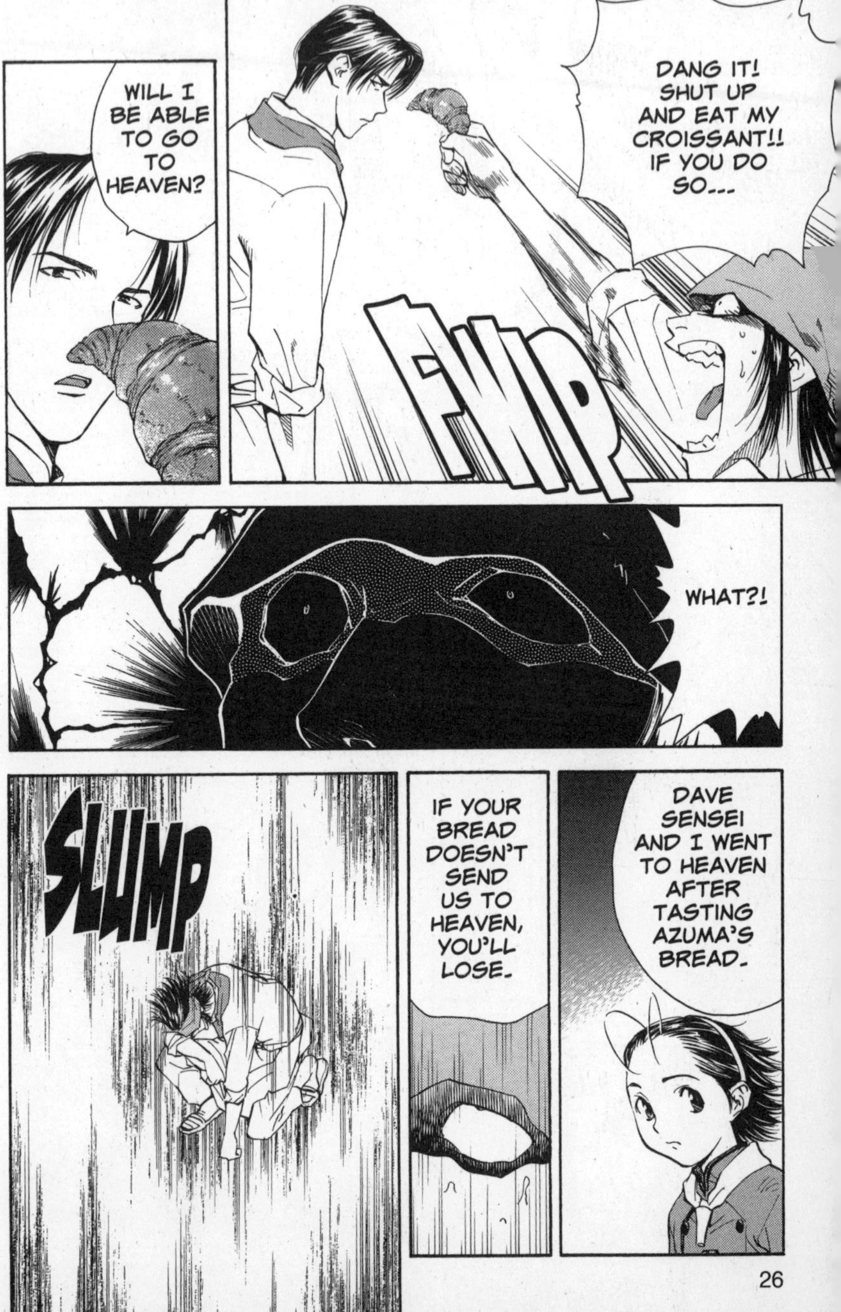
DANG IT! SHUT UP AND EAT MY CROISSANT!! IF YOU DO SO...
FWIP
WILL I BE ABLE TO GO TO HEAVEN?
WHAT?!
DAVE SENSEI AND I WENT TO HEAVEN AFTER TASTING AZUMA'S BREAD.
IF YOUR BREAD DOESN'T SEND US TO HEAVEN, YOU'LL LOSE.
SLUMP

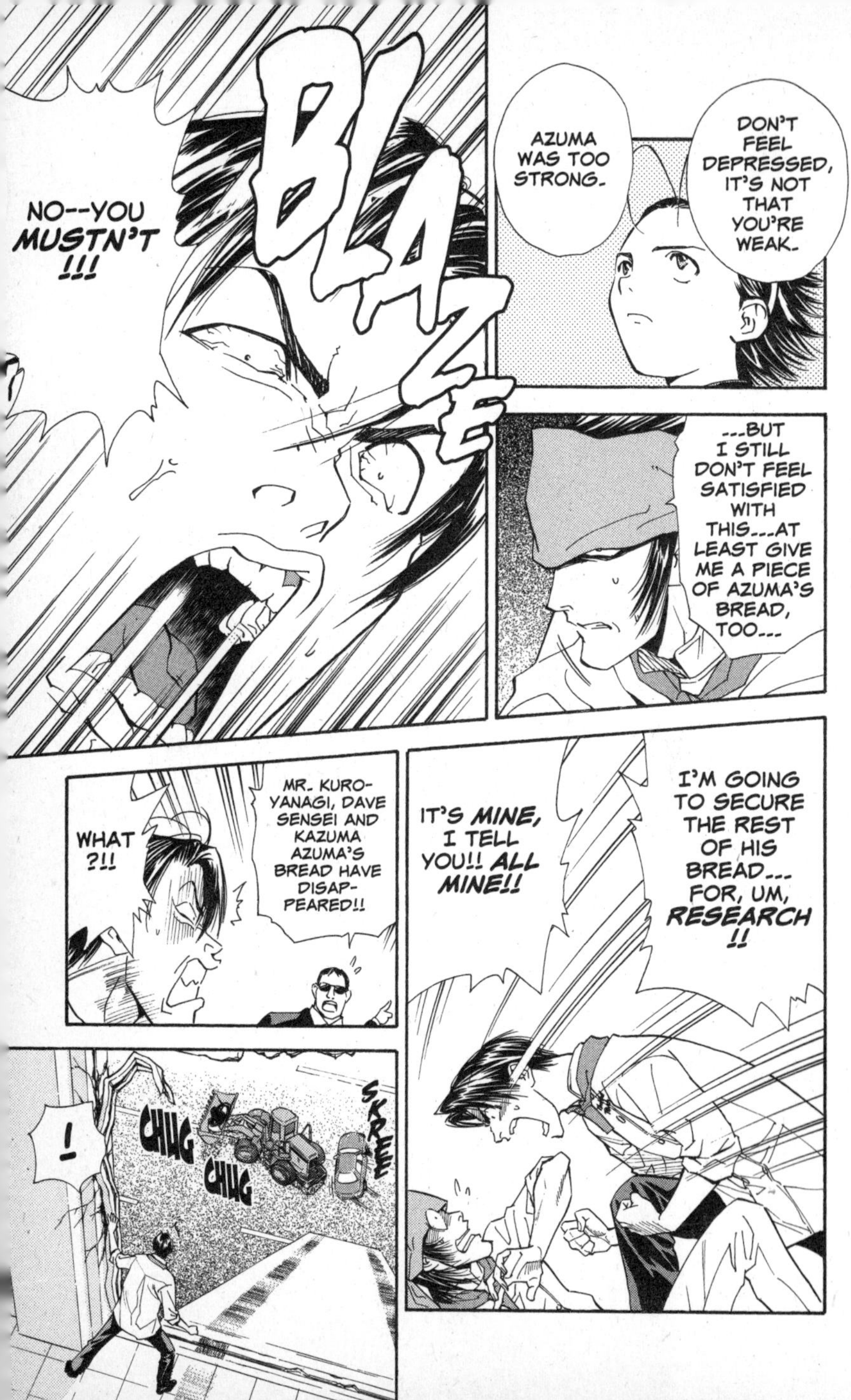
DON'T FEEL DEPRESSED, IT'S NOT THAT YOU'RE WEAK.
AZUMA WAS TOO STRONG.
...BUT I STILL DON'T FEEL SATISFIED WITH THIS...AT LEAST GIVE ME A PIECE OF AZUMA'S BREAD, TOO...
BLAZE
NO--YOU MUSTN'T !!!
I'M GOING TO SECURE THE REST OF HIS BREAD... FOR, UM, RESEARCH !!
IT'S MINE, I TELL YOU!! ALL MINE!!
MR. KURO-YANAGI, DAVE SENSEI AND KAZUMA AZUMA'S BREAD HAVE DISAP-PEARED!!
WHAT ?!!
SKREE
CHUG
CHUG
!

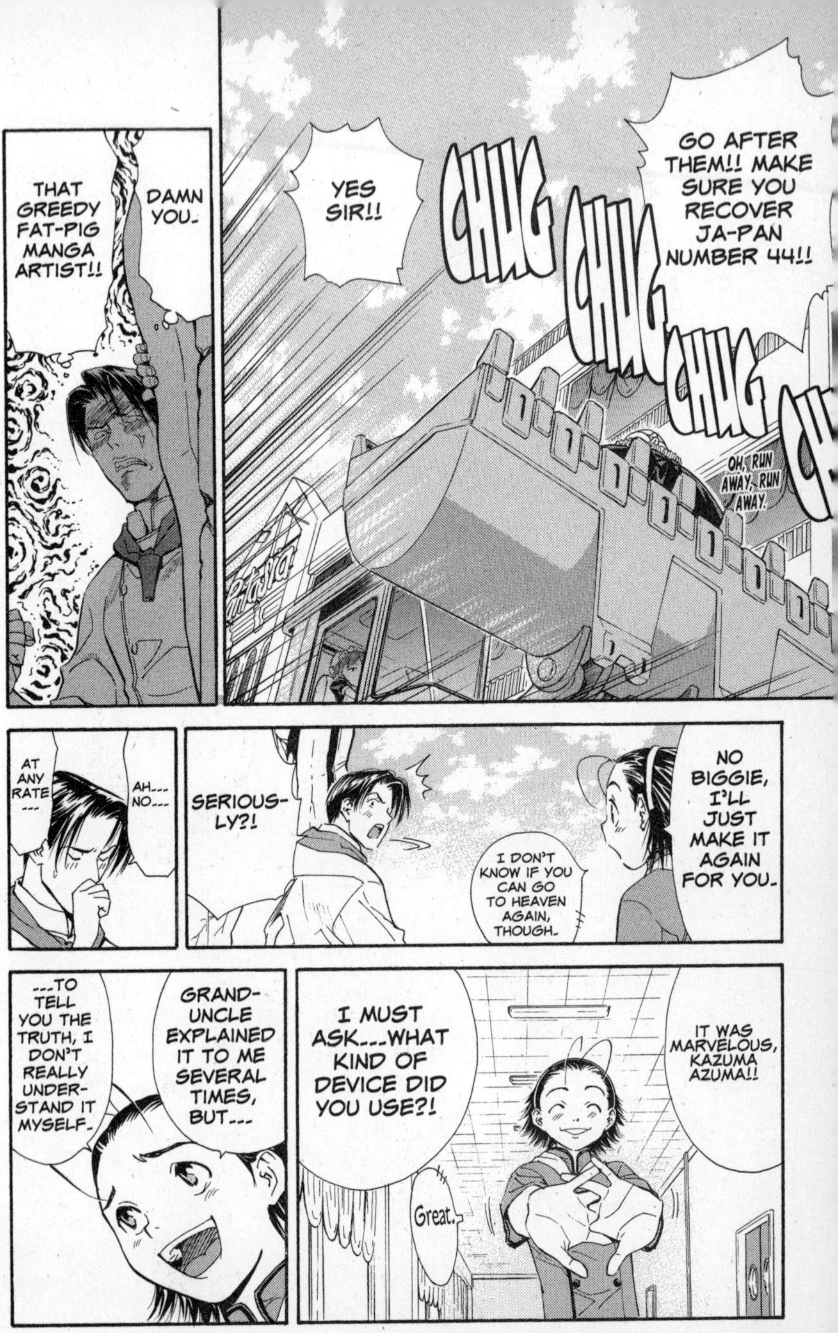
GO AFTER THEM!! MAKE SURE YOU RECOVER JA-PAN NUMBER 44!!
CHUG CHUG CHUG CHUG CH
YES SIR!!
OH, RUN AWAY. RUN AWAY.
DAMN YOU.
THAT GREEDY FAT-PIG MANGA ARTIST!!
NO BIGGIE, I'LL JUST MAKE IT AGAIN FOR YOU.
I DON'T KNOW IF YOU CAN GO TO HEAVEN AGAIN, THOUGH.
SERIOUS-LY?!
AH... NO...
AT ANY RATE...
IT WAS MARVELOUS, KAZUMA AZUMA!!
I MUST ASK...WHAT KIND OF DEVICE DID YOU USE?!
Great.
GRAND-UNCLE EXPLAINED IT TO ME SEVERAL TIMES, BUT...
...TO TELL YOU THE TRUTH, I DON'T REALLY UNDER-STAND IT MYSELF.

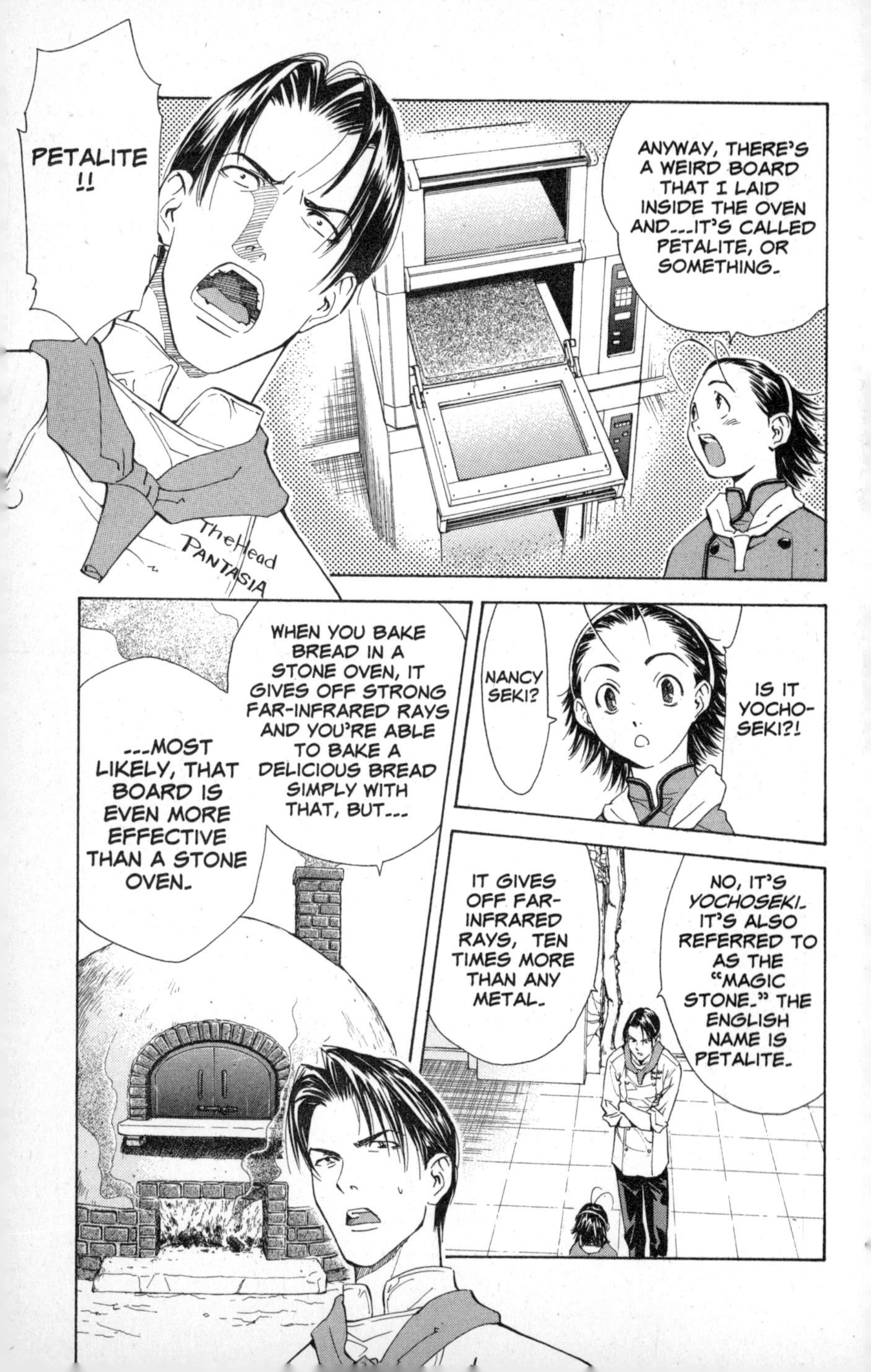
ANYWAY, THERE'S A WEIRD BOARD THAT I LAID INSIDE THE OVEN AND...IT'S CALLED PETALITE, OR SOMETHING.
PETALITE !!
TheHead PANTASIA
IS IT YOCHO-SEKI?!
NANCY SEKI?
NO, IT'S *YOCHOSEKI*. IT'S ALSO REFERRED TO AS THE "MAGIC STONE." THE ENGLISH NAME IS PETALITE.
IT GIVES OFF FAR-INFRARED RAYS, TEN TIMES MORE THAN ANY METAL.
WHEN YOU BAKE BREAD IN A STONE OVEN, IT GIVES OFF STRONG FAR-INFRARED RAYS AND YOU'RE ABLE TO BAKE A DELICIOUS BREAD SIMPLY WITH THAT, BUT...
...MOST LIKELY, THAT BOARD IS EVEN MORE EFFECTIVE THAN A STONE OVEN.

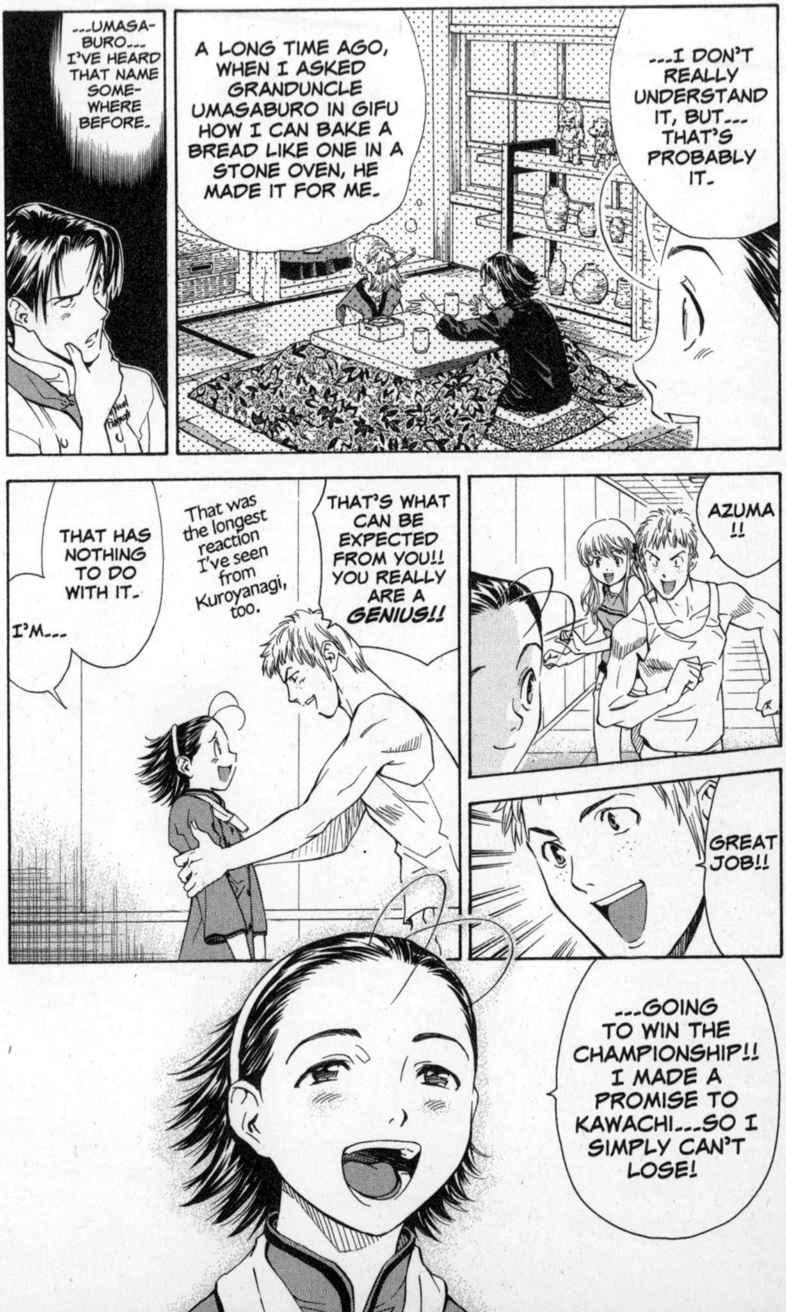
...I DON'T REALLY UNDERSTAND IT, BUT... THAT'S PROBABLY IT.
A LONG TIME AGO, WHEN I ASKED GRANDUNCLE UMASABURO IN GIFU HOW I CAN BAKE A BREAD LIKE ONE IN A STONE OVEN, HE MADE IT FOR ME.
...UMASABURO... I'VE HEARD THAT NAME SOMEWHERE BEFORE.
AZUMA!!
GREAT JOB!!
THAT'S WHAT CAN BE EXPECTED FROM YOU!! YOU REALLY ARE A GENIUS!!
That was the longest reaction I've seen from Kuroyanagi, too.
THAT HAS NOTHING TO DO WITH IT.
I'M...
...GOING TO WIN THE CHAMPIONSHIP!! I MADE A PROMISE TO KAWACHI...SO I SIMPLY CAN'T LOSE!

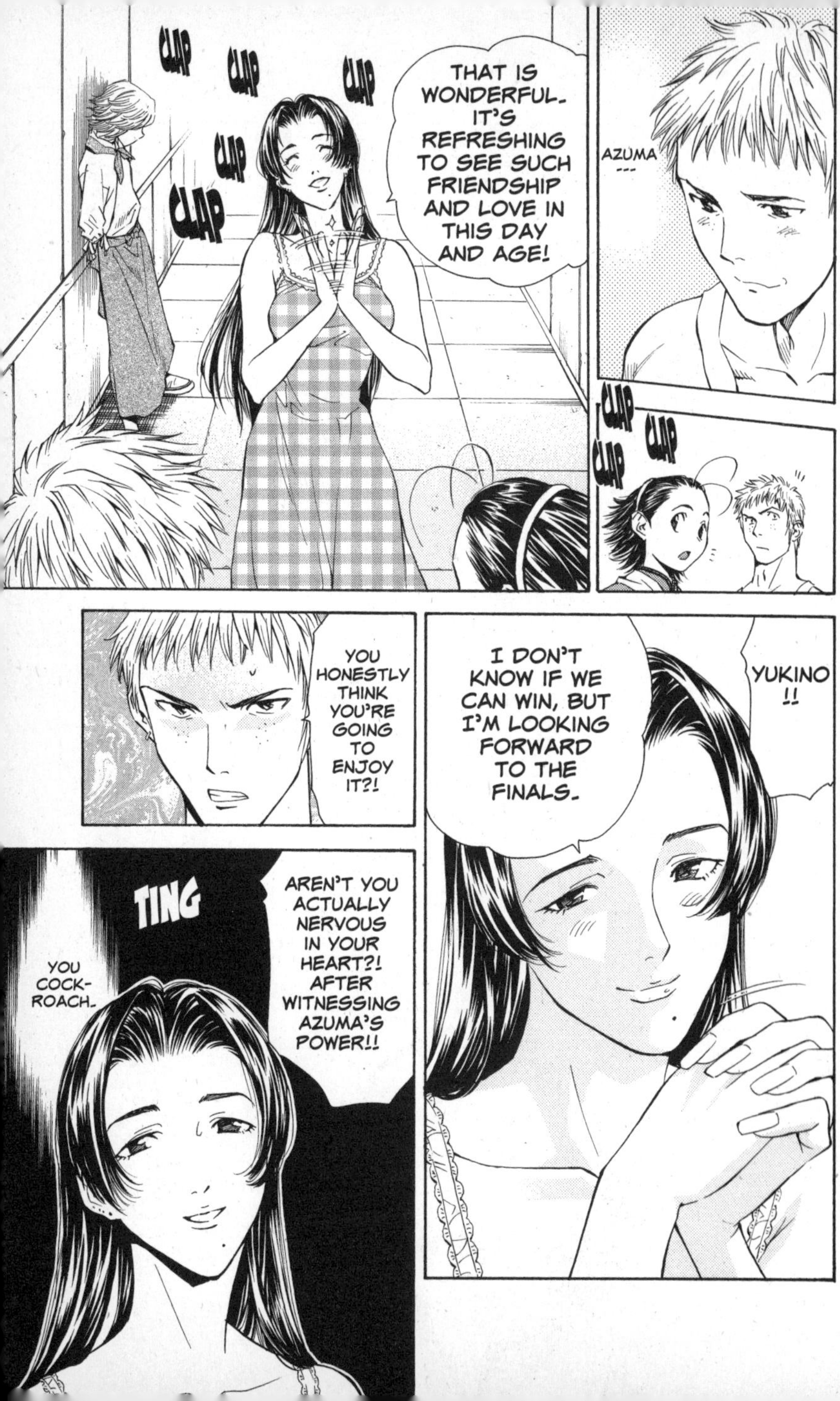
AZUMA ---
CLAP
CLAP
CLAP
CLAP
CLAP
CLAP
CLAP
CLAP
THAT IS WONDERFUL. IT'S REFRESHING TO SEE SUCH FRIENDSHIP AND LOVE IN THIS DAY AND AGE!
YUKINO !!
I DON'T KNOW IF WE CAN WIN, BUT I'M LOOKING FORWARD TO THE FINALS.
YOU HONESTLY THINK YOU'RE GOING TO ENJOY IT?!
AREN'T YOU ACTUALLY NERVOUS IN YOUR HEART?! AFTER WITNESSING AZUMA'S POWER!!
TING
YOU COCK-ROACH.

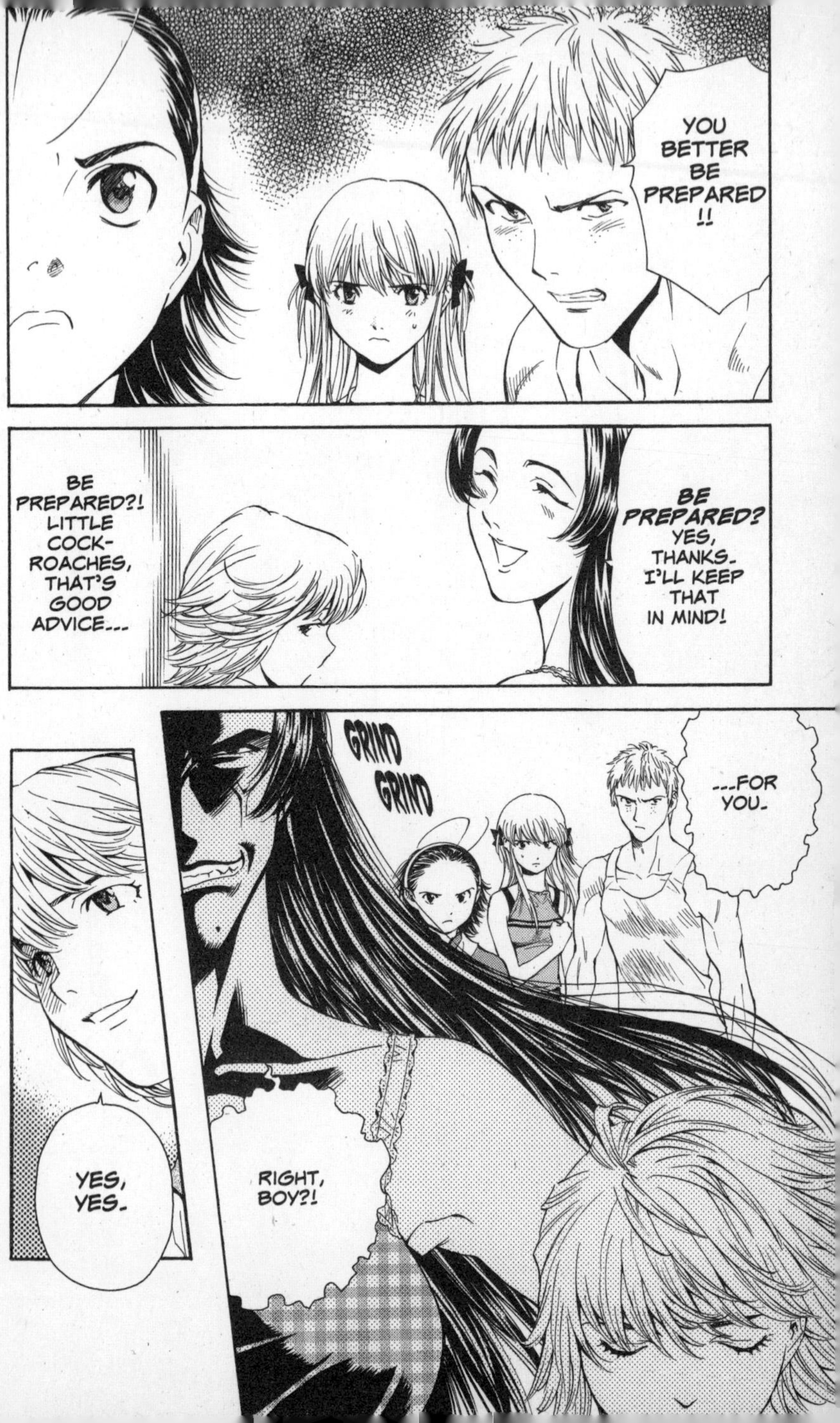
YOU BETTER BE PREPARED !!
BE PREPARED? YES, THANKS. I'LL KEEP THAT IN MIND!
BE PREPARED?! LITTLE COCK-ROACHES, THAT'S GOOD ADVICE...
...FOR YOU.
GRIND GRIND
RIGHT, BOY?!
YES, YES.

Story 43: Take It Easy?

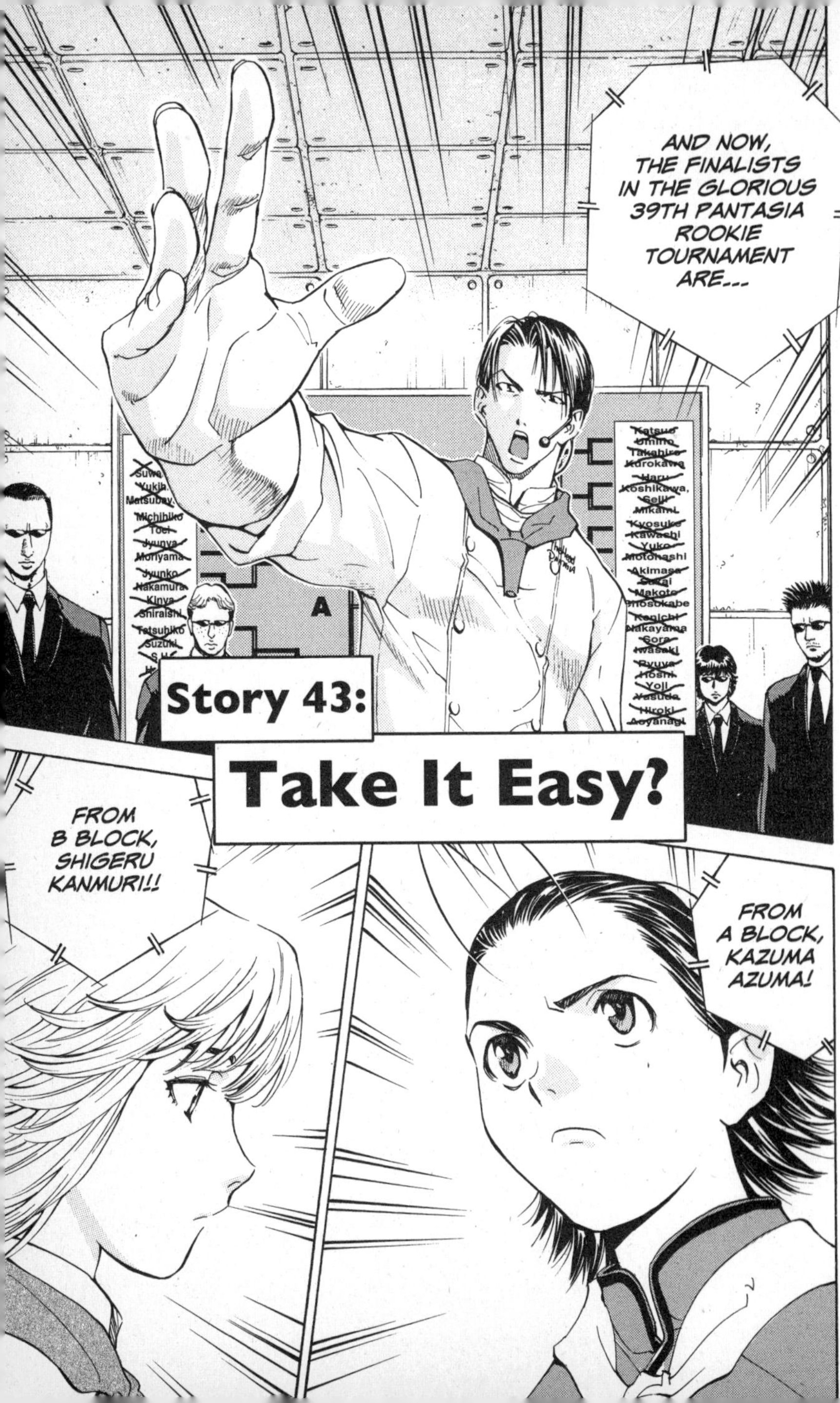
AND NOW, THE FINALISTS IN THE GLORIOUS 39TH PANTASIA ROOKIE TOURNAMENT ARE...
A
FROM A BLOCK, KAZUMA AZUMA!
FROM B BLOCK, SHIGERU KANMURI!!

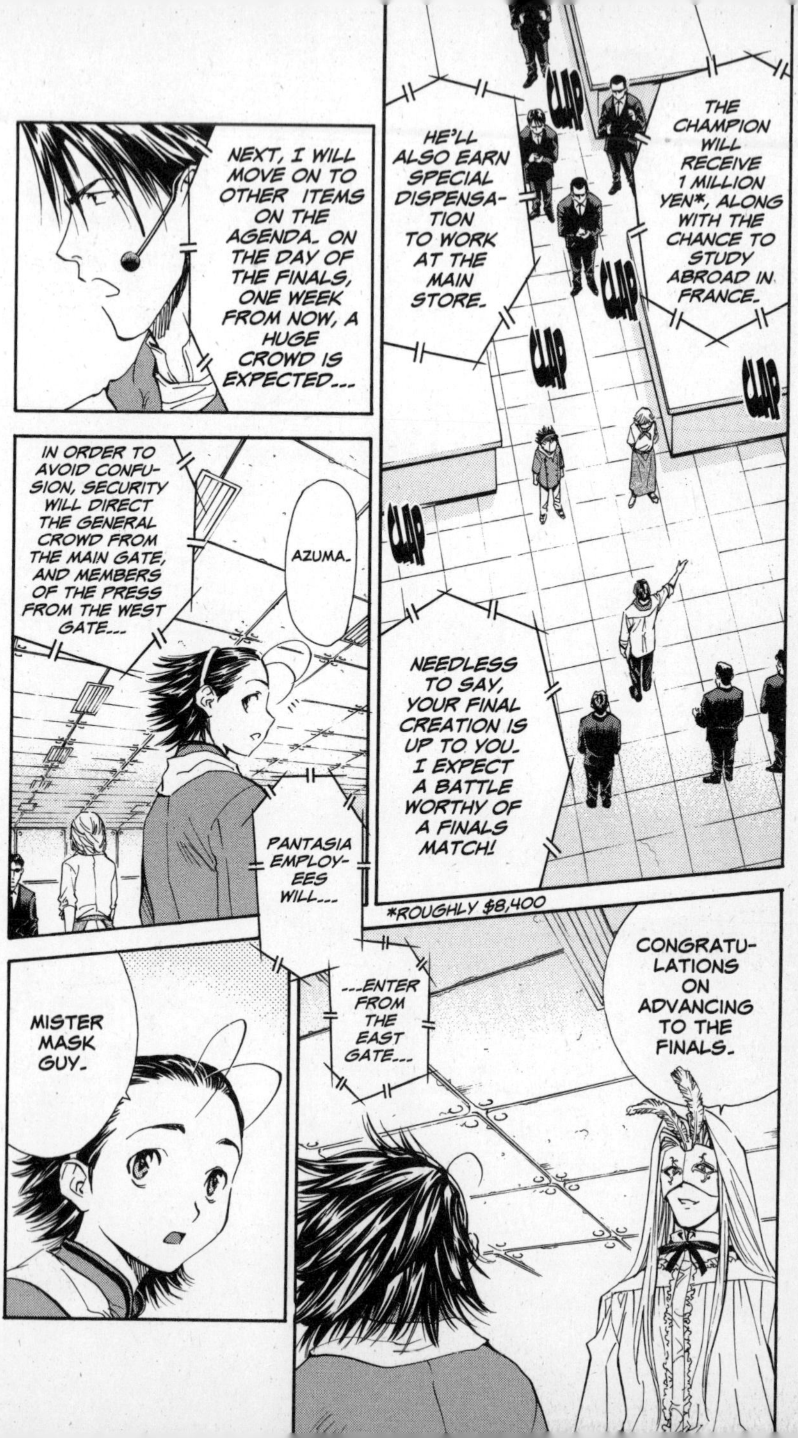
CLAP
THE CHAMPION WILL RECEIVE 1 MILLION YEN*, ALONG WITH THE CHANCE TO STUDY ABROAD IN FRANCE.
HE'LL ALSO EARN SPECIAL DISPENSATION TO WORK AT THE MAIN STORE.
CLAP
CLAP
CLAP
CLAP
NEEDLESS TO SAY, YOUR FINAL CREATION IS UP TO YOU. I EXPECT A BATTLE WORTHY OF A FINALS MATCH!
*ROUGHLY $8,400
NEXT, I WILL MOVE ON TO OTHER ITEMS ON THE AGENDA. ON THE DAY OF THE FINALS, ONE WEEK FROM NOW, A HUGE CROWD IS EXPECTED...
IN ORDER TO AVOID CONFUSION, SECURITY WILL DIRECT THE GENERAL CROWD FROM THE MAIN GATE, AND MEMBERS OF THE PRESS FROM THE WEST GATE...
AZUMA.
PANTASIA EMPLOYEES WILL...
CONGRATULATIONS ON ADVANCING TO THE FINALS.
...ENTER FROM THE EAST GATE...
MISTER MASK GUY.

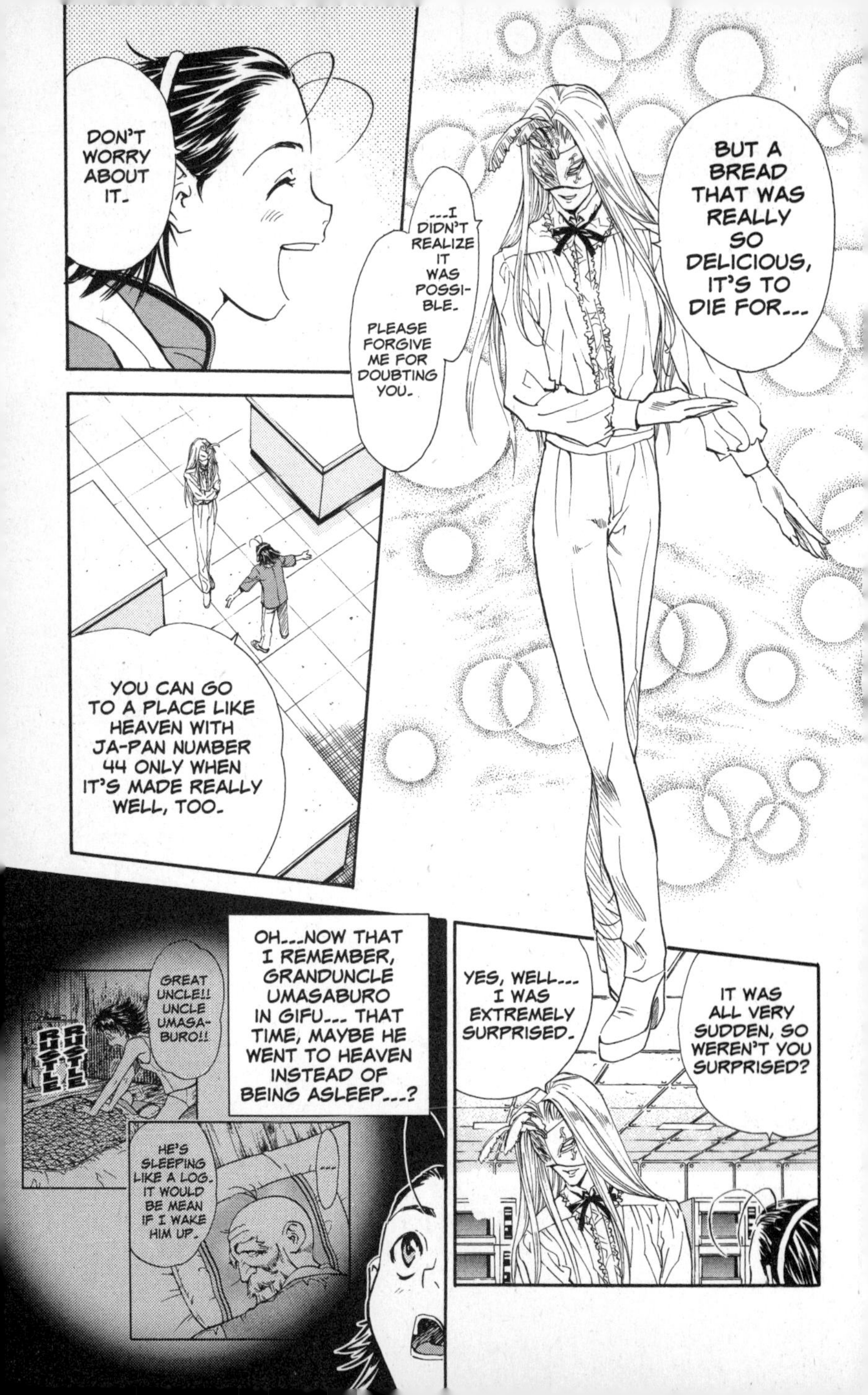
BUT A BREAD THAT WAS REALLY SO DELICIOUS, IT'S TO DIE FOR...
...I DIDN'T REALIZE IT WAS POSSIBLE.
PLEASE FORGIVE ME FOR DOUBTING YOU.
DON'T WORRY ABOUT IT.
YOU CAN GO TO A PLACE LIKE HEAVEN WITH JA-PAN NUMBER 44 ONLY WHEN IT'S MADE REALLY WELL, TOO.
IT WAS ALL VERY SUDDEN, SO WEREN'T YOU SURPRISED?
YES, WELL... I WAS EXTREMELY SURPRISED.
OH...NOW THAT I REMEMBER, GRANDUNCLE UMASABURO IN GIFU... THAT TIME, MAYBE HE WENT TO HEAVEN INSTEAD OF BEING ASLEEP...?
GREAT UNCLE!! UNCLE UMASABURO!!
RUSTLE
RUSTLE
...
HE'S SLEEPING LIKE A LOG. IT WOULD BE MEAN IF I WAKE HIM UP.

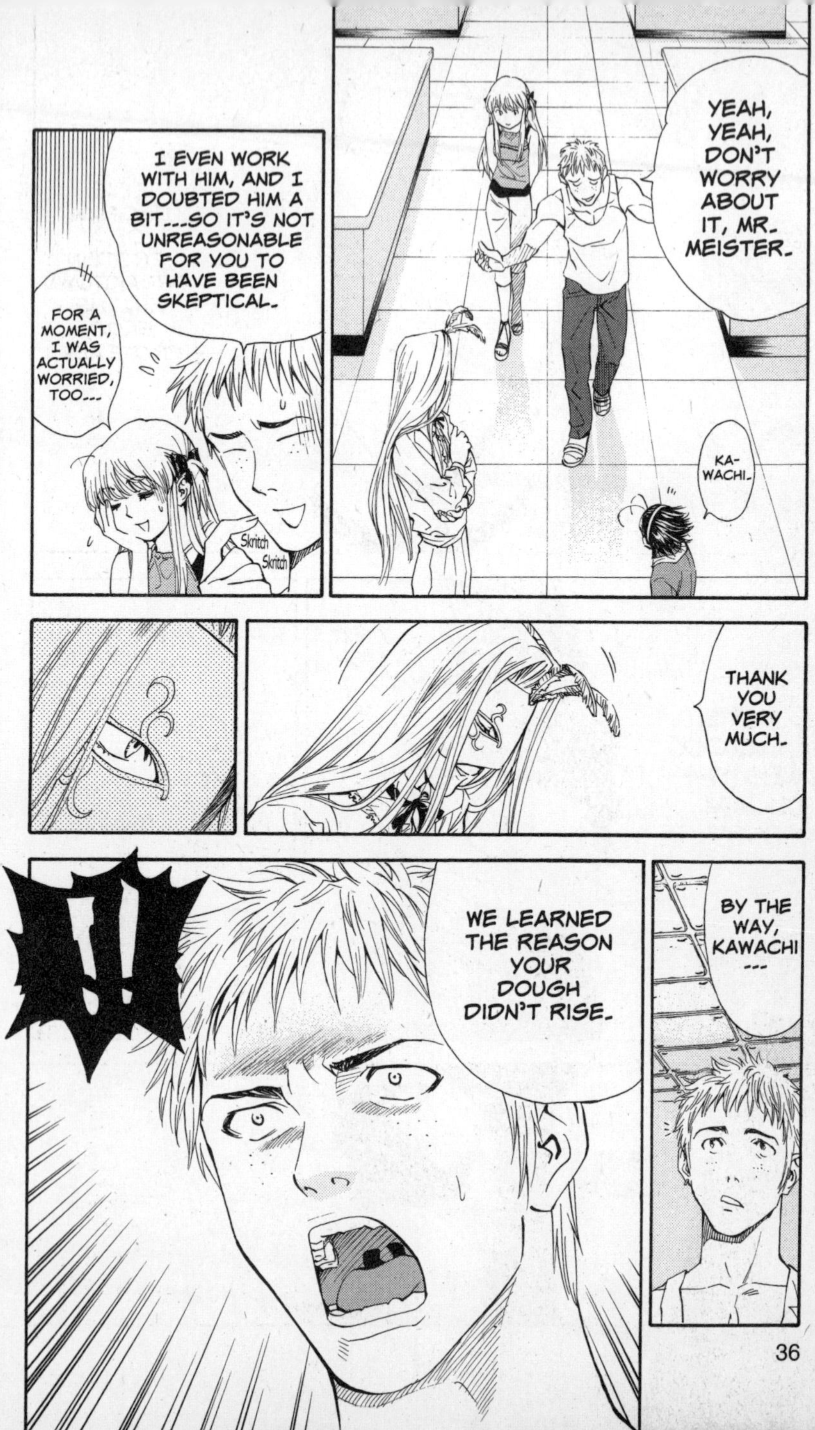
YEAH, YEAH, DON'T WORRY ABOUT IT, MR. MEISTER.
KA-WACHI.
I EVEN WORK WITH HIM, AND I DOUBTED HIM A BIT...SO IT'S NOT UNREASONABLE FOR YOU TO HAVE BEEN SKEPTICAL.
FOR A MOMENT, I WAS ACTUALLY WORRIED, TOO...
Skritch Skritch
THANK YOU VERY MUCH.
BY THE WAY, KAWACHI ---
WE LEARNED THE REASON YOUR DOUGH DIDN'T RISE.
!!

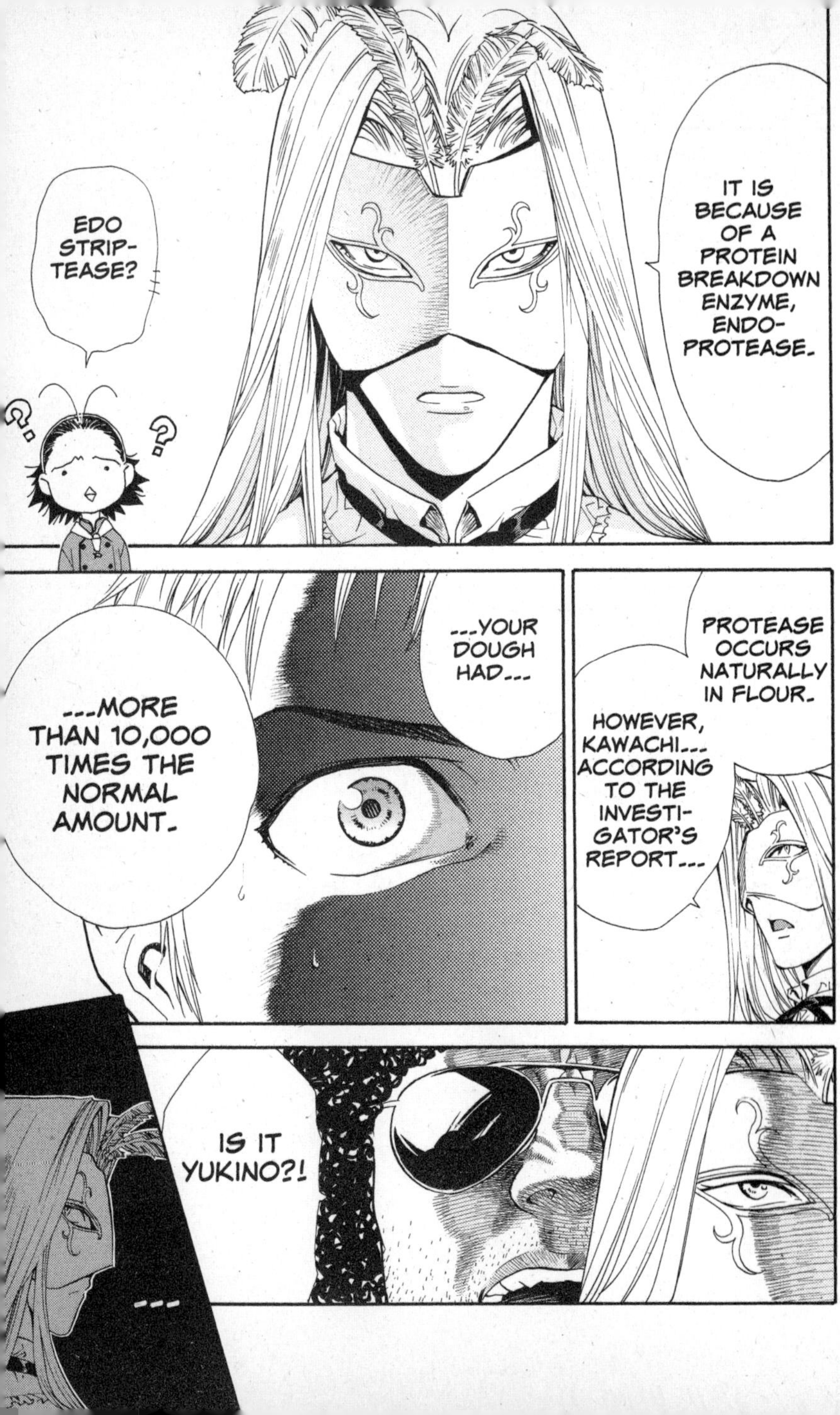

IT IS BECAUSE OF A PROTEIN BREAKDOWN ENZYME, ENDO-PROTEASE.
EDO STRIP-TEASE?
PROTEASE OCCURS NATURALLY IN FLOUR.
HOWEVER, KAWACHI... ACCORDING TO THE INVESTI-GATOR'S REPORT...
...YOUR DOUGH HAD...
...MORE THAN 10,000 TIMES THE NORMAL AMOUNT.
IS IT YUKINO?!
...

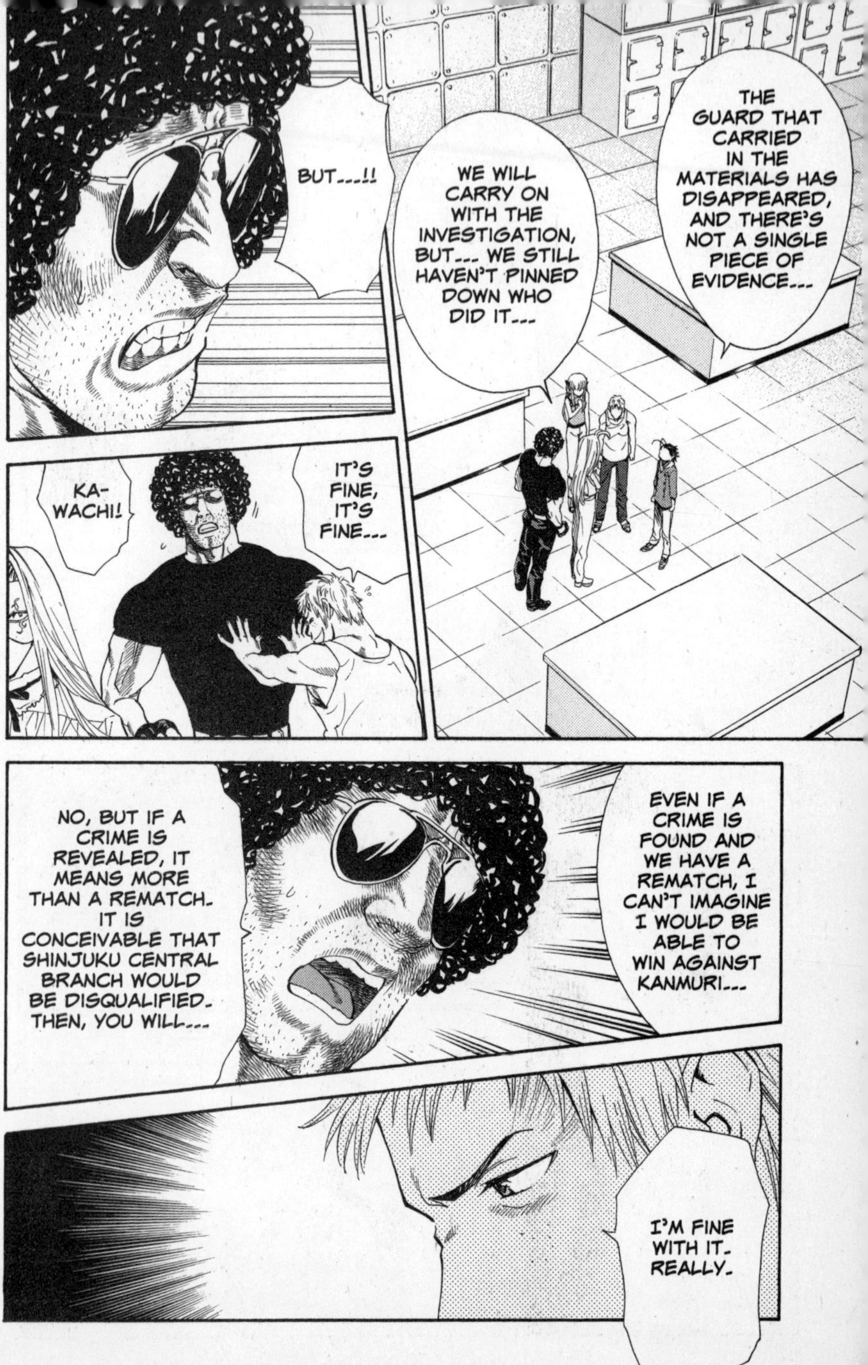
THE GUARD THAT CARRIED IN THE MATERIALS HAS DISAPPEARED, AND THERE'S NOT A SINGLE PIECE OF EVIDENCE...
WE WILL CARRY ON WITH THE INVESTIGATION, BUT... WE STILL HAVEN'T PINNED DOWN WHO DID IT...
BUT...!!
IT'S FINE, IT'S FINE...
KA-WACHI!
EVEN IF A CRIME IS FOUND AND WE HAVE A REMATCH, I CAN'T IMAGINE I WOULD BE ABLE TO WIN AGAINST KANMURI...
NO, BUT IF A CRIME IS REVEALED, IT MEANS MORE THAN A REMATCH. IT IS CONCEIVABLE THAT SHINJUKU CENTRAL BRANCH WOULD BE DISQUALIFIED. THEN, YOU WILL...
I'M FINE WITH IT. REALLY.

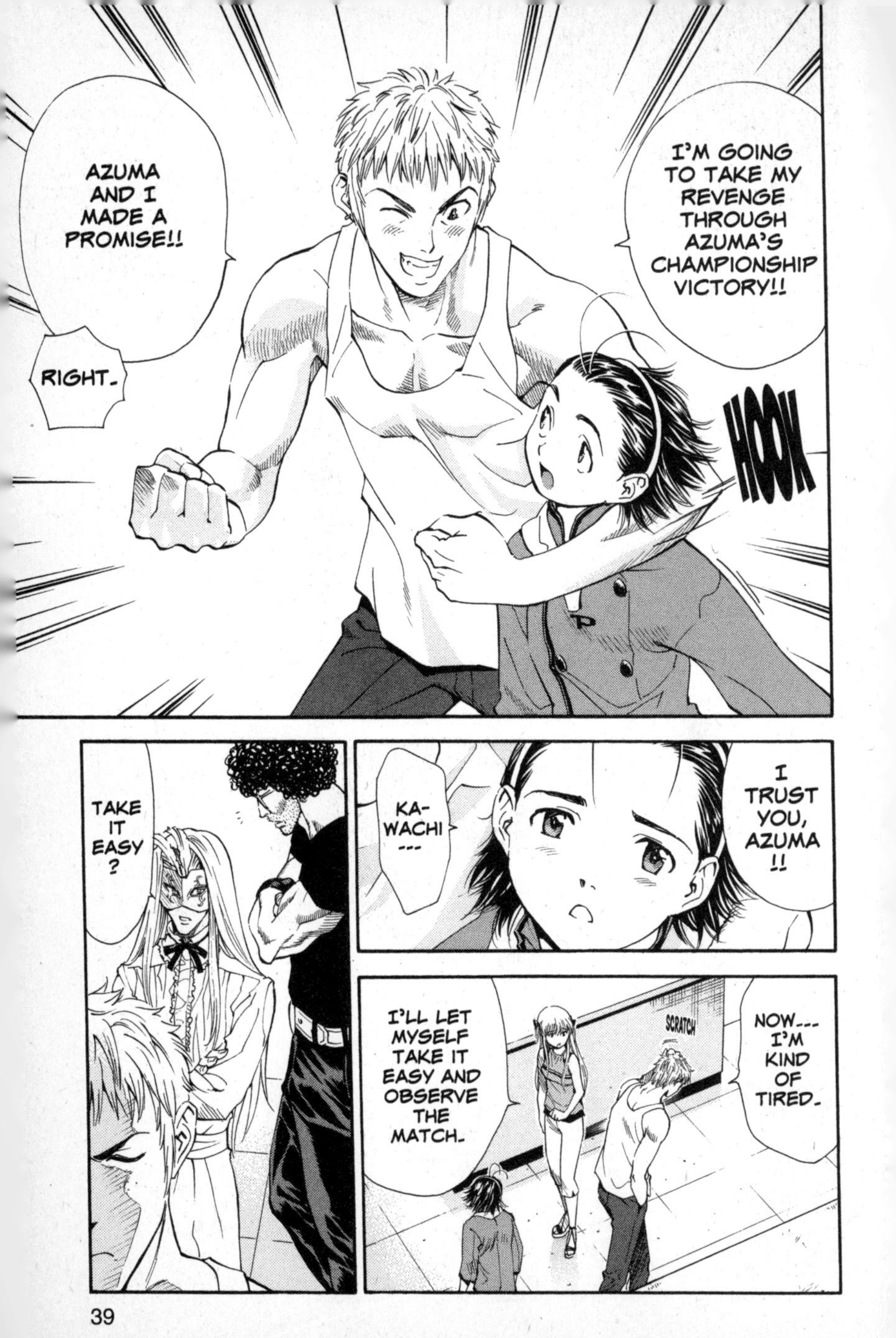
I'M GOING TO TAKE MY REVENGE THROUGH AZUMA'S CHAMPIONSHIP VICTORY!!
AZUMA AND I MADE A PROMISE!!
RIGHT.
HOOK
I TRUST YOU, AZUMA!!
KA-WACHI...
NOW... I'M KIND OF TIRED.
SCRATCH
I'LL LET MYSELF TAKE IT EASY AND OBSERVE THE MATCH.
TAKE IT EASY?

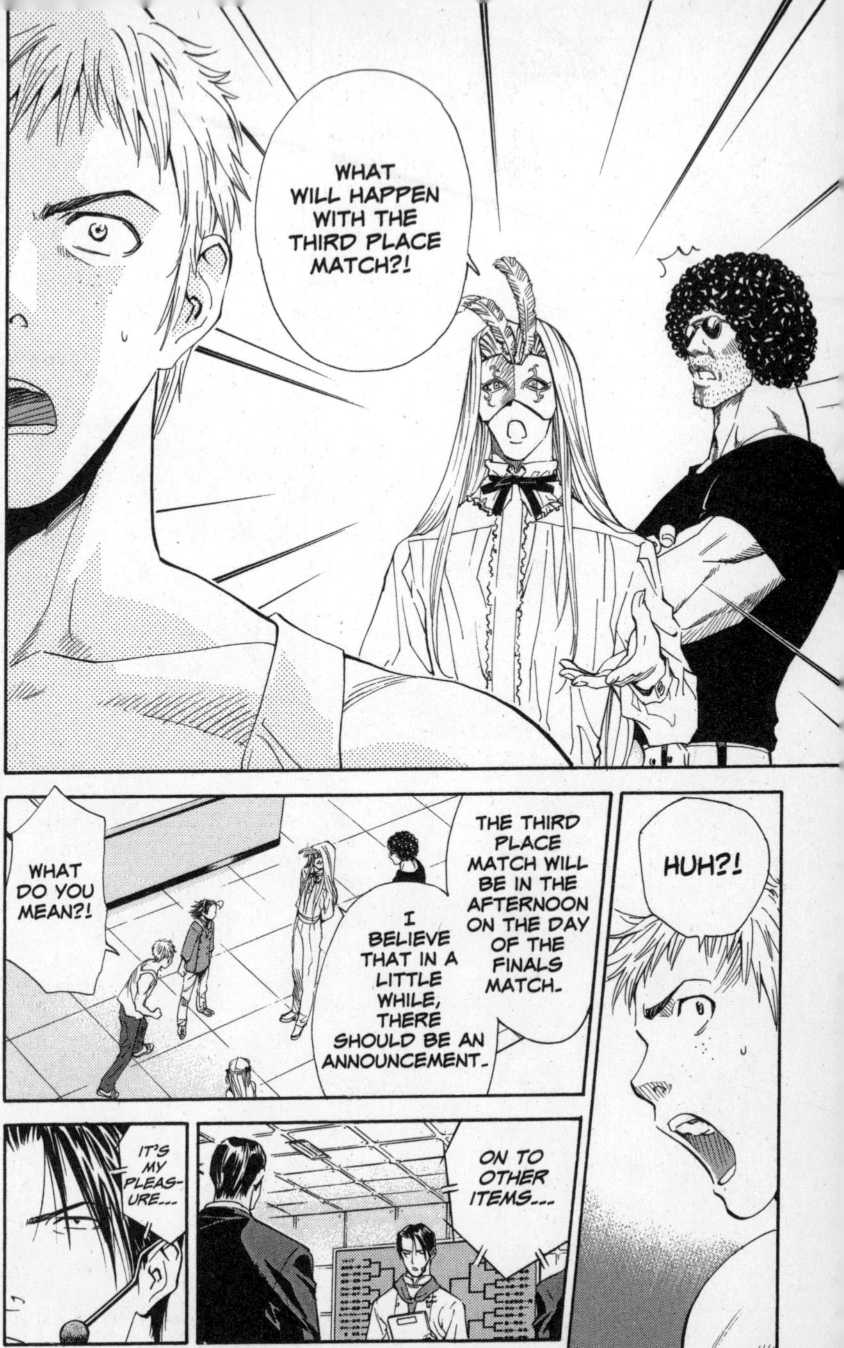
WHAT WILL HAPPEN WITH THE THIRD PLACE MATCH?!
HUH?!
WHAT DO YOU MEAN?!
THE THIRD PLACE MATCH WILL BE IN THE AFTERNOON ON THE DAY OF THE FINALS MATCH.
I BELIEVE THAT IN A LITTLE WHILE, THERE SHOULD BE AN ANNOUNCEMENT.
ON TO OTHER ITEMS...
IT'S MY PLEASURE...

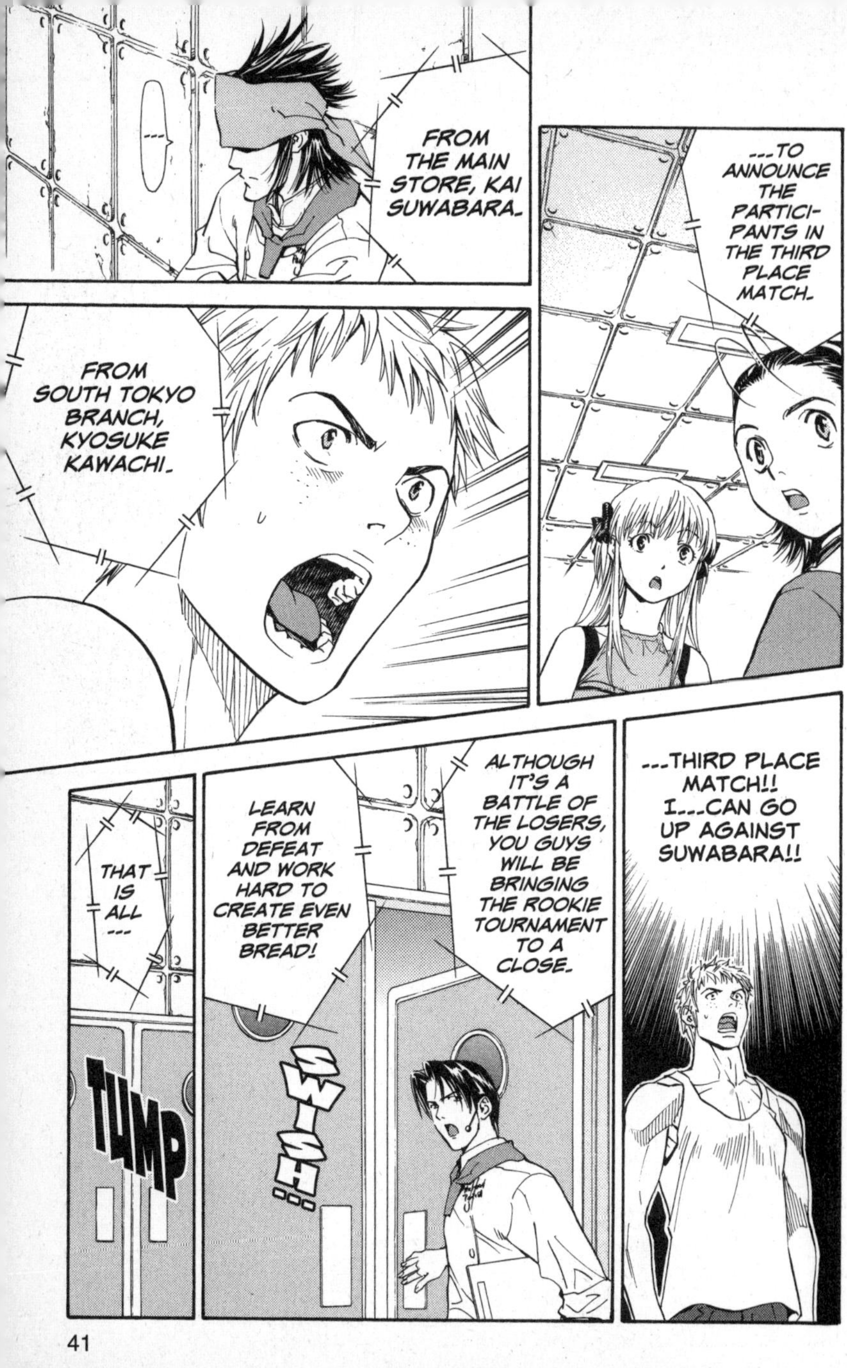
---TO ANNOUNCE THE PARTICIPANTS IN THE THIRD PLACE MATCH-
FROM THE MAIN STORE, KAI SUWABARA-

FROM SOUTH TOKYO BRANCH, KYOSUKE KAWACHI-
---THIRD PLACE MATCH!! I---CAN GO UP AGAINST SUWABARA!!
ALTHOUGH IT'S A BATTLE OF THE LOSERS, YOU GUYS WILL BE BRINGING THE ROOKIE TOURNAMENT TO A CLOSE-
LEARN FROM DEFEAT AND WORK HARD TO CREATE EVEN BETTER BREAD!
SWISH---
THAT IS ALL ---
THUMP

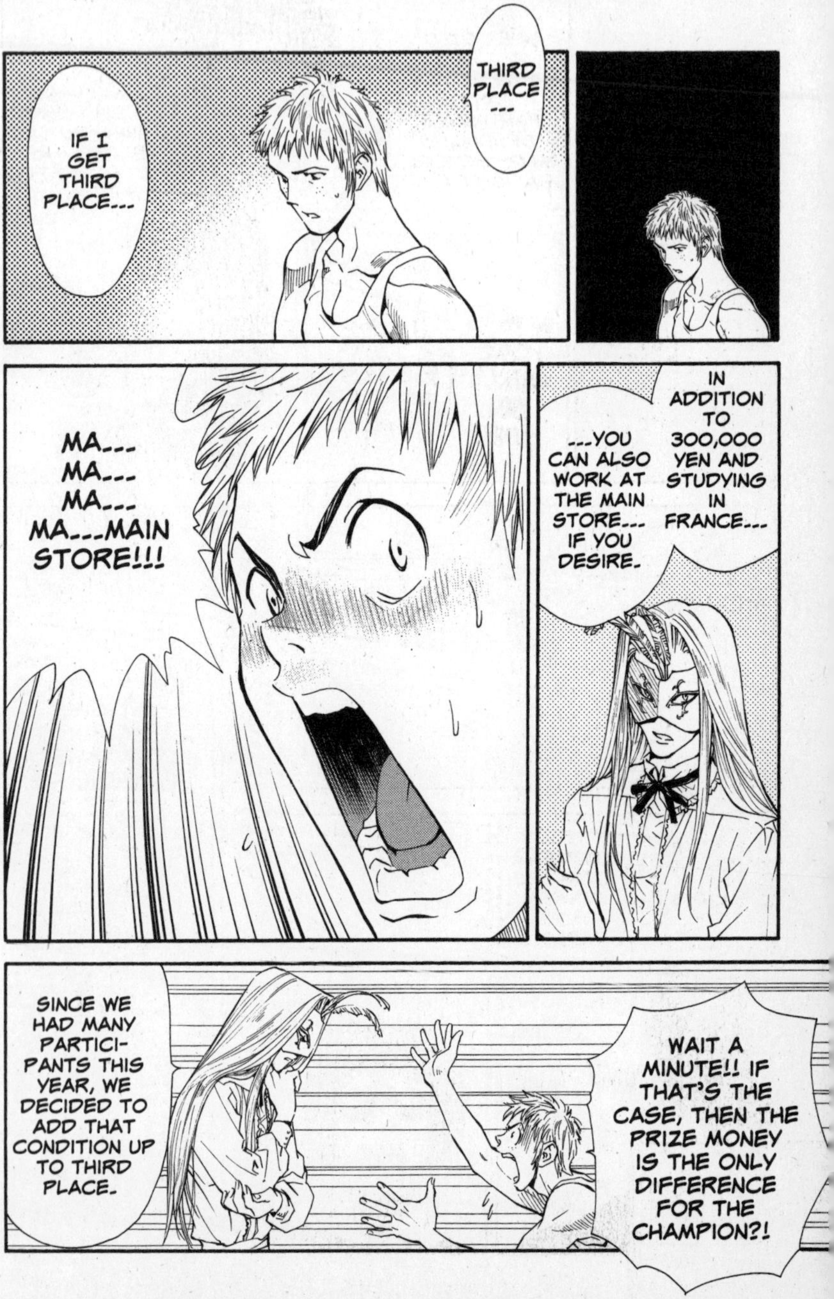
THIRD PLACE...
IF I GET THIRD PLACE...
IN ADDITION TO 300,000 YEN AND STUDYING IN FRANCE...
...YOU CAN ALSO WORK AT THE MAIN STORE... IF YOU DESIRE.
MA... MA... MA... MA...MAIN STORE!!!
WAIT A MINUTE!! IF THAT'S THE CASE, THEN THE PRIZE MONEY IS THE ONLY DIFFERENCE FOR THE CHAMPION?!
SINCE WE HAD MANY PARTICI-PANTS THIS YEAR, WE DECIDED TO ADD THAT CONDITION UP TO THIRD PLACE.

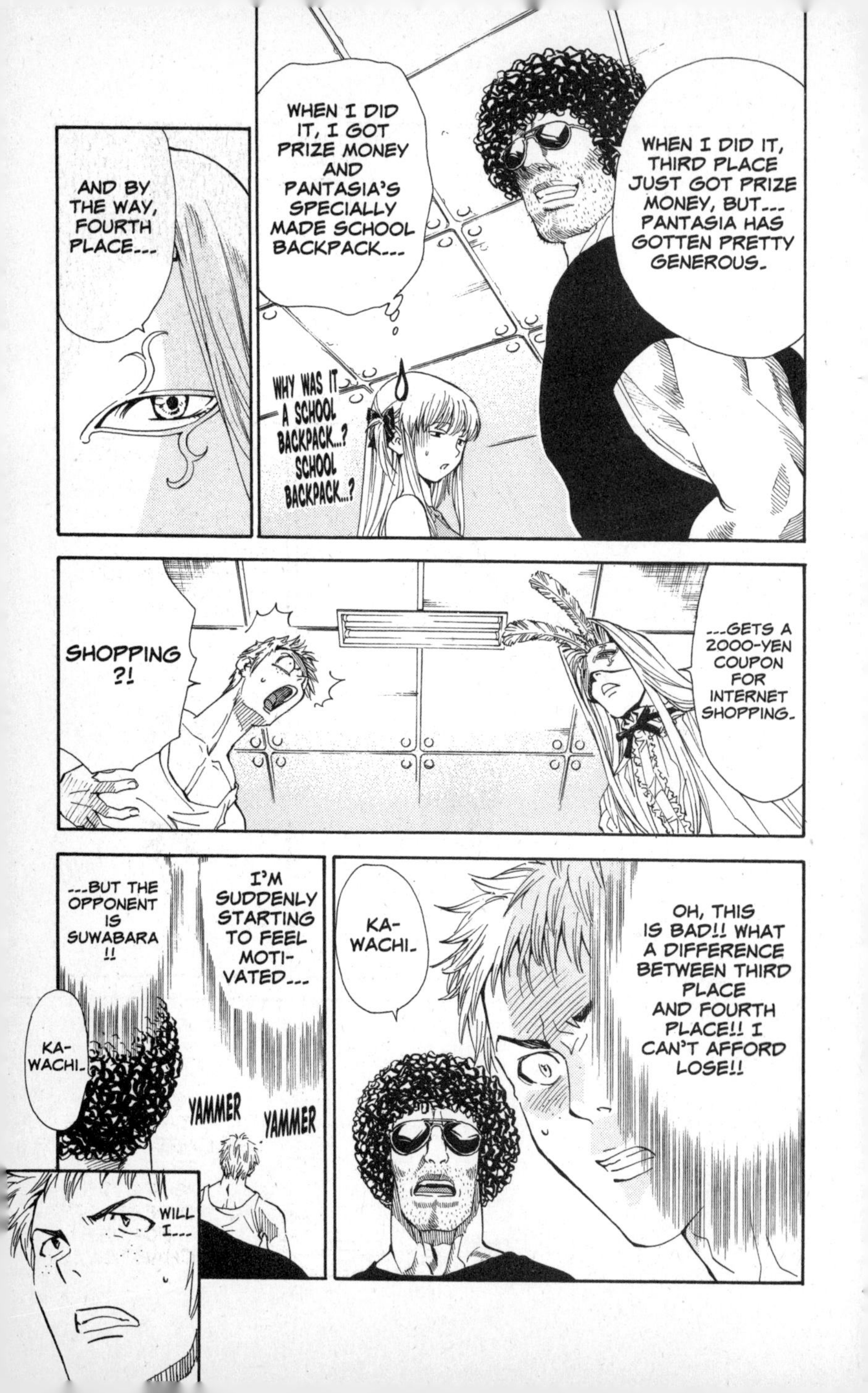
WHEN I DID IT, THIRD PLACE JUST GOT PRIZE MONEY, BUT... PANTASIA HAS GOTTEN PRETTY GENEROUS.
WHEN I DID IT, I GOT PRIZE MONEY AND PANTASIA'S SPECIALLY MADE SCHOOL BACKPACK...
WHY WAS IT A SCHOOL BACKPACK..? SCHOOL BACKPACK..?
AND BY THE WAY, FOURTH PLACE...
...GETS A 2000-YEN COUPON FOR INTERNET SHOPPING.
SHOPPING ?!
OH, THIS IS BAD!! WHAT A DIFFERENCE BETWEEN THIRD PLACE AND FOURTH PLACE!! I CAN'T AFFORD LOSE!!
KA-WACHI.
I'M SUDDENLY STARTING TO FEEL MOTI-VATED...
...BUT THE OPPONENT IS SUWABARA!!
KA-WACHI.
YAMMER
YAMMER
WILL I...

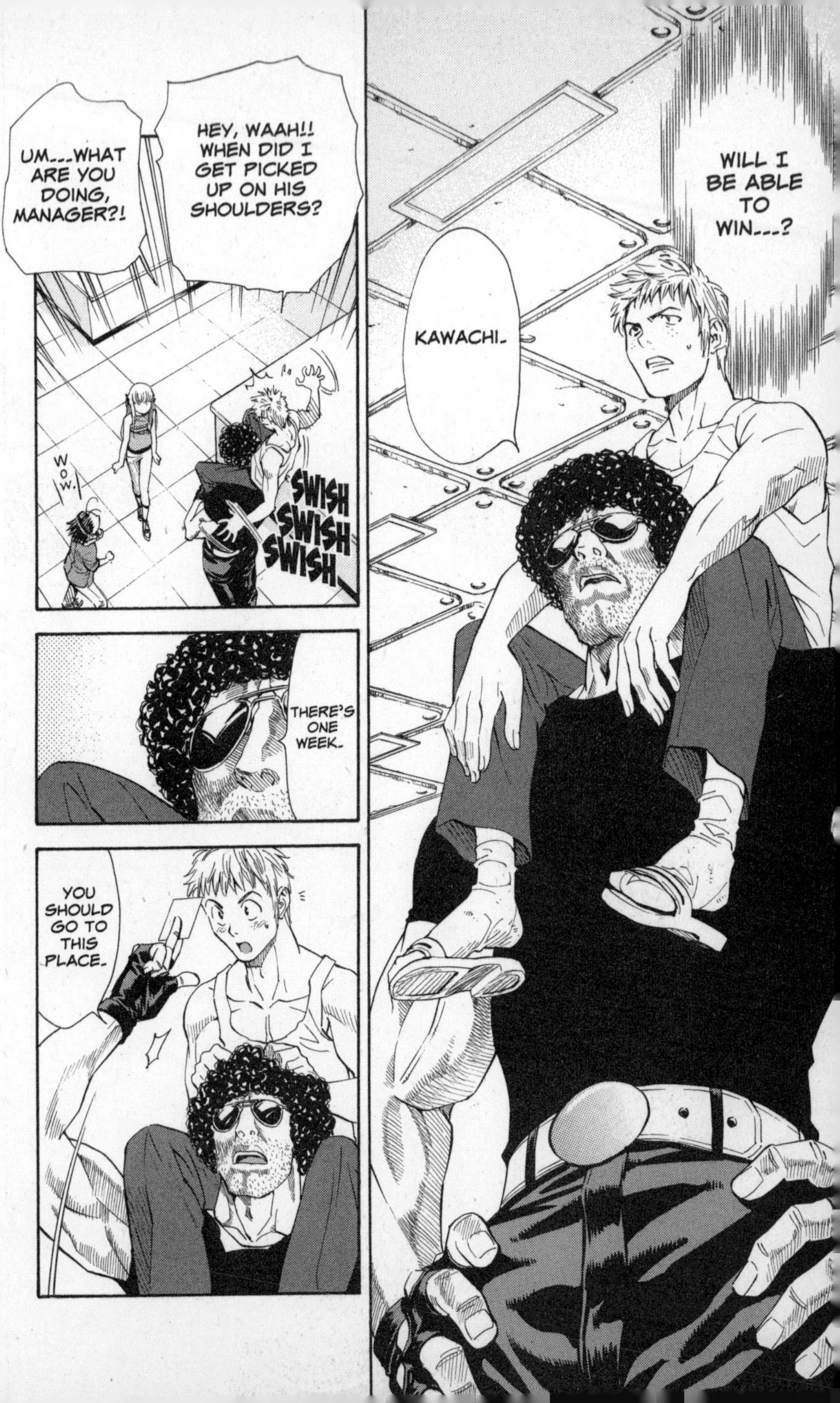
WILL I BE ABLE TO WIN...?
KAWACHI...
HEY, WAAH!! WHEN DID I GET PICKED UP ON HIS SHOULDERS?
UM...WHAT ARE YOU DOING, MANAGER?!
WOW.
SWISH SWISH SWISH
THERE'S ONE WEEK.
YOU SHOULD GO TO THIS PLACE.

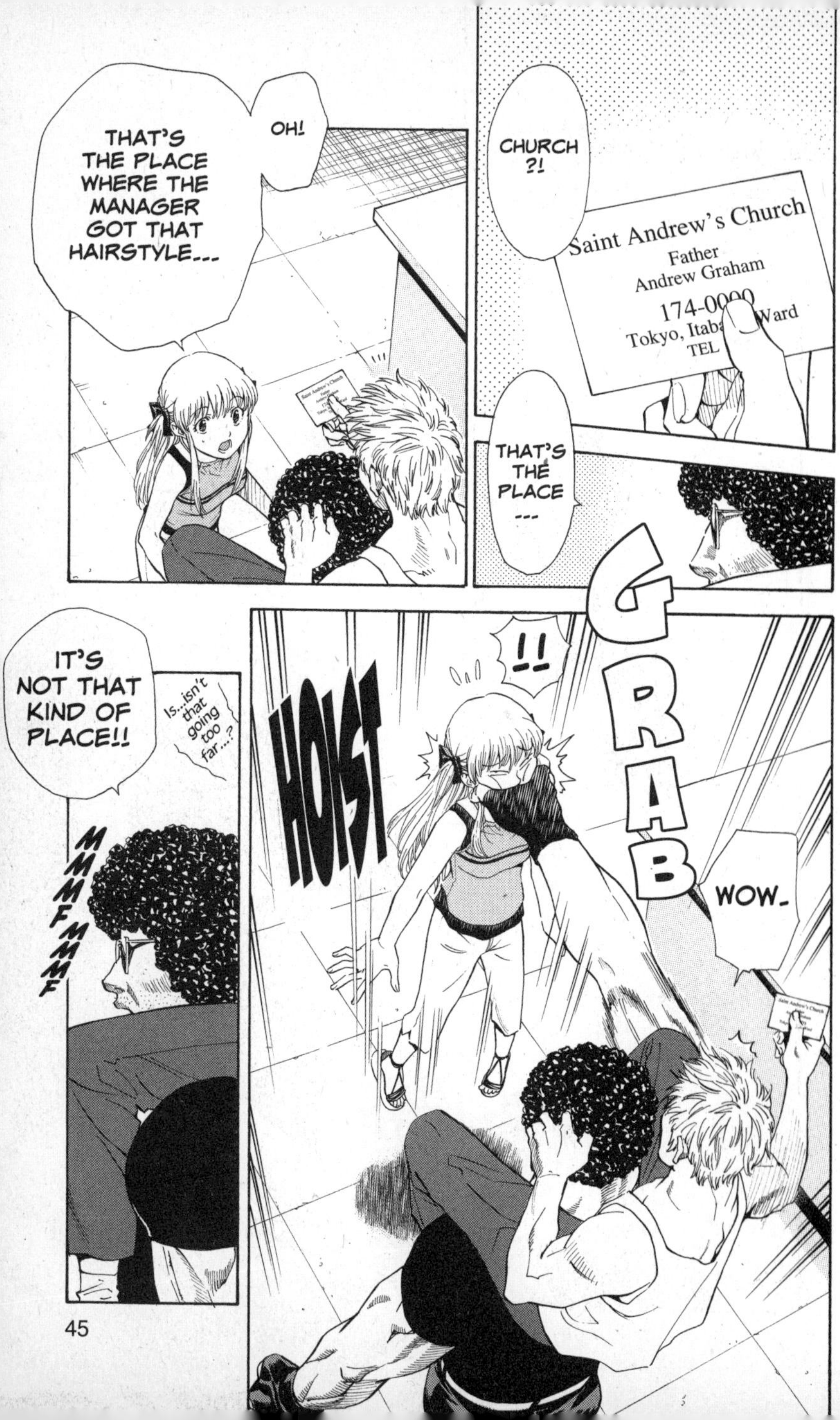
CHURCH ?!
Saint Andrew's Church
Father
Andrew Graham
174-0000
Tokyo, Itaba Ward
TEL
THAT'S THE PLACE ...
OH!
THAT'S THE PLACE WHERE THE MANAGER GOT THAT HAIRSTYLE...
GRAB
!!
HOIST
WOW...
IT'S NOT THAT KIND OF PLACE!!
Is...isn't that going too far...?
MMMF MMMF

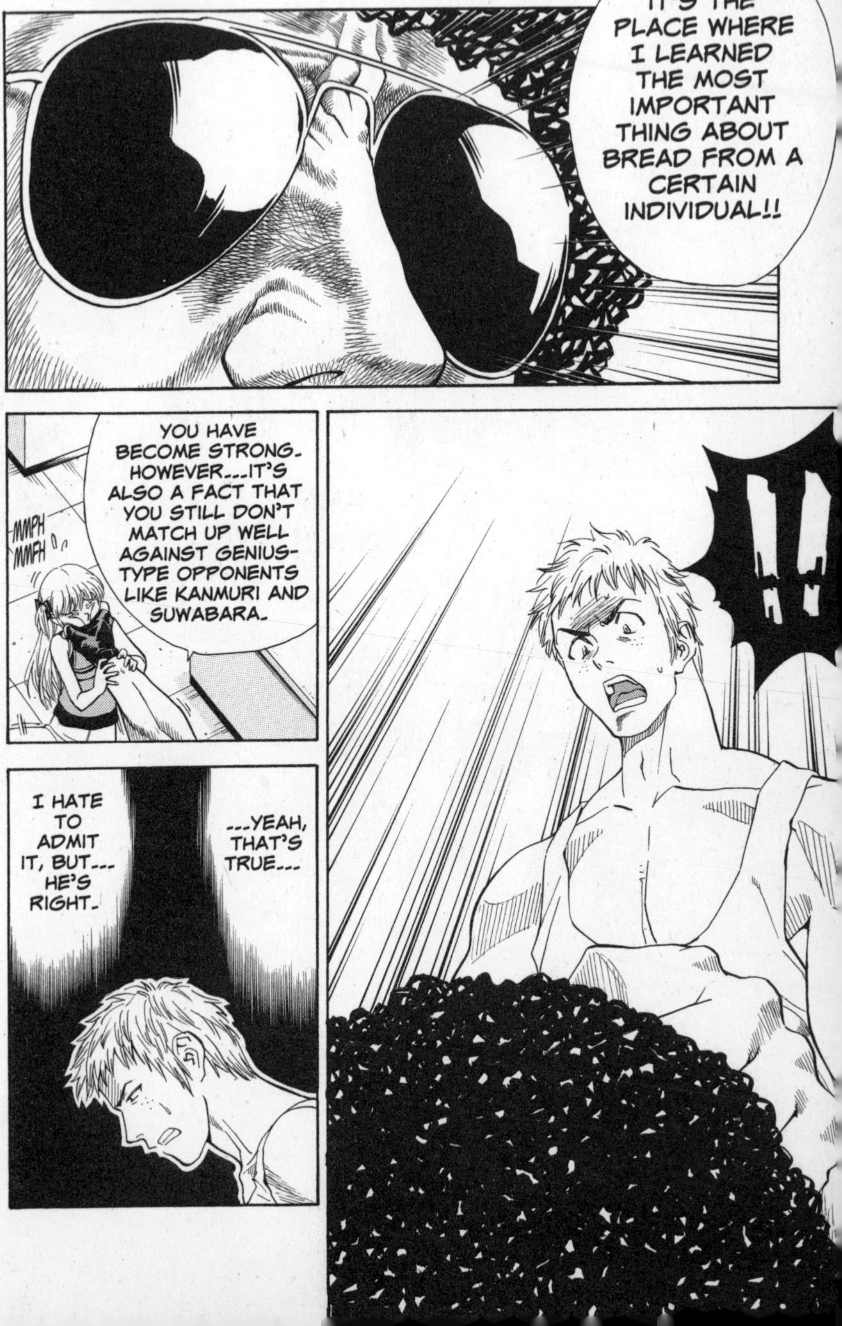
IT'S THE PLACE WHERE I LEARNED THE MOST IMPORTANT THING ABOUT BREAD FROM A CERTAIN INDIVIDUAL!!
!!
YOU HAVE BECOME STRONG. HOWEVER...IT'S ALSO A FACT THAT YOU STILL DON'T MATCH UP WELL AGAINST GENIUS-TYPE OPPONENTS LIKE KANMURI AND SUWABARA.
MMPH MMFH
...YEAH, THAT'S TRUE...
I HATE TO ADMIT IT, BUT... HE'S RIGHT.

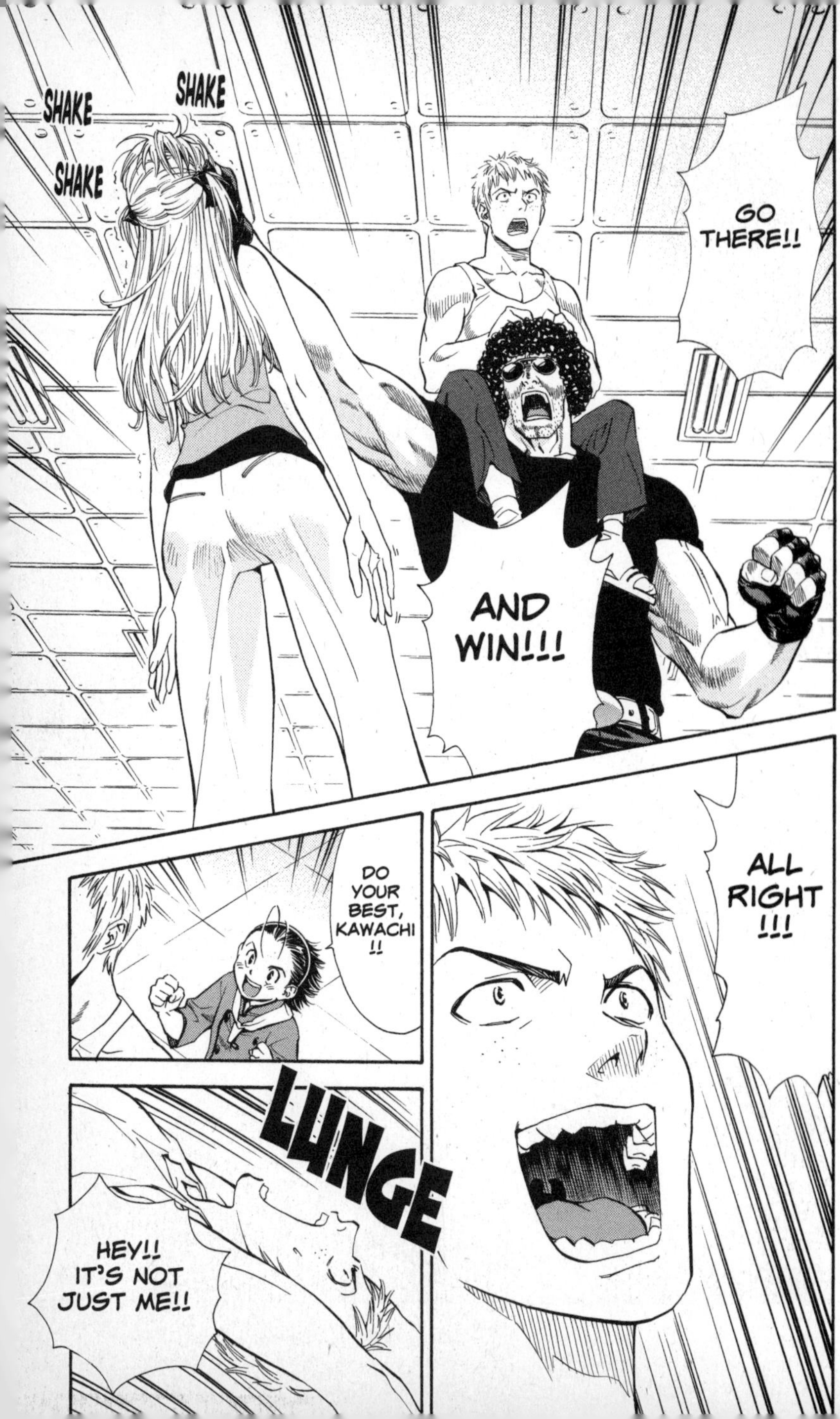
GO THERE!!
SHAKE
SHAKE
SHAKE
AND WIN!!!
ALL RIGHT!!!
DO YOUR BEST, KAWACHI!!
LUNGE
HEY!! IT'S NOT JUST ME!!

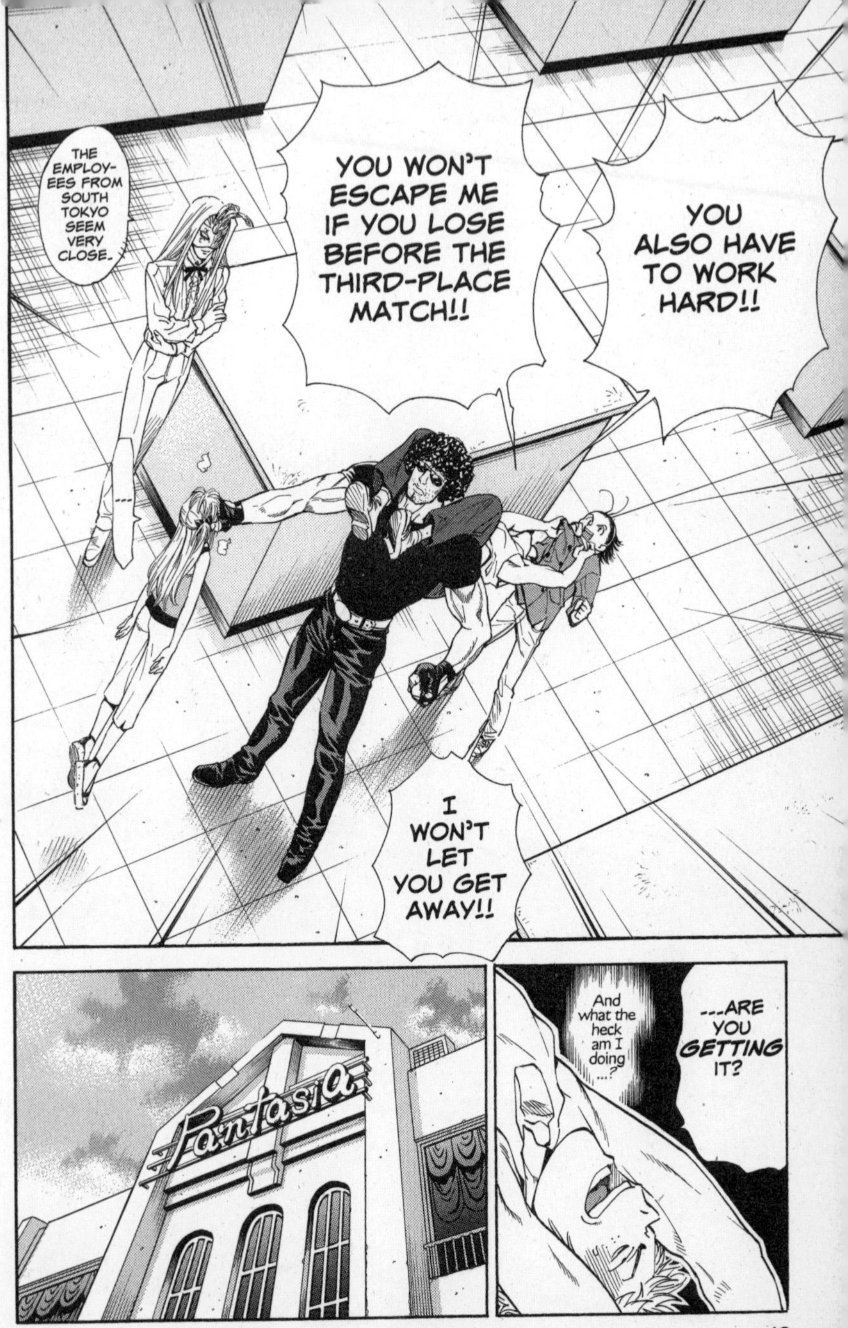
YOU ALSO HAVE TO WORK HARD!!
YOU WON'T ESCAPE ME IF YOU LOSE BEFORE THE THIRD-PLACE MATCH!!
THE EMPLOY-EES FROM SOUTH TOKYO SEEM VERY CLOSE.

I WON'T LET YOU GET AWAY!!
---ARE YOU GETTING IT?
And what the heck am I doing...?
Pantasia

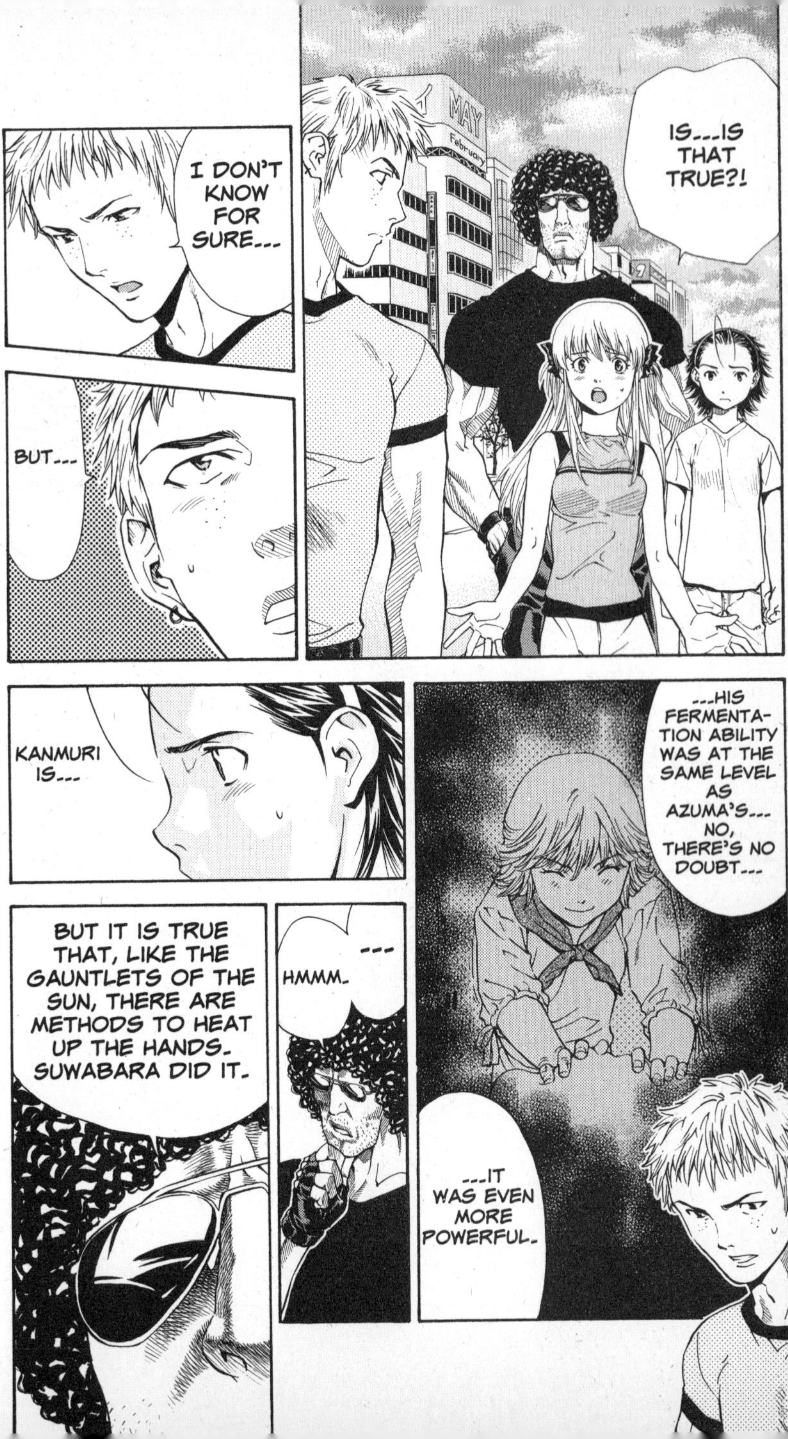
IS...IS THAT TRUE?!
I DON'T KNOW FOR SURE...
BUT...
...HIS FERMENTATION ABILITY WAS AT THE SAME LEVEL AS AZUMA'S... NO, THERE'S NO DOUBT...
...IT WAS EVEN MORE POWERFUL.
KANMURI IS...
...
HMMM.
BUT IT IS TRUE THAT, LIKE THE GAUNTLETS OF THE SUN, THERE ARE METHODS TO HEAT UP THE HANDS. SUWABARA DID IT.

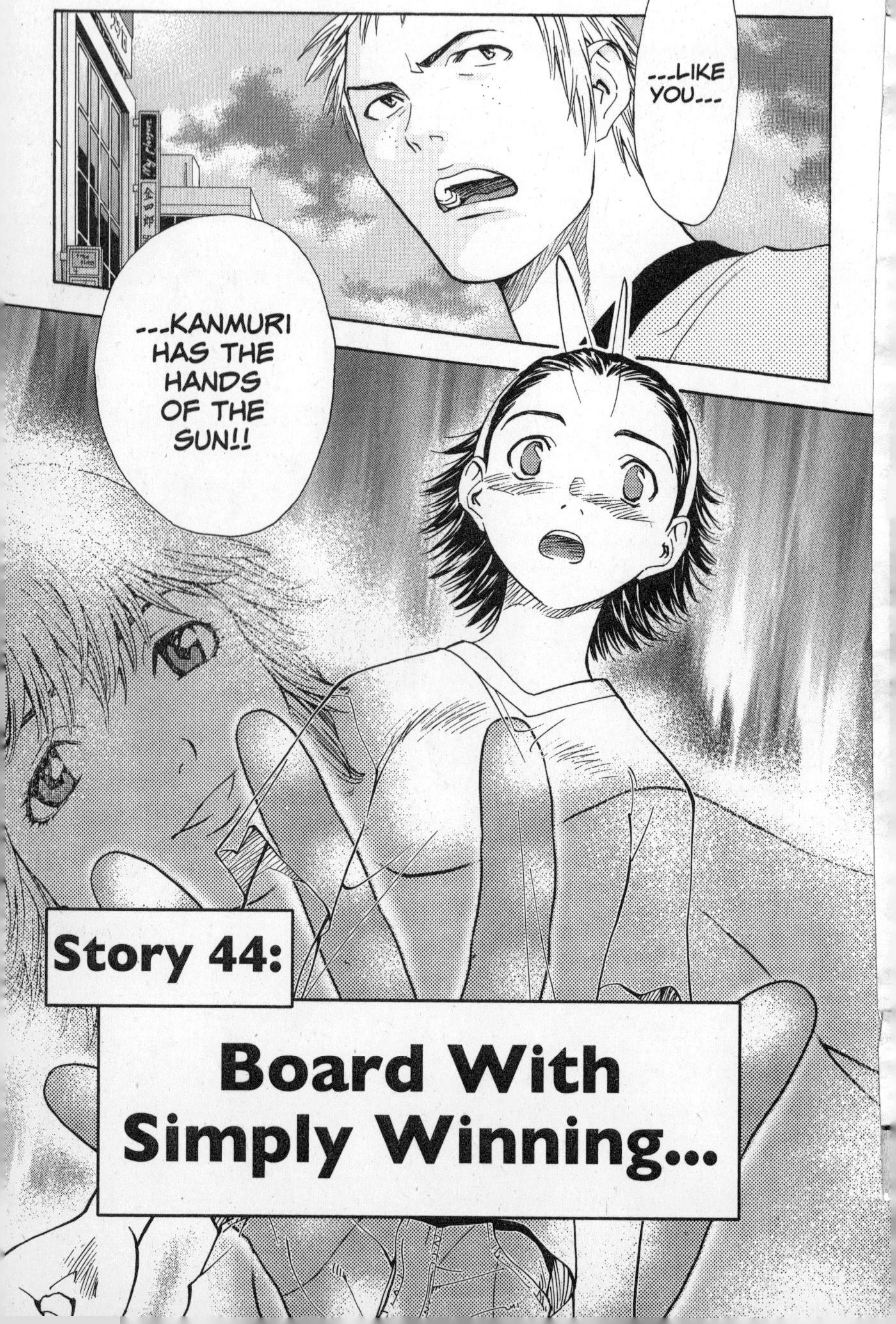
---LIKE YOU---
---KANMURI HAS THE HANDS OF THE SUN!!
Story 44:
Board With Simply Winning...

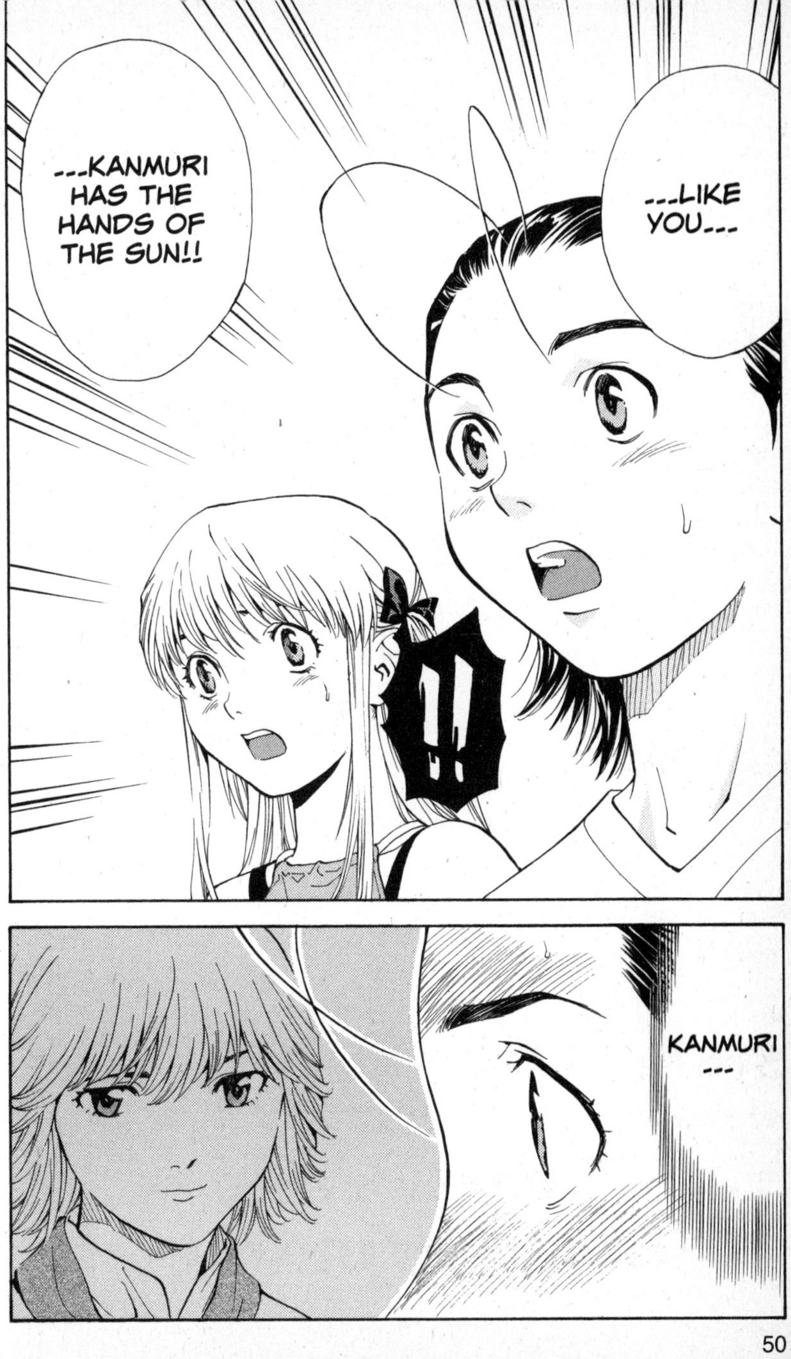
---LIKE YOU---
---KANMURI HAS THE HANDS OF THE SUN!!
!!
KANMURI ---

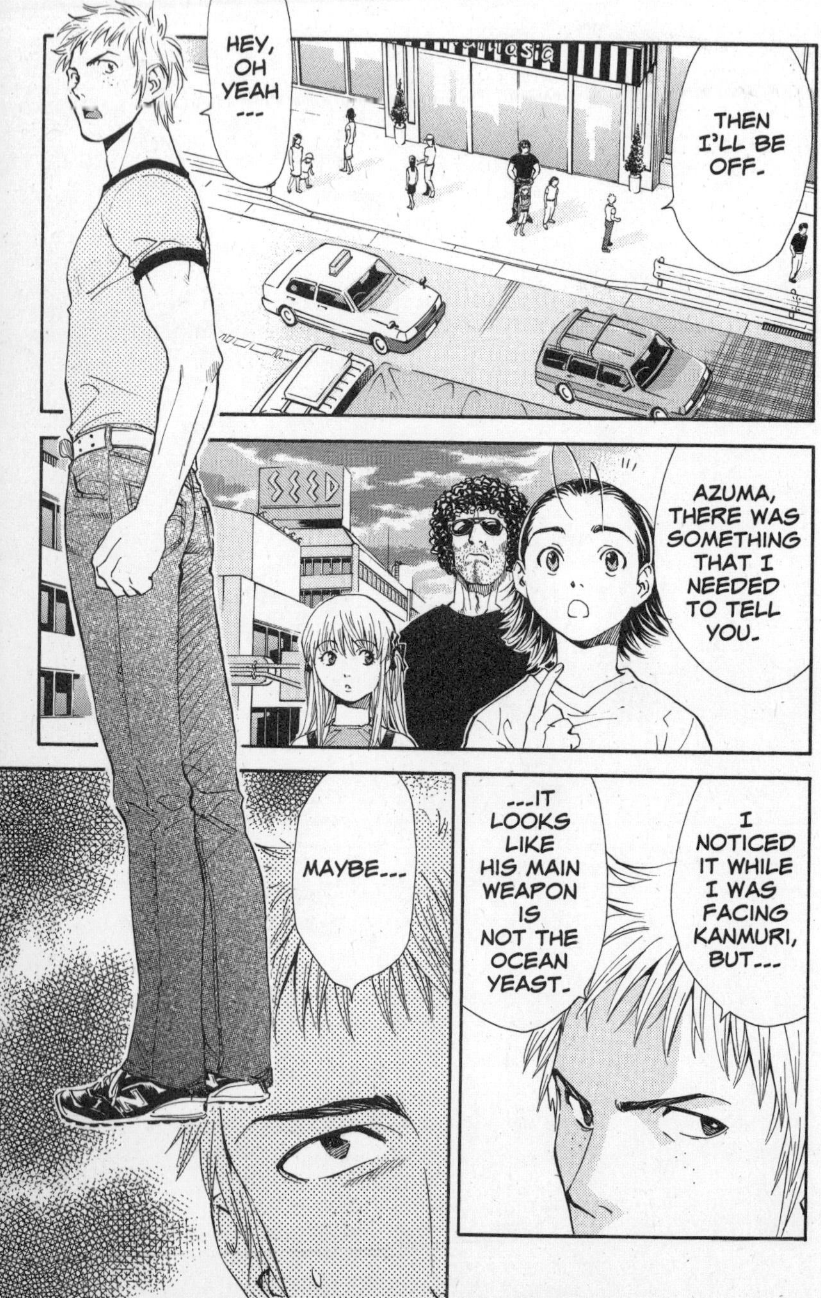
THEN I'LL BE OFF.
HEY, OH YEAH---
SEED
AZUMA, THERE WAS SOMETHING THAT I NEEDED TO TELL YOU.
I NOTICED IT WHILE I WAS FACING KANMURI, BUT...
...IT LOOKS LIKE HIS MAIN WEAPON IS NOT THE OCEAN YEAST.
MAYBE...

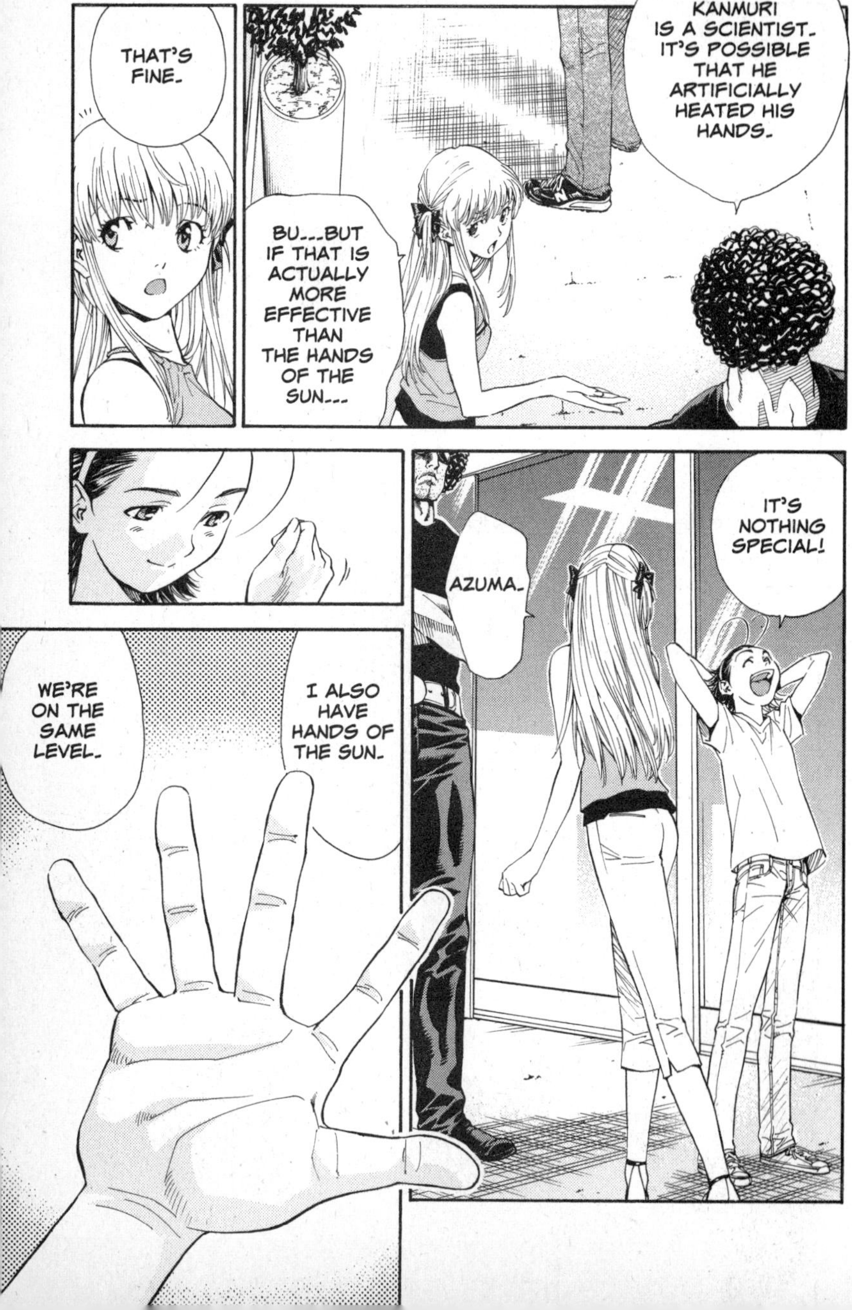
KANMURI IS A SCIENTIST. IT'S POSSIBLE THAT HE ARTIFICIALLY HEATED HIS HANDS.
BU...BUT IF THAT IS ACTUALLY MORE EFFECTIVE THAN THE HANDS OF THE SUN...
THAT'S FINE.
IT'S NOTHING SPECIAL!
AZUMA.
I ALSO HAVE HANDS OF THE SUN.
WE'RE ON THE SAME LEVEL.

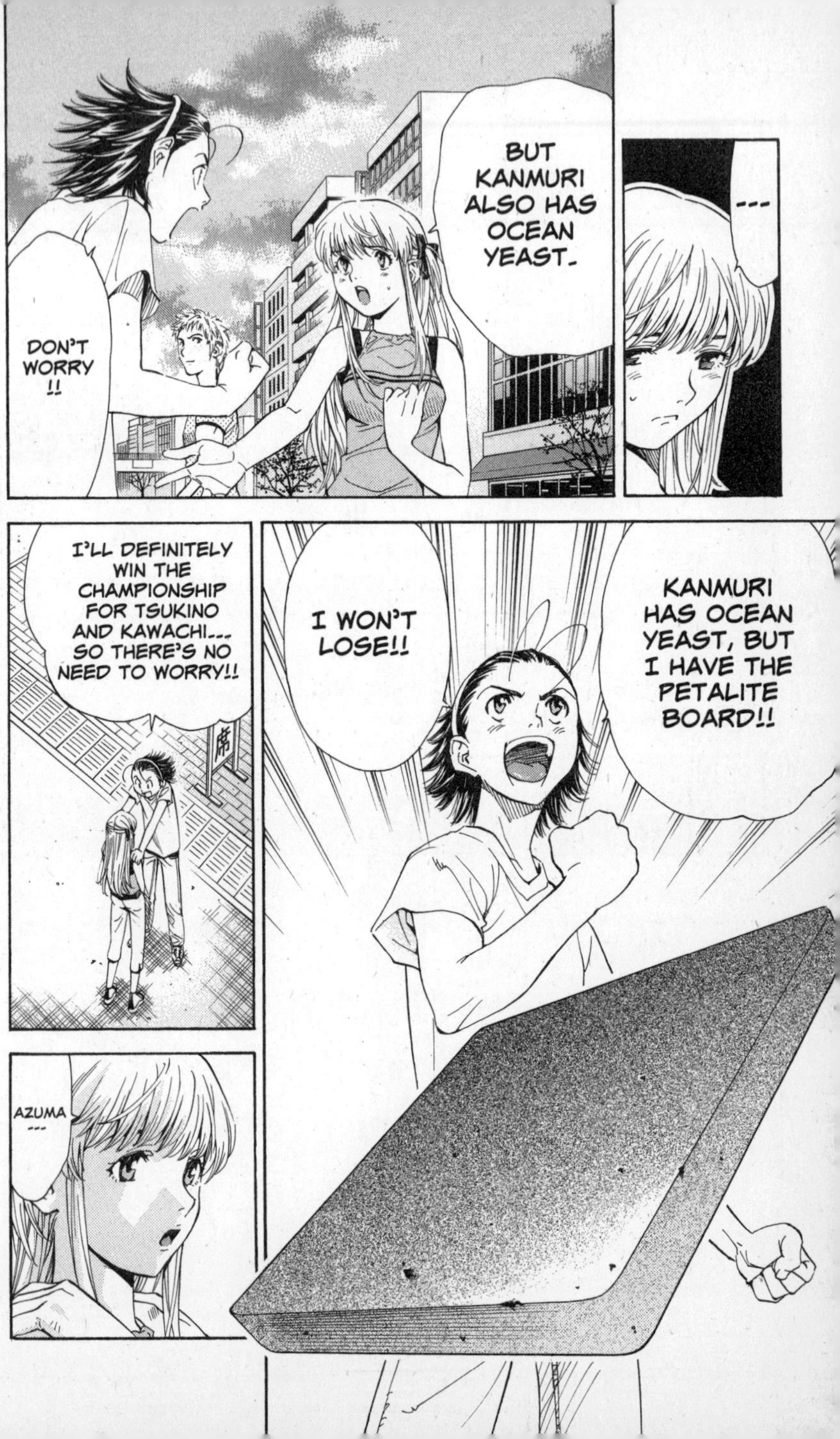

BUT KANMURI ALSO HAS OCEAN YEAST.
DON'T WORRY !!
KANMURI HAS OCEAN YEAST, BUT I HAVE THE PETALITE BOARD!!
I WON'T LOSE!!
I'LL DEFINITELY WIN THE CHAMPIONSHIP FOR TSUKINO AND KAWACHI... SO THERE'S NO NEED TO WORRY!!
AZUMA ---

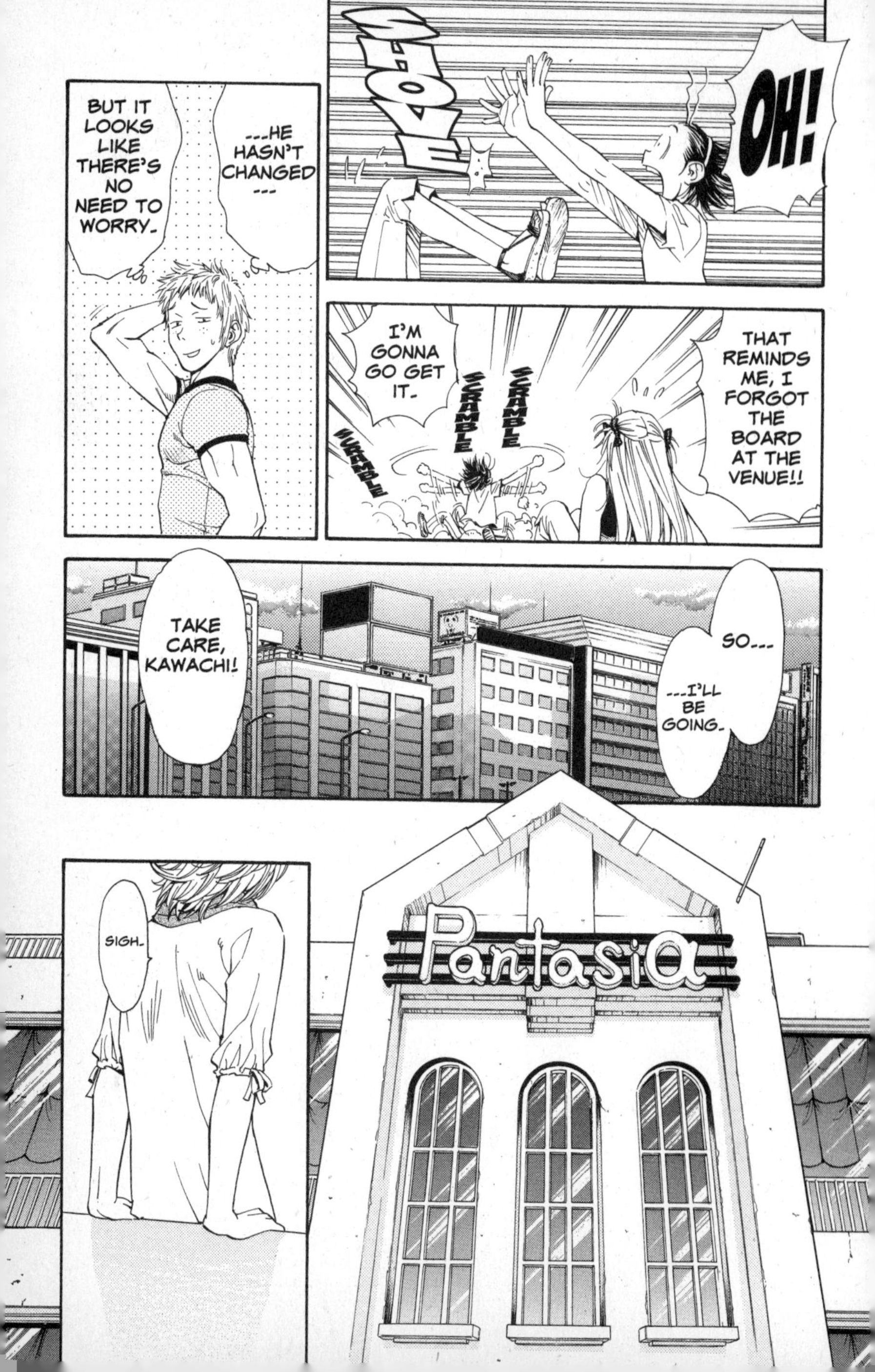
OH!
SHOVE
...HE HASN'T CHANGED...
BUT IT LOOKS LIKE THERE'S NO NEED TO WORRY.
THAT REMINDS ME, I FORGOT THE BOARD AT THE VENUE!!
SCRAMBLE
SCRAMBLE
I'M GONNA GO GET IT.
SCRAMBLE
SO...
...I'LL BE GOING.
TAKE CARE, KAWACHI!
SIGH.
Pantasia

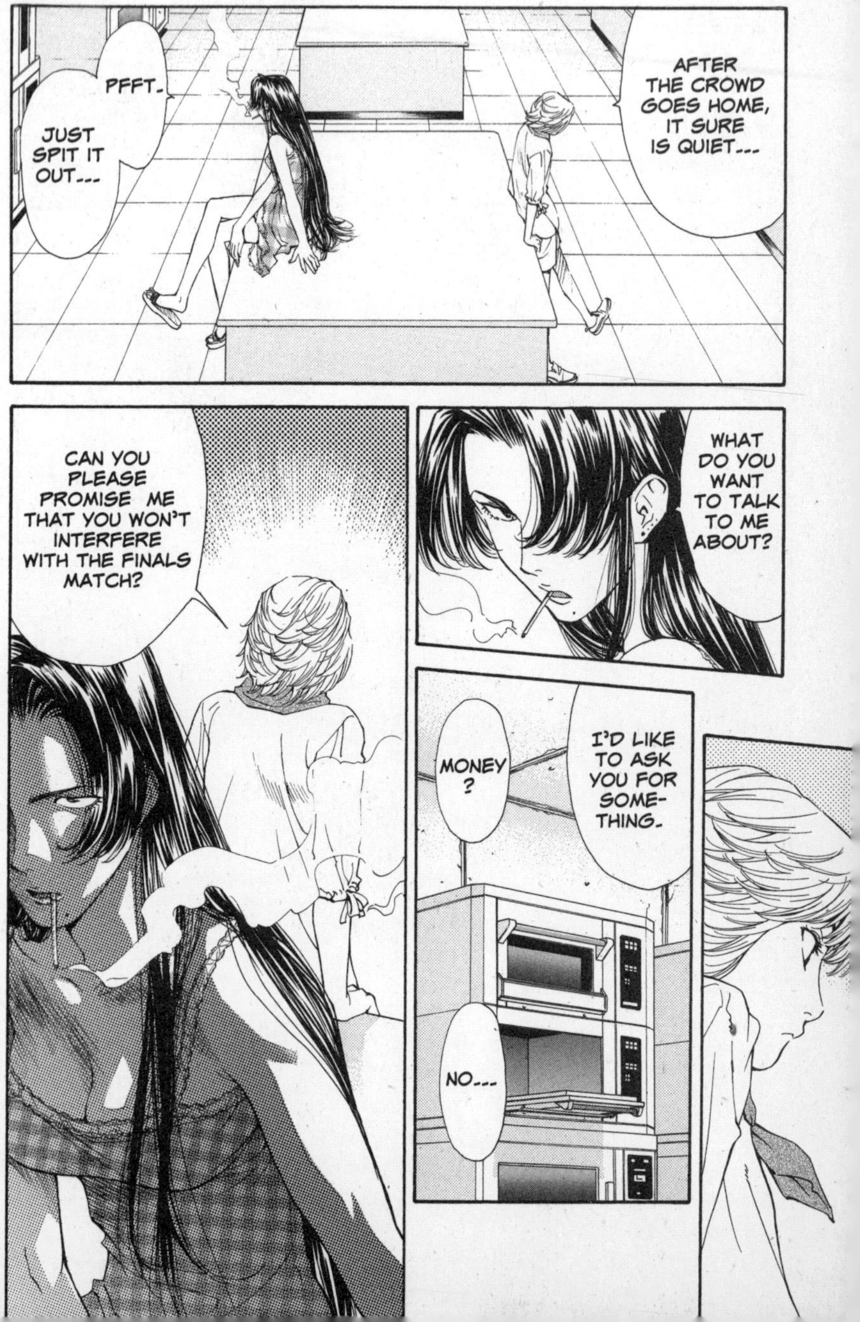
AFTER THE CROWD GOES HOME, IT SURE IS QUIET...
PFFT.
JUST SPIT IT OUT...
WHAT DO YOU WANT TO TALK TO ME ABOUT?
I'D LIKE TO ASK YOU FOR SOME-THING.
MONEY?
NO...
CAN YOU PLEASE PROMISE ME THAT YOU WON'T INTERFERE WITH THE FINALS MATCH?

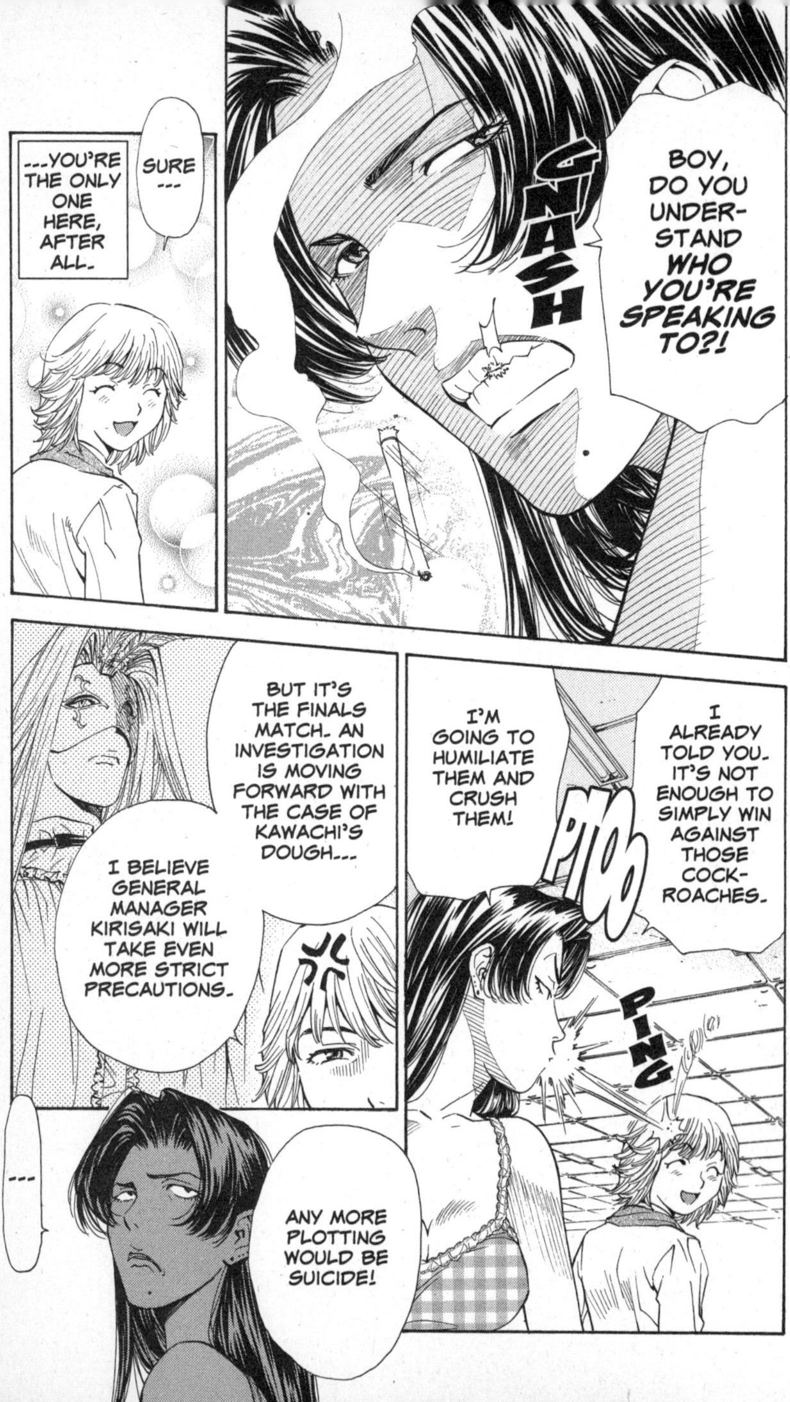
BOY, DO YOU UNDER-STAND WHO YOU'RE SPEAKING TO?!
GNASH
SURE ---
---YOU'RE THE ONLY ONE HERE, AFTER ALL.
I ALREADY TOLD YOU. IT'S NOT ENOUGH TO SIMPLY WIN AGAINST THOSE COCK-ROACHES.
I'M GOING TO HUMILIATE THEM AND CRUSH THEM!
PTOO
PING
BUT IT'S THE FINALS MATCH. AN INVESTIGATION IS MOVING FORWARD WITH THE CASE OF KAWACHI'S DOUGH...
I BELIEVE GENERAL MANAGER KIRISAKI WILL TAKE EVEN MORE STRICT PRECAUTIONS.
ANY MORE PLOTTING WOULD BE SUICIDE!

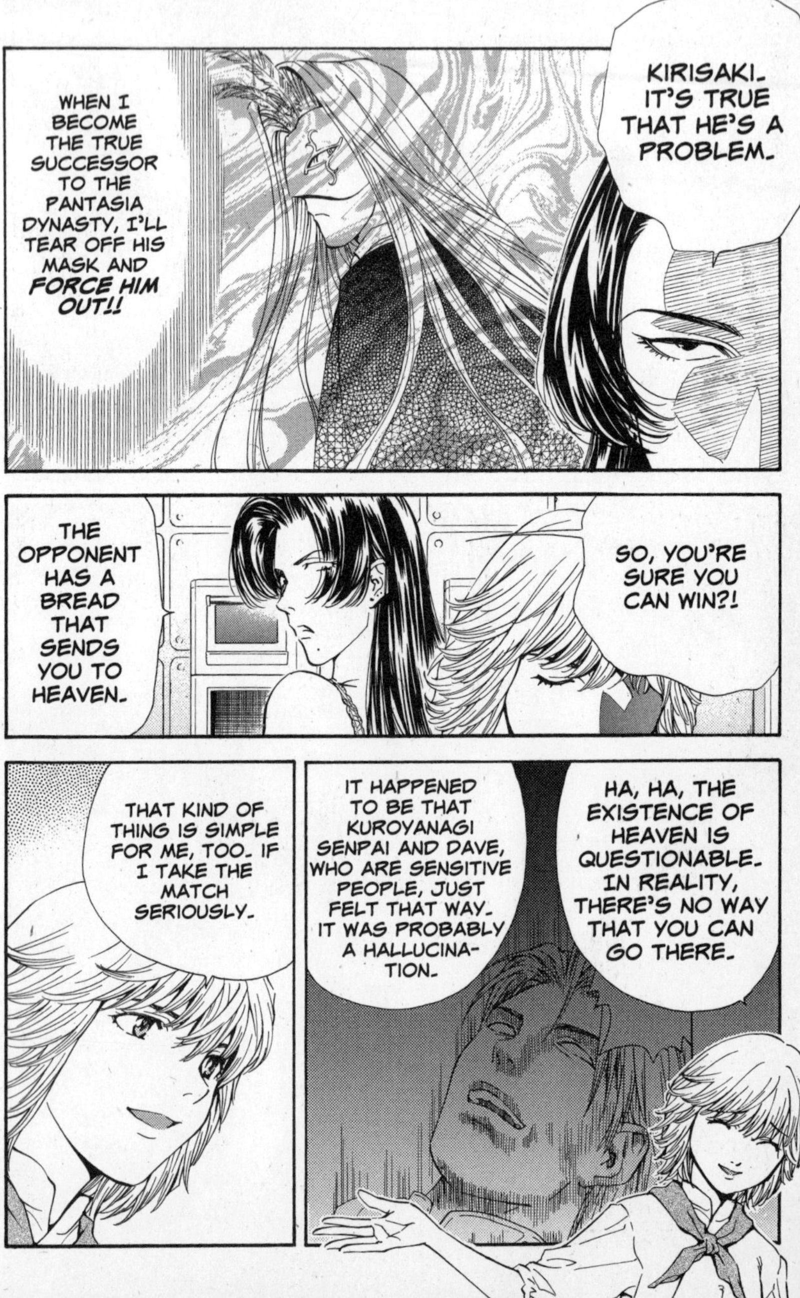
KIRISAKI... IT'S TRUE THAT HE'S A PROBLEM...
WHEN I BECOME THE TRUE SUCCESSOR TO THE PANTASIA DYNASTY, I'LL TEAR OFF HIS MASK AND *FORCE HIM OUT!!*
SO, YOU'RE SURE YOU CAN WIN?!
THE OPPONENT HAS A BREAD THAT SENDS YOU TO HEAVEN...
HA, HA, THE EXISTENCE OF HEAVEN IS QUESTIONABLE... IN REALITY, THERE'S NO WAY THAT YOU CAN GO THERE...
IT HAPPENED TO BE THAT KUROYANAGI SENPAI AND DAVE, WHO ARE SENSITIVE PEOPLE, JUST FELT THAT WAY... IT WAS PROBABLY A HALLUCINATION...
THAT KIND OF THING IS SIMPLE FOR ME, TOO... IF I TAKE THE MATCH SERIOUSLY...

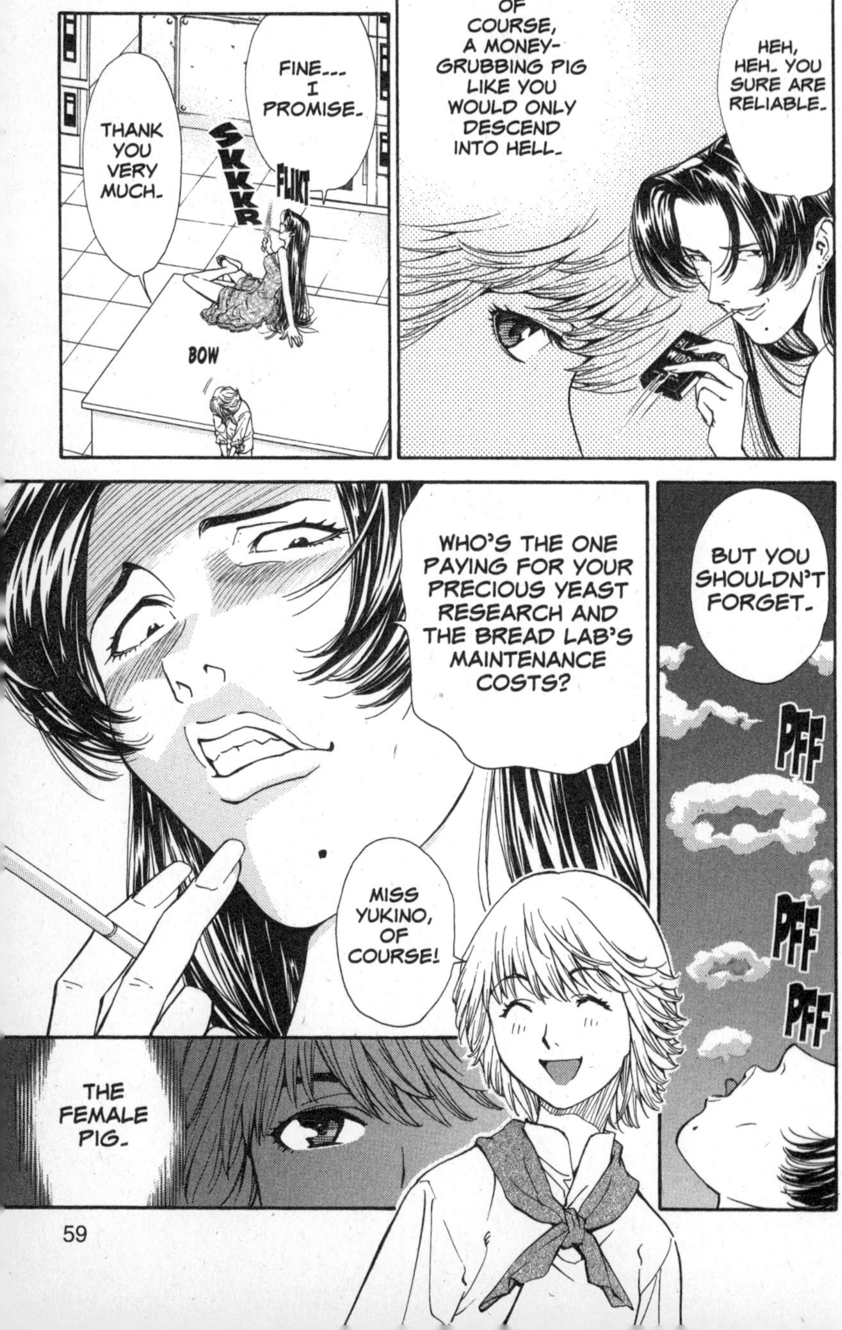
HEH, HEH. YOU SURE ARE RELIABLE.
OF COURSE, A MONEY-GRUBBING PIG LIKE YOU WOULD ONLY DESCEND INTO HELL.
FINE... I PROMISE.
SKKKR
FLIKT
THANK YOU VERY MUCH.
BOW
BUT YOU SHOULDN'T FORGET.
PFF
PFF
PFF
WHO'S THE ONE PAYING FOR YOUR PRECIOUS YEAST RESEARCH AND THE BREAD LAB'S MAINTENANCE COSTS?
MISS YUKINO, OF COURSE!
THE FEMALE PIG.

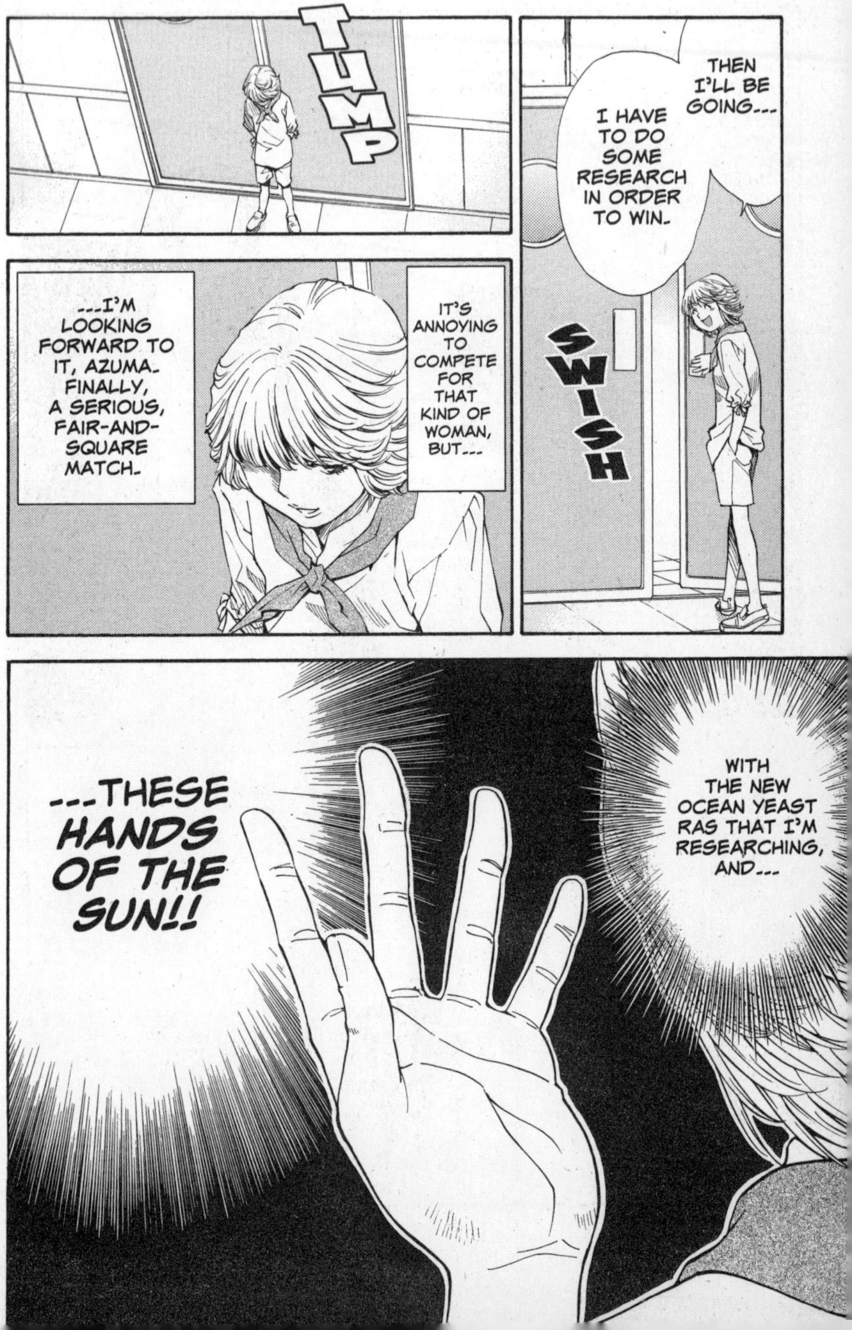
THEN I'LL BE GOING...
I HAVE TO DO SOME RESEARCH IN ORDER TO WIN.
SWISH
TUMP
IT'S ANNOYING TO COMPETE FOR THAT KIND OF WOMAN, BUT...
...I'M LOOKING FORWARD TO IT, AZUMA. FINALLY, A SERIOUS, FAIR-AND-SQUARE MATCH.
WITH THE NEW OCEAN YEAST RAS THAT I'M RESEARCHING, AND...
...THESE HANDS OF THE SUN!!

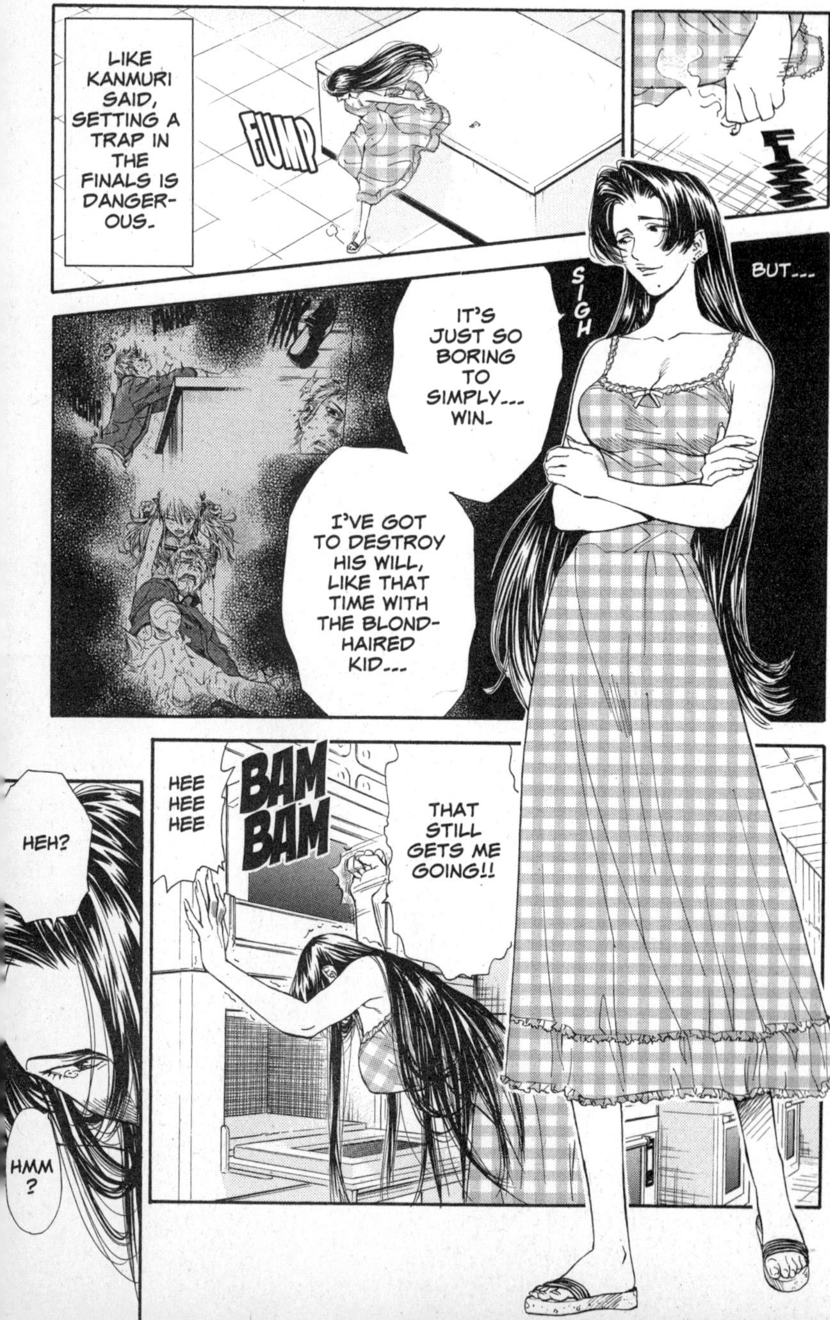
LIKE KANMURI SAID, SETTING A TRAP IN THE FINALS IS DANGEROUS.
FUMP
BUT...
SIGH
IT'S JUST SO BORING TO SIMPLY... WIN.
I'VE GOT TO DESTROY HIS WILL, LIKE THAT TIME WITH THE BLOND-HAIRED KID...
THAT STILL GETS ME GOING!!
BAM BAM
HEE HEE HEE
HEH?
HMM ?

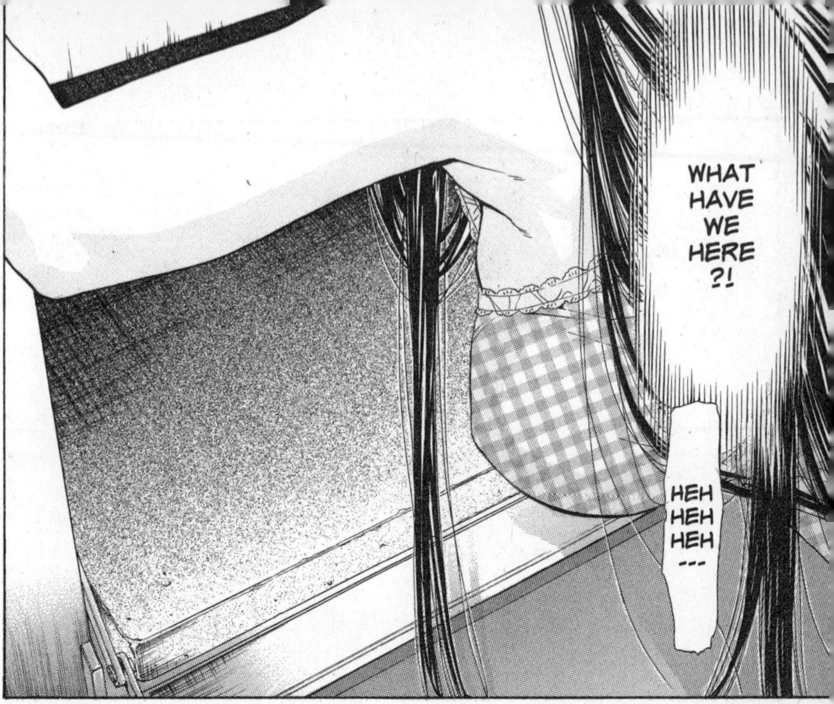
WHAT HAVE WE HERE ?!
HEH HEH HEH ---

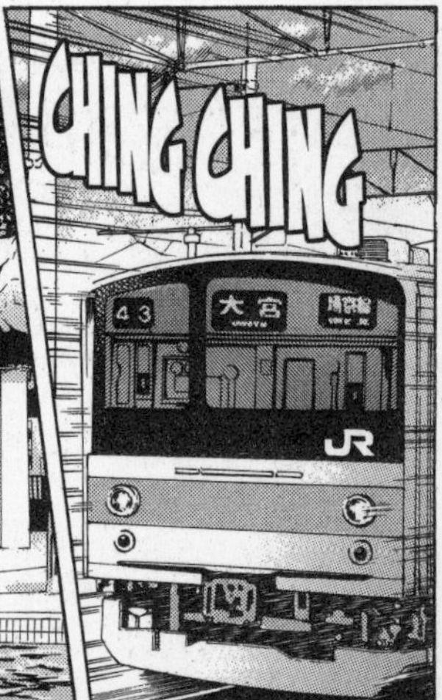
CHING CHING
大宮

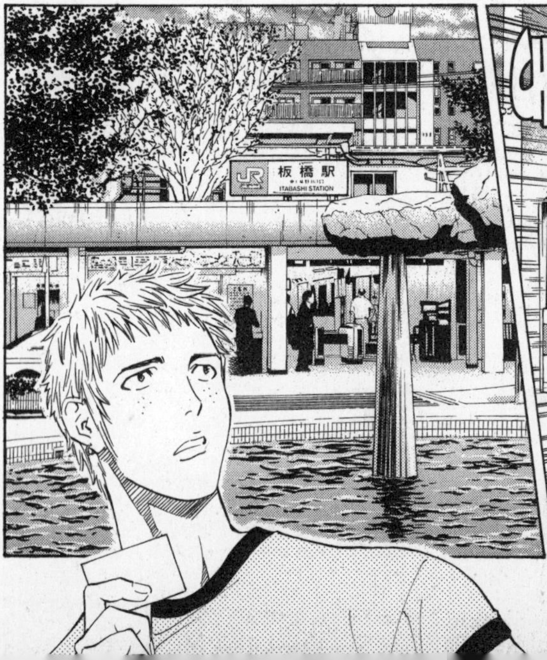
板橋駅
ITABASHI STATION

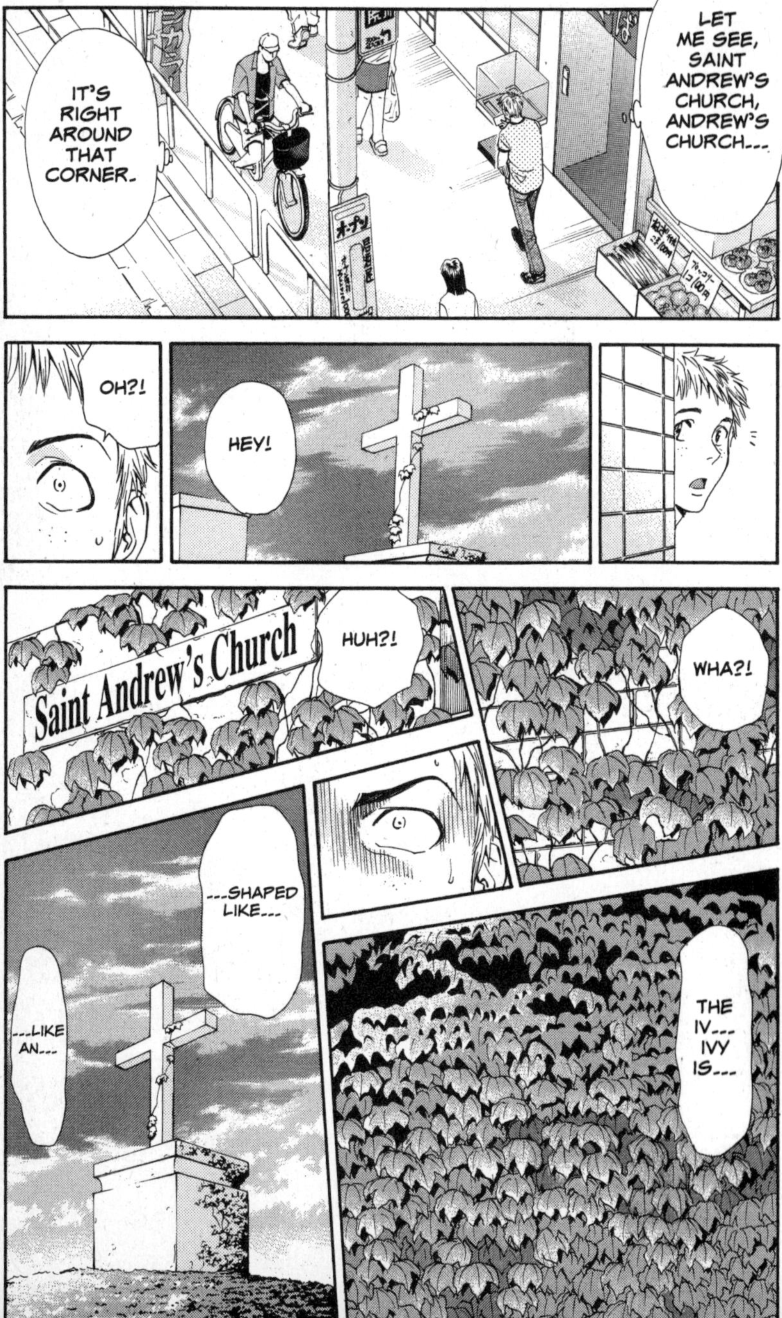
LET ME SEE, SAINT ANDREW'S CHURCH, ANDREW'S CHURCH...
IT'S RIGHT AROUND THAT CORNER.
HEY!
OH?!
WHA?!
Saint Andrew's Church
HUH?!
THE IV... IVY IS...
...SHAPED LIKE...
...LIKE AN...

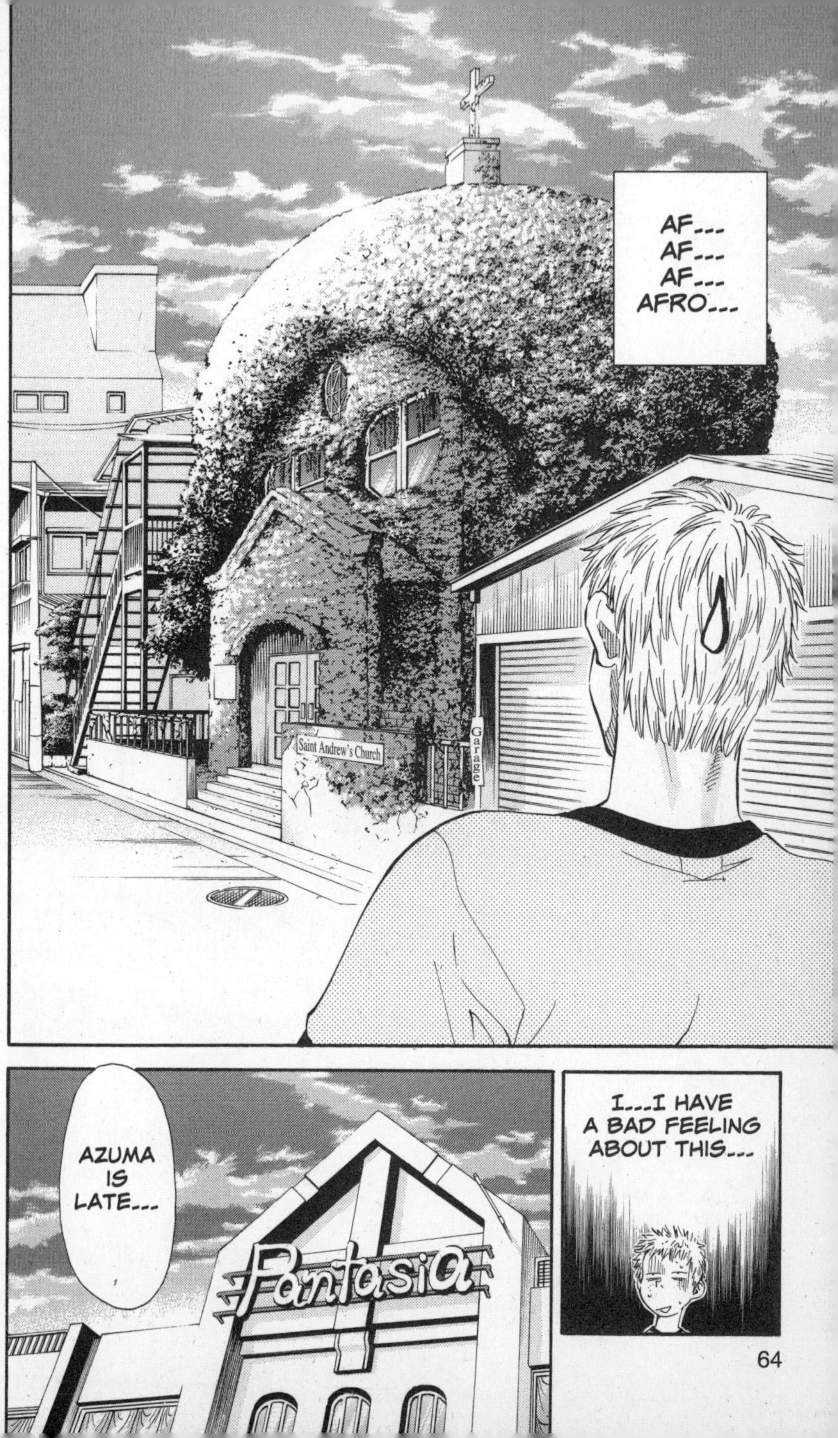
AF... AF... AF... AFRO...
Saint Andrew's Church
Garage
I...I HAVE A BAD FEELING ABOUT THIS...
AZUMA IS LATE...
Pantasia

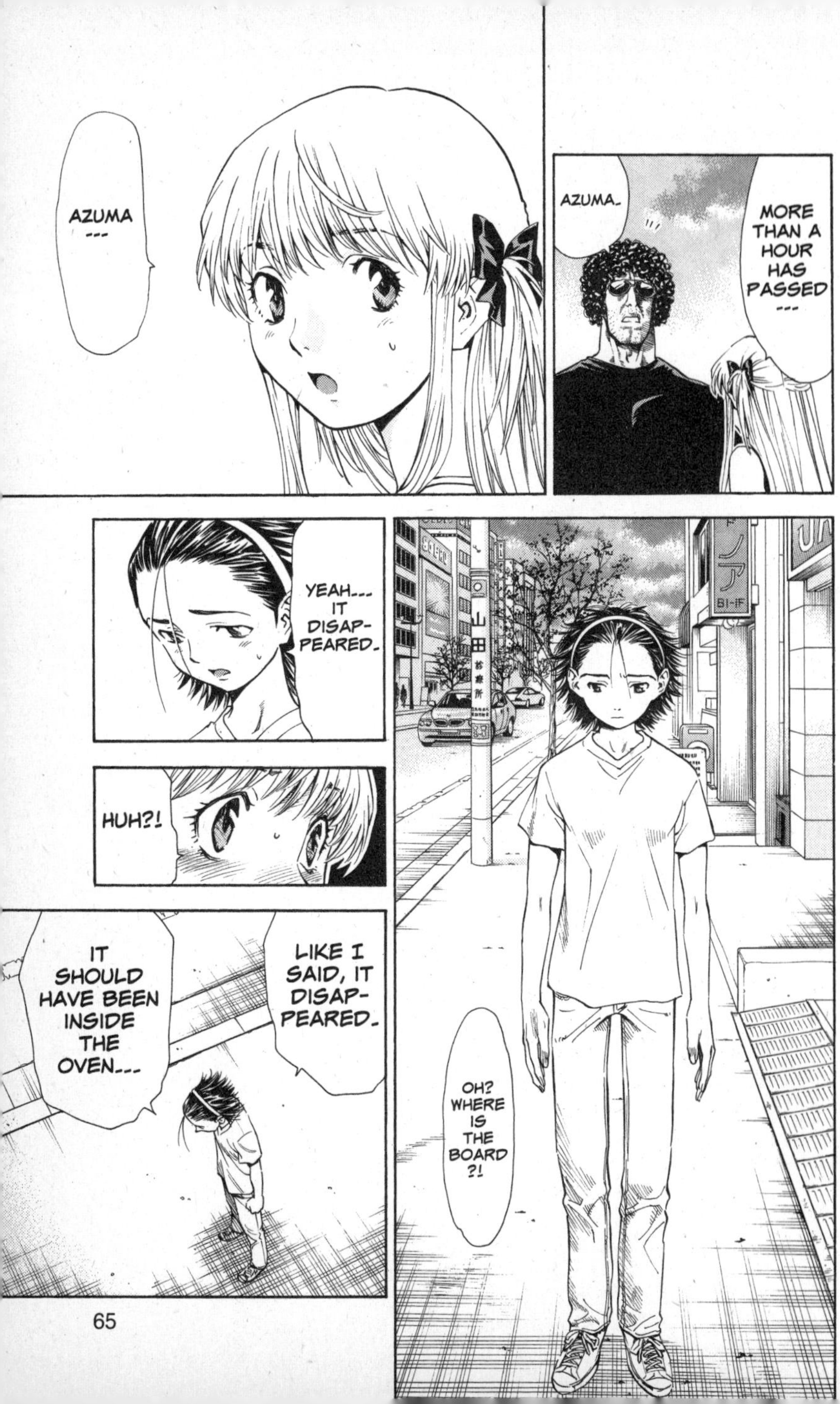
MORE THAN A HOUR HAS PASSED---
AZUMA_
AZUMA---
OH? WHERE IS THE BOARD?!
YEAH... IT DISAPPEARED.
HUH?!
LIKE I SAID, IT DISAPPEARED.
IT SHOULD HAVE BEEN INSIDE THE OVEN...

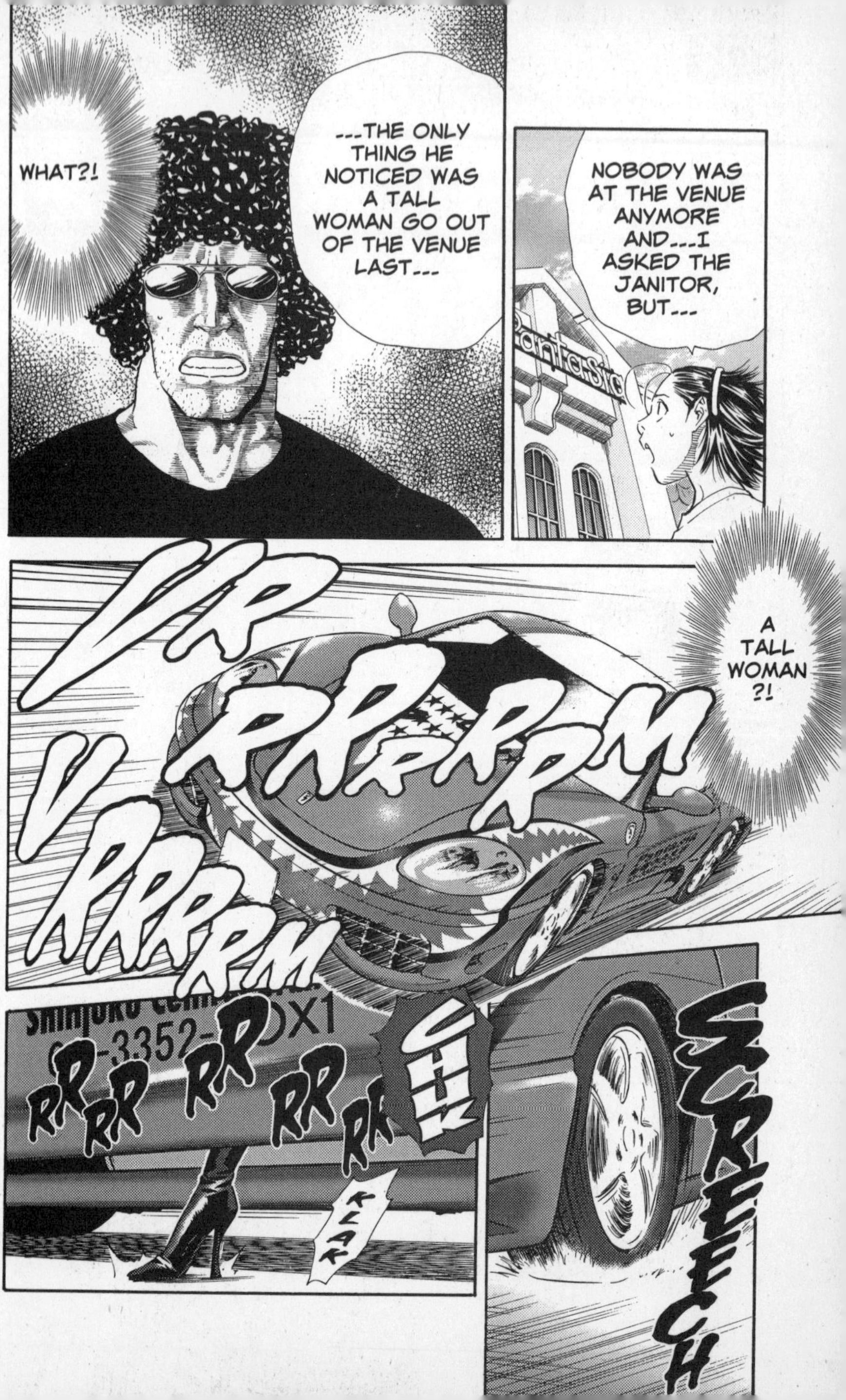
NOBODY WAS AT THE VENUE ANYMORE AND...I ASKED THE JANITOR, BUT...
...THE ONLY THING HE NOTICED WAS A TALL WOMAN GO OUT OF THE VENUE LAST...
WHAT?!
A TALL WOMAN?!
VRRRRRRM
VRRRRRM
SCREECH
CHK
KLAK
RR RR RR RR RR

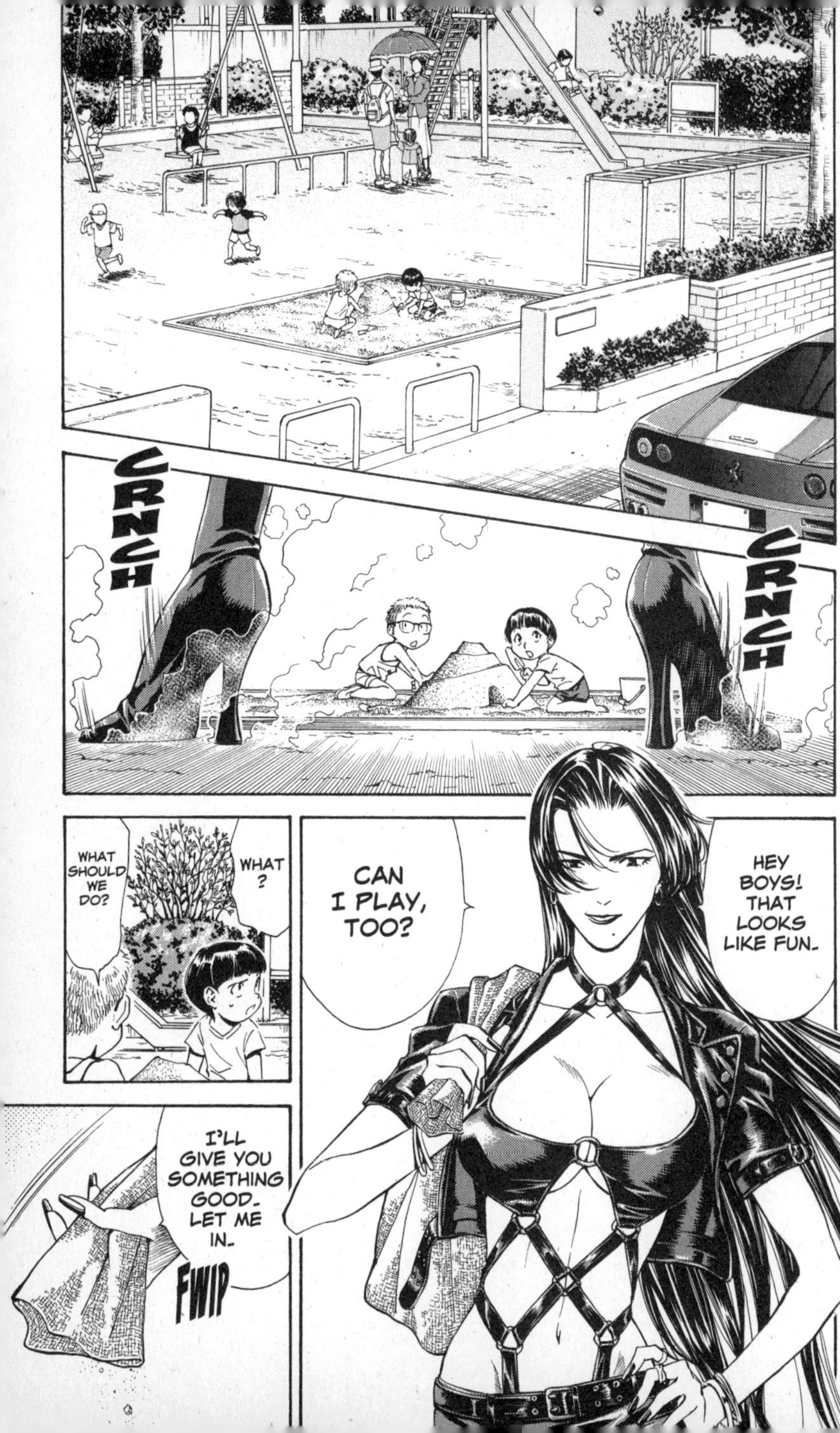
CRNCH
CRNCH
HEY BOYS! THAT LOOKS LIKE FUN.
CAN I PLAY, TOO?
WHAT?
WHAT SHOULD WE DO?
I'LL GIVE YOU SOMETHING GOOD. LET ME IN.
FWIP

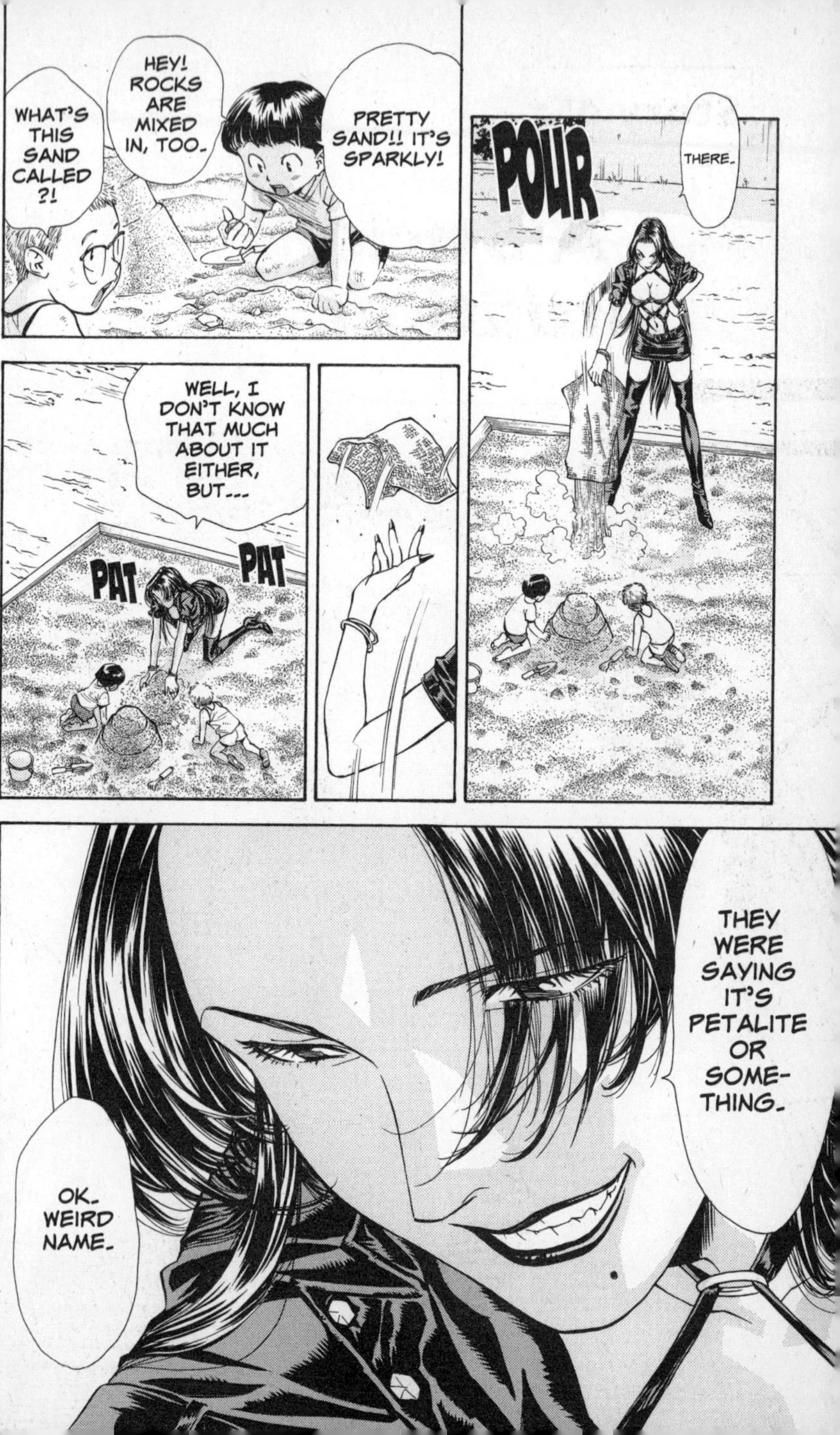
POUR
THERE.
PRETTY SAND!! IT'S SPARKLY!
HEY! ROCKS ARE MIXED IN, TOO.
WHAT'S THIS SAND CALLED?!
WELL, I DON'T KNOW THAT MUCH ABOUT IT EITHER, BUT...
PAT
PAT
THEY WERE SAYING IT'S PETALITE OR SOME-THING.
OK. WEIRD NAME.

Story 45: A Sticky Situation...

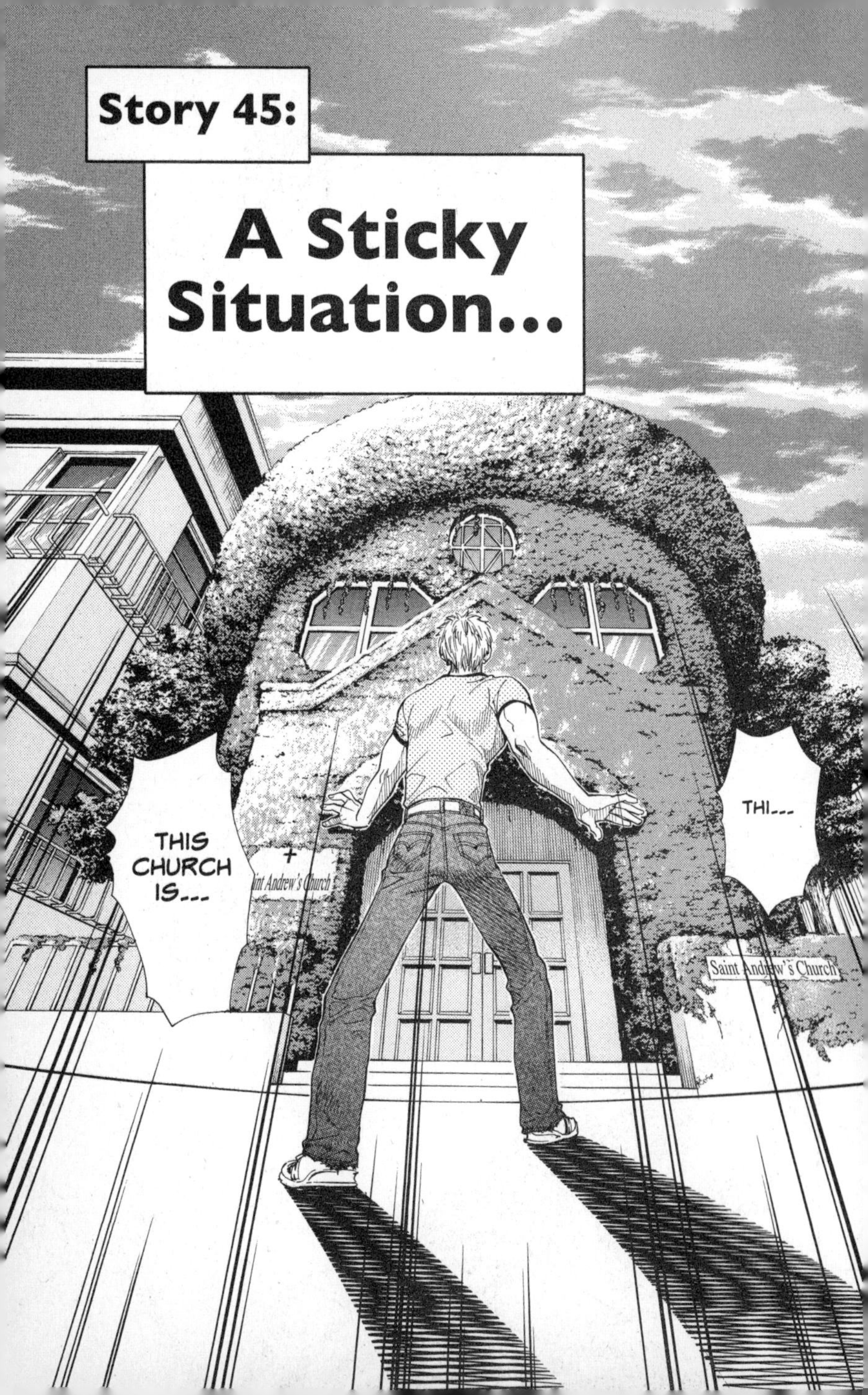
THI---
THIS CHURCH IS---
Saint Andrew's Church

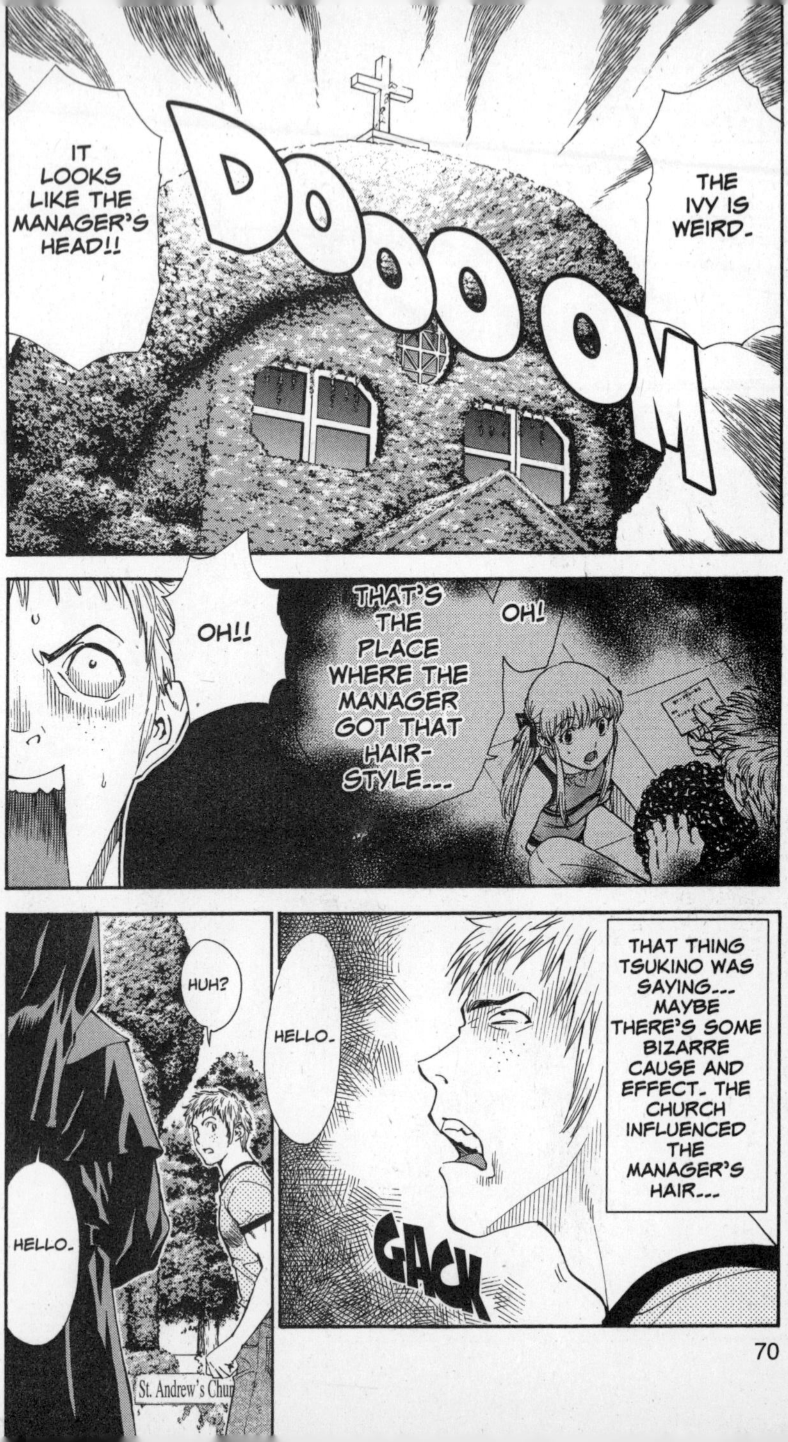
THE IVY IS WEIRD.
IT LOOKS LIKE THE MANAGER'S HEAD!!
DOOOOOM
OH!
THAT'S THE PLACE WHERE THE MANAGER GOT THAT HAIR-STYLE...
OH!!
THAT THING TSUKINO WAS SAYING... MAYBE THERE'S SOME BIZARRE CAUSE AND EFFECT. THE CHURCH INFLUENCED THE MANAGER'S HAIR...
GACK
HELLO.
HUH?
HELLO.
St. Andrew's Chur

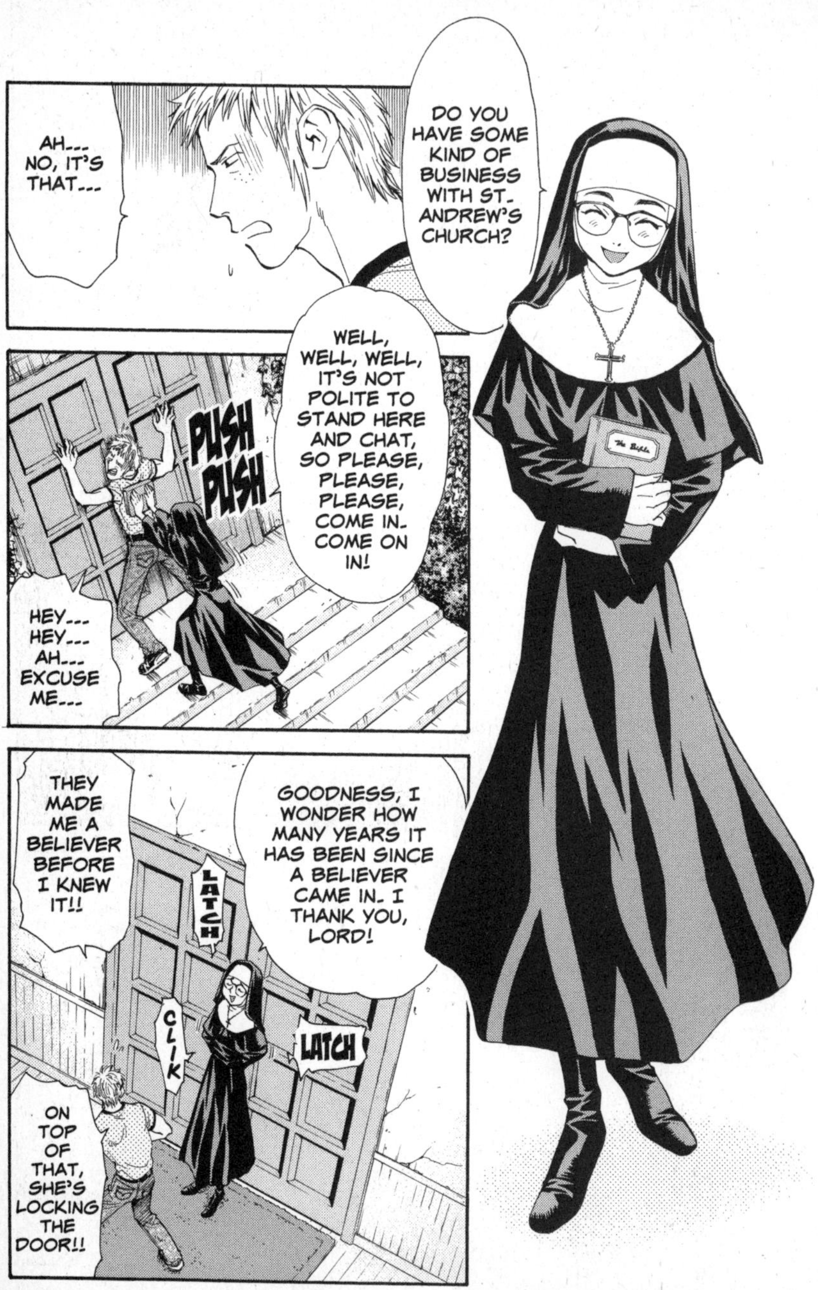
DO YOU HAVE SOME KIND OF BUSINESS WITH ST. ANDREW'S CHURCH?
AH... NO, IT'S THAT...
WELL, WELL, WELL, IT'S NOT POLITE TO STAND HERE AND CHAT, SO PLEASE, PLEASE, PLEASE, COME IN. COME ON IN!
PUSH PUSH
HEY... HEY... AH... EXCUSE ME...
GOODNESS, I WONDER HOW MANY YEARS IT HAS BEEN SINCE A BELIEVER CAME IN. I THANK YOU, LORD!
THEY MADE ME A BELIEVER BEFORE I KNEW IT!!
LATCH
LATCH
CLIK
ON TOP OF THAT, SHE'S LOCKING THE DOOR!!

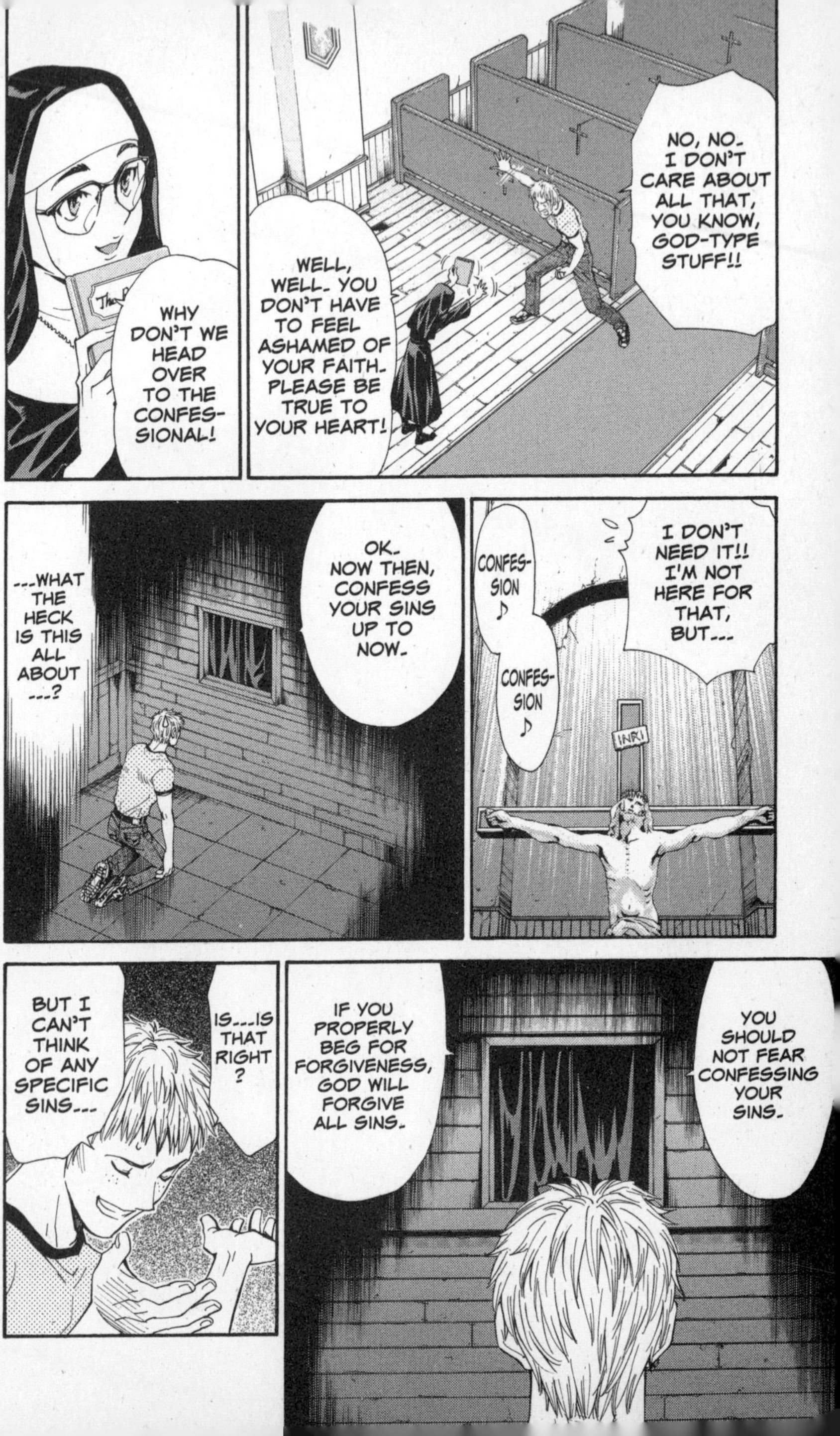
NO, NO. I DON'T CARE ABOUT ALL THAT, YOU KNOW, GOD-TYPE STUFF!!
WELL, WELL. YOU DON'T HAVE TO FEEL ASHAMED OF YOUR FAITH. PLEASE BE TRUE TO YOUR HEART!
WHY DON'T WE HEAD OVER TO THE CONFESSIONAL!
I DON'T NEED IT!! I'M NOT HERE FOR THAT, BUT...
CONFESSION ♪
CONFESSION ♪
INRI
OK. NOW THEN, CONFESS YOUR SINS UP TO NOW.
...WHAT THE HECK IS THIS ALL ABOUT...?
YOU SHOULD NOT FEAR CONFESSING YOUR SINS.
IF YOU PROPERLY BEG FOR FORGIVENESS, GOD WILL FORGIVE ALL SINS.
IS...IS THAT RIGHT?
BUT I CAN'T THINK OF ANY SPECIFIC SINS...

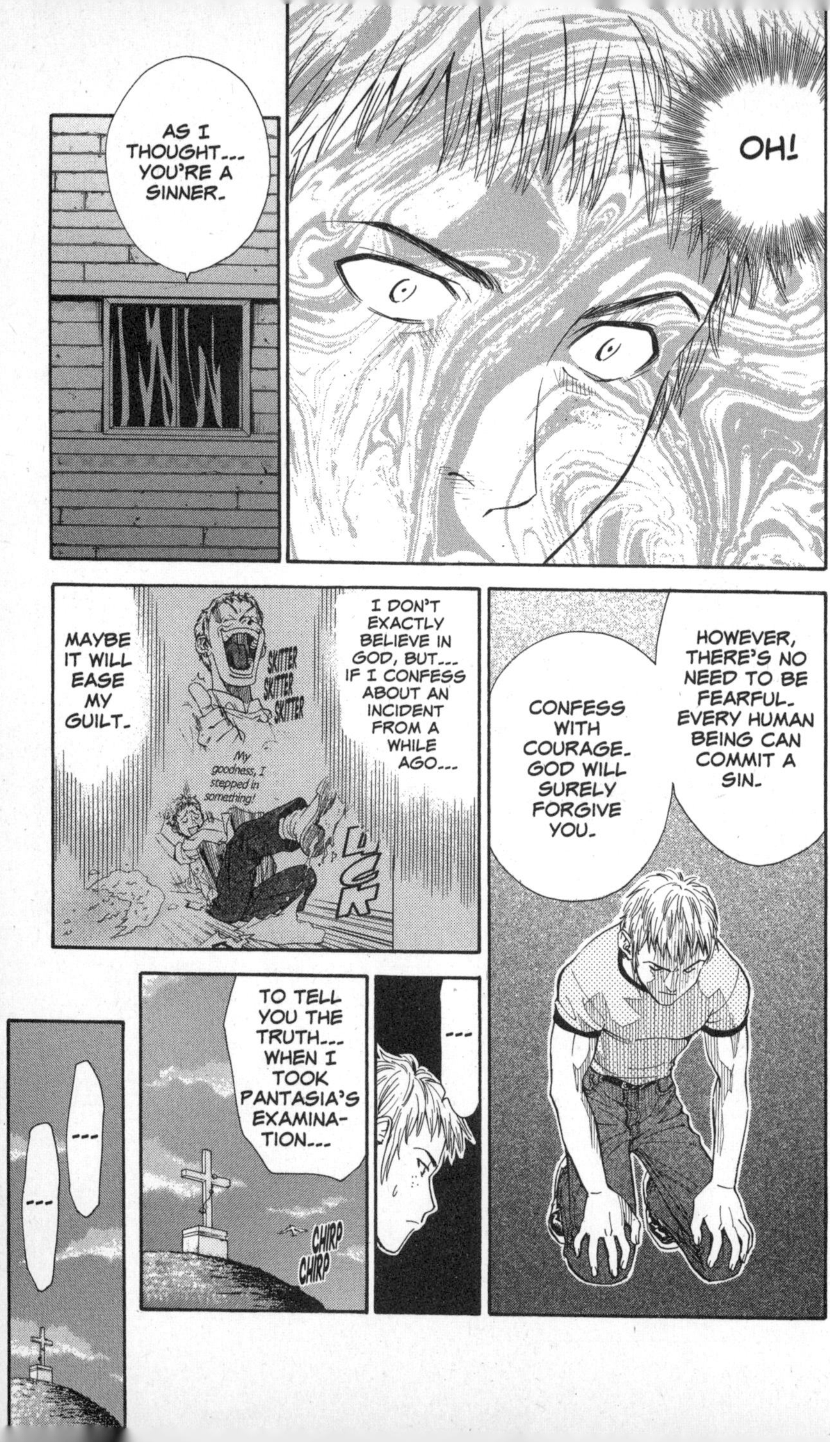
OH!
AS I THOUGHT... YOU'RE A SINNER.
HOWEVER, THERE'S NO NEED TO BE FEARFUL. EVERY HUMAN BEING CAN COMMIT A SIN.
CONFESS WITH COURAGE. GOD WILL SURELY FORGIVE YOU.
I DON'T EXACTLY BELIEVE IN GOD, BUT... IF I CONFESS ABOUT AN INCIDENT FROM A WHILE AGO...
MAYBE IT WILL EASE MY GUILT.
SKITTER SKITTER SKITTER
My goodness, I stepped in something!
...
TO TELL YOU THE TRUTH... WHEN I TOOK PANTASIA'S EXAMINATION...
CHIRP CHIRP
...
...

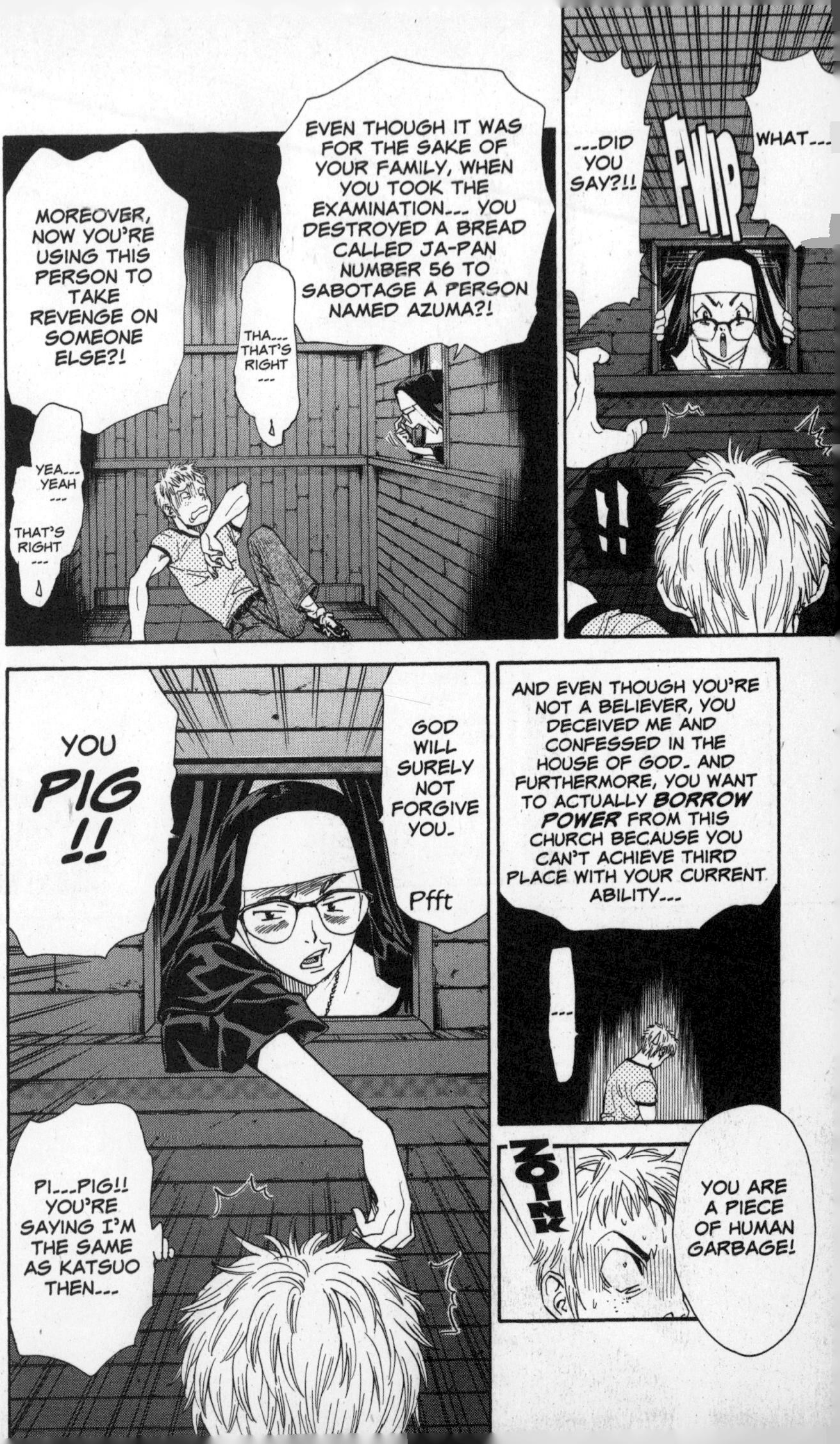
WHAT...
FWIP
...DID YOU SAY?!!
!!
EVEN THOUGH IT WAS FOR THE SAKE OF YOUR FAMILY, WHEN YOU TOOK THE EXAMINATION... YOU DESTROYED A BREAD CALLED JA-PAN NUMBER 56 TO SABOTAGE A PERSON NAMED AZUMA?!
MOREOVER, NOW YOU'RE USING THIS PERSON TO TAKE REVENGE ON SOMEONE ELSE?!
THA... THAT'S RIGHT ...
YEA... YEAH ...
THAT'S RIGHT ...
AND EVEN THOUGH YOU'RE NOT A BELIEVER, YOU DECEIVED ME AND CONFESSED IN THE HOUSE OF GOD. AND FURTHERMORE, YOU WANT TO ACTUALLY BORROW POWER FROM THIS CHURCH BECAUSE YOU CAN'T ACHIEVE THIRD PLACE WITH YOUR CURRENT ABILITY...
...
ZOINK
YOU ARE A PIECE OF HUMAN GARBAGE!
GOD WILL SURELY NOT FORGIVE YOU.
Pfft
YOU PIG!!
PI...PIG!! YOU'RE SAYING I'M THE SAME AS KATSUO THEN...

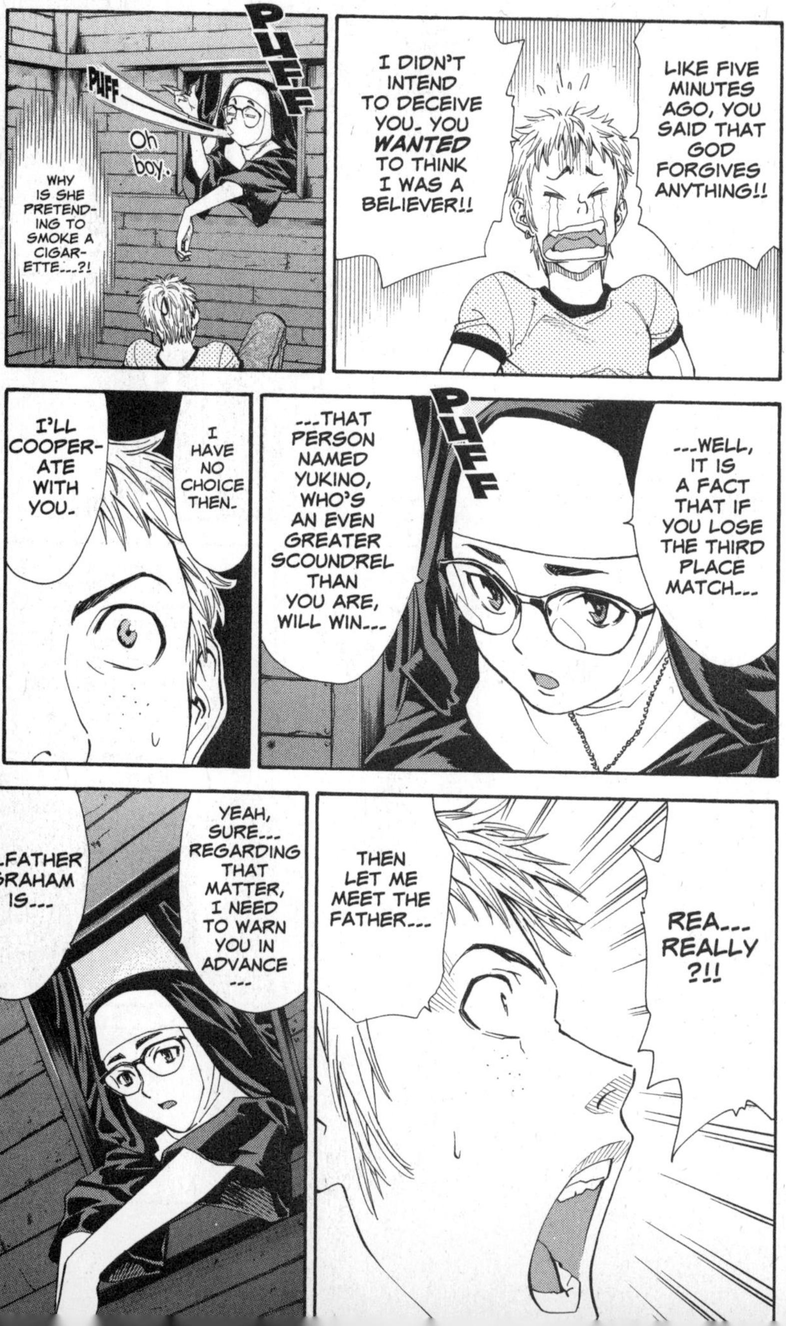
LIKE FIVE MINUTES AGO, YOU SAID THAT GOD FORGIVES ANYTHING!!
I DIDN'T INTEND TO DECEIVE YOU. YOU *WANTED* TO THINK I WAS A BELIEVER!!
PUFF
PUFF
Oh boy.
WHY IS SHE PRETEND-ING TO SMOKE A CIGAR-ETTE...?!
PUFF
...WELL, IT IS A FACT THAT IF YOU LOSE THE THIRD PLACE MATCH...
...THAT PERSON NAMED YUKINO, WHO'S AN EVEN GREATER SCOUNDREL THAN YOU ARE, WILL WIN...
I HAVE NO CHOICE THEN.
I'LL COOPER-ATE WITH YOU.
REA... REALLY ?!!
THEN LET ME MEET THE FATHER...
YEAH, SURE... REGARDING THAT MATTER, I NEED TO WARN YOU IN ADVANCE ...
...FATHER GRAHAM IS...

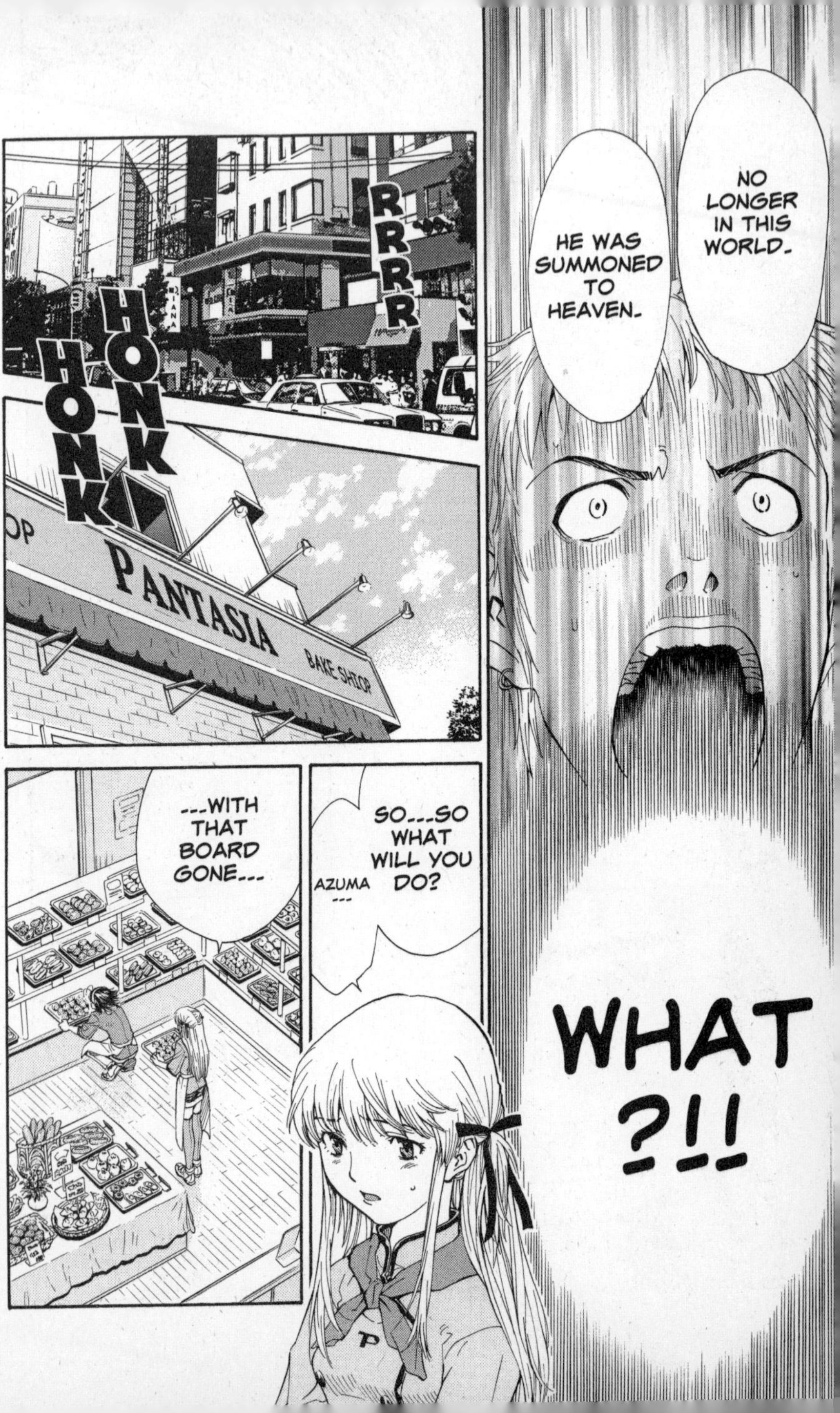

NO LONGER IN THIS WORLD.
HE WAS SUMMONED TO HEAVEN.
WHAT?!!
RRRR
HONK
HONK
PANTASIA
BAKE SHOP
SO...SO WHAT WILL YOU DO?
AZUMA...
...WITH THAT BOARD GONE...

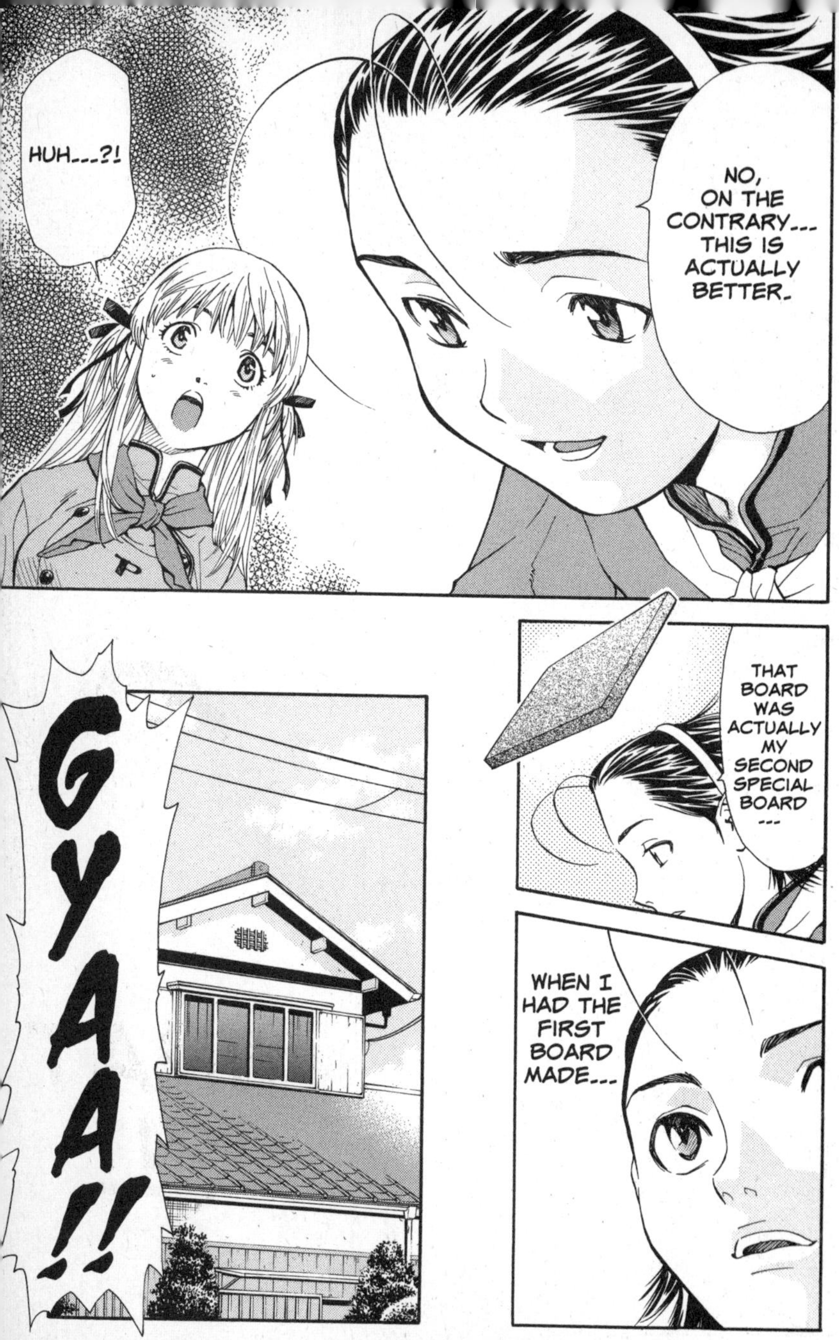
NO, ON THE CONTRARY... THIS IS ACTUALLY BETTER.
HUH...?!
THAT BOARD WAS ACTUALLY MY SECOND SPECIAL BOARD...
WHEN I HAD THE FIRST BOARD MADE...
GYAAA!!

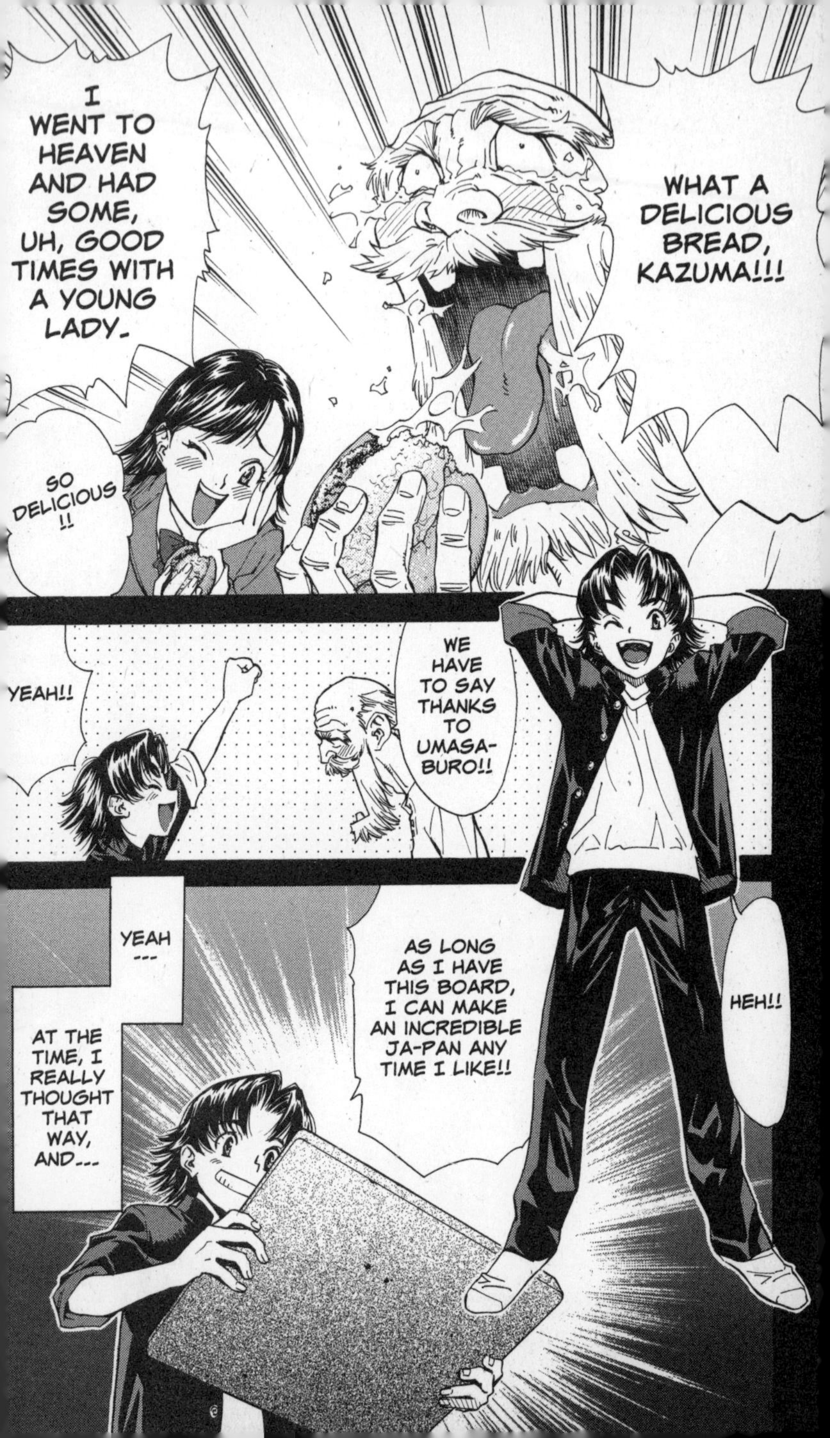
WHAT A DELICIOUS BREAD, KAZUMA!!!
I WENT TO HEAVEN AND HAD SOME, UH, GOOD TIMES WITH A YOUNG LADY.
SO DELICIOUS !!
WE HAVE TO SAY THANKS TO UMASA-BURO!!
YEAH!!
HEH!!
AS LONG AS I HAVE THIS BOARD, I CAN MAKE AN INCREDIBLE JA-PAN ANY TIME I LIKE!!
YEAH ---
AT THE TIME, I REALLY THOUGHT THAT WAY, AND---

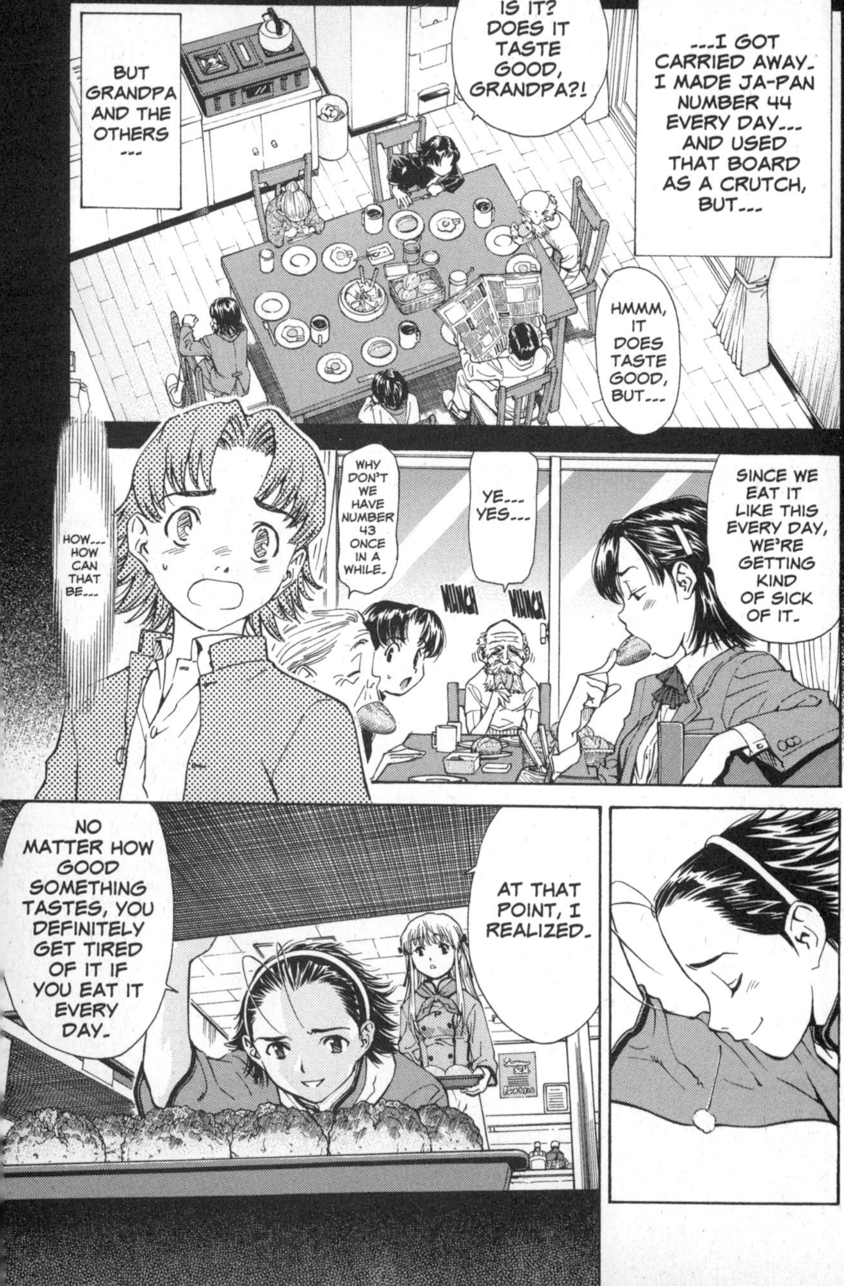
...I GOT CARRIED AWAY. I MADE JA-PAN NUMBER 44 EVERY DAY... AND USED THAT BOARD AS A CRUTCH, BUT...
HOW IS IT? DOES IT TASTE GOOD, GRANDPA?!
BUT GRANDPA AND THE OTHERS ...
HMMM, IT DOES TASTE GOOD, BUT...
SINCE WE EAT IT LIKE THIS EVERY DAY, WE'RE GETTING KIND OF SICK OF IT.
YE... YES...
MUNCH
MUNCH
WHY DON'T WE HAVE NUMBER 43 ONCE IN A WHILE.
HOW... HOW CAN THAT BE...
AT THAT POINT, I REALIZED.
NO MATTER HOW GOOD SOMETHING TASTES, YOU DEFINITELY GET TIRED OF IT IF YOU EAT IT EVERY DAY.

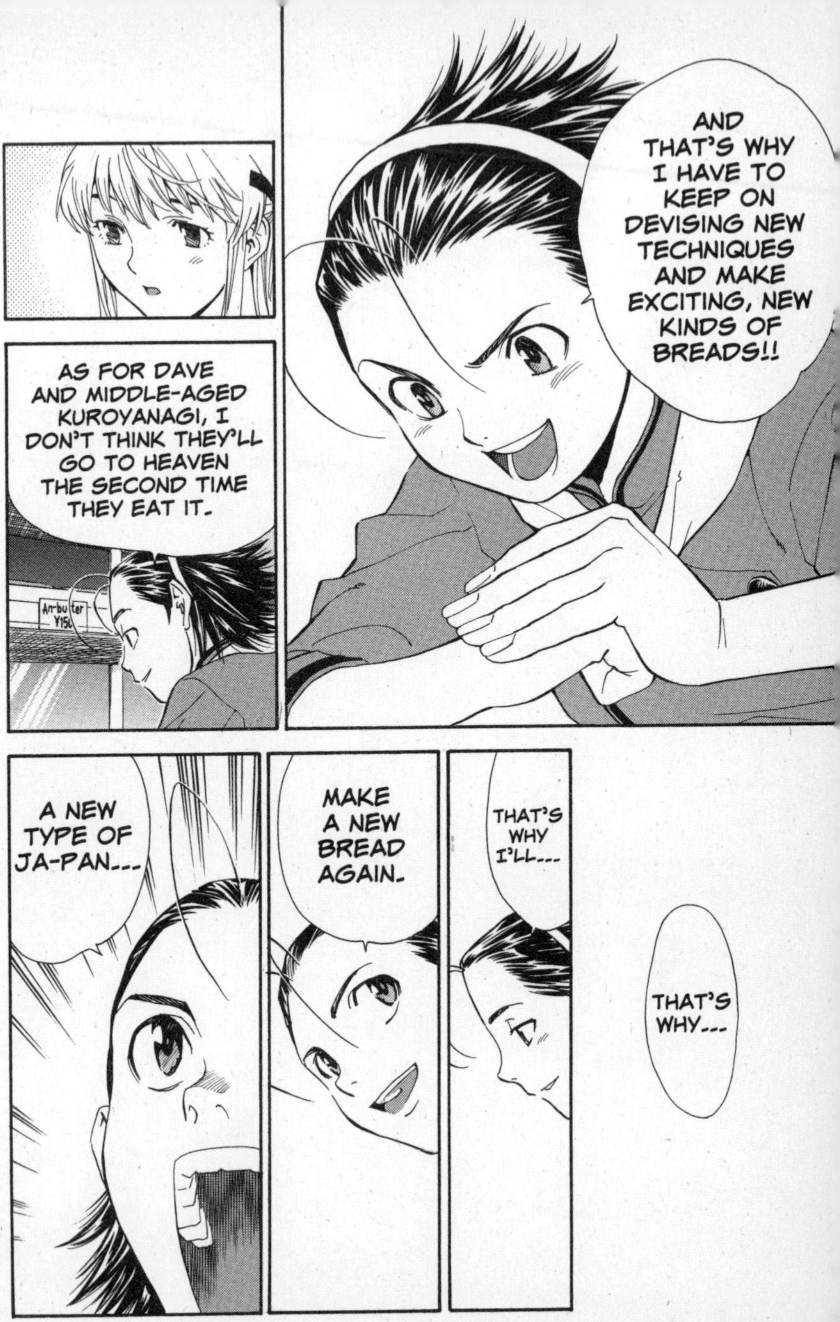
AND THAT'S WHY I HAVE TO KEEP ON DEVISING NEW TECHNIQUES AND MAKE EXCITING, NEW KINDS OF BREADS!!
AS FOR DAVE AND MIDDLE-AGED KUROYANAGI, I DON'T THINK THEY'LL GO TO HEAVEN THE SECOND TIME THEY EAT IT.
An-butter
THAT'S WHY...
THAT'S WHY I'LL...
MAKE A NEW BREAD AGAIN.
A NEW TYPE OF JA-PAN...

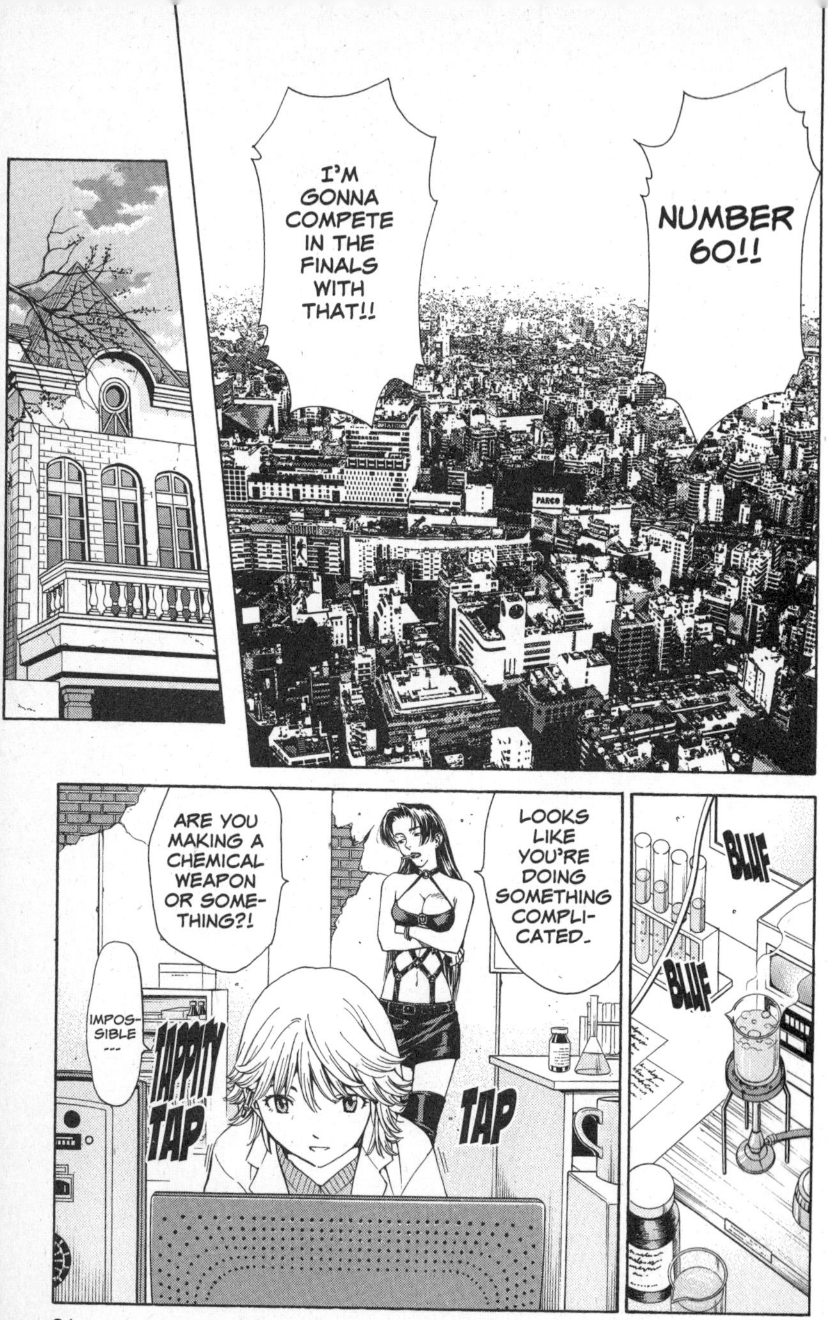
NUMBER 60!!
I'M GONNA COMPETE IN THE FINALS WITH THAT!!
BLUF
BLUF
LOOKS LIKE YOU'RE DOING SOMETHING COMPLICATED.
ARE YOU MAKING A CHEMICAL WEAPON OR SOMETHING?!
TAP
TAPPITY TAP
IMPOSSIBLE...

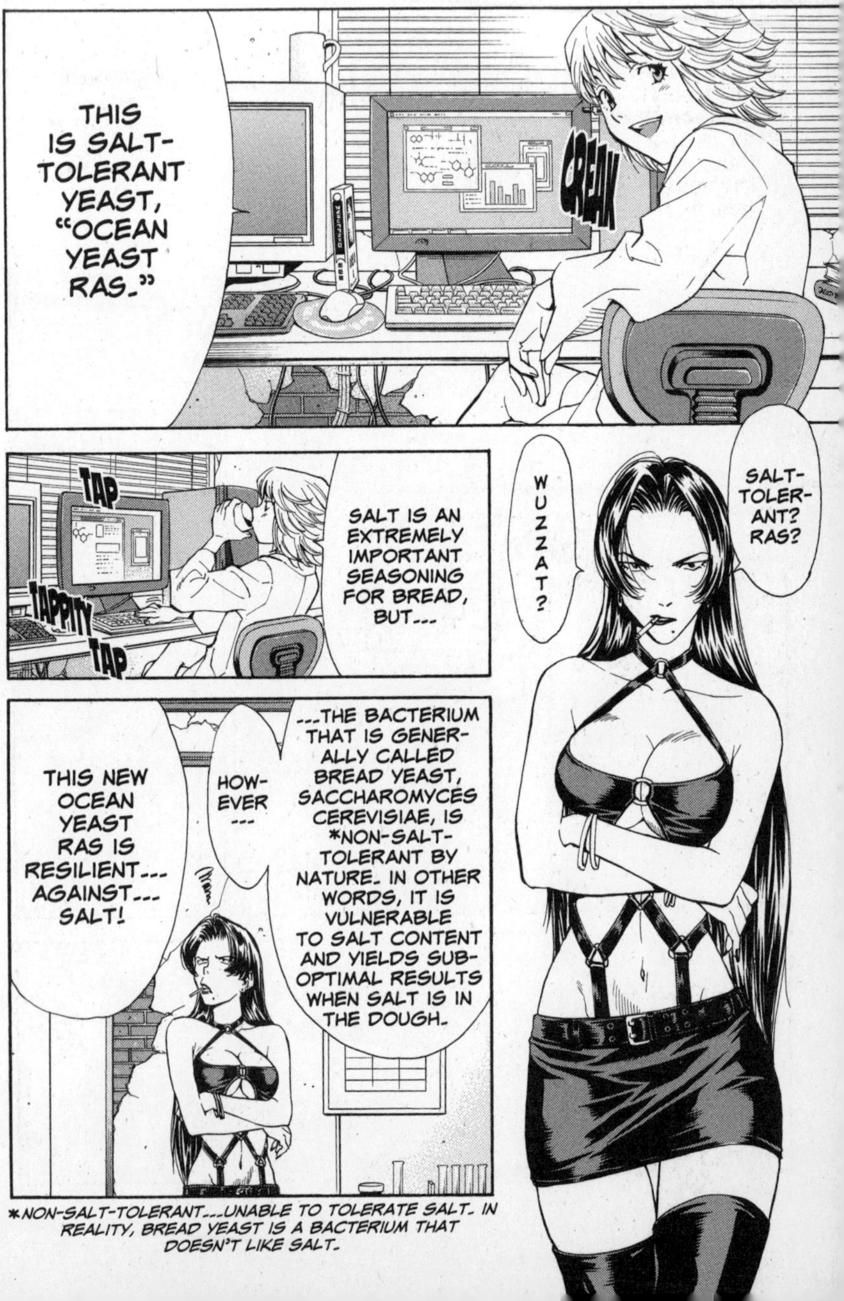
THIS IS SALT-TOLERANT YEAST, "OCEAN YEAST RAS."
CREAK
SALT-TOLERANT? RAS?
WUZZAT?
TAP
TAPPITY TAP
SALT IS AN EXTREMELY IMPORTANT SEASONING FOR BREAD, BUT...
...THE BACTERIUM THAT IS GENERALLY CALLED BREAD YEAST, SACCHAROMYCES CEREVISIAE, IS *NON-SALT-TOLERANT BY NATURE. IN OTHER WORDS, IT IS VULNERABLE TO SALT CONTENT AND YIELDS SUBOPTIMAL RESULTS WHEN SALT IS IN THE DOUGH.
HOWEVER ...
THIS NEW OCEAN YEAST RAS IS RESILIENT... AGAINST... SALT!

*NON-SALT-TOLERANT...UNABLE TO TOLERATE SALT. IN REALITY, BREAD YEAST IS A BACTERIUM THAT DOESN'T LIKE SALT.

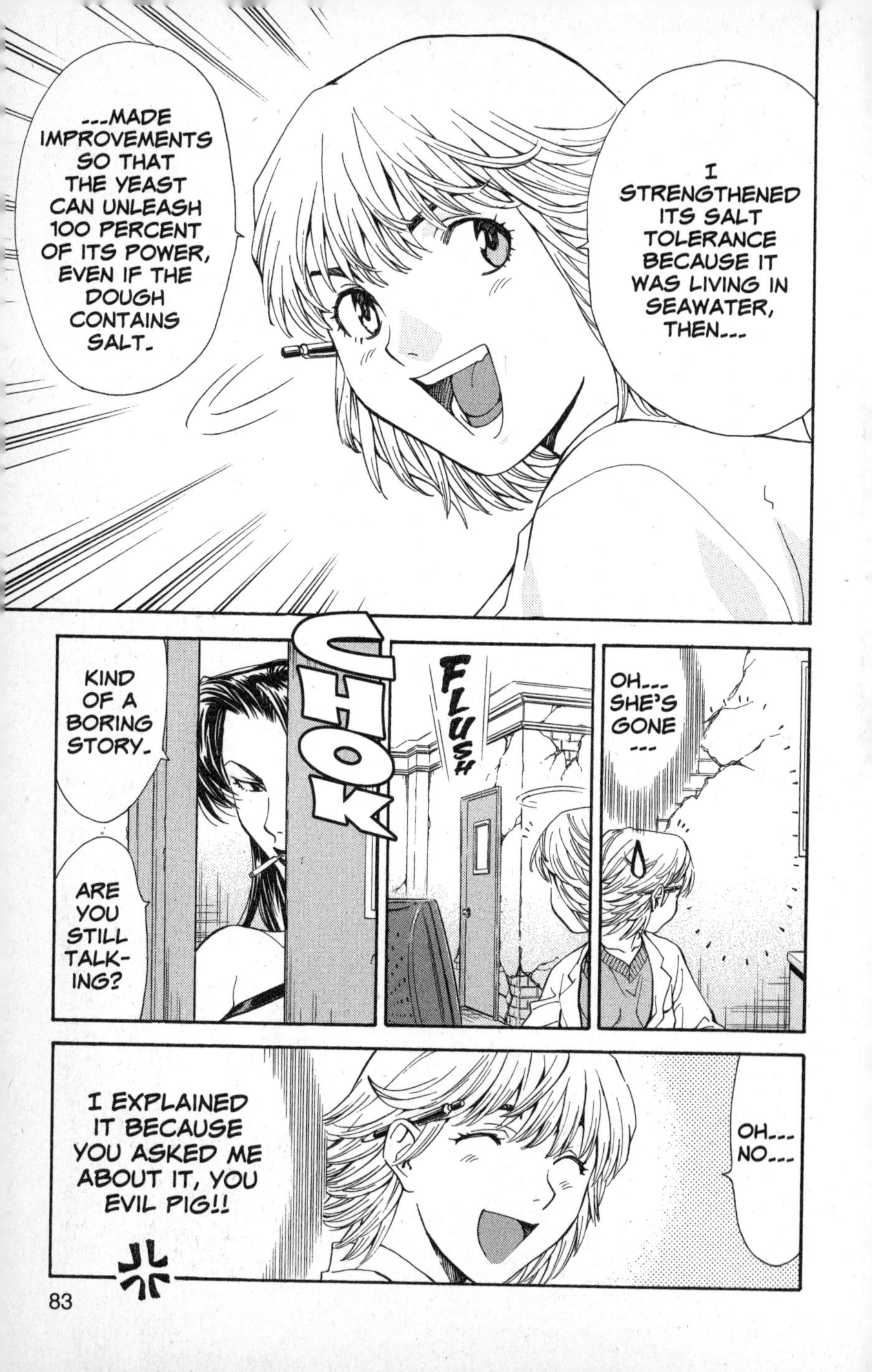
I STRENGTHENED ITS SALT TOLERANCE BECAUSE IT WAS LIVING IN SEAWATER, THEN---
---MADE IMPROVEMENTS SO THAT THE YEAST CAN UNLEASH 100 PERCENT OF ITS POWER, EVEN IF THE DOUGH CONTAINS SALT.
OH--- SHE'S GONE ---
FLUSH
CHOK
KIND OF A BORING STORY.
ARE YOU STILL TALK-ING?
OH--- NO---
I EXPLAINED IT BECAUSE YOU ASKED ME ABOUT IT, YOU EVIL PIG!!

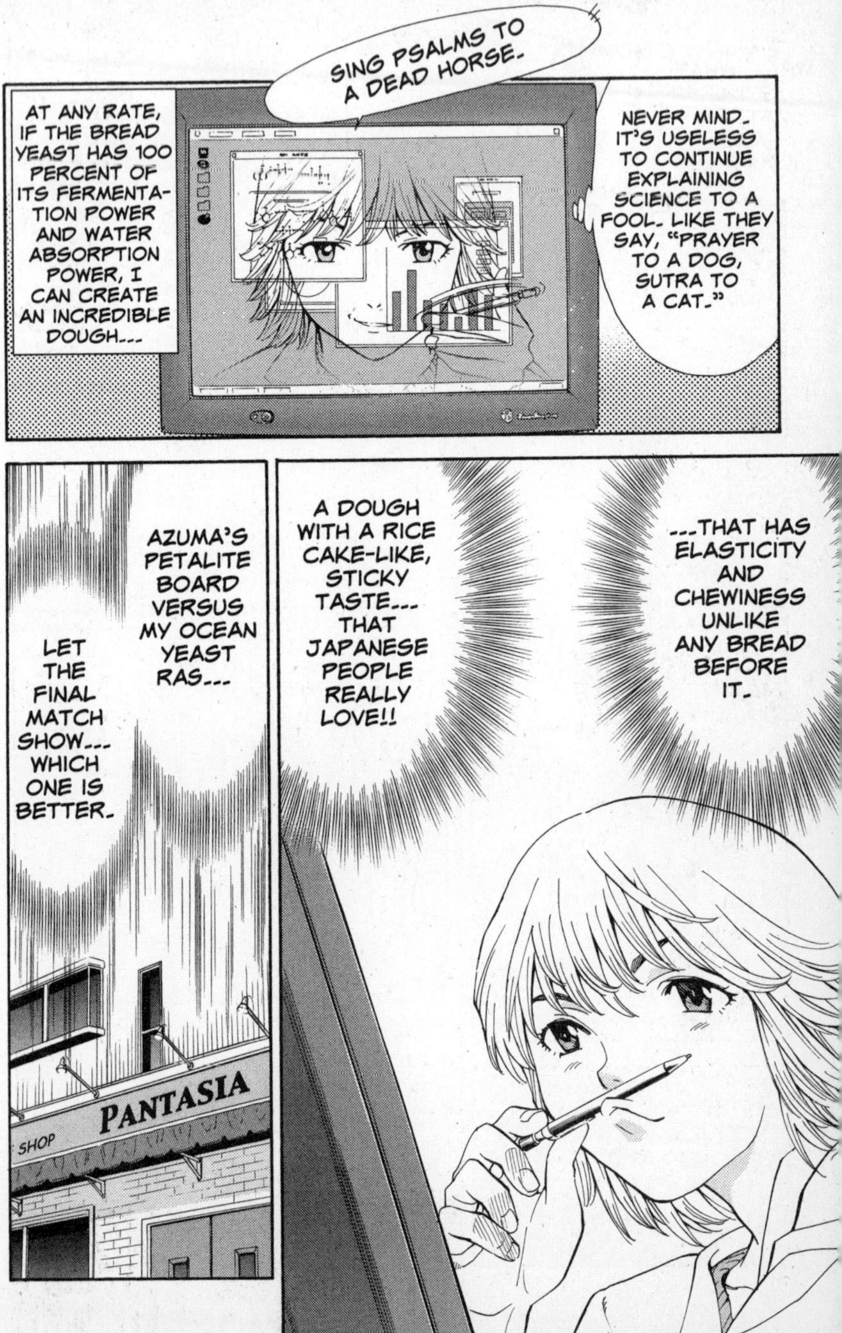
NEVER MIND. IT'S USELESS TO CONTINUE EXPLAINING SCIENCE TO A FOOL. LIKE THEY SAY, "PRAYER TO A DOG, SUTRA TO A CAT."
SING PSALMS TO A DEAD HORSE.
AT ANY RATE, IF THE BREAD YEAST HAS 100 PERCENT OF ITS FERMENTATION POWER AND WATER ABSORPTION POWER, I CAN CREATE AN INCREDIBLE DOUGH...
...THAT HAS ELASTICITY AND CHEWINESS UNLIKE ANY BREAD BEFORE IT.
A DOUGH WITH A RICE CAKE-LIKE, STICKY TASTE... THAT JAPANESE PEOPLE REALLY LOVE!!
AZUMA'S PETALITE BOARD VERSUS MY OCEAN YEAST RAS...
LET THE FINAL MATCH SHOW... WHICH ONE IS BETTER.
PANTASIA
SHOP

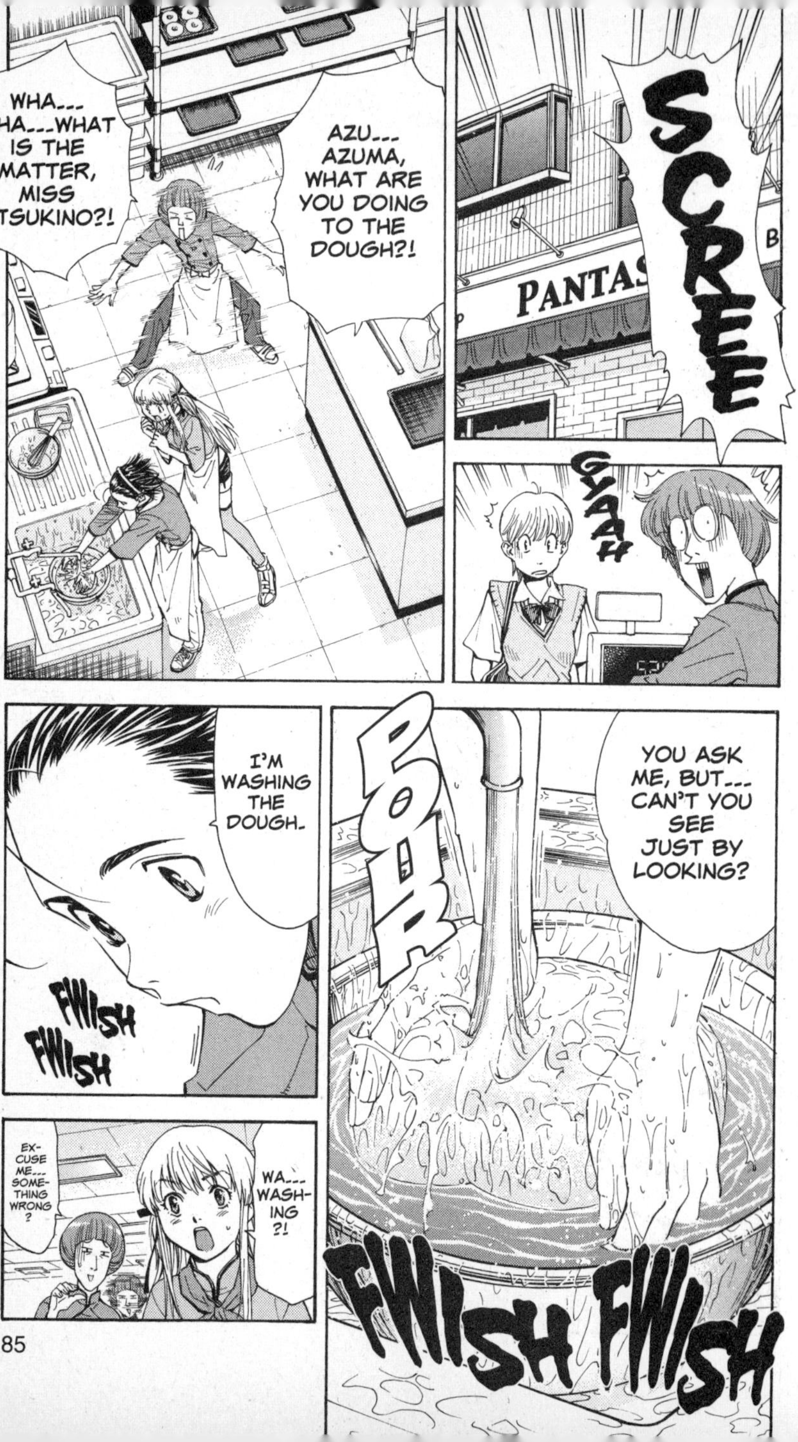
SCREE
PANTAS
GYAAH
AZU... AZUMA, WHAT ARE YOU DOING TO THE DOUGH?!
WHA... WHA...WHAT IS THE MATTER, MISS TSUKINO?!
YOU ASK ME, BUT... CAN'T YOU SEE JUST BY LOOKING?
POUR
FWISH FWISH
I'M WASHING THE DOUGH.
FWISH FWISH
WA... WASHING?!
EX-CUSE ME... SOME-THING WRONG?

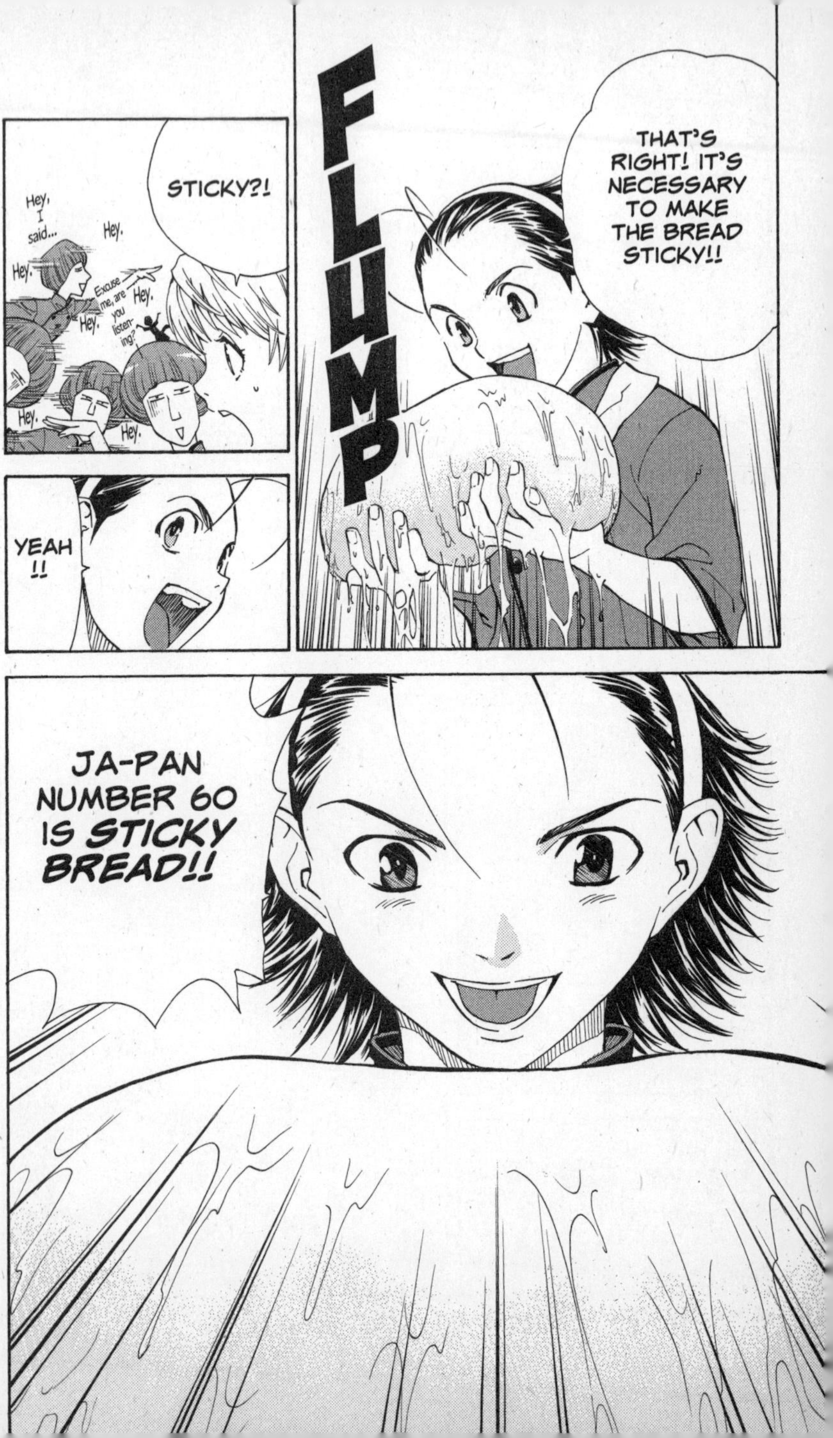
FLUMP
THAT'S RIGHT! IT'S NECESSARY TO MAKE THE BREAD STICKY!!
STICKY?!
Hey.
Hey.
Hey, I said...
Excuse me, are you listening?
Hey.
Hey.
Hey.
Hey.
YEAH!!
JA-PAN NUMBER 60 IS *STICKY BREAD!!*

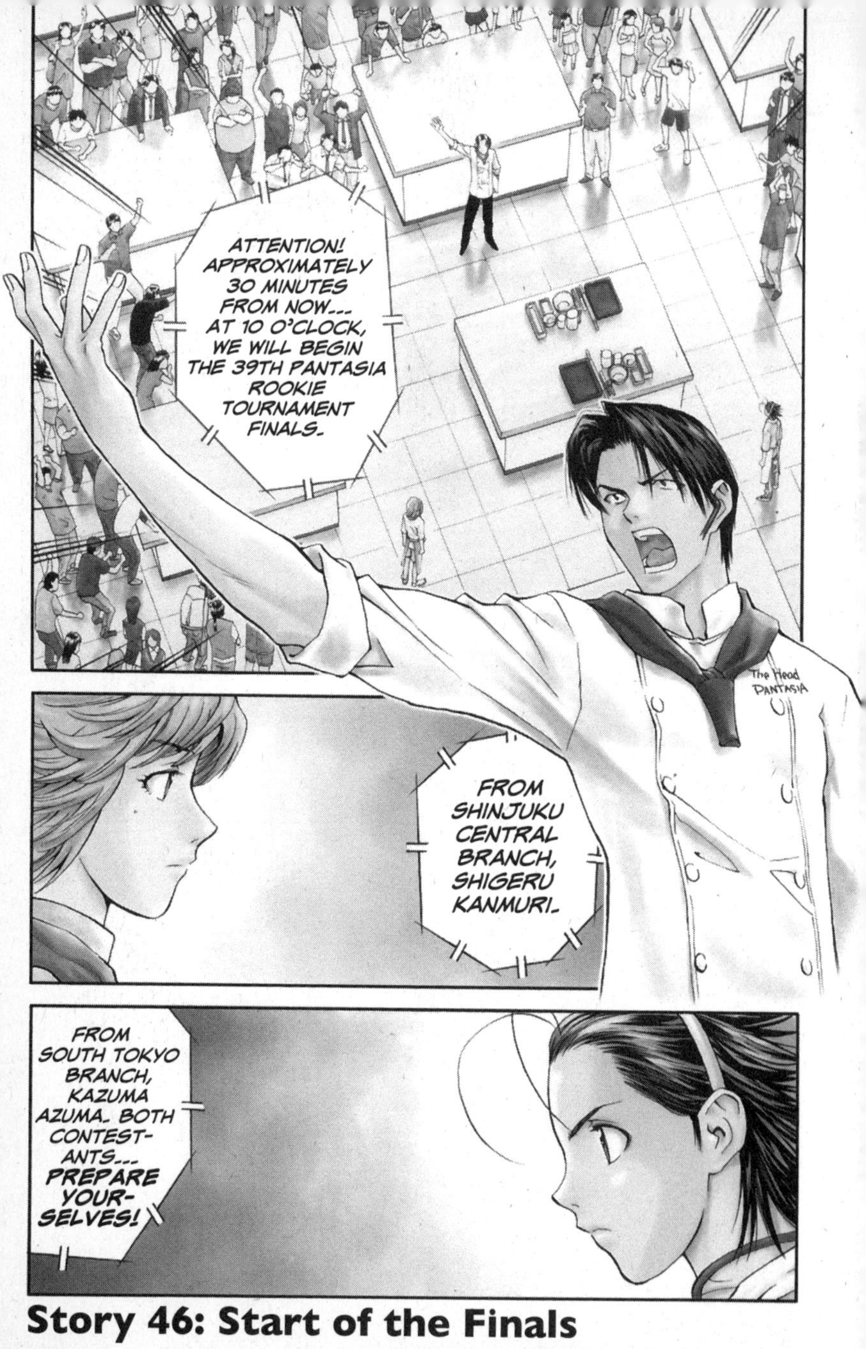
ATTENTION! APPROXIMATELY 30 MINUTES FROM NOW... AT 10 O'CLOCK, WE WILL BEGIN THE 39TH PANTASIA ROOKIE TOURNAMENT FINALS.
The Head PANTASIA
FROM SHINJUKU CENTRAL BRANCH, SHIGERU KANMURI.
FROM SOUTH TOKYO BRANCH, KAZUMA AZUMA. BOTH CONTEST-ANTS... PREPARE YOUR-SELVES!

Story 46: Start of the Finals

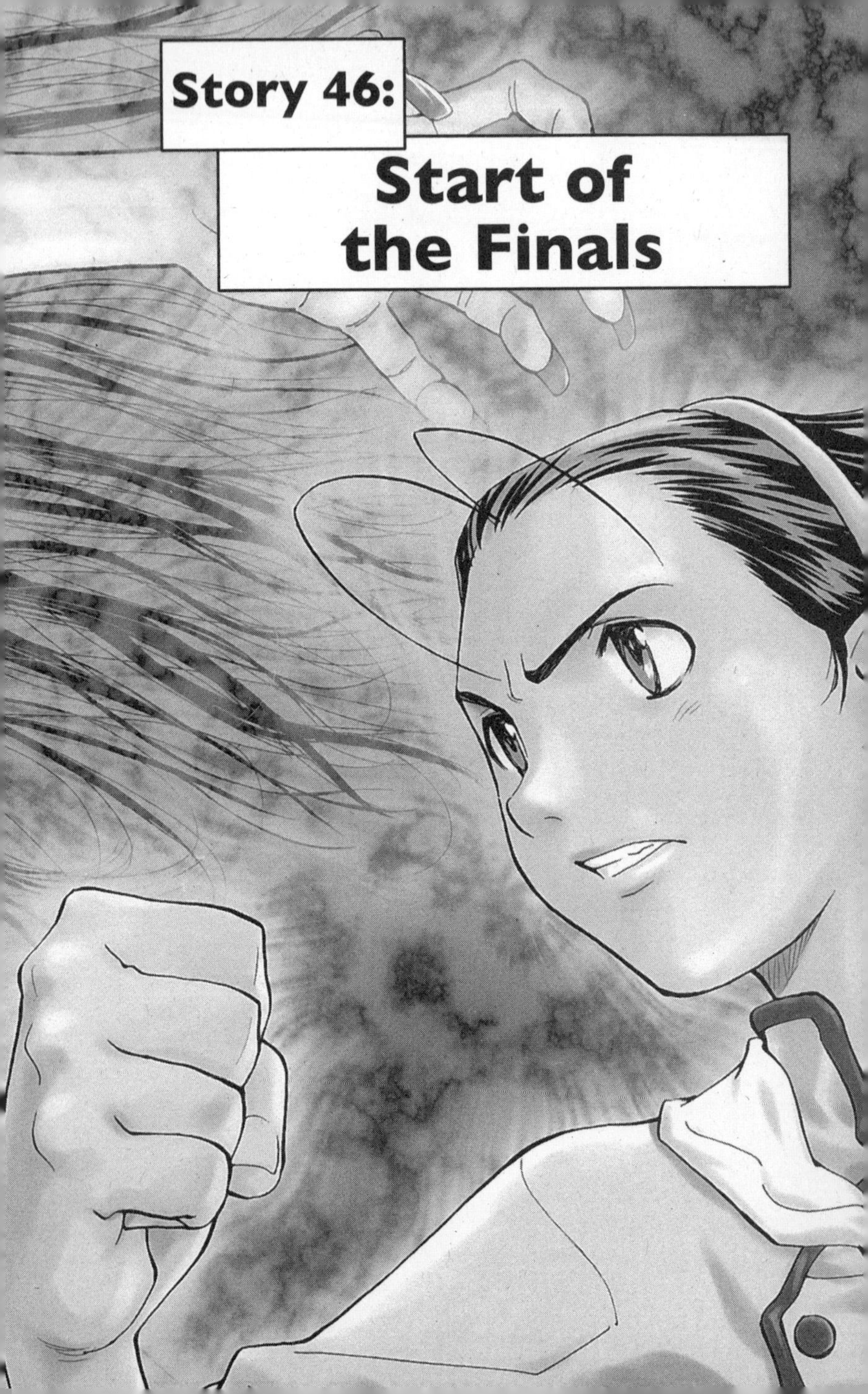
Story 46:
Start of the Finals

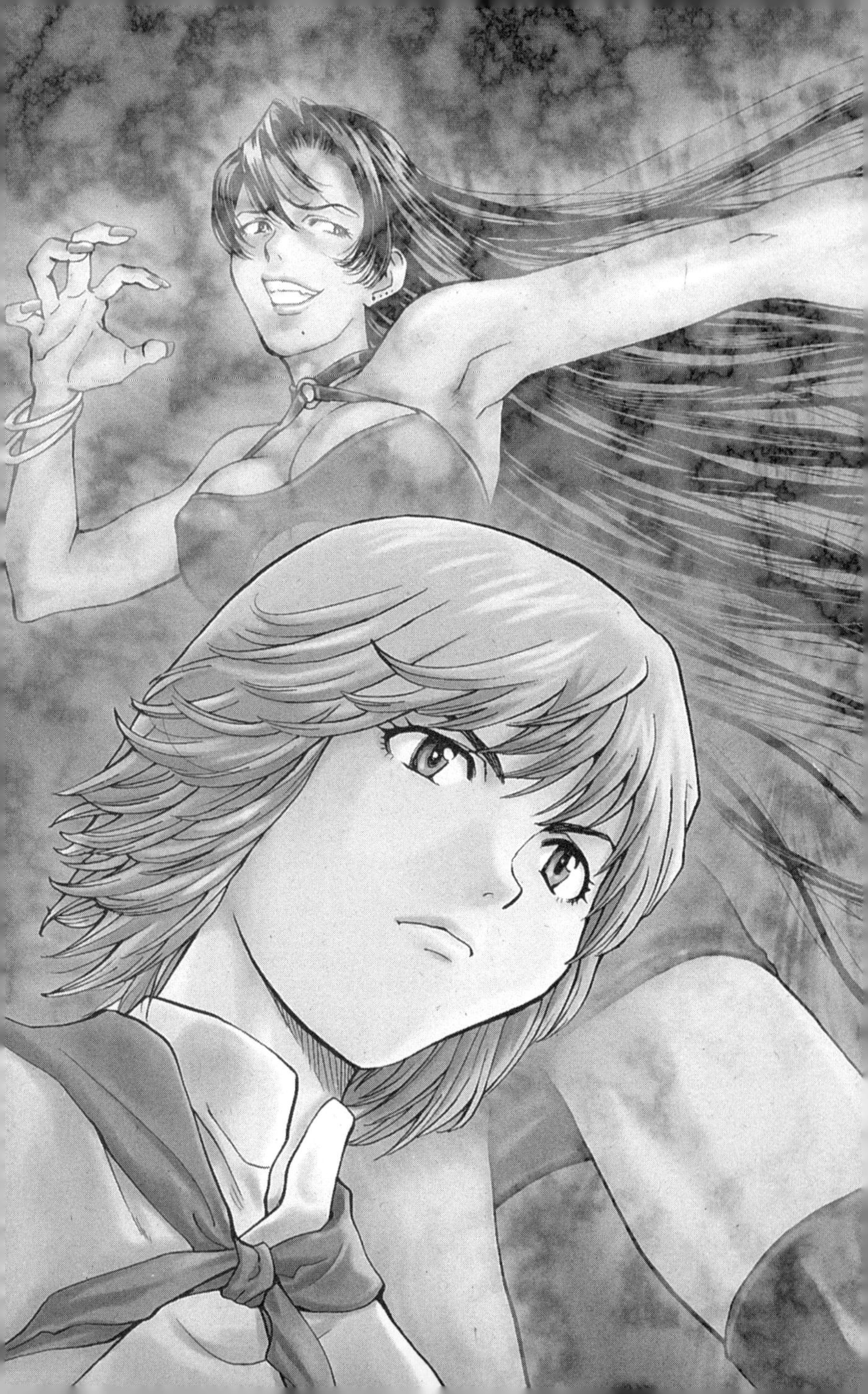

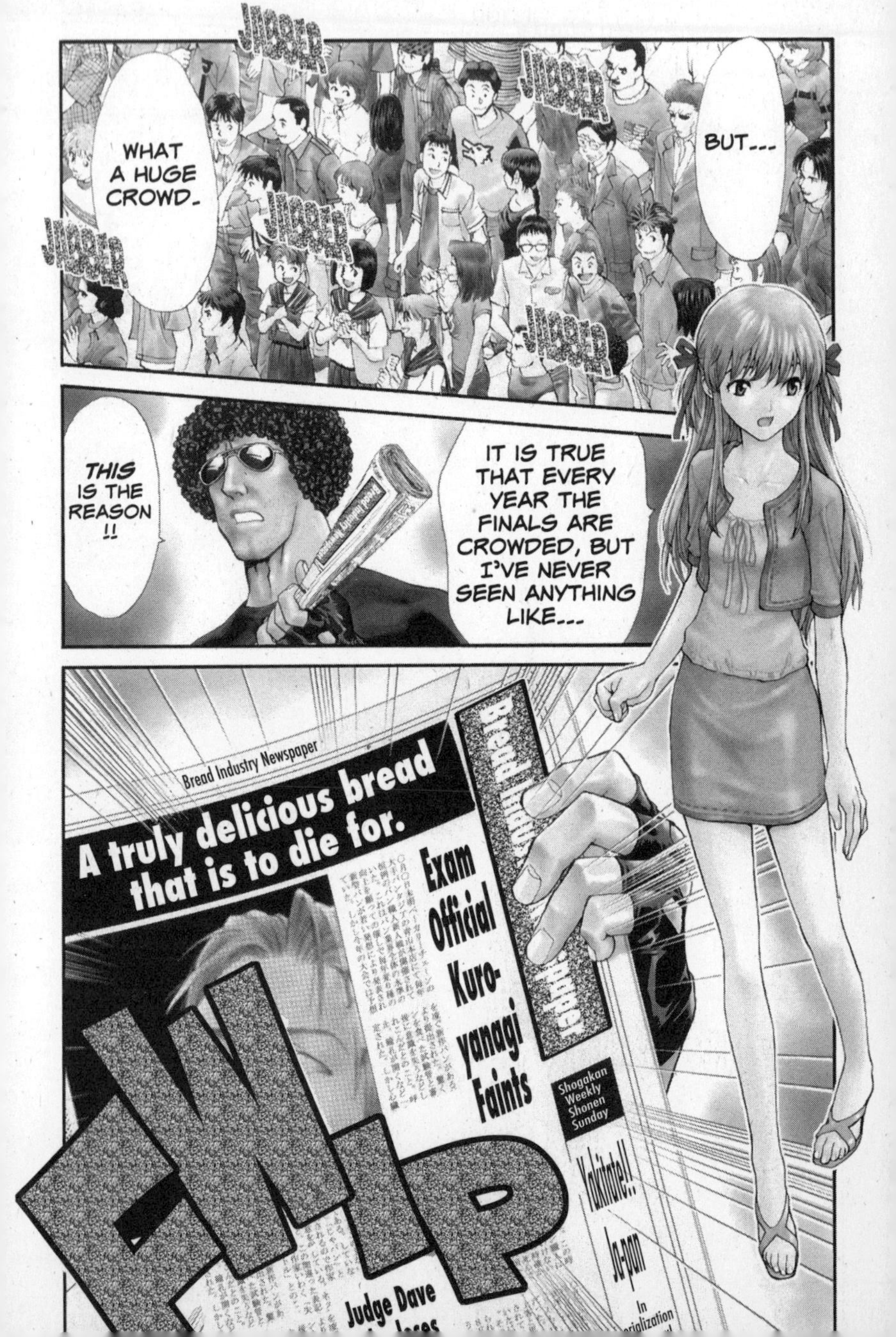
BUT...
JABBER
JABBER
JABBER
WHAT A HUGE CROWD.
JABBER
JABBER
IT IS TRUE THAT EVERY YEAR THE FINALS ARE CROWDED, BUT I'VE NEVER SEEN ANYTHING LIKE...
THIS IS THE REASON !!
Bread Industry Newspaper
A truly delicious bread that is to die for.
Exam Official Kuro-yanagi Faints
Shogakan Weekly Shonen Sunday
Yakitate!! Ja-pan
WHIP
Judge Dave

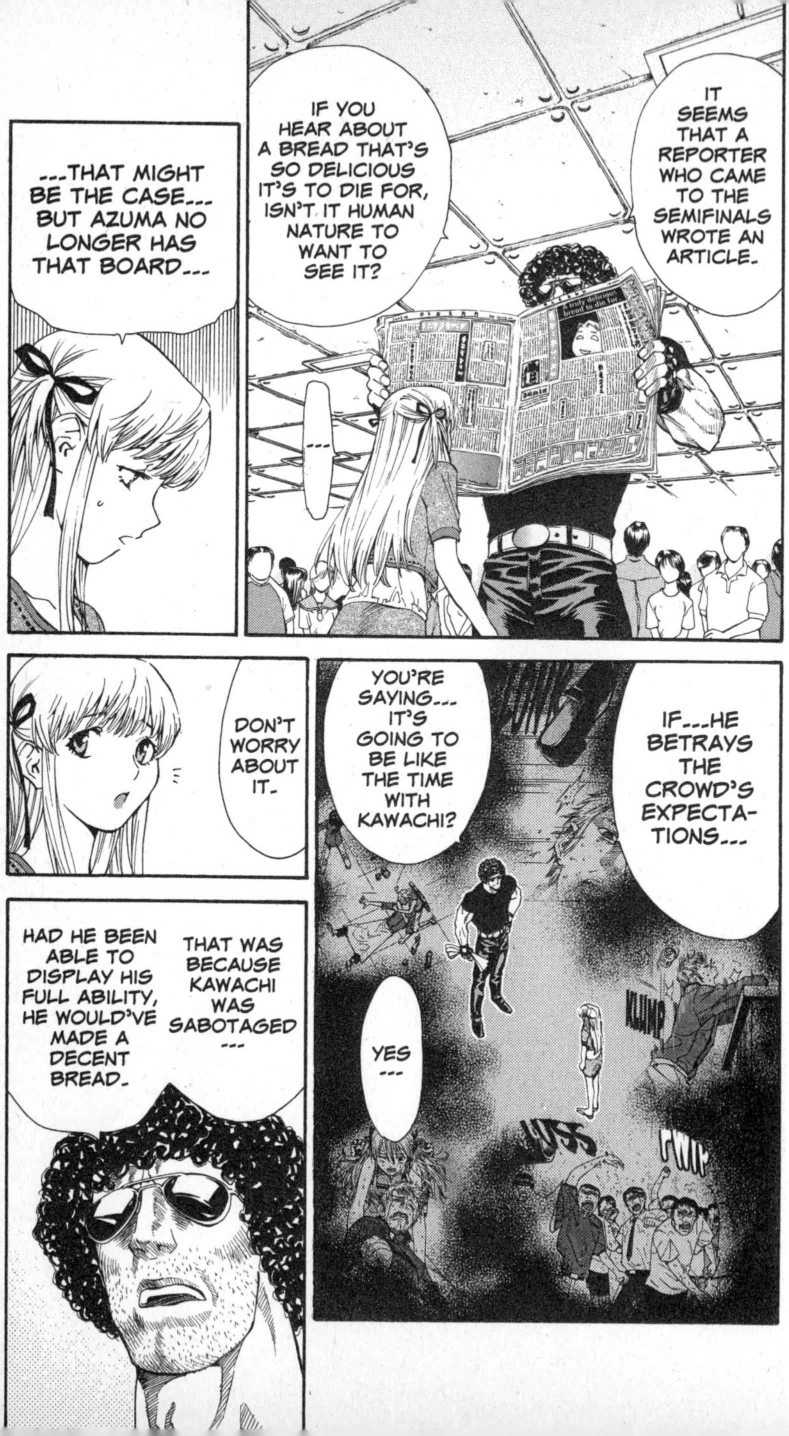
IT SEEMS THAT A REPORTER WHO CAME TO THE SEMIFINALS WROTE AN ARTICLE.
A truly delicious bread to die for
IF YOU HEAR ABOUT A BREAD THAT'S SO DELICIOUS IT'S TO DIE FOR, ISN'T IT HUMAN NATURE TO WANT TO SEE IT?
...
...THAT MIGHT BE THE CASE... BUT AZUMA NO LONGER HAS THAT BOARD...
IF...HE BETRAYS THE CROWD'S EXPECTATIONS...
YOU'RE SAYING... IT'S GOING TO BE LIKE THE TIME WITH KAWACHI?
KLUMP
YES ...
FWIP
DON'T WORRY ABOUT IT.
THAT WAS BECAUSE KAWACHI WAS SABOTAGED ...
HAD HE BEEN ABLE TO DISPLAY HIS FULL ABILITY, HE WOULD'VE MADE A DECENT BREAD.

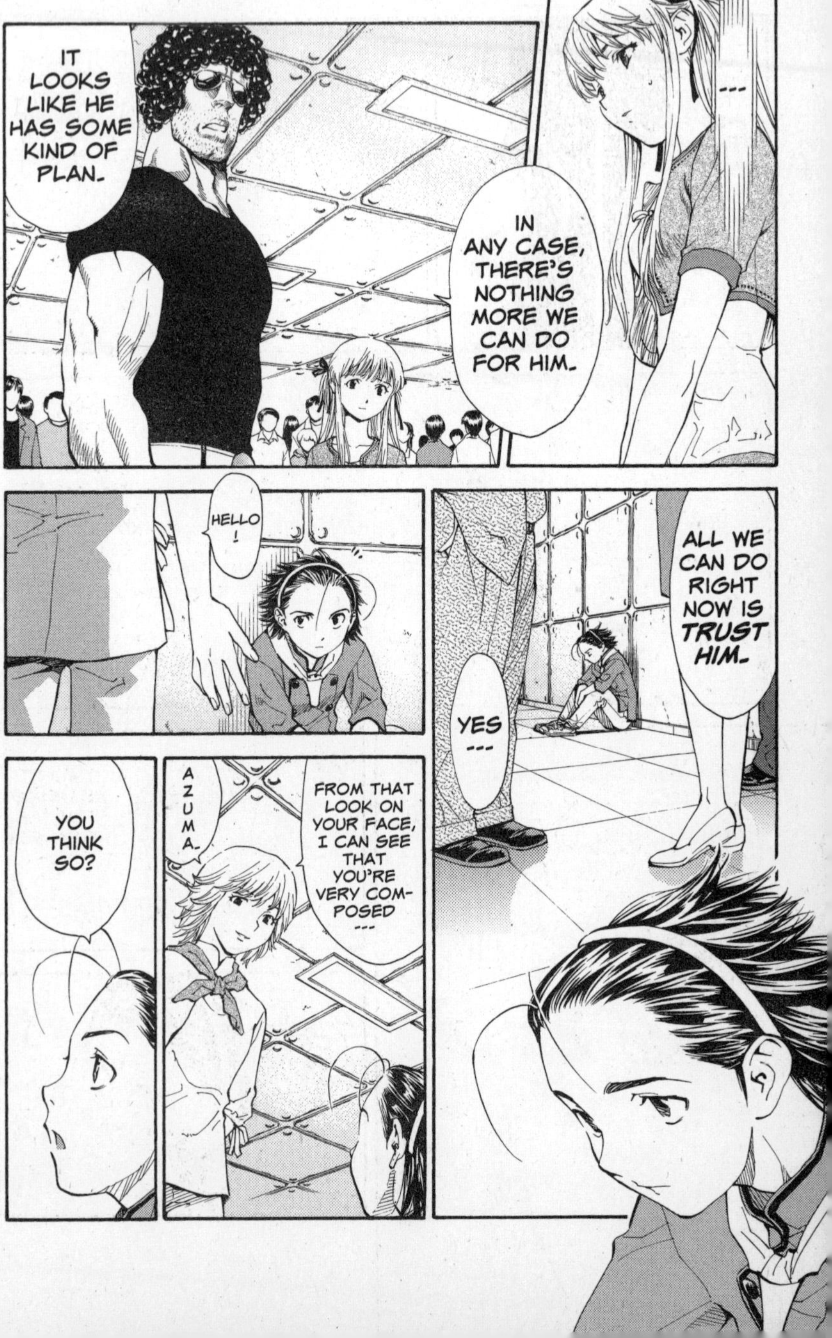

IN ANY CASE, THERE'S NOTHING MORE WE CAN DO FOR HIM.
IT LOOKS LIKE HE HAS SOME KIND OF PLAN.
ALL WE CAN DO RIGHT NOW IS *TRUST* HIM.
YES ---
HELLO!
AZUMA.
FROM THAT LOOK ON YOUR FACE, I CAN SEE THAT YOU'RE VERY COMPOSED ---
YOU THINK SO?

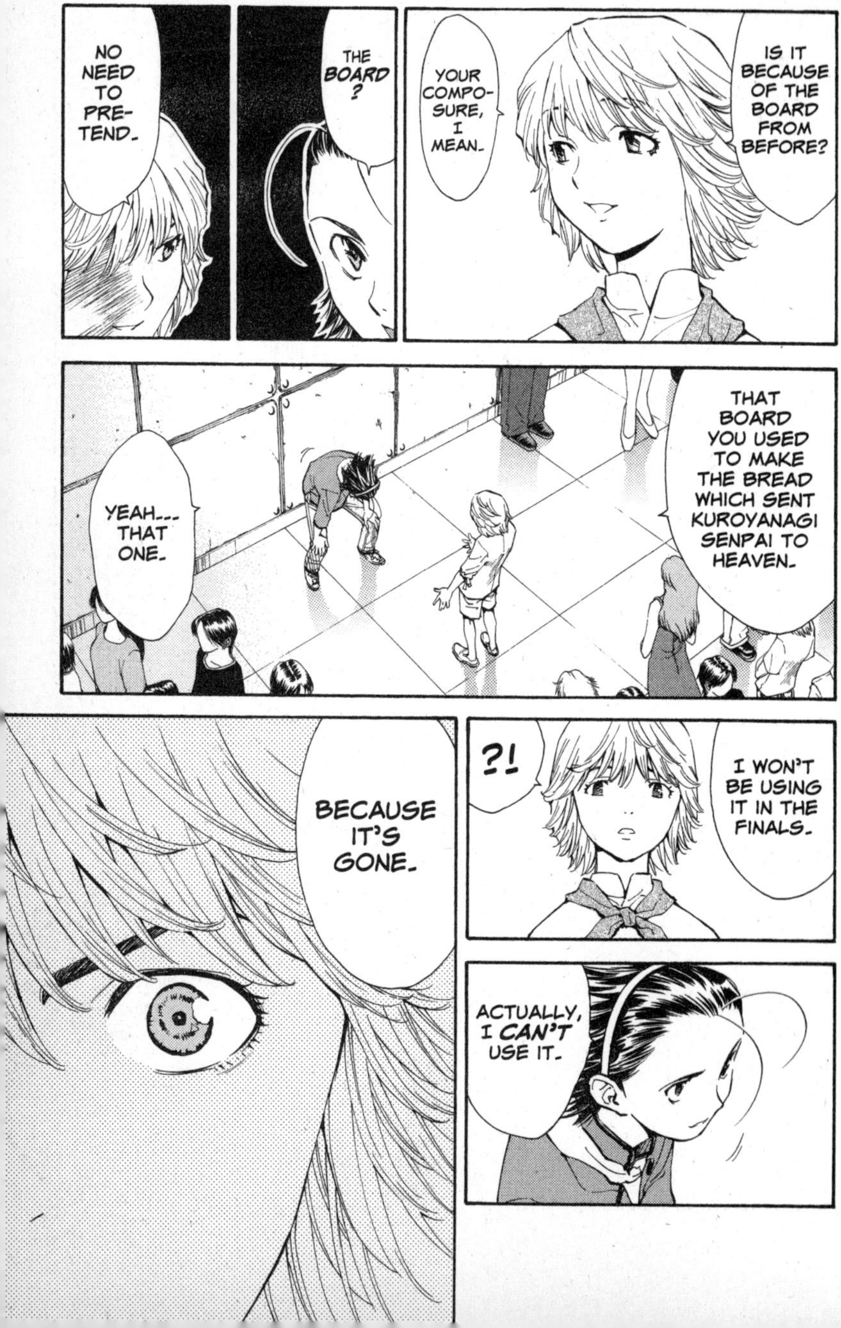
IS IT BECAUSE OF THE BOARD FROM BEFORE?
YOUR COMPOSURE, I MEAN.
THE *BOARD*?
NO NEED TO PRETEND.
THAT BOARD YOU USED TO MAKE THE BREAD WHICH SENT KUROYANAGI SENPAI TO HEAVEN.
YEAH... THAT ONE.
I WON'T BE USING IT IN THE FINALS.
?!
ACTUALLY, I *CAN'T* USE IT.
BECAUSE IT'S GONE.

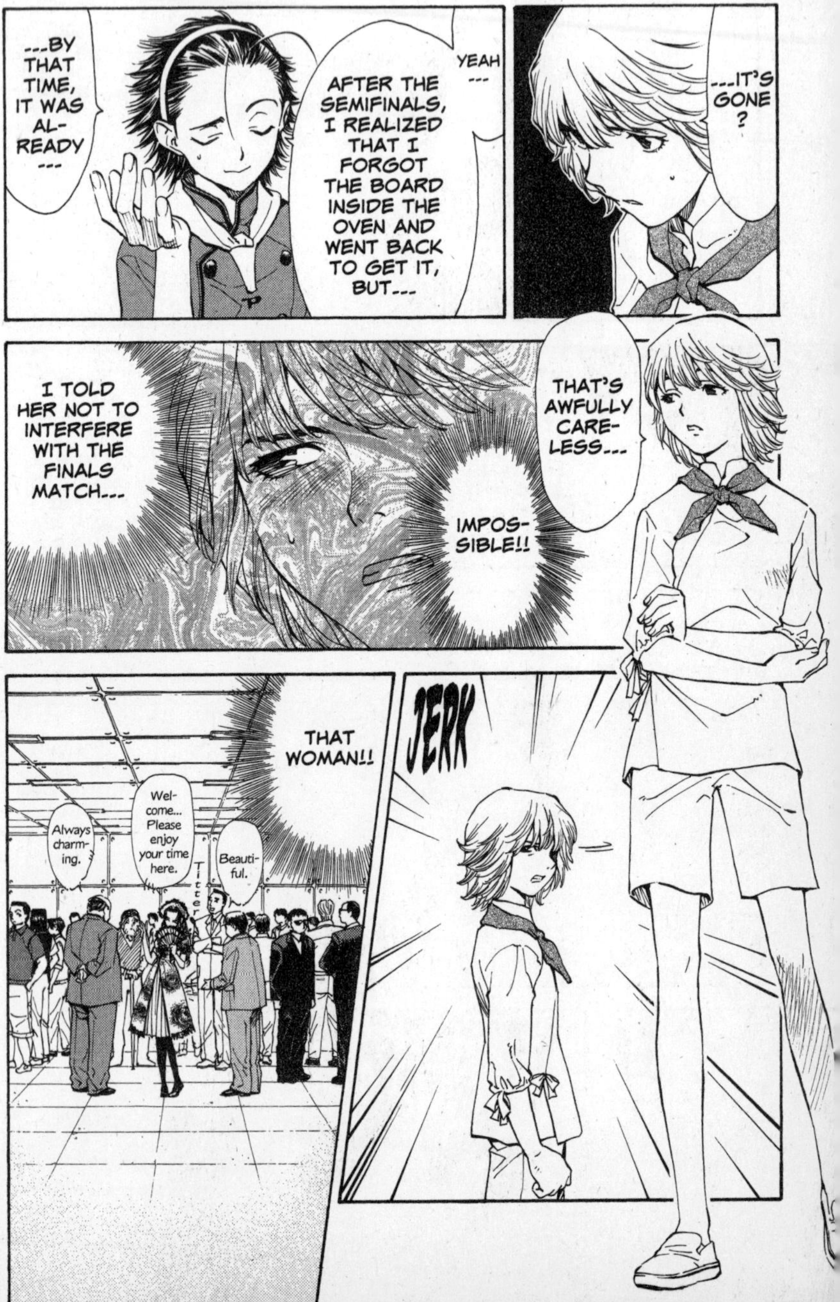
---IT'S GONE ?
YEAH ---
AFTER THE SEMIFINALS, I REALIZED THAT I FORGOT THE BOARD INSIDE THE OVEN AND WENT BACK TO GET IT, BUT---
---BY THAT TIME, IT WAS AL- READY ---
THAT'S AWFULLY CARE- LESS---
IMPOS- SIBLE!!
I TOLD HER NOT TO INTERFERE WITH THE FINALS MATCH---
JERK
THAT WOMAN!!
Beauti- ful.
Titter
Wel- come... Please enjoy your time here.
Always charm- ing.

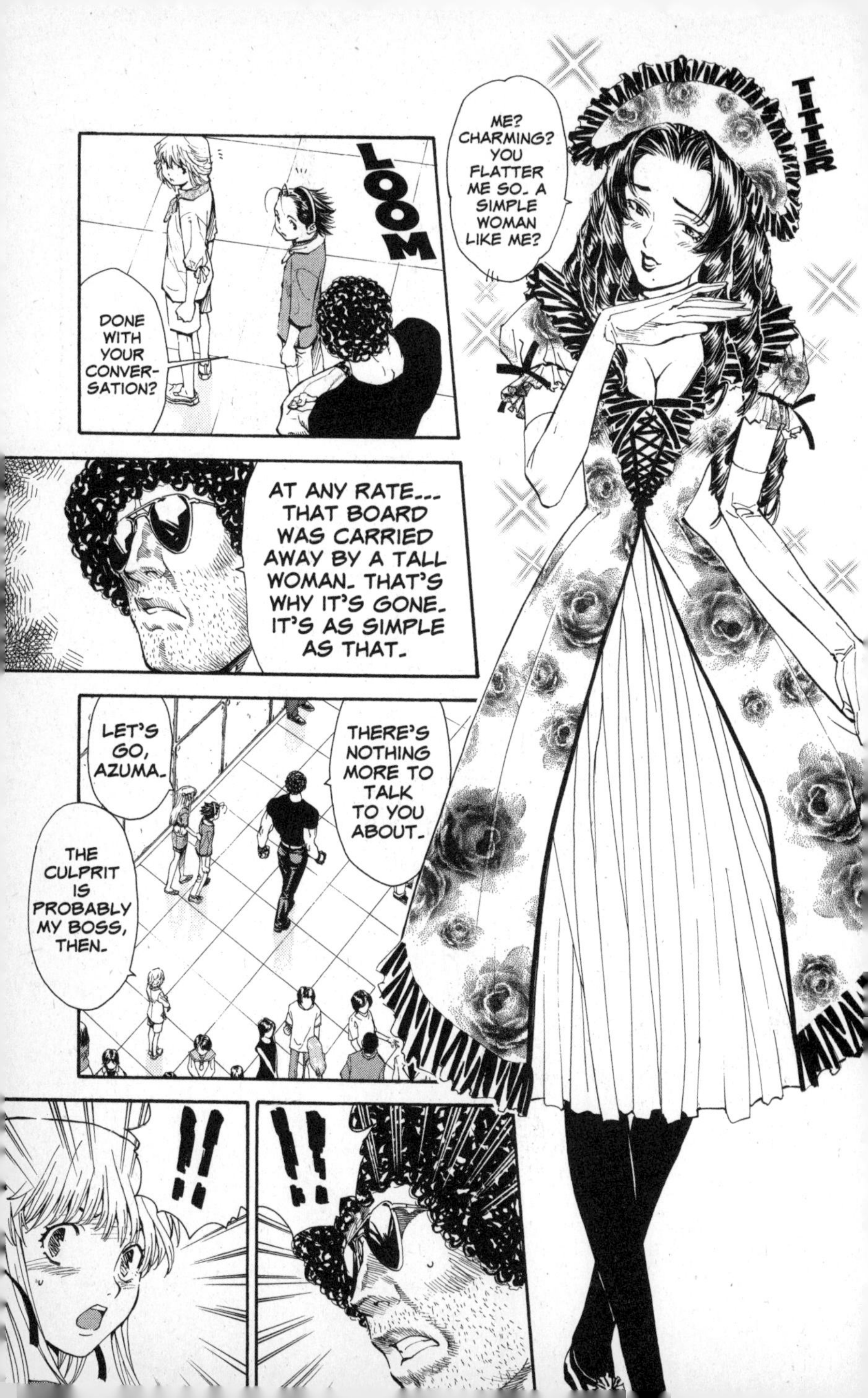
TITTER
ME? CHARMING? YOU FLATTER ME SO. A SIMPLE WOMAN LIKE ME?
LOOM
DONE WITH YOUR CONVER-SATION?
AT ANY RATE... THAT BOARD WAS CARRIED AWAY BY A TALL WOMAN. THAT'S WHY IT'S GONE. IT'S AS SIMPLE AS THAT.
THERE'S NOTHING MORE TO TALK TO YOU ABOUT.
LET'S GO, AZUMA.
THE CULPRIT IS PROBABLY MY BOSS, THEN.
!!
!!

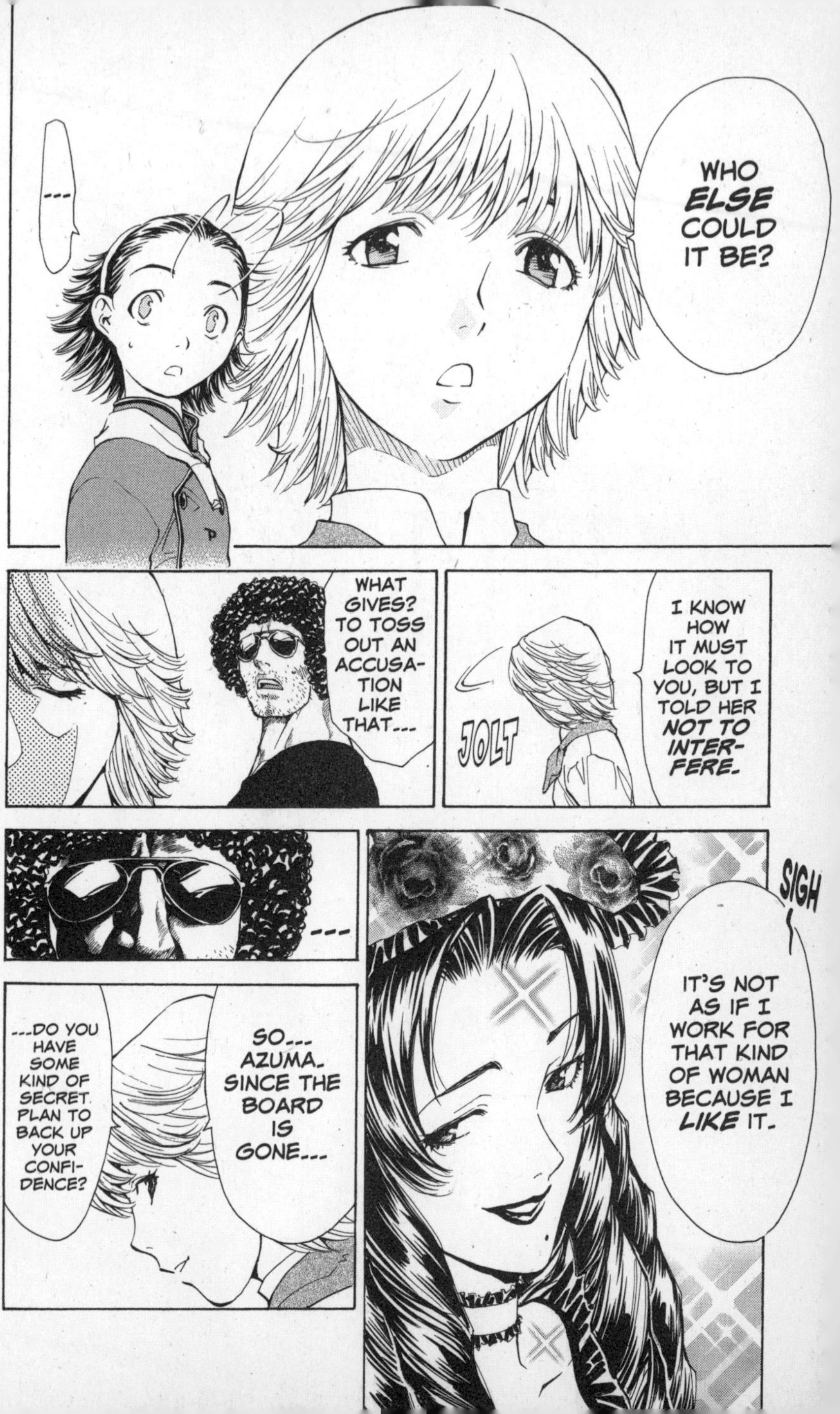
WHO ELSE COULD IT BE?
...
I KNOW HOW IT MUST LOOK TO YOU, BUT I TOLD HER NOT TO INTERFERE.
JOLT
WHAT GIVES? TO TOSS OUT AN ACCUSATION LIKE THAT...
SIGH
IT'S NOT AS IF I WORK FOR THAT KIND OF WOMAN BECAUSE I LIKE IT.
...
SO... AZUMA. SINCE THE BOARD IS GONE...
...DO YOU HAVE SOME KIND OF SECRET PLAN TO BACK UP YOUR CONFIDENCE?

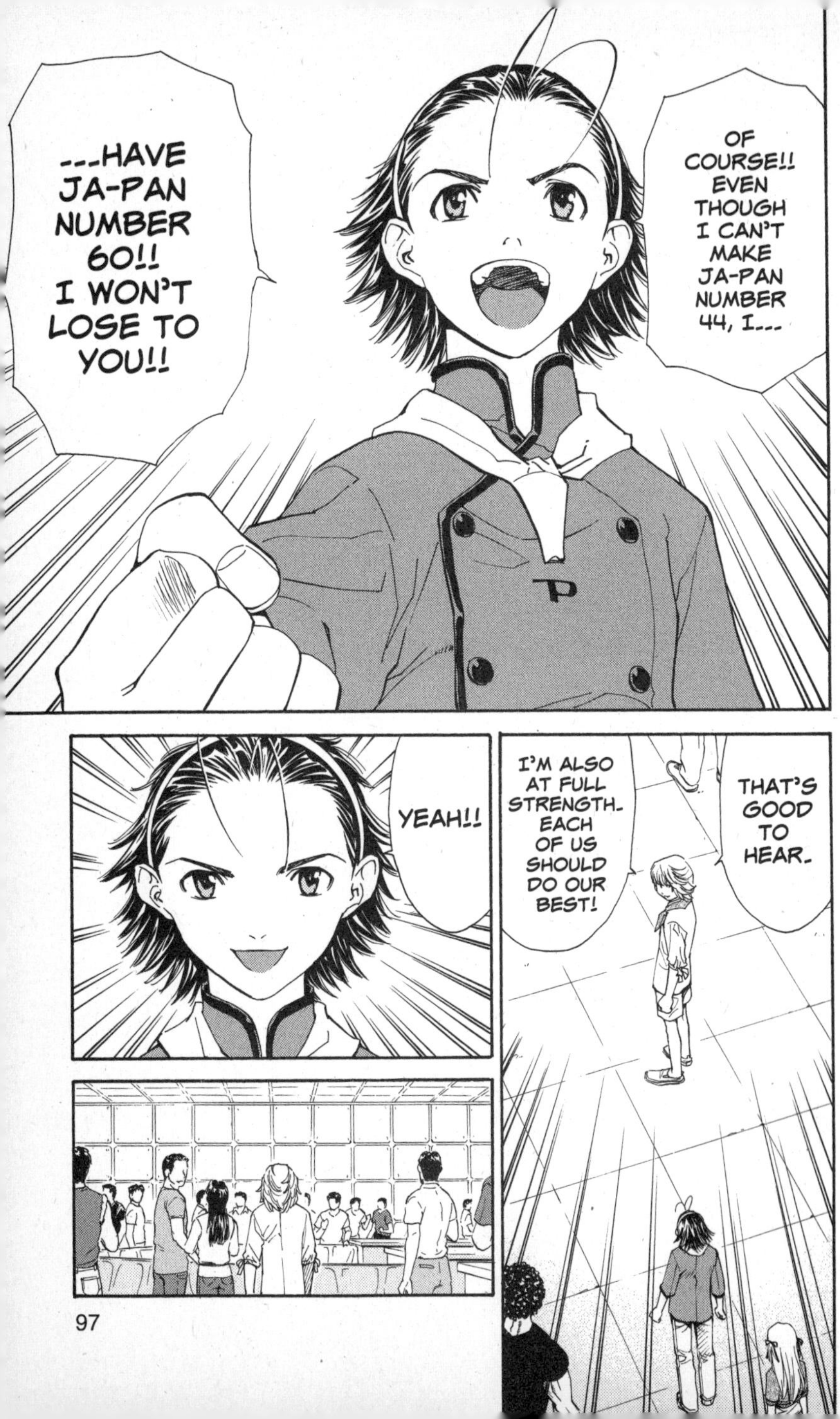
OF COURSE!! EVEN THOUGH I CAN'T MAKE JA-PAN NUMBER 44, I---
---HAVE JA-PAN NUMBER 60!! I WON'T LOSE TO YOU!!
THAT'S GOOD TO HEAR.
I'M ALSO AT FULL STRENGTH. EACH OF US SHOULD DO OUR BEST!
YEAH!!

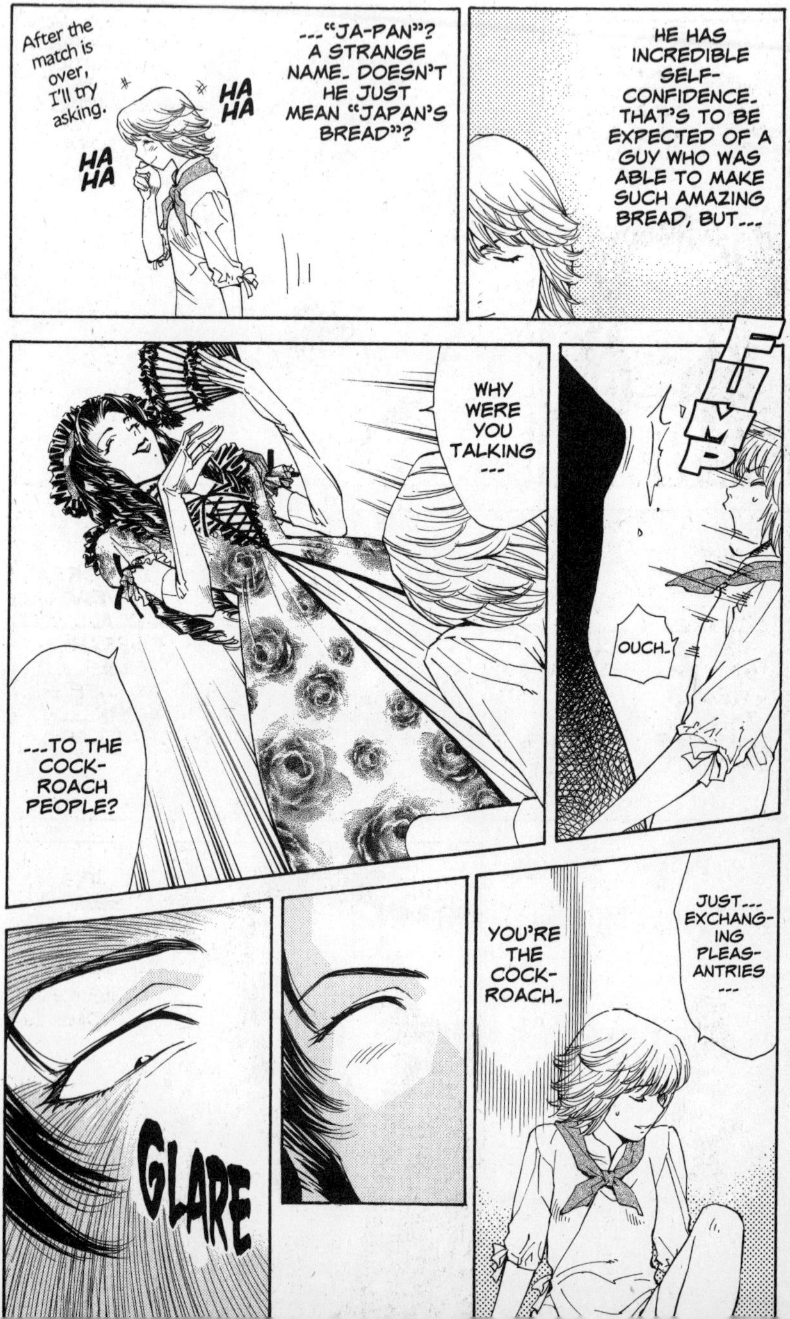
HE HAS INCREDIBLE SELF-CONFIDENCE. THAT'S TO BE EXPECTED OF A GUY WHO WAS ABLE TO MAKE SUCH AMAZING BREAD, BUT...
---"JA-PAN"? A STRANGE NAME. DOESN'T HE JUST MEAN "JAPAN'S BREAD"?
HA HA
After the match is over, I'll try asking.
HA HA
FUMP
OUCH.
WHY WERE YOU TALKING ---
---TO THE COCKROACH PEOPLE?
JUST... EXCHANGING PLEASANTRIES ---
YOU'RE THE COCKROACH.
GLARE

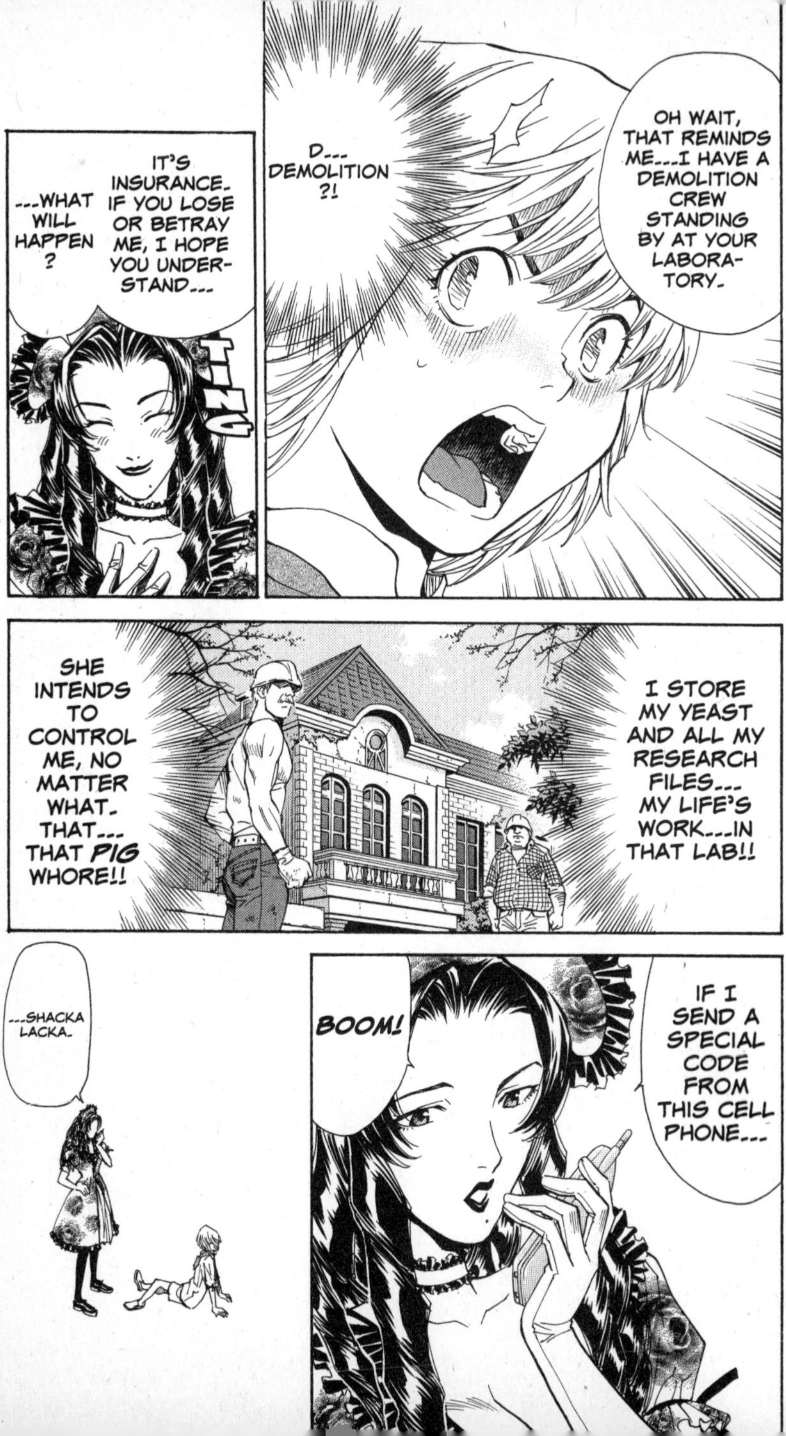
OH WAIT, THAT REMINDS ME...I HAVE A DEMOLITION CREW STANDING BY AT YOUR LABORATORY.
D... DEMOLITION ?!
IT'S INSURANCE. IF YOU LOSE OR BETRAY ME, I HOPE YOU UNDERSTAND...
...WHAT WILL HAPPEN ?
TING
I STORE MY YEAST AND ALL MY RESEARCH FILES... MY LIFE'S WORK...IN THAT LAB!!
SHE INTENDS TO CONTROL ME, NO MATTER WHAT. THAT... THAT *PIG* WHORE!!
IF I SEND A SPECIAL CODE FROM THIS CELL PHONE...
BOOM!
...SHACKA LACKA.

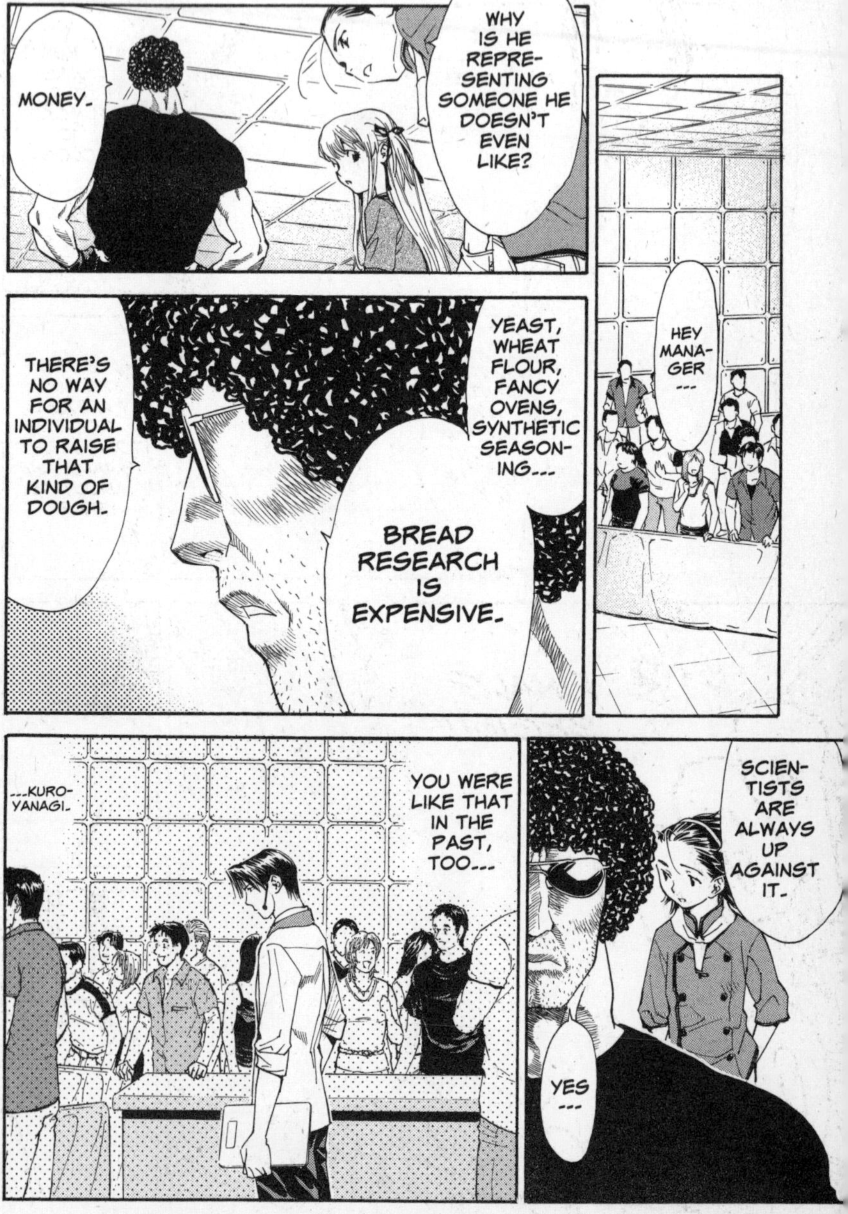
HEY MANAGER---
WHY IS HE REPRESENTING SOMEONE HE DOESN'T EVEN LIKE?
MONEY.
YEAST, WHEAT FLOUR, FANCY OVENS, SYNTHETIC SEASONING...
BREAD RESEARCH IS EXPENSIVE.
THERE'S NO WAY FOR AN INDIVIDUAL TO RAISE THAT KIND OF DOUGH.
SCIENTISTS ARE ALWAYS UP AGAINST IT.
YES---
YOU WERE LIKE THAT IN THE PAST, TOO...
...KURO-YANAGI.

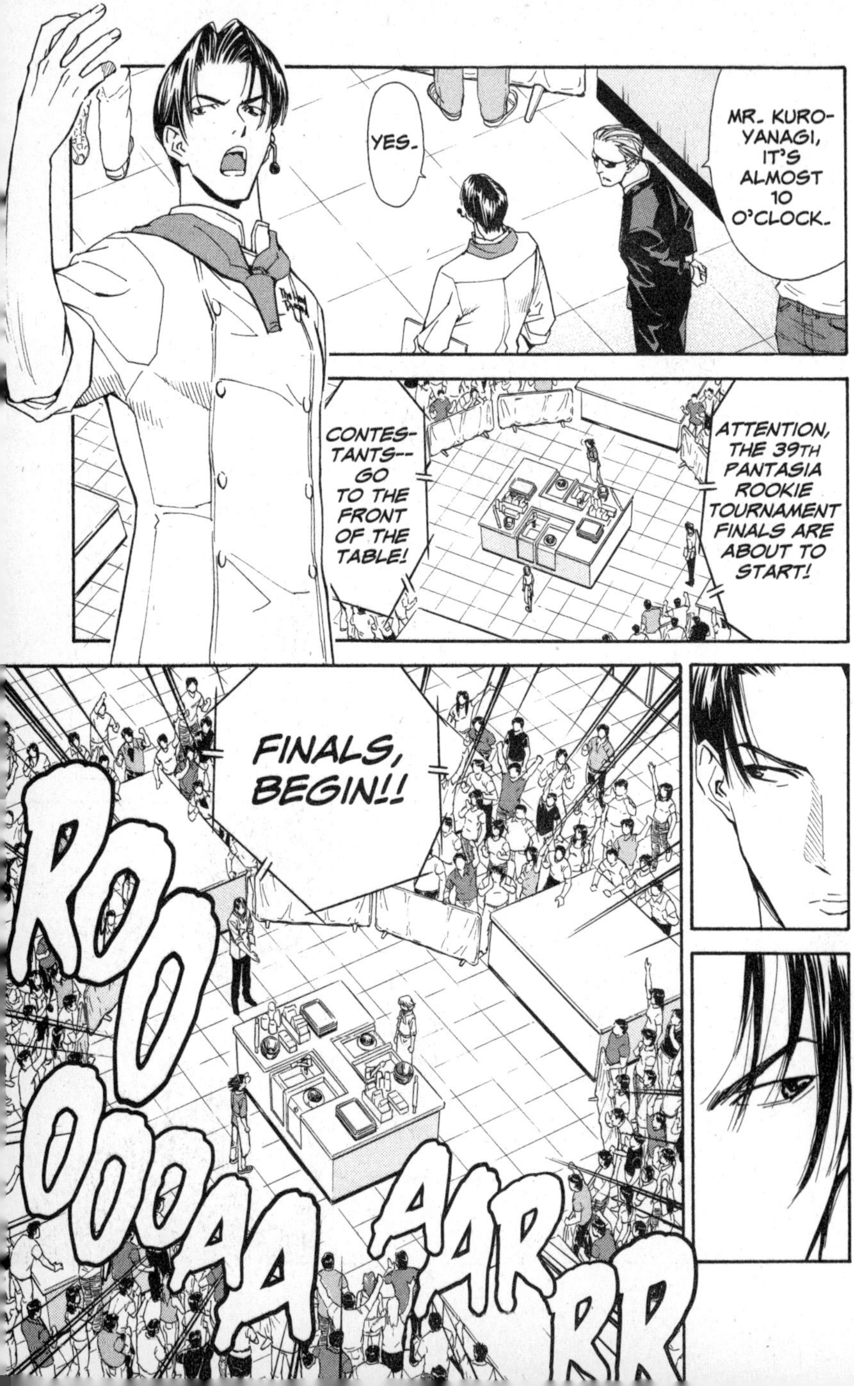
MR. KURO-YANAGI, IT'S ALMOST 10 O'CLOCK.
YES.
ATTENTION, THE 39TH PANTASIA ROOKIE TOURNAMENT FINALS ARE ABOUT TO START!
CONTES-TANTS--GO TO THE FRONT OF THE TABLE!
FINALS, BEGIN!!
ROOOOOAAAARRR

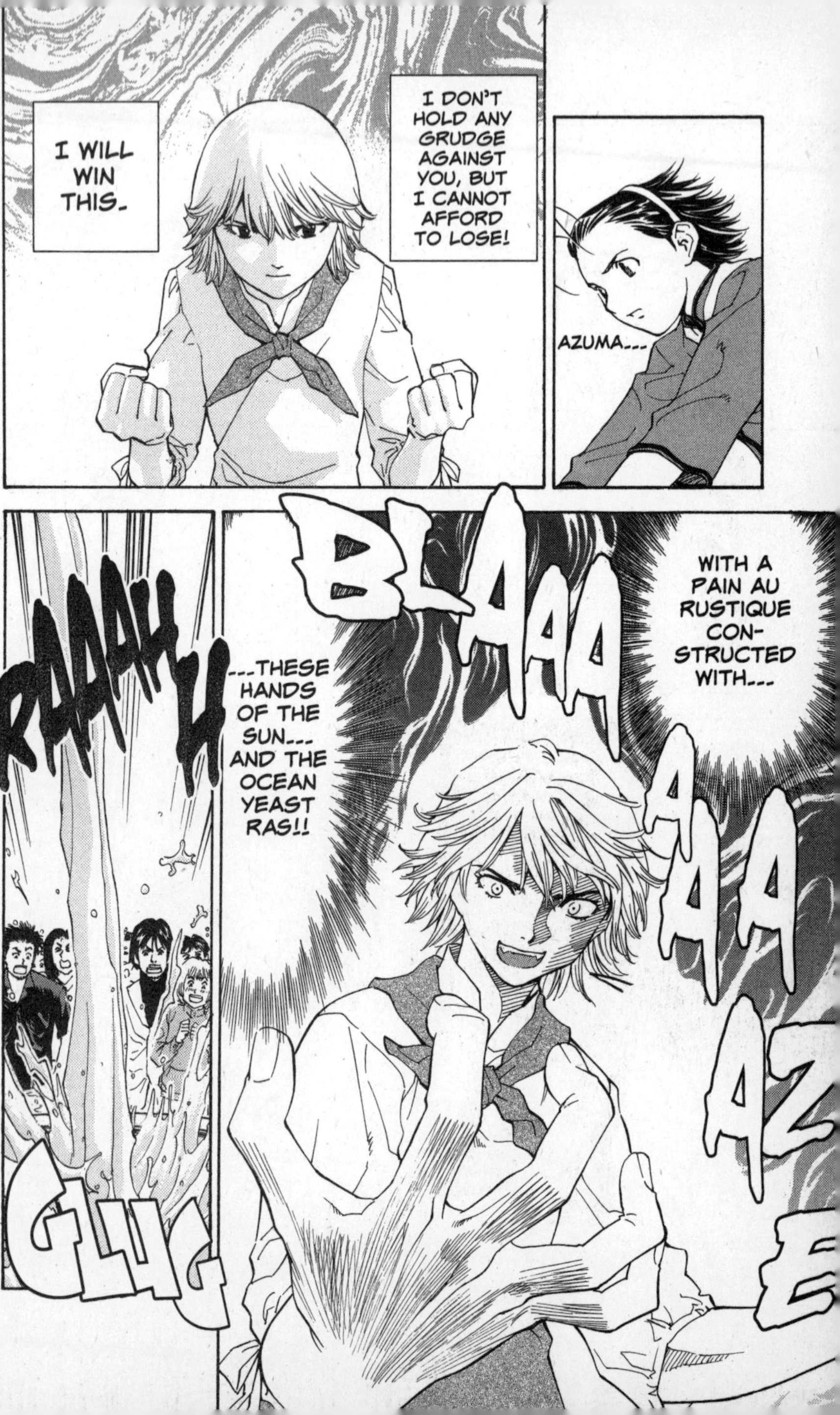
AZUMA...
I DON'T HOLD ANY GRUDGE AGAINST YOU, BUT I CANNOT AFFORD TO LOSE!
I WILL WIN THIS.
BLAAAAAAAZE
WITH A PAIN AU RUSTIQUE CON-STRUCTED WITH...
...THESE HANDS OF THE SUN... AND THE OCEAN YEAST RAS!!
RAAAHH
GLUG

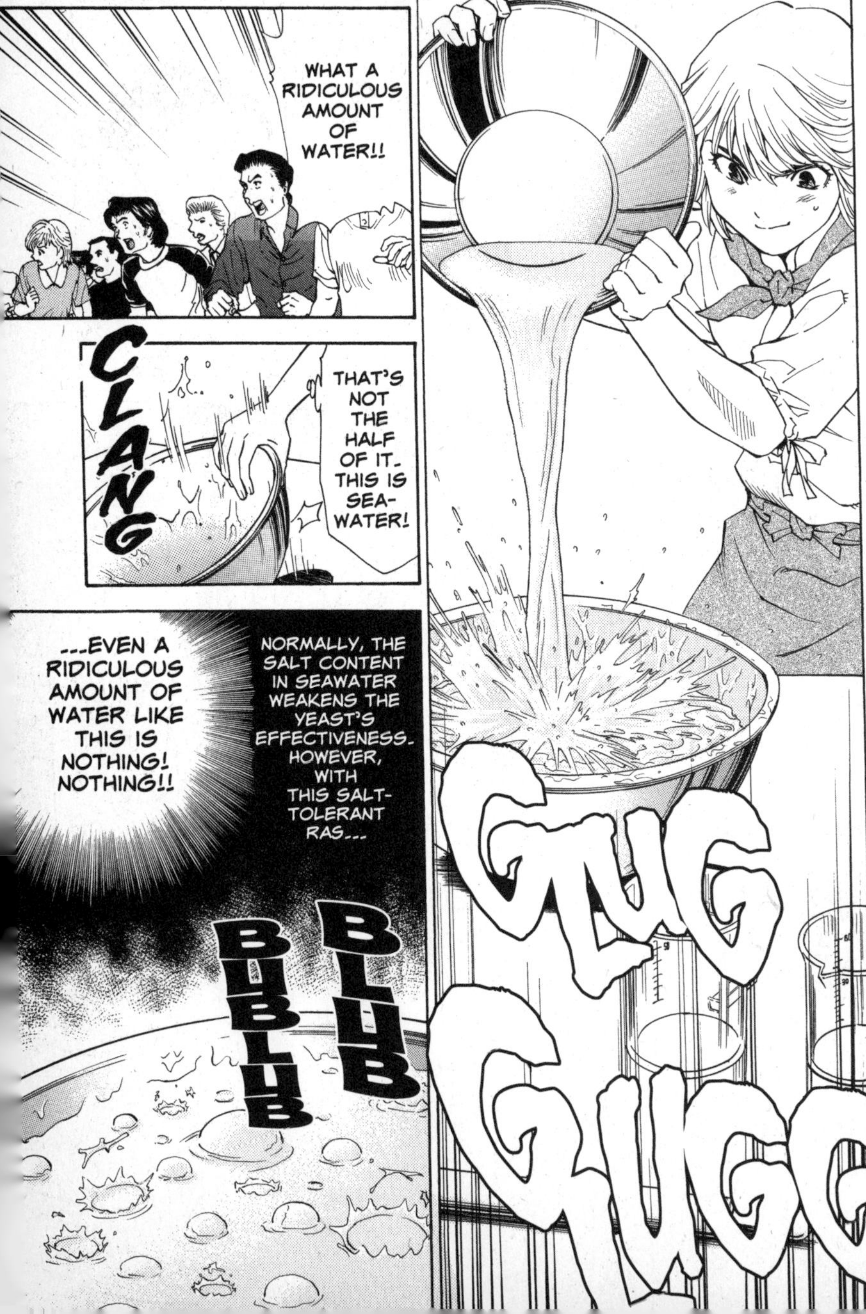
GLUG
GLUGG
WHAT A RIDICULOUS AMOUNT OF WATER!!
CLANG
THAT'S NOT THE HALF OF IT. THIS IS SEA-WATER!
NORMALLY, THE SALT CONTENT IN SEAWATER WEAKENS THE YEAST'S EFFECTIVENESS. HOWEVER, WITH THIS SALT-TOLERANT RAS...
...EVEN A RIDICULOUS AMOUNT OF WATER LIKE THIS IS NOTHING! NOTHING!!
BLUB
BUBLUB

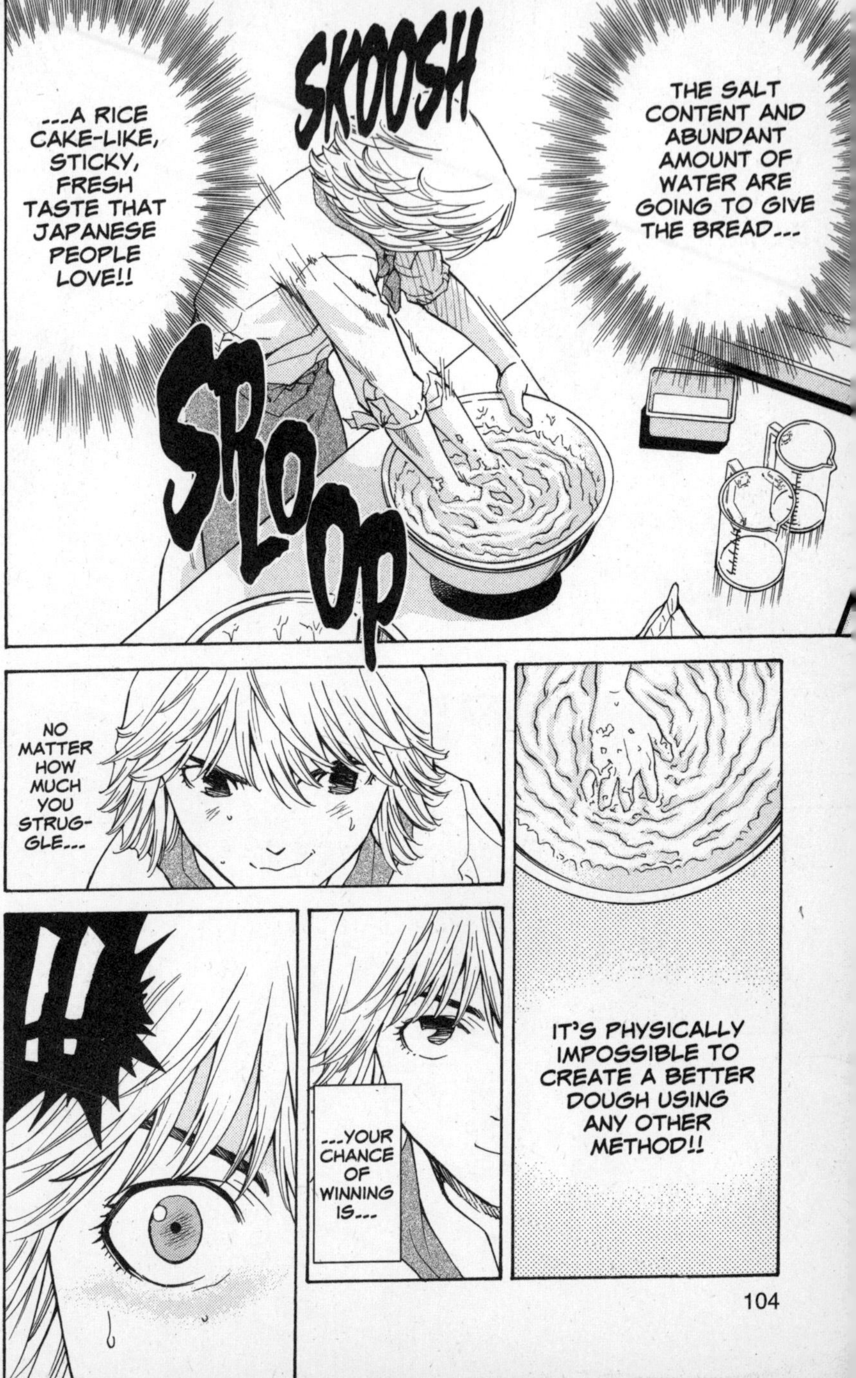
THE SALT CONTENT AND ABUNDANT AMOUNT OF WATER ARE GOING TO GIVE THE BREAD...
SKOOSH
...A RICE CAKE-LIKE, STICKY, FRESH TASTE THAT JAPANESE PEOPLE LOVE!!
SRLOOP
IT'S PHYSICALLY IMPOSSIBLE TO CREATE A BETTER DOUGH USING ANY OTHER METHOD!!
NO MATTER HOW MUCH YOU STRUGGLE...
...YOUR CHANCE OF WINNING IS...
!!

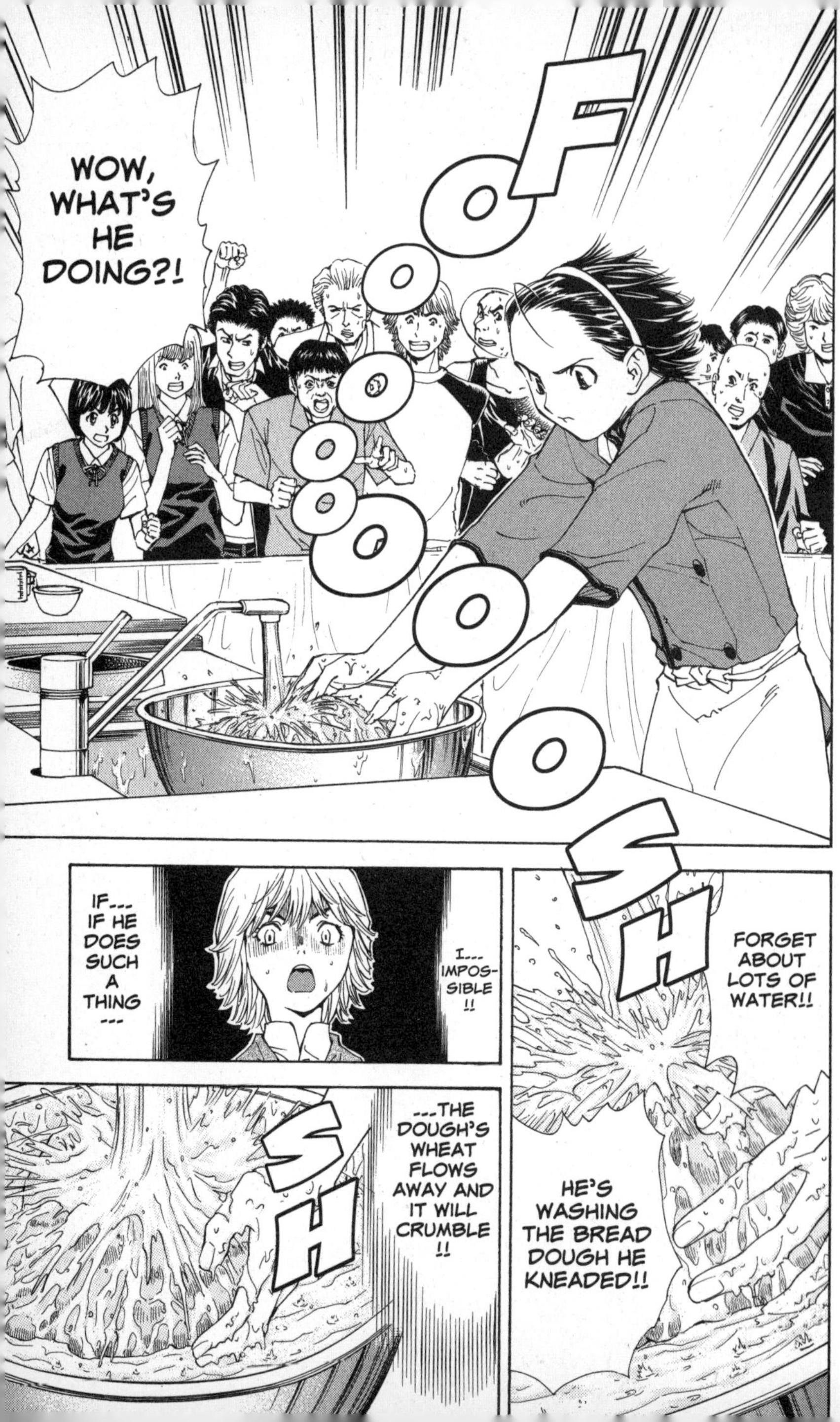

FOOOOOOOOSH
WOW, WHAT'S HE DOING?!
FORGET ABOUT LOTS OF WATER!!
HE'S WASHING THE BREAD DOUGH HE KNEADED!!
I... IMPOSSIBLE!!
IF... IF HE DOES SUCH A THING...
...THE DOUGH'S WHEAT FLOWS AWAY AND IT WILL CRUMBLE!!
SH

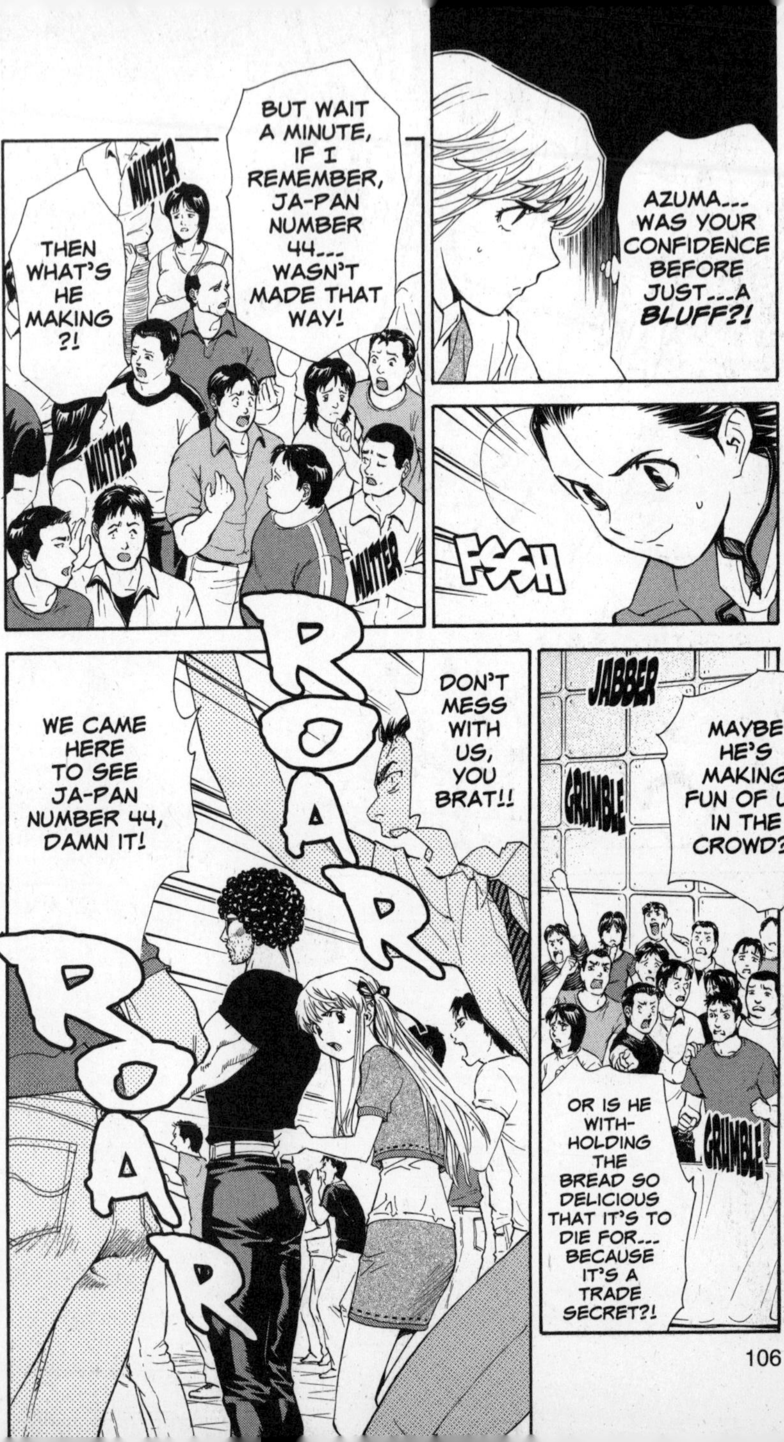
AZUMA... WAS YOUR CONFIDENCE BEFORE JUST...A BLUFF?!
FSSH
BUT WAIT A MINUTE, IF I REMEMBER, JA-PAN NUMBER 44... WASN'T MADE THAT WAY!
MUTTER
THEN WHAT'S HE MAKING?!
MUTTER
MUTTER
JABBER
MAYBE HE'S MAKING FUN OF US IN THE CROWD?!
GRUMBLE
OR IS HE WITH-HOLDING THE BREAD SO DELICIOUS THAT IT'S TO DIE FOR... BECAUSE IT'S A TRADE SECRET?!
GRUMBLE
DON'T MESS WITH US, YOU BRAT!!
ROAR
WE CAME HERE TO SEE JA-PAN NUMBER 44, DAMN IT!
ROAR

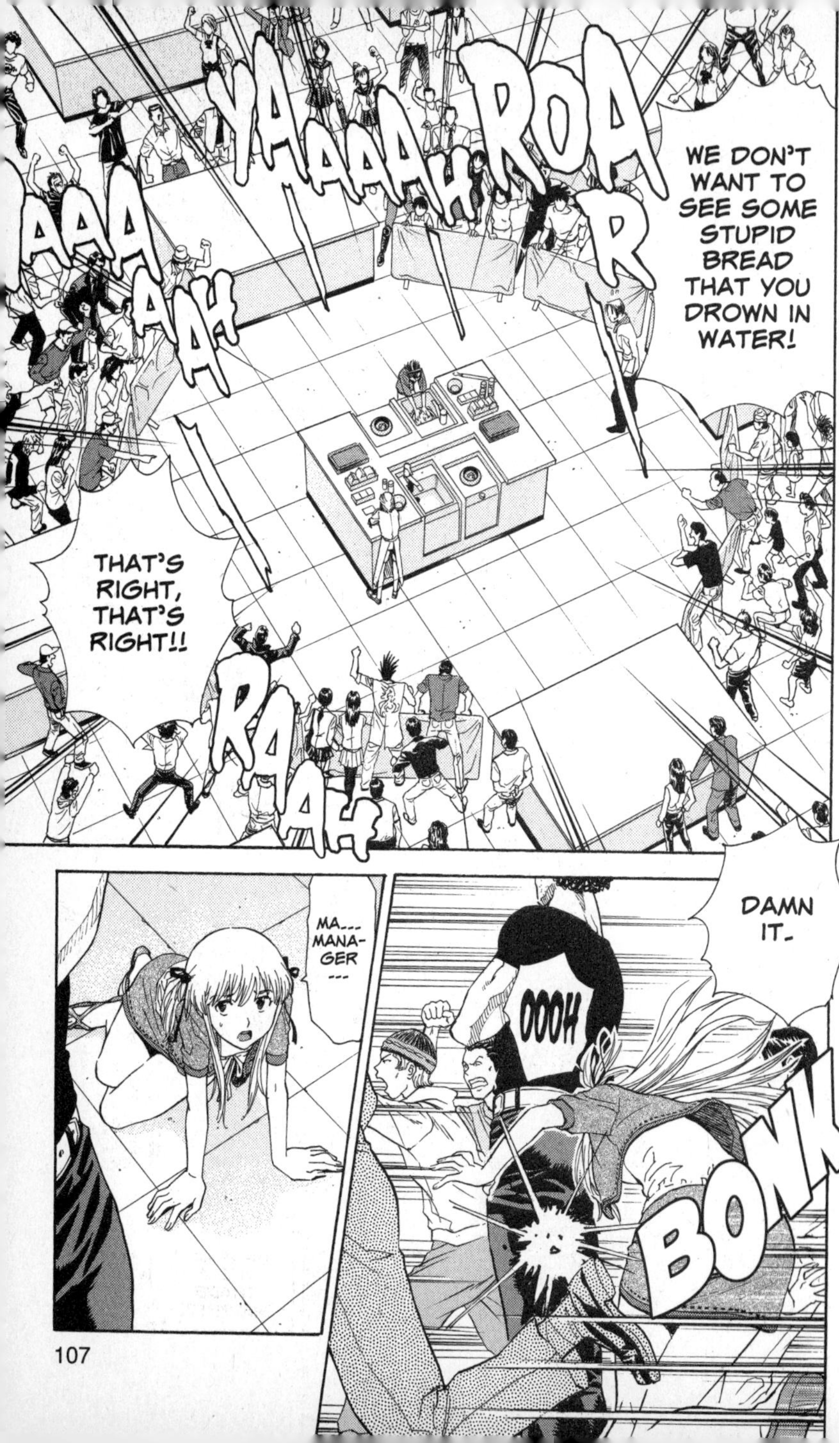

WE DON'T WANT TO SEE SOME STUPID BREAD THAT YOU DROWN IN WATER!
YAAAAAHROAR
AAAAAH
THAT'S RIGHT, THAT'S RIGHT!!
RAAAH
DAMN IT.
OOOH
BONK
MA... MANAGER...

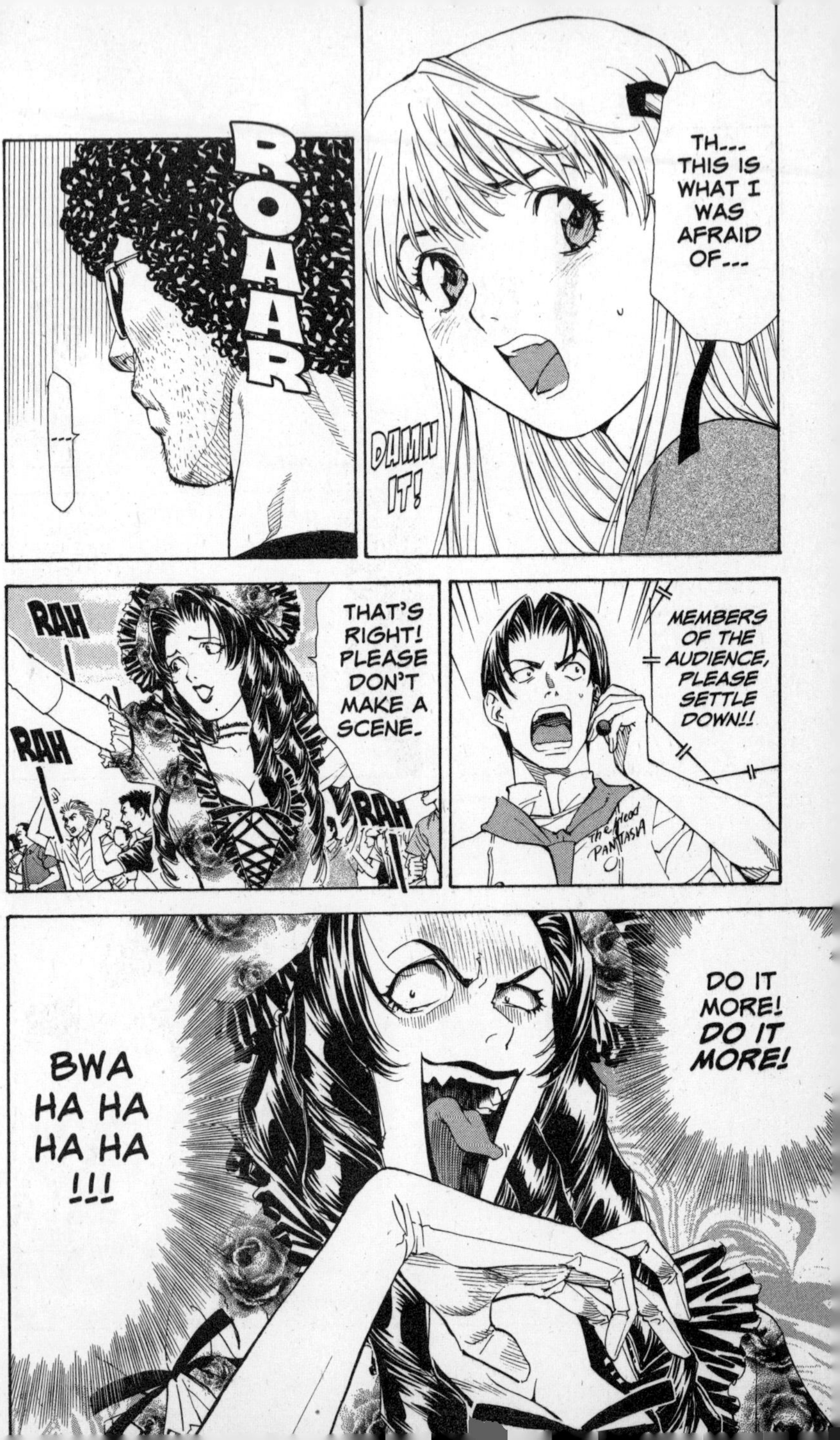
TH... THIS IS WHAT I WAS AFRAID OF...
DAMN IT!
ROAAR
...
MEMBERS OF THE AUDIENCE, PLEASE SETTLE DOWN!!
The Head PANTASIA
THAT'S RIGHT! PLEASE DON'T MAKE A SCENE.
RAH
RAH
RAH
DO IT MORE! DO IT MORE!
BWA HA HA HA HA !!!

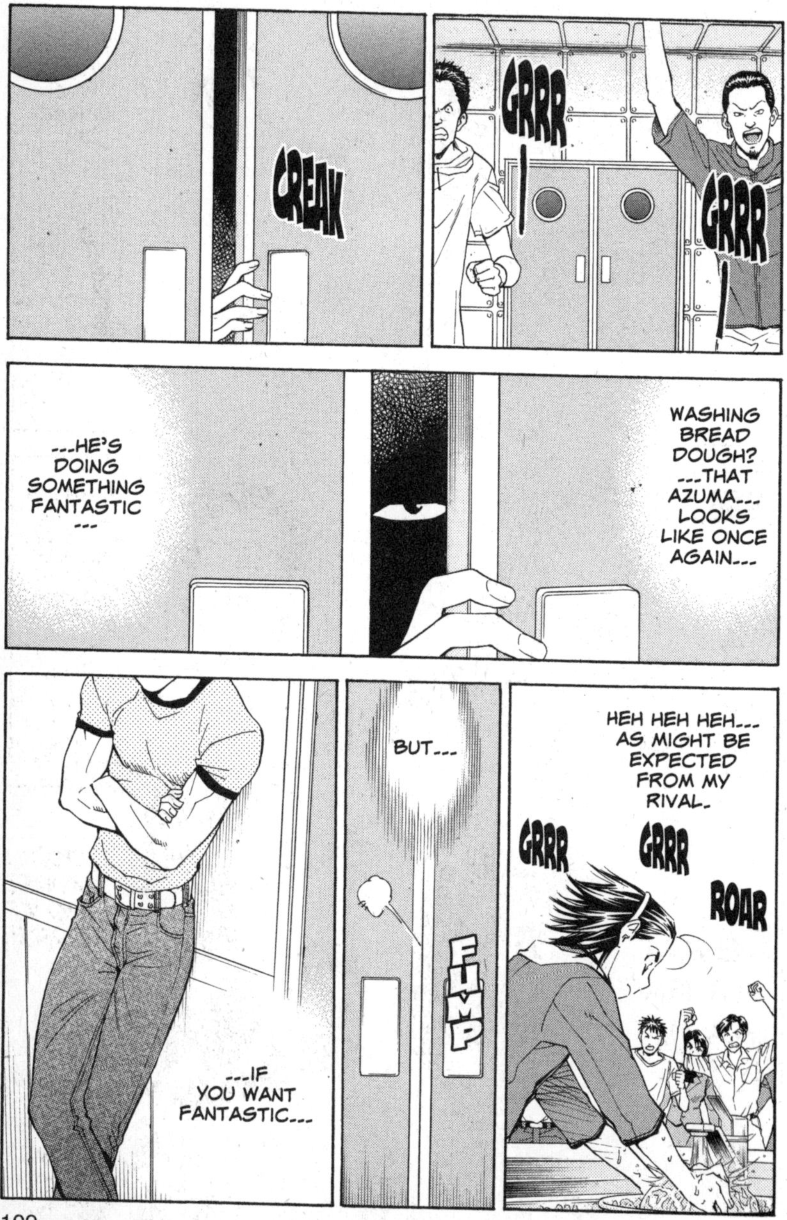
GRRR
GRRR
CREAK
WASHING BREAD DOUGH? ...THAT AZUMA... LOOKS LIKE ONCE AGAIN...
...HE'S DOING SOMETHING FANTASTIC ...
HEH HEH HEH... AS MIGHT BE EXPECTED FROM MY RIVAL.
GRRR
GRRR
ROAR
BUT...
FUMP
...IF YOU WANT FANTASTIC...

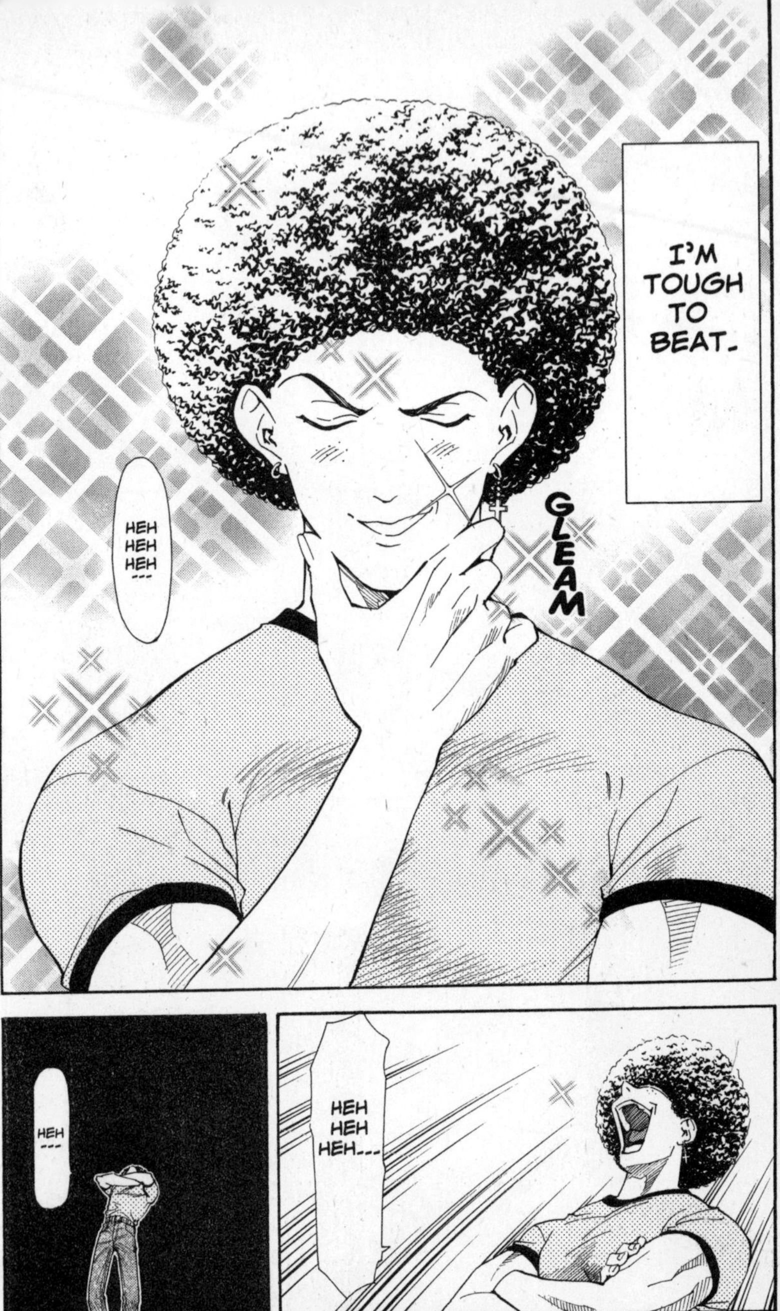
I'M TOUGH TO BEAT.
GLEAM
HEH HEH HEH...
HEH HEH HEH...
HEH...

Story 47: Swan Lake

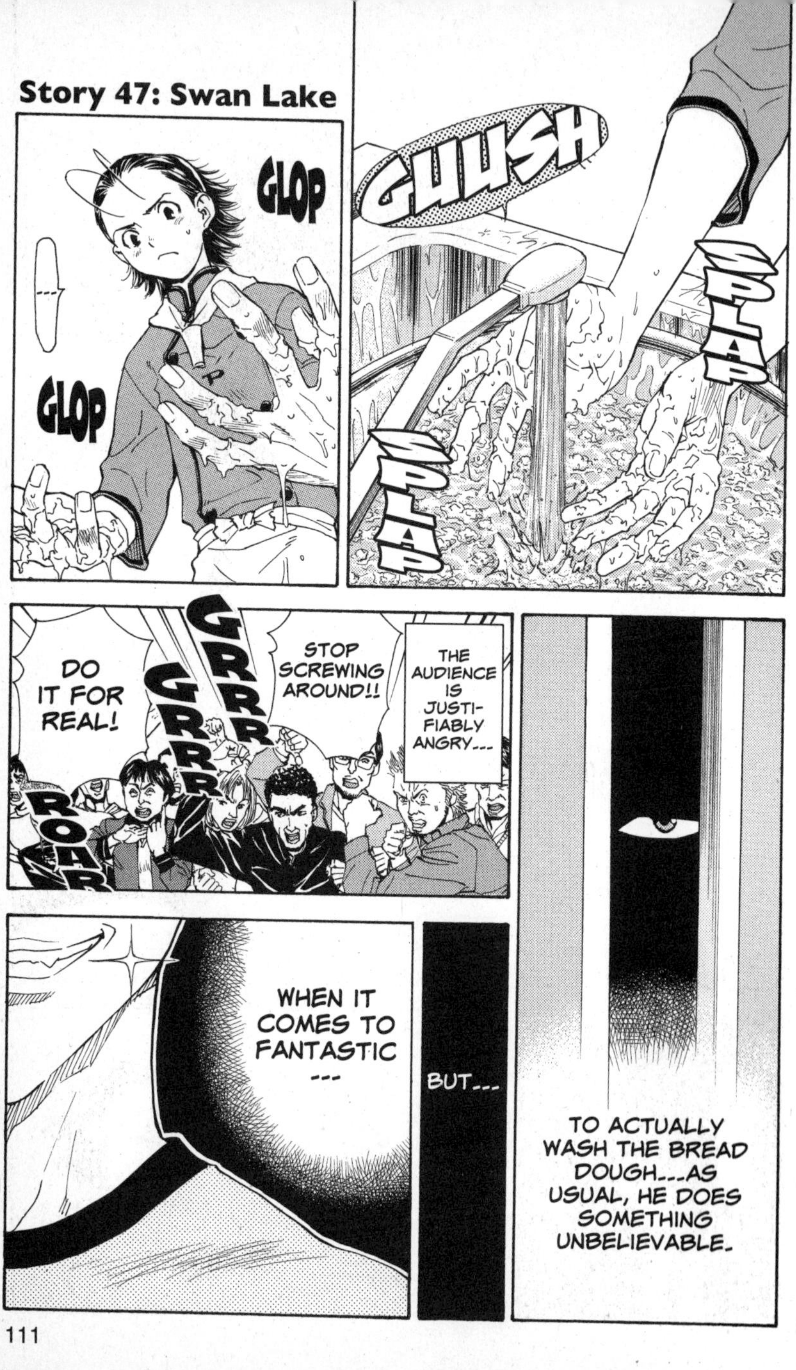

GUUSH
SPLAP
SPLAP
GLOP
...
GLOP
TO ACTUALLY WASH THE BREAD DOUGH...AS USUAL, HE DOES SOMETHING UNBELIEVABLE.
THE AUDIENCE IS JUSTI-FIABLY ANGRY...
STOP SCREWING AROUND!!
GRRR
GRRR
DO IT FOR REAL!
ROAR
BUT...
WHEN IT COMES TO FANTASTIC---

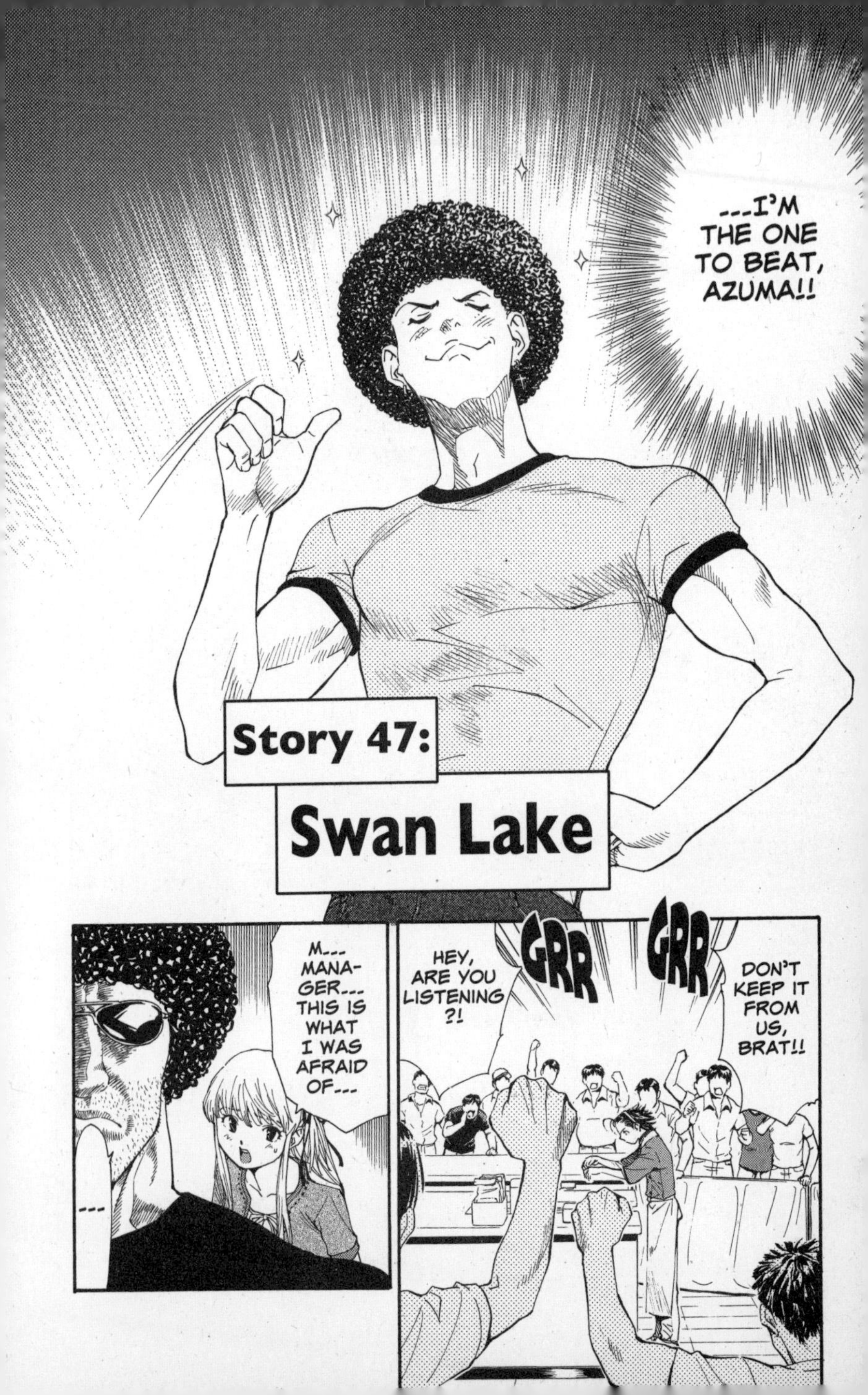
---I'M THE ONE TO BEAT, AZUMA!!
Story 47:
Swan Lake
DON'T KEEP IT FROM US, BRAT!!
GRR
GRR
HEY, ARE YOU LISTENING ?!
M--- MANAGER--- THIS IS WHAT I WAS AFRAID OF---

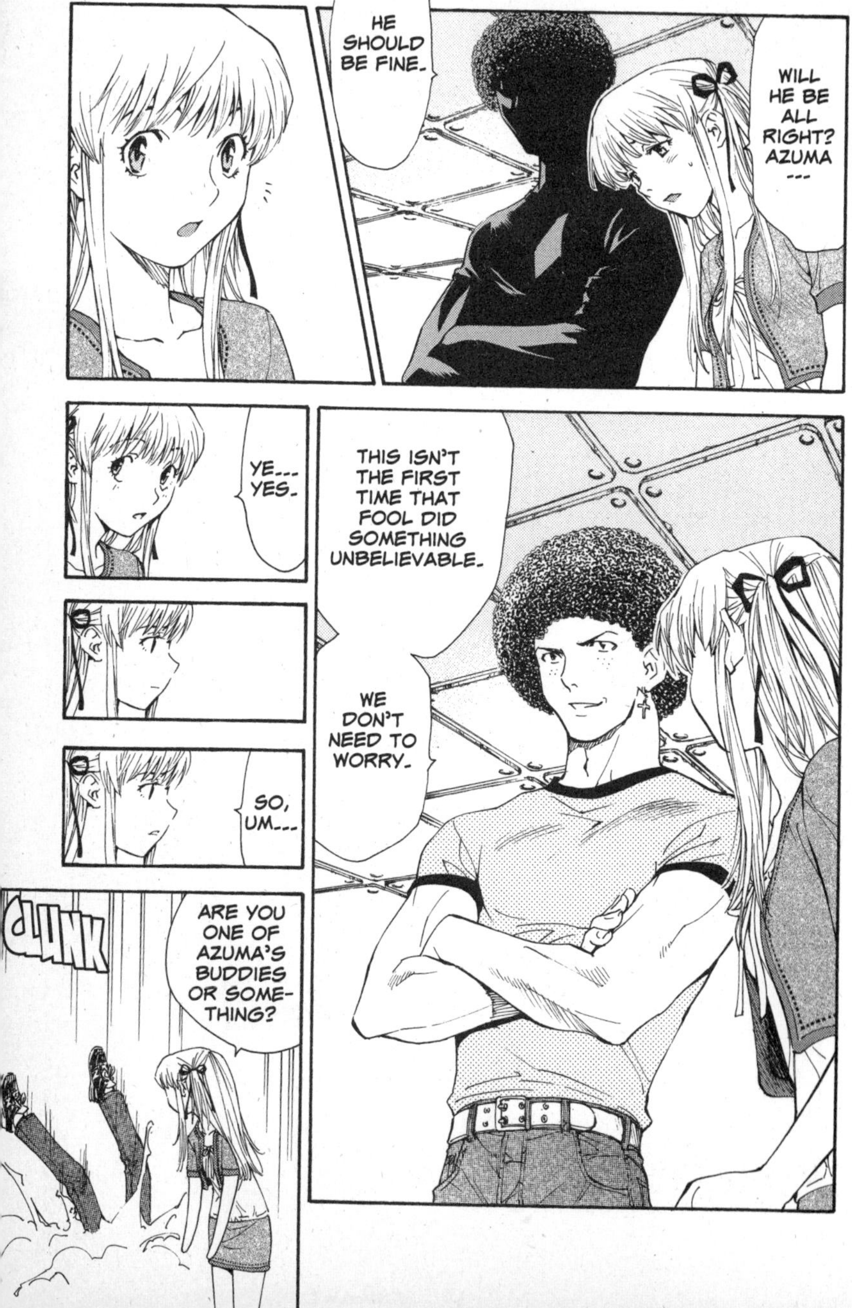
WILL HE BE ALL RIGHT? AZUMA ---
HE SHOULD BE FINE.
THIS ISN'T THE FIRST TIME THAT FOOL DID SOMETHING UNBELIEVABLE.
WE DON'T NEED TO WORRY.
YE--- YES.
SO, UM---
CLUNK
ARE YOU ONE OF AZUMA'S BUDDIES OR SOMETHING?

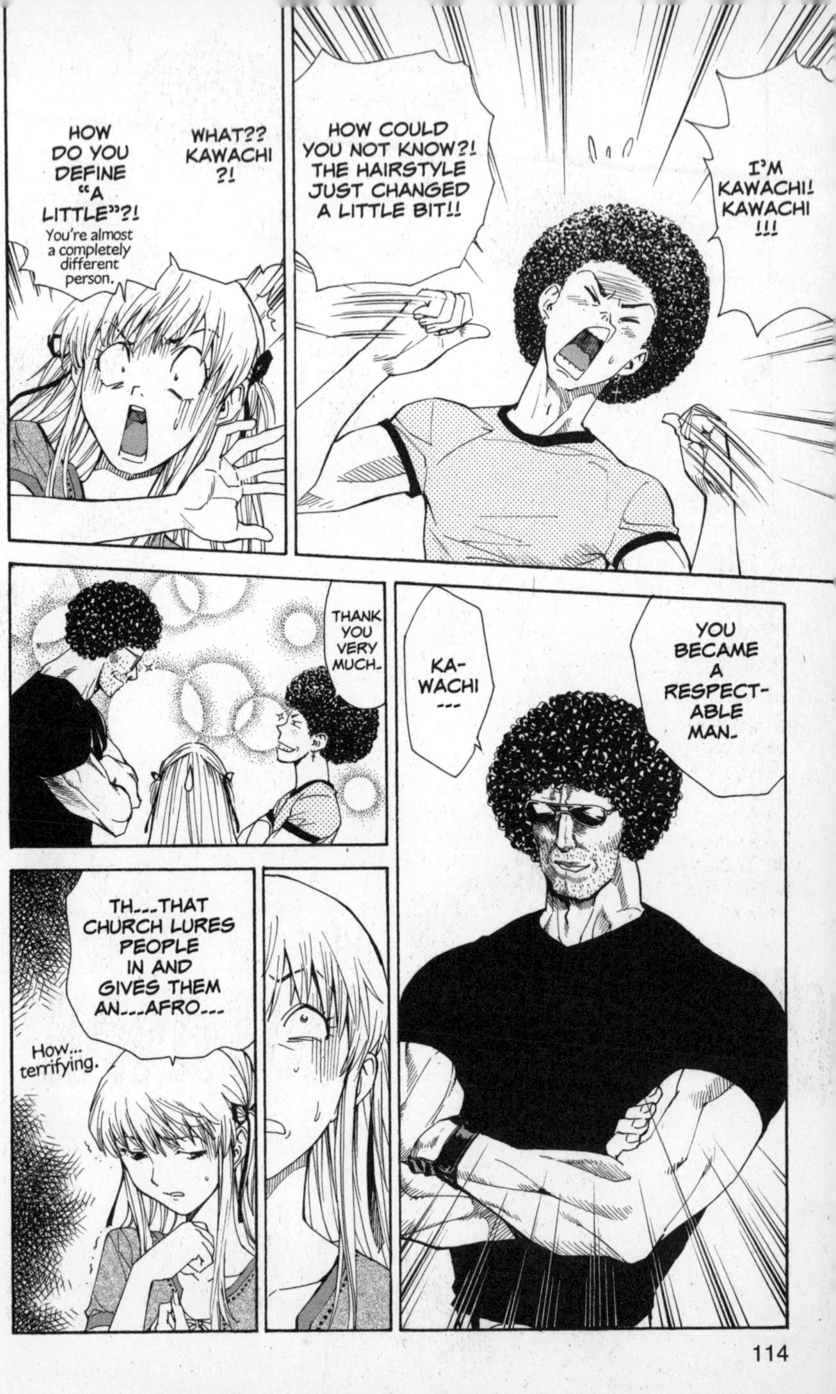
I'M KAWACHI! KAWACHI !!!
HOW COULD YOU NOT KNOW?! THE HAIRSTYLE JUST CHANGED A LITTLE BIT!!
WHAT?? KAWACHI ?!
HOW DO YOU DEFINE "A LITTLE"?!
You're almost a completely different person.
YOU BECAME A RESPECT-ABLE MAN.
KA-WACHI...
THANK YOU VERY MUCH.
TH...THAT CHURCH LURES PEOPLE IN AND GIVES THEM AN...AFRO...
How... terrifying.

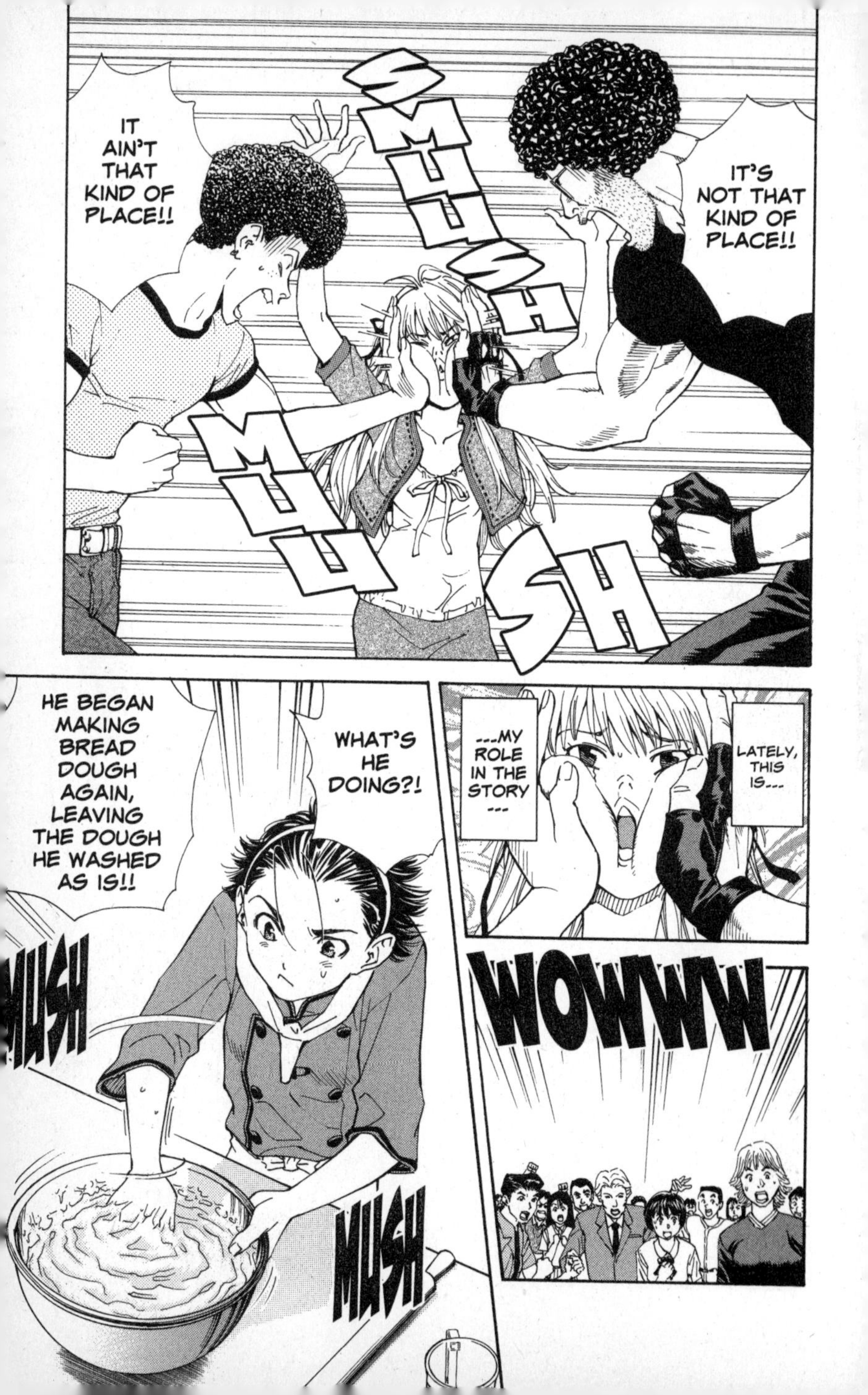
IT'S NOT THAT KIND OF PLACE!!
IT AIN'T THAT KIND OF PLACE!!
SMUUSH
MUUUSH
LATELY, THIS IS---
---MY ROLE IN THE STORY---
WOWWW
WHAT'S HE DOING?!
HE BEGAN MAKING BREAD DOUGH AGAIN, LEAVING THE DOUGH HE WASHED AS IS!!
MUSH
MUSH

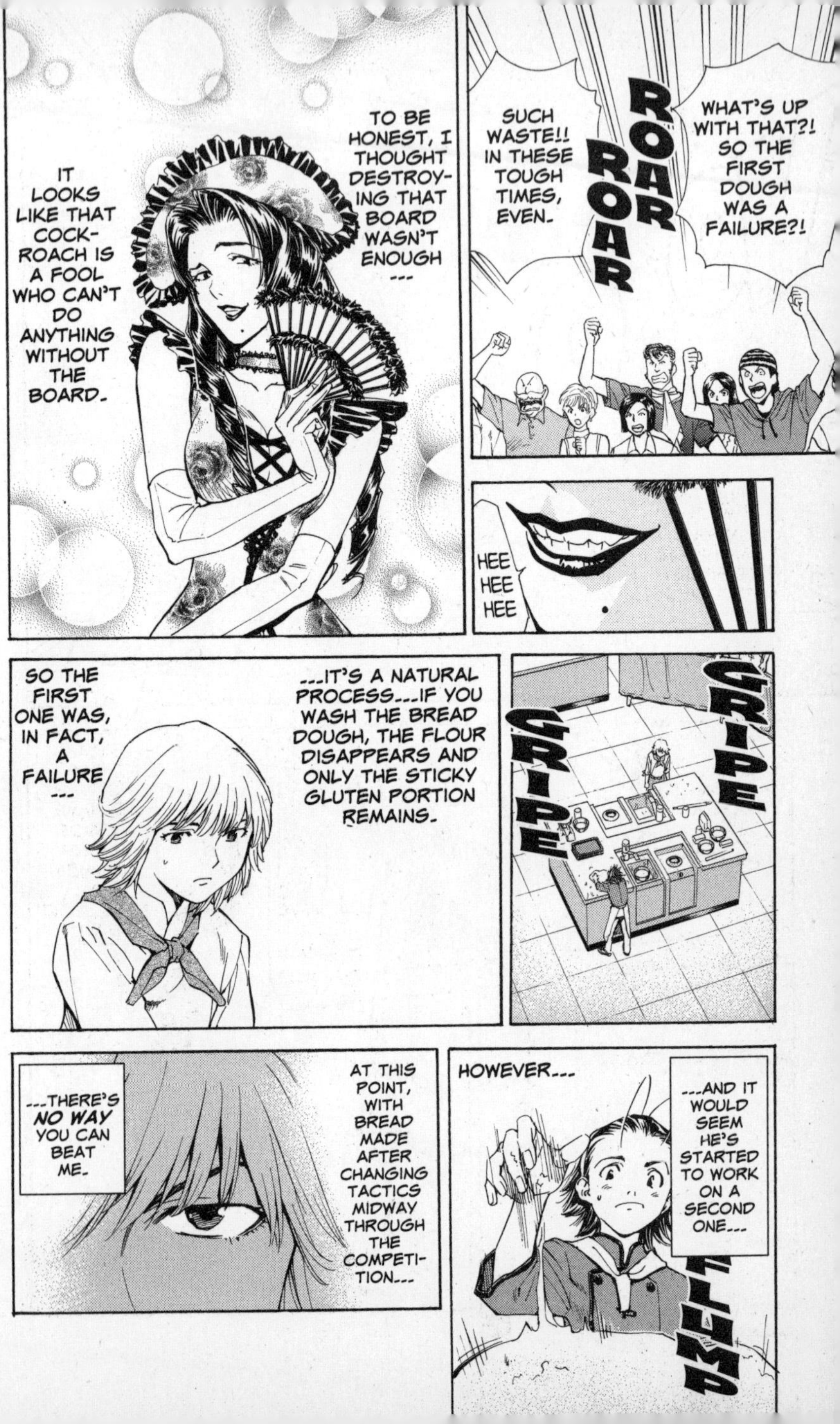
WHAT'S UP WITH THAT?! SO THE FIRST DOUGH WAS A FAILURE?!
ROAR
ROAR
ROAR
SUCH WASTE!! IN THESE TOUGH TIMES, EVEN.
HEE HEE HEE
TO BE HONEST, I THOUGHT DESTROYING THAT BOARD WASN'T ENOUGH ---
IT LOOKS LIKE THAT COCKROACH IS A FOOL WHO CAN'T DO ANYTHING WITHOUT THE BOARD.
GRIPE
GRIPE
---IT'S A NATURAL PROCESS---IF YOU WASH THE BREAD DOUGH, THE FLOUR DISAPPEARS AND ONLY THE STICKY GLUTEN PORTION REMAINS.
SO THE FIRST ONE WAS, IN FACT, A FAILURE ---
HOWEVER---
---AND IT WOULD SEEM HE'S STARTED TO WORK ON A SECOND ONE---
FLUMP
AT THIS POINT, WITH BREAD MADE AFTER CHANGING TACTICS MIDWAY THROUGH THE COMPETITION---
---THERE'S ***NO WAY*** YOU CAN BEAT ME.

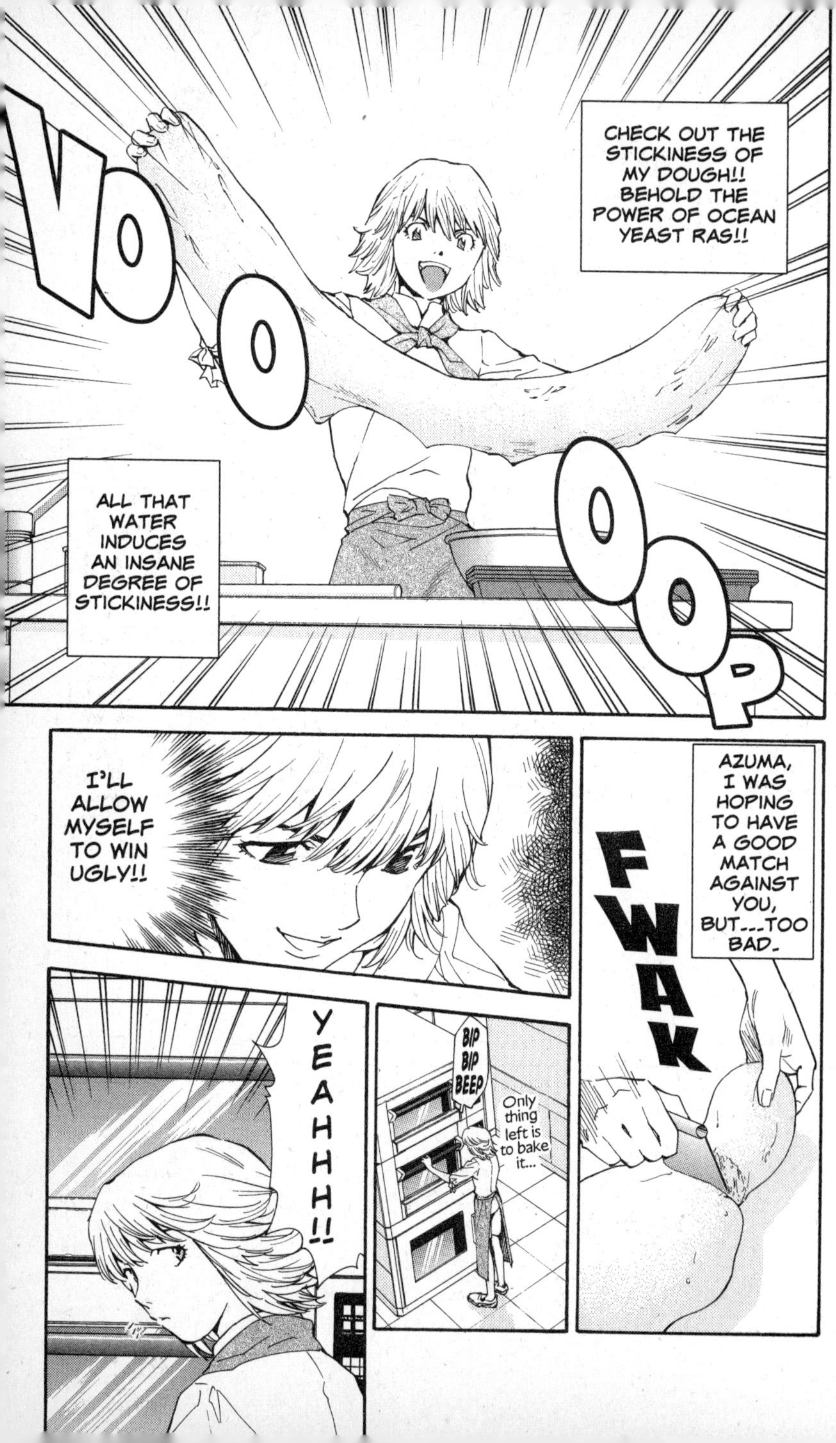
CHECK OUT THE STICKINESS OF MY DOUGH!! BEHOLD THE POWER OF OCEAN YEAST RAS!!
VOOOOOOP
ALL THAT WATER INDUCES AN INSANE DEGREE OF STICKINESS!!
AZUMA, I WAS HOPING TO HAVE A GOOD MATCH AGAINST YOU, BUT...TOO BAD.
FWAK
I'LL ALLOW MYSELF TO WIN UGLY!!
BIP BIP BEEP
Only thing left is to bake it...
YEAHHHH!!

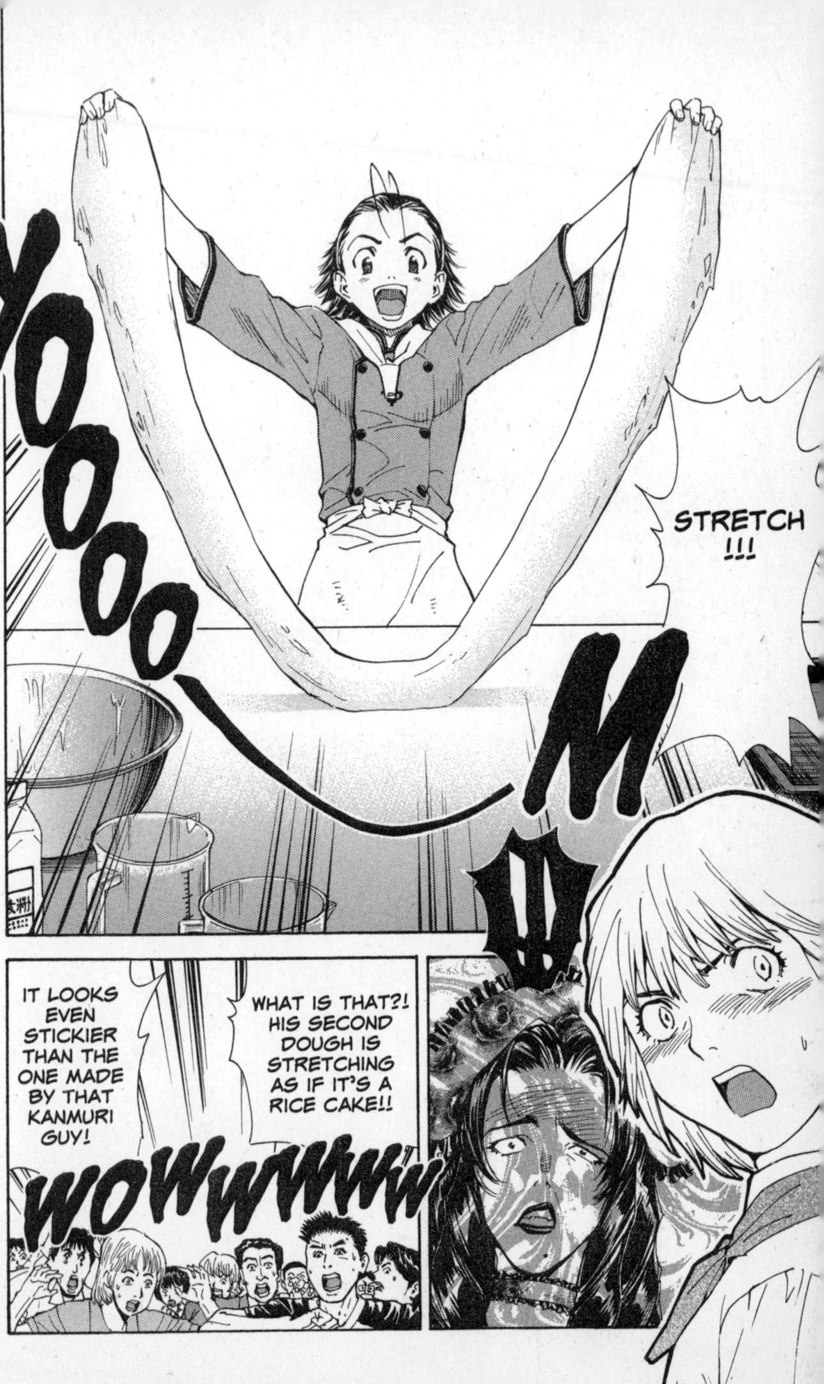
YOOOOO—M
STRETCH!!!
WHAT IS THAT?! HIS SECOND DOUGH IS STRETCHING AS IF IT'S A RICE CAKE!!
IT LOOKS EVEN STICKIER THAN THE ONE MADE BY THAT KANMURI GUY!
WOWWWWWW

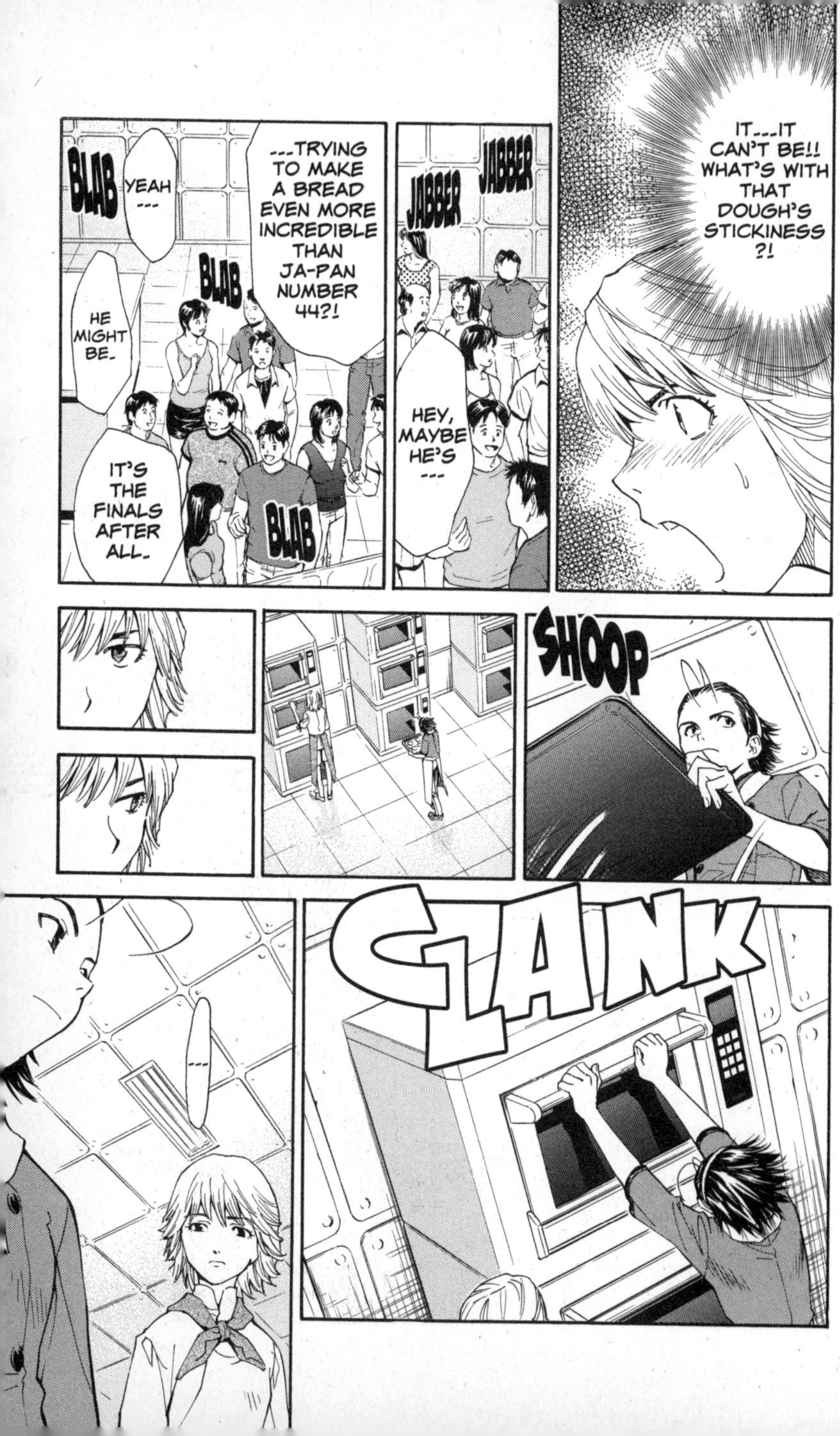
IT---IT CAN'T BE!! WHAT'S WITH THAT DOUGH'S STICKINESS ?!
JABBER
JABBER
HEY, MAYBE HE'S ---
---TRYING TO MAKE A BREAD EVEN MORE INCREDIBLE THAN JA-PAN NUMBER 44?!
BLAB
YEAH ---
BLAB
HE MIGHT BE.
BLAB
IT'S THE FINALS AFTER ALL.
SHOOP
CLANK

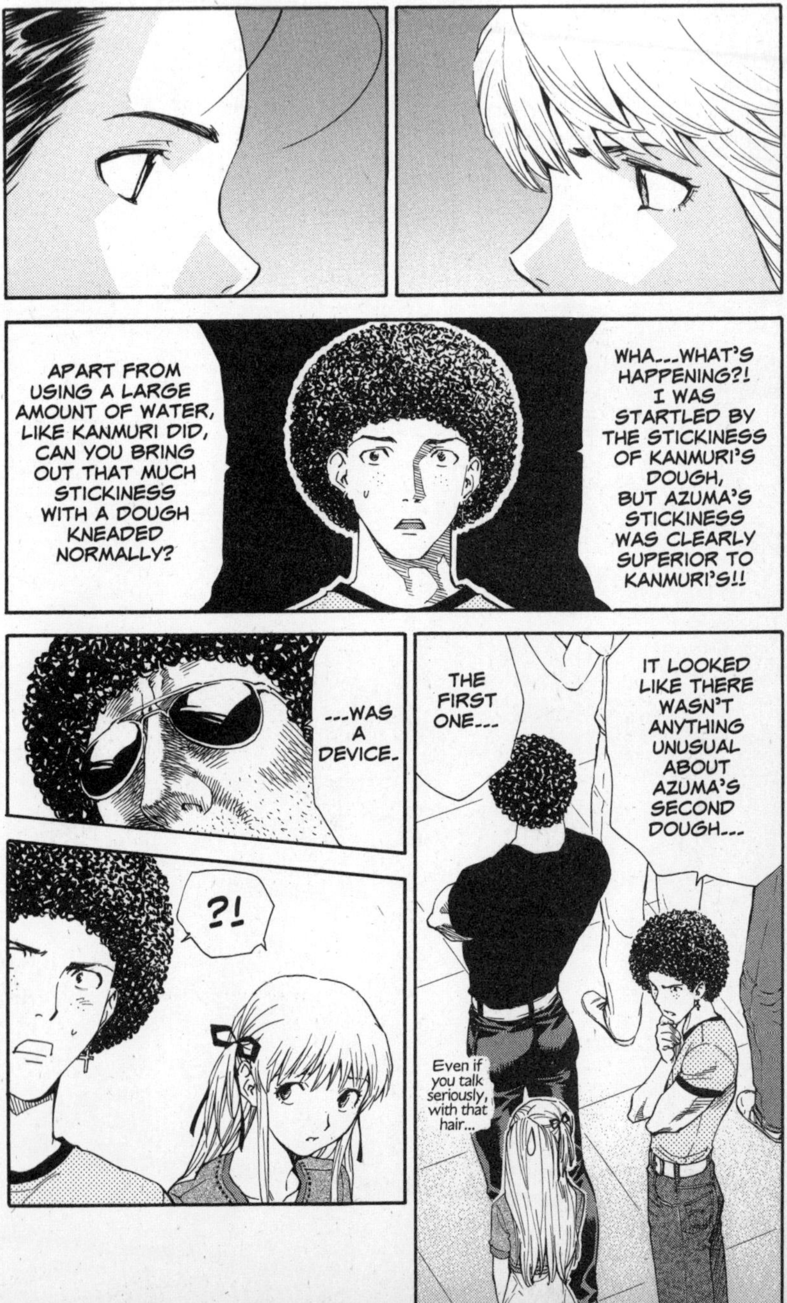
WHA...WHAT'S HAPPENING?! I WAS STARTLED BY THE STICKINESS OF KANMURI'S DOUGH, BUT AZUMA'S STICKINESS WAS CLEARLY SUPERIOR TO KANMURI'S!!
APART FROM USING A LARGE AMOUNT OF WATER, LIKE KANMURI DID, CAN YOU BRING OUT THAT MUCH STICKINESS WITH A DOUGH KNEADED NORMALLY?
IT LOOKED LIKE THERE WASN'T ANYTHING UNUSUAL ABOUT AZUMA'S SECOND DOUGH...
THE FIRST ONE...
Even if you talk seriously, with that hair...
...WAS A DEVICE.
?!

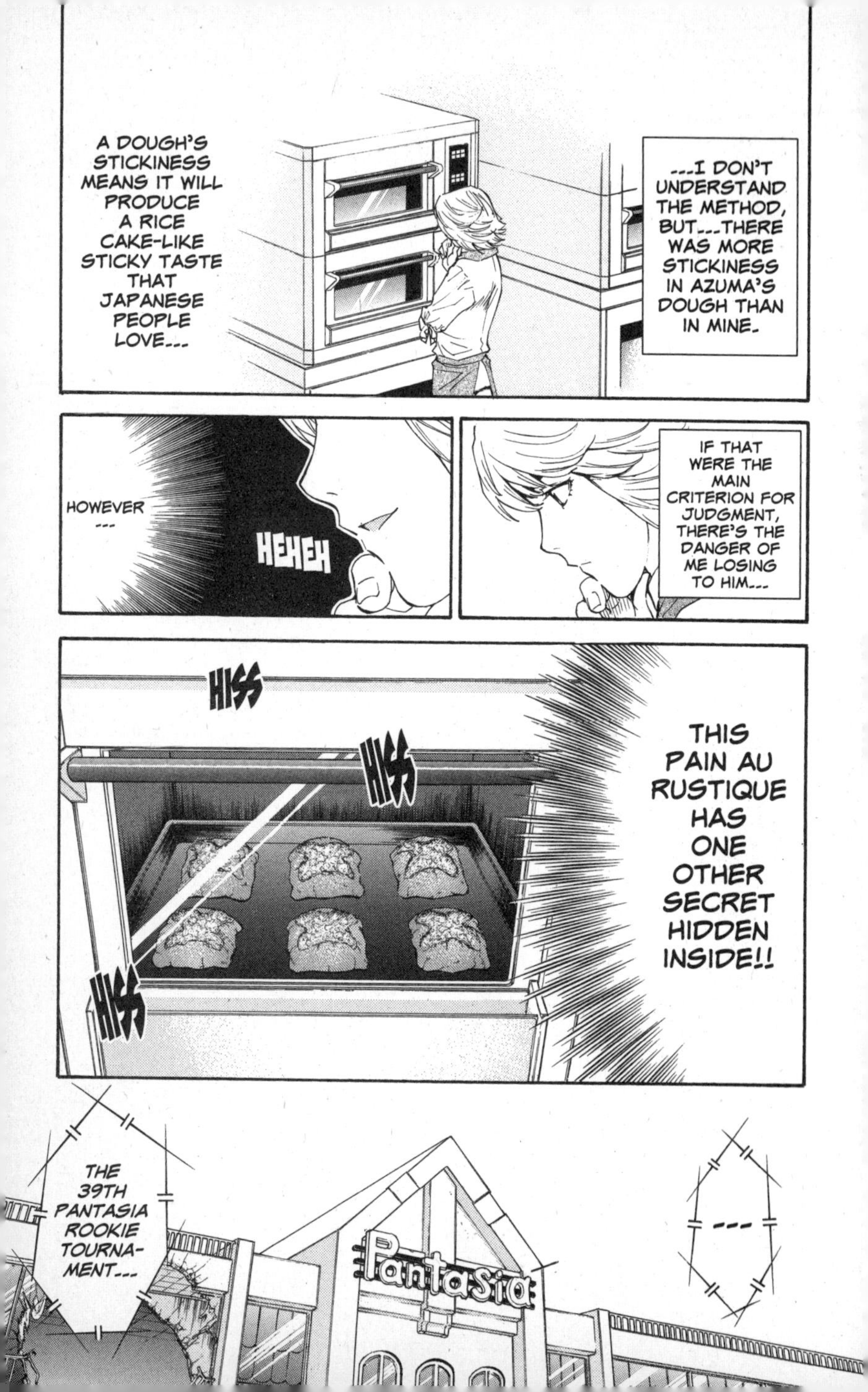

...I DON'T UNDERSTAND THE METHOD, BUT...THERE WAS MORE STICKINESS IN AZUMA'S DOUGH THAN IN MINE.
A DOUGH'S STICKINESS MEANS IT WILL PRODUCE A RICE CAKE-LIKE STICKY TASTE THAT JAPANESE PEOPLE LOVE...
IF THAT WERE THE MAIN CRITERION FOR JUDGMENT, THERE'S THE DANGER OF ME LOSING TO HIM...
HOWEVER ...
HEHEH
THIS PAIN AU RUSTIQUE HAS ONE OTHER SECRET HIDDEN INSIDE!!
HISS
HISS
HISS
...
THE 39TH PANTASIA ROOKIE TOURNAMENT...
Pantasia

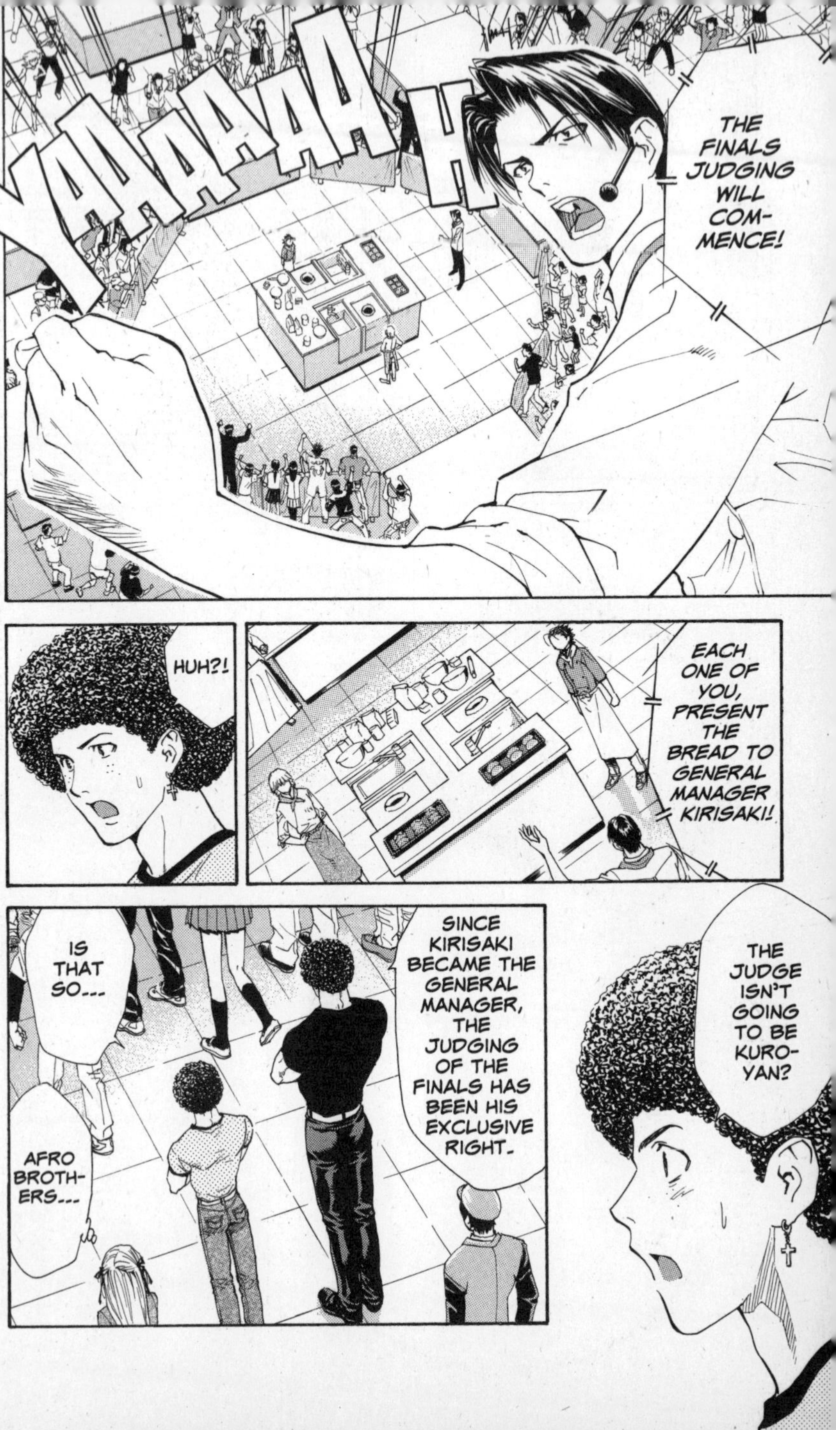
THE FINALS JUDGING WILL COMMENCE!
YAAAAAH
EACH ONE OF YOU, PRESENT THE BREAD TO GENERAL MANAGER KIRISAKI!
HUH?!
THE JUDGE ISN'T GOING TO BE KURO-YAN?
SINCE KIRISAKI BECAME THE GENERAL MANAGER, THE JUDGING OF THE FINALS HAS BEEN HIS EXCLUSIVE RIGHT.
IS THAT SO...
AFRO BROTHERS...

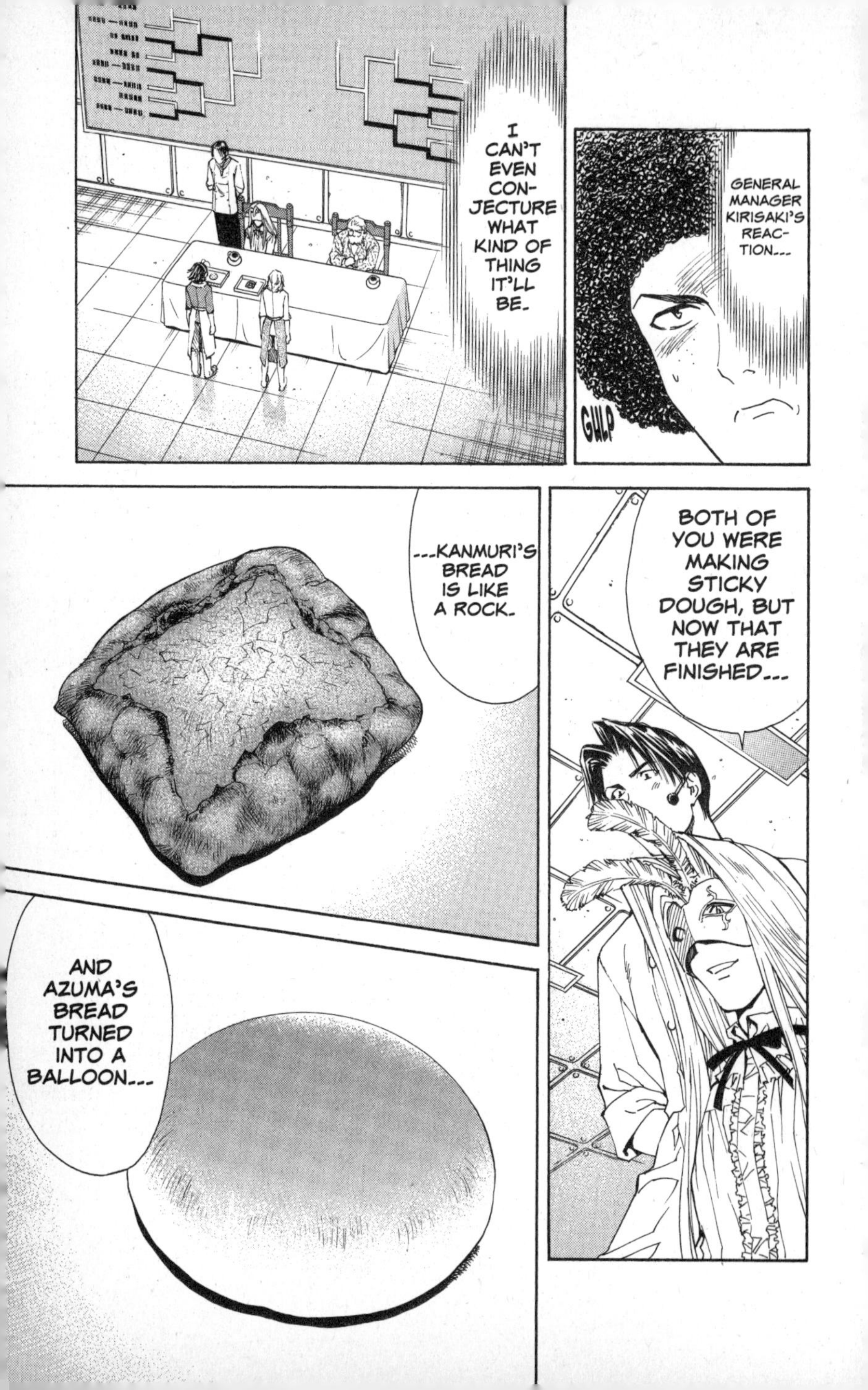
GENERAL MANAGER KIRISAKI'S REACTION...
GULP
I CAN'T EVEN CONJECTURE WHAT KIND OF THING IT'LL BE.
BOTH OF YOU WERE MAKING STICKY DOUGH, BUT NOW THAT THEY ARE FINISHED...
...KANMURI'S BREAD IS LIKE A ROCK.
AND AZUMA'S BREAD TURNED INTO A BALLOON...

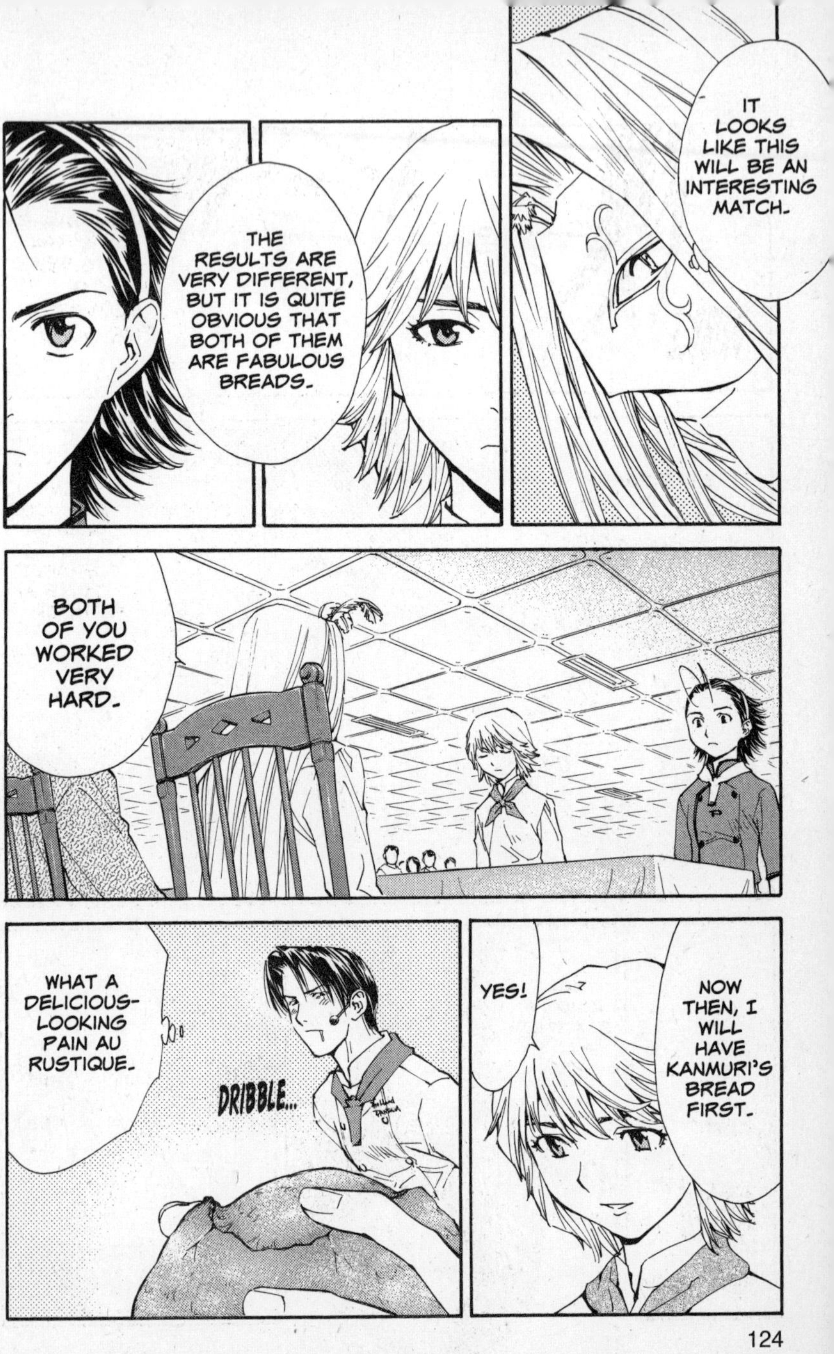
IT LOOKS LIKE THIS WILL BE AN INTERESTING MATCH.
THE RESULTS ARE VERY DIFFERENT, BUT IT IS QUITE OBVIOUS THAT BOTH OF THEM ARE FABULOUS BREADS.
BOTH OF YOU WORKED VERY HARD.
NOW THEN, I WILL HAVE KANMURI'S BREAD FIRST.
YES!
WHAT A DELICIOUS-LOOKING PAIN AU RUSTIQUE.
DRIBBLE...

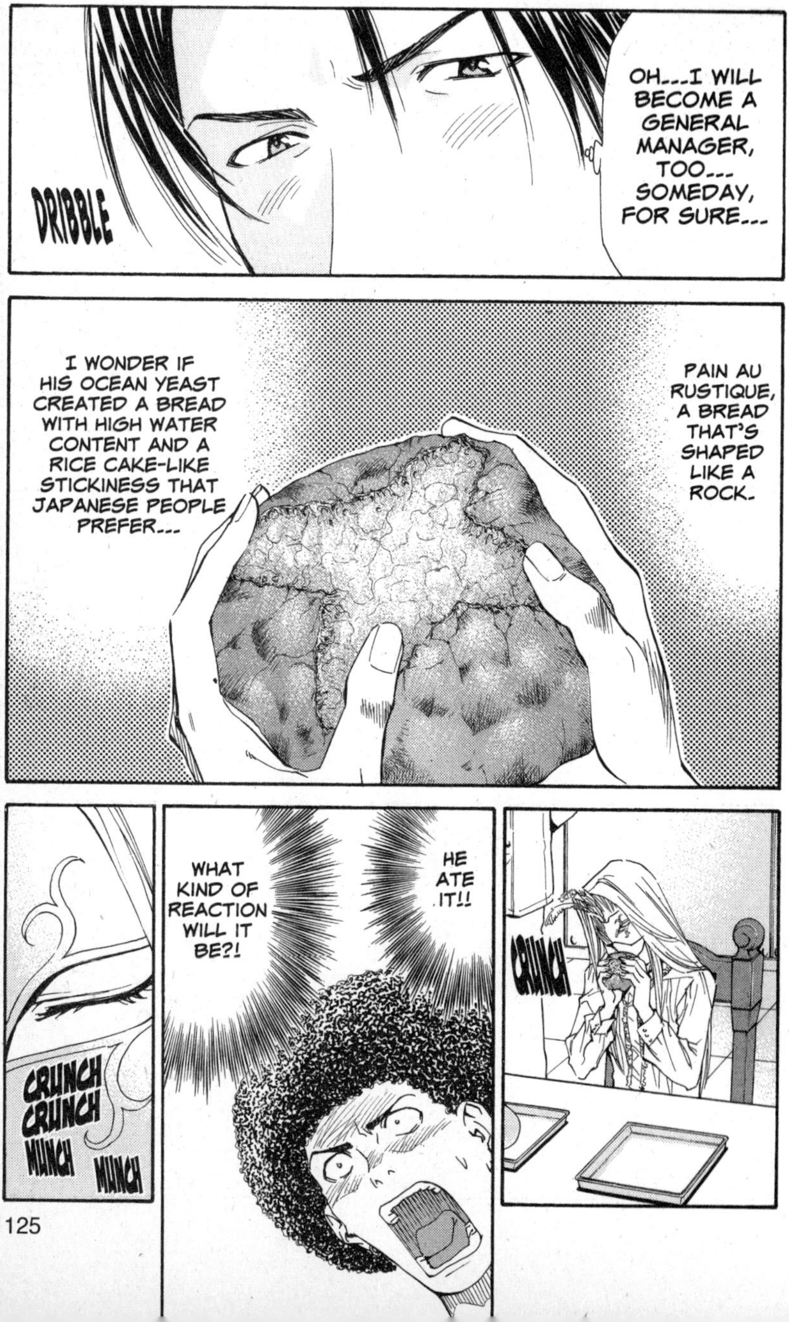

OH...I WILL BECOME A GENERAL MANAGER, TOO... SOMEDAY, FOR SURE...
DRIBBLE
PAIN AU RUSTIQUE, A BREAD THAT'S SHAPED LIKE A ROCK.
I WONDER IF HIS OCEAN YEAST CREATED A BREAD WITH HIGH WATER CONTENT AND A RICE CAKE-LIKE STICKINESS THAT JAPANESE PEOPLE PREFER...
CRUNCH
HE ATE IT!!
WHAT KIND OF REACTION WILL IT BE?!
CRUNCH CRUNCH
MUNCH
MUNCH

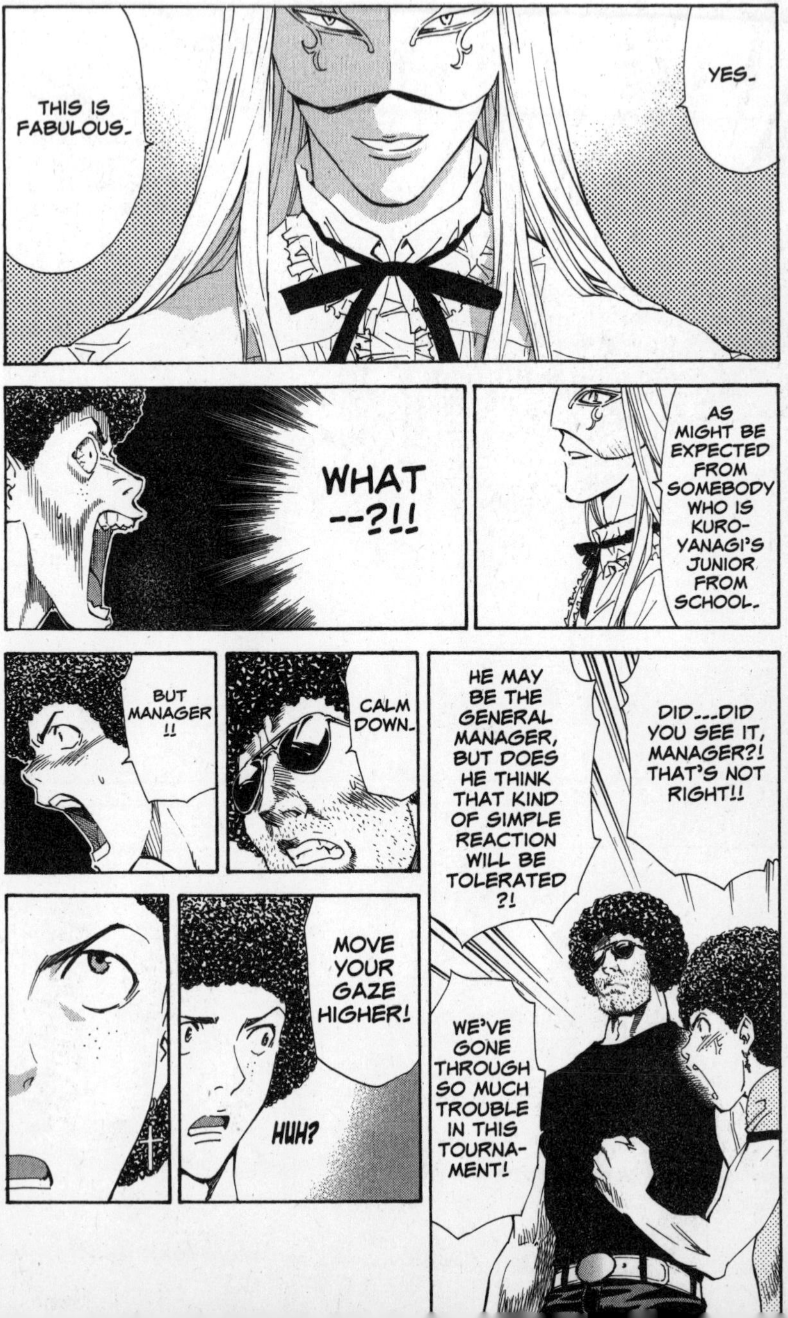
YES.
THIS IS FABULOUS.
AS MIGHT BE EXPECTED FROM SOMEBODY WHO IS KURO-YANAGI'S JUNIOR FROM SCHOOL.
WHAT --?!!
DID...DID YOU SEE IT, MANAGER?! THAT'S NOT RIGHT!!
HE MAY BE THE GENERAL MANAGER, BUT DOES HE THINK THAT KIND OF SIMPLE REACTION WILL BE TOLERATED ?!
WE'VE GONE THROUGH SO MUCH TROUBLE IN THIS TOURNA-MENT!
CALM DOWN.
BUT MANAGER !!
MOVE YOUR GAZE HIGHER!
HUH?

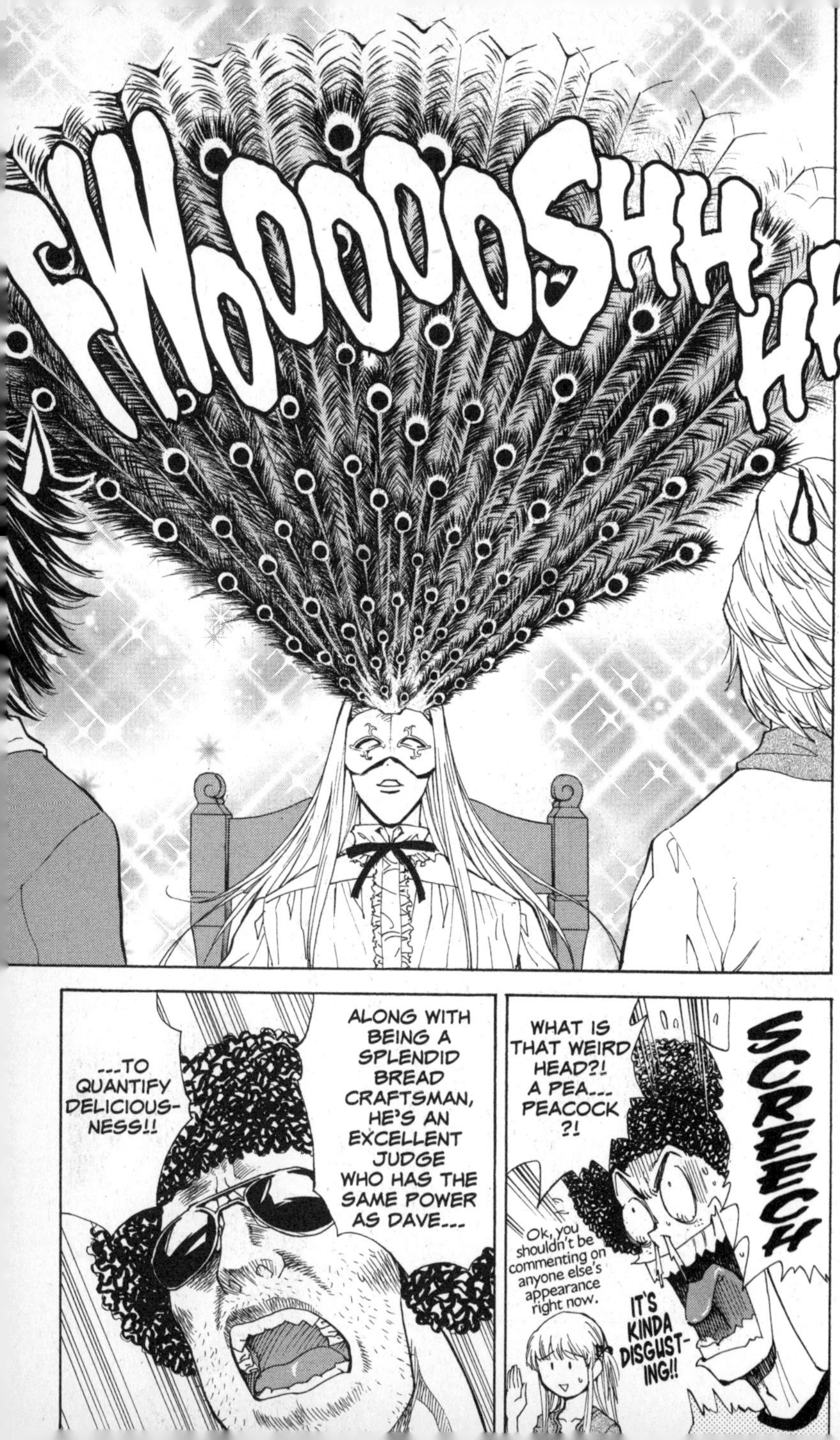
WOOOOOSHHHH
SCREEECH
WHAT IS THAT WEIRD HEAD?! A PEA... PEACOCK ?!
IT'S KINDA DISGUSTING!!
Ok, you shouldn't be commenting on anyone else's appearance right now.
ALONG WITH BEING A SPLENDID BREAD CRAFTSMAN, HE'S AN EXCELLENT JUDGE WHO HAS THE SAME POWER AS DAVE...
...TO QUANTIFY DELICIOUS-NESS!!

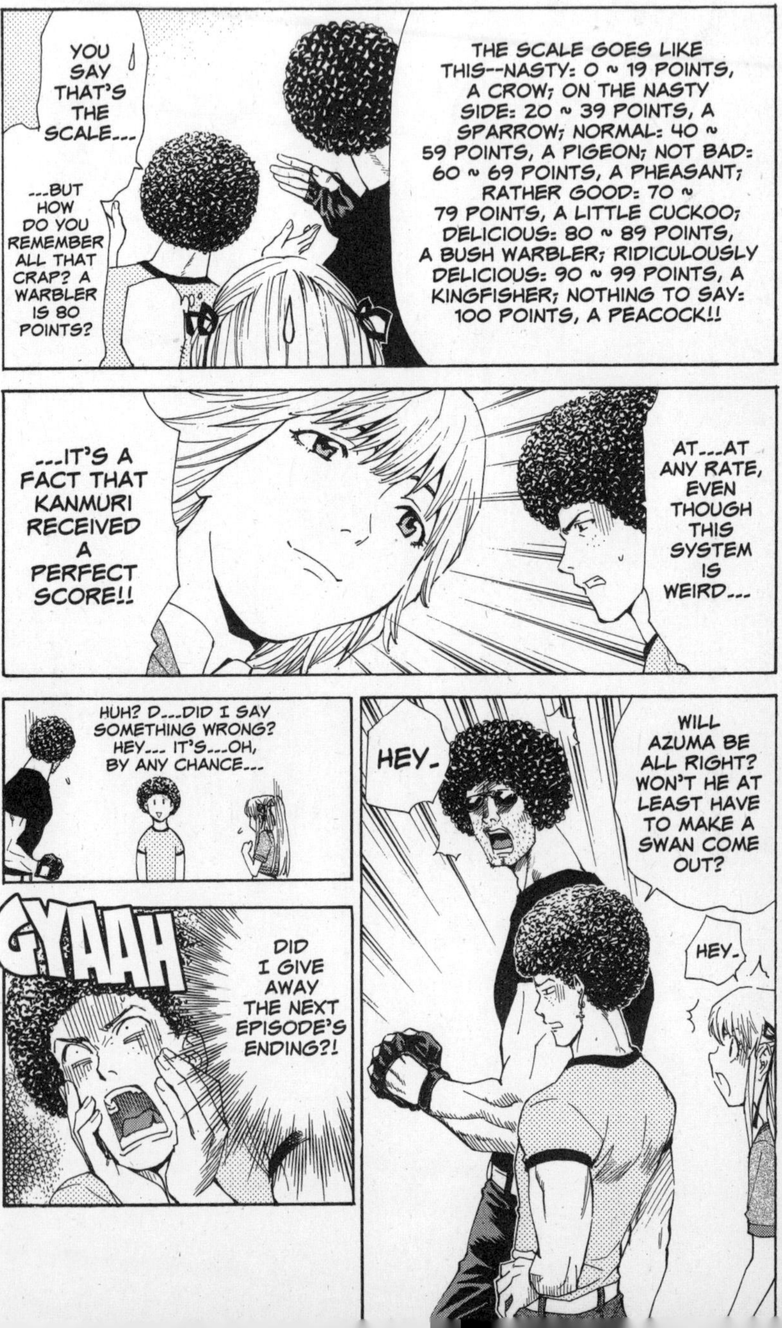
THE SCALE GOES LIKE THIS--NASTY: 0 ~ 19 POINTS, A CROW; ON THE NASTY SIDE: 20 ~ 39 POINTS, A SPARROW; NORMAL: 40 ~ 59 POINTS, A PIGEON; NOT BAD: 60 ~ 69 POINTS, A PHEASANT; RATHER GOOD: 70 ~ 79 POINTS, A LITTLE CUCKOO; DELICIOUS: 80 ~ 89 POINTS, A BUSH WARBLER; RIDICULOUSLY DELICIOUS: 90 ~ 99 POINTS, A KINGFISHER; NOTHING TO SAY: 100 POINTS, A PEACOCK!!
YOU SAY THAT'S THE SCALE...
...BUT HOW DO YOU REMEMBER ALL THAT CRAP? A WARBLER IS 80 POINTS?
AT...AT ANY RATE, EVEN THOUGH THIS SYSTEM IS WEIRD...
...IT'S A FACT THAT KANMURI RECEIVED A PERFECT SCORE!!
WILL AZUMA BE ALL RIGHT? WON'T HE AT LEAST HAVE TO MAKE A SWAN COME OUT?
HEY.
HEY.
HUH? D...DID I SAY SOMETHING WRONG? HEY... IT'S...OH, BY ANY CHANCE...
GYAAH
DID I GIVE AWAY THE NEXT EPISODE'S ENDING?!

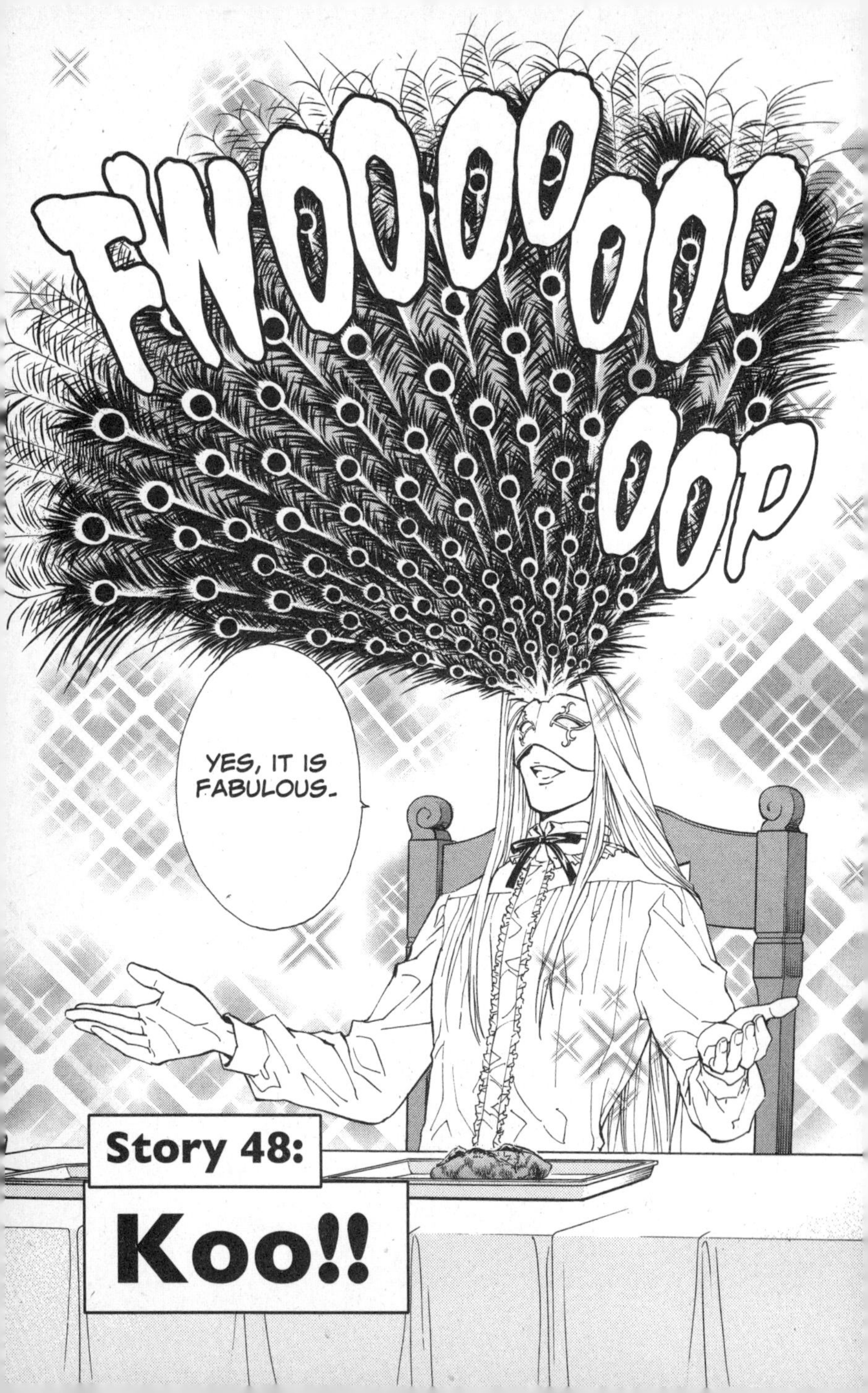
F'WOOOOOOOOOOP
YES, IT IS FABULOUS.
Story 48:
Koo!!

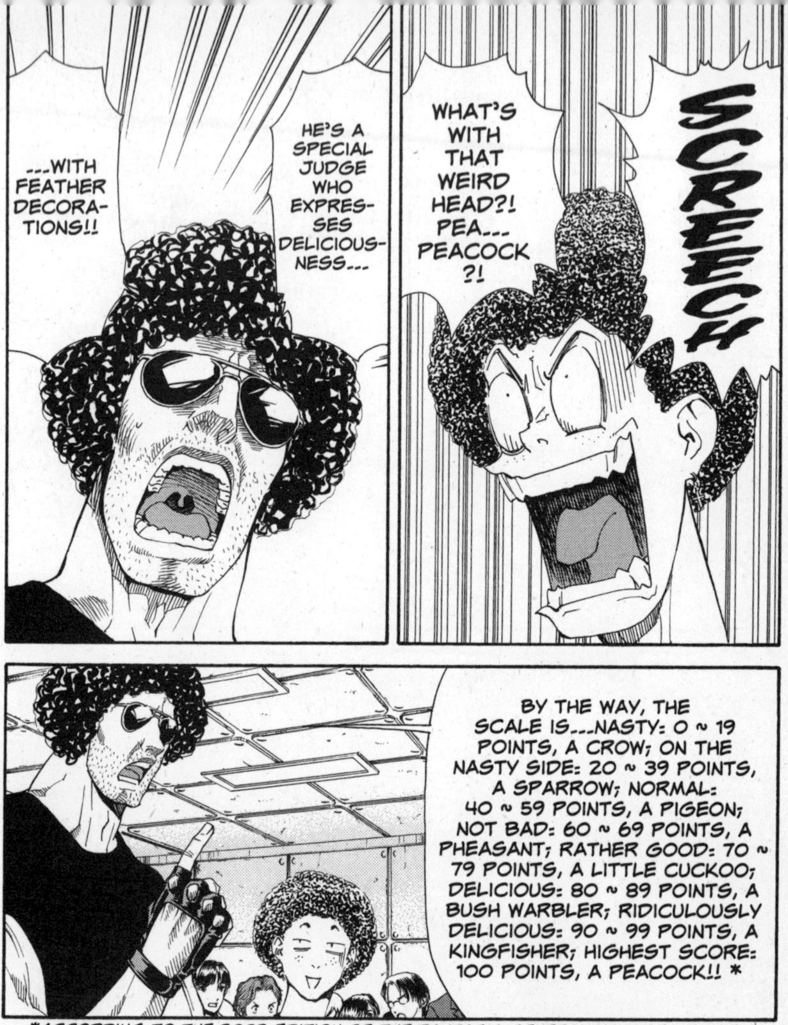

SCREECH
WHAT'S WITH THAT WEIRD HEAD?! PEA... PEACOCK?!
HE'S A SPECIAL JUDGE WHO EXPRESSES DELICIOUSNESS...
...WITH FEATHER DECORATIONS!!
BY THE WAY, THE SCALE IS...NASTY: 0 ~ 19 POINTS, A CROW; ON THE NASTY SIDE: 20 ~ 39 POINTS, A SPARROW; NORMAL: 40 ~ 59 POINTS, A PIGEON; NOT BAD: 60 ~ 69 POINTS, A PHEASANT; RATHER GOOD: 70 ~ 79 POINTS, A LITTLE CUCKOO; DELICIOUS: 80 ~ 89 POINTS, A BUSH WARBLER; RIDICULOUSLY DELICIOUS: 90 ~ 99 POINTS, A KINGFISHER; HIGHEST SCORE: 100 POINTS, A PEACOCK!! *
*ACCORDING TO THE 2002 EDITION OF THE PANTASIA GENERAL MANAGER GUIDE.
I...I HAVE NO INTENTION OF REMEMBERING THE RELATIONSHIP BETWEEN BIRDS AND POINTS, EVEN IF YOU TELL ME, BUT...
IT'S CLEAR THAT KANMURI HAS GOTTEN A PERFECT SCORE.
AZUMA...

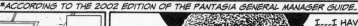

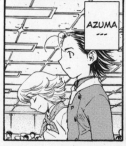

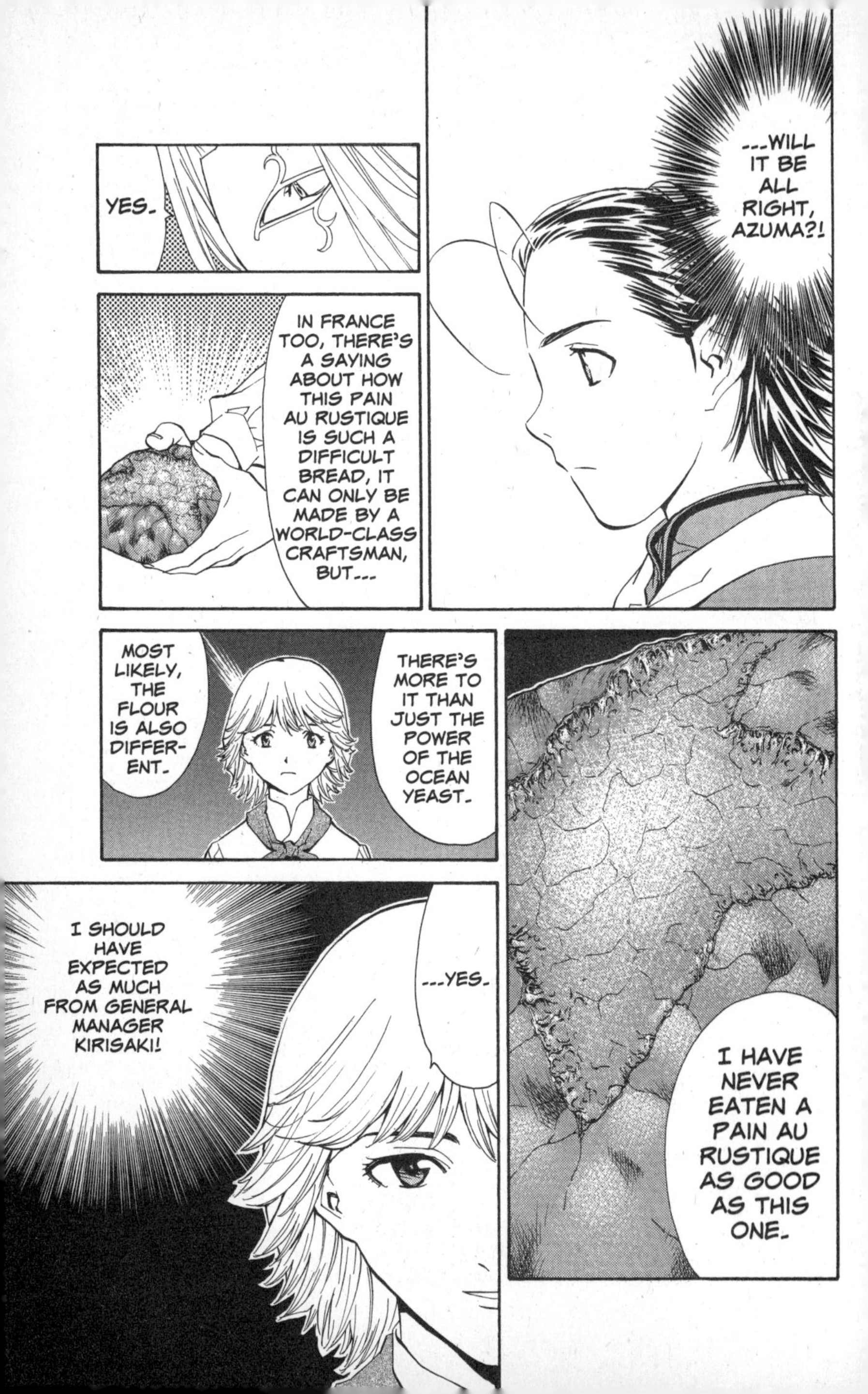
---WILL IT BE ALL RIGHT, AZUMA?!
YES.
IN FRANCE TOO, THERE'S A SAYING ABOUT HOW THIS PAIN AU RUSTIQUE IS SUCH A DIFFICULT BREAD, IT CAN ONLY BE MADE BY A WORLD-CLASS CRAFTSMAN, BUT---
I HAVE NEVER EATEN A PAIN AU RUSTIQUE AS GOOD AS THIS ONE.
THERE'S MORE TO IT THAN JUST THE POWER OF THE OCEAN YEAST.
MOST LIKELY, THE FLOUR IS ALSO DIFFERENT.
---YES.
I SHOULD HAVE EXPECTED AS MUCH FROM GENERAL MANAGER KIRISAKI!

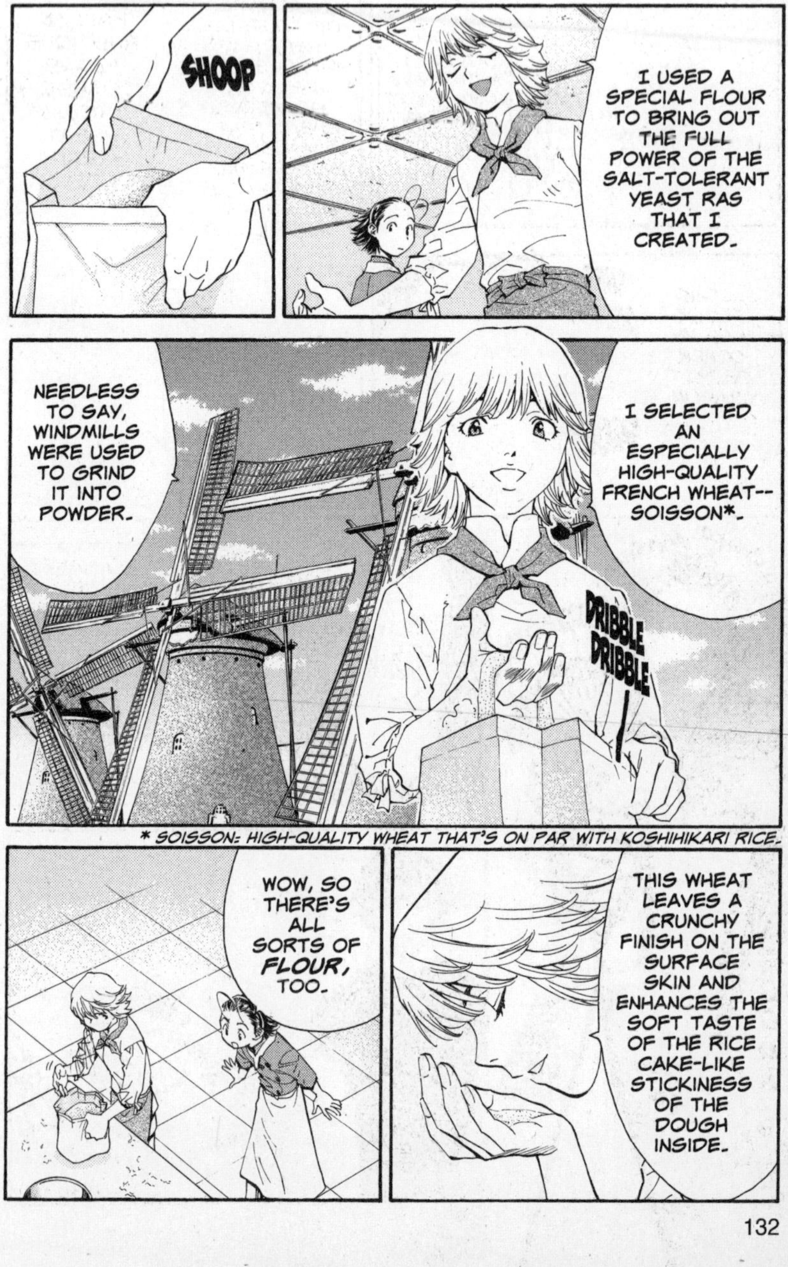
I USED A SPECIAL FLOUR TO BRING OUT THE FULL POWER OF THE SALT-TOLERANT YEAST RAS THAT I CREATED.
SHOOP
I SELECTED AN ESPECIALLY HIGH-QUALITY FRENCH WHEAT--SOISSON*.
DRIBBLE DRIBBLE
NEEDLESS TO SAY, WINDMILLS WERE USED TO GRIND IT INTO POWDER.
* SOISSON: HIGH-QUALITY WHEAT THAT'S ON PAR WITH KOSHIHIKARI RICE.
THIS WHEAT LEAVES A CRUNCHY FINISH ON THE SURFACE SKIN AND ENHANCES THE SOFT TASTE OF THE RICE CAKE-LIKE STICKINESS OF THE DOUGH INSIDE.
WOW, SO THERE'S ALL SORTS OF FLOUR, TOO.

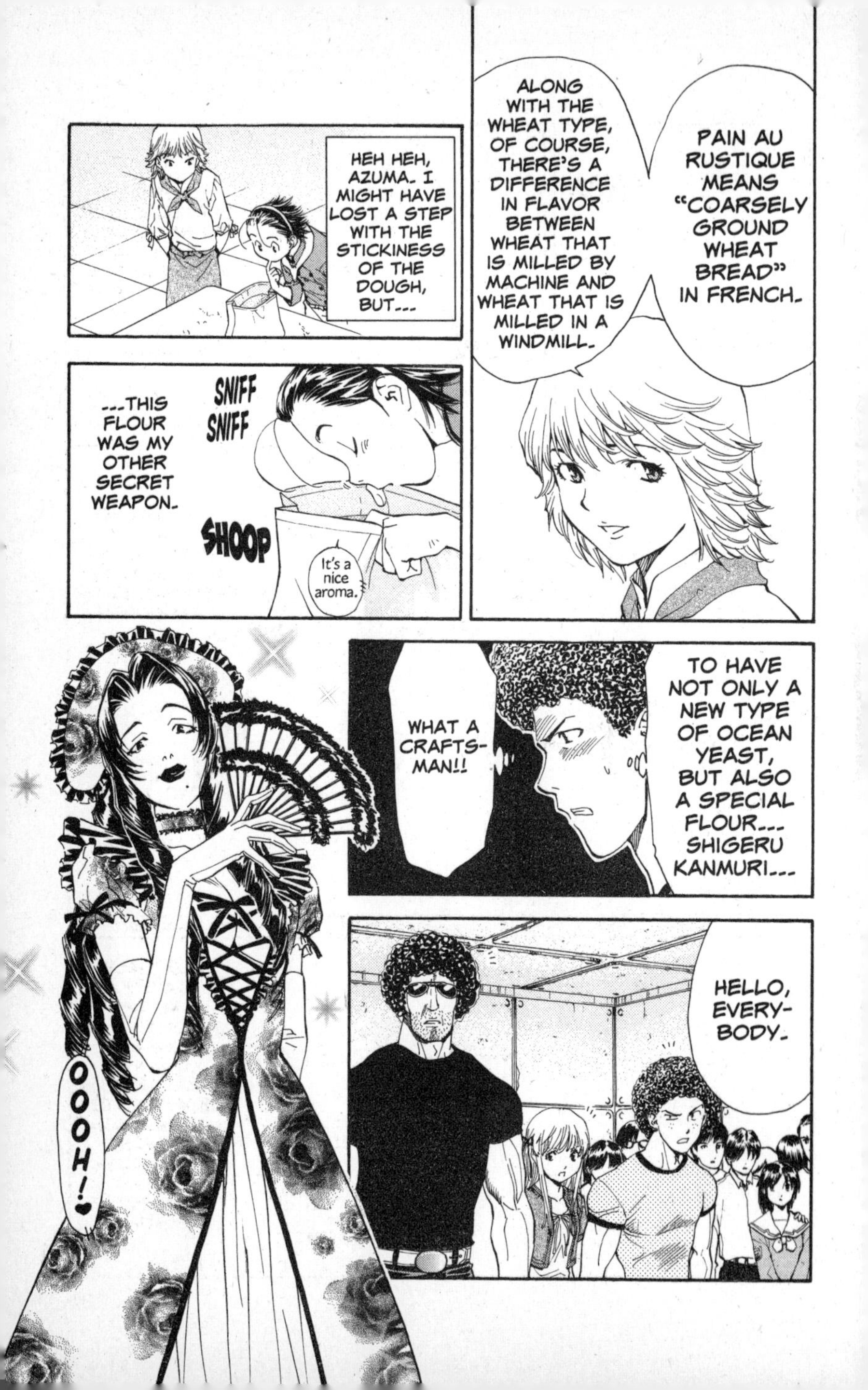
PAIN AU RUSTIQUE MEANS "COARSELY GROUND WHEAT BREAD" IN FRENCH.
ALONG WITH THE WHEAT TYPE, OF COURSE, THERE'S A DIFFERENCE IN FLAVOR BETWEEN WHEAT THAT IS MILLED BY MACHINE AND WHEAT THAT IS MILLED IN A WINDMILL.
HEH HEH, AZUMA. I MIGHT HAVE LOST A STEP WITH THE STICKINESS OF THE DOUGH, BUT...
...THIS FLOUR WAS MY OTHER SECRET WEAPON.
SNIFF SNIFF
SHOOP
It's a nice aroma.
TO HAVE NOT ONLY A NEW TYPE OF OCEAN YEAST, BUT ALSO A SPECIAL FLOUR... SHIGERU KANMURI...
WHAT A CRAFTSMAN!!
HELLO, EVERYBODY.
OOOH!

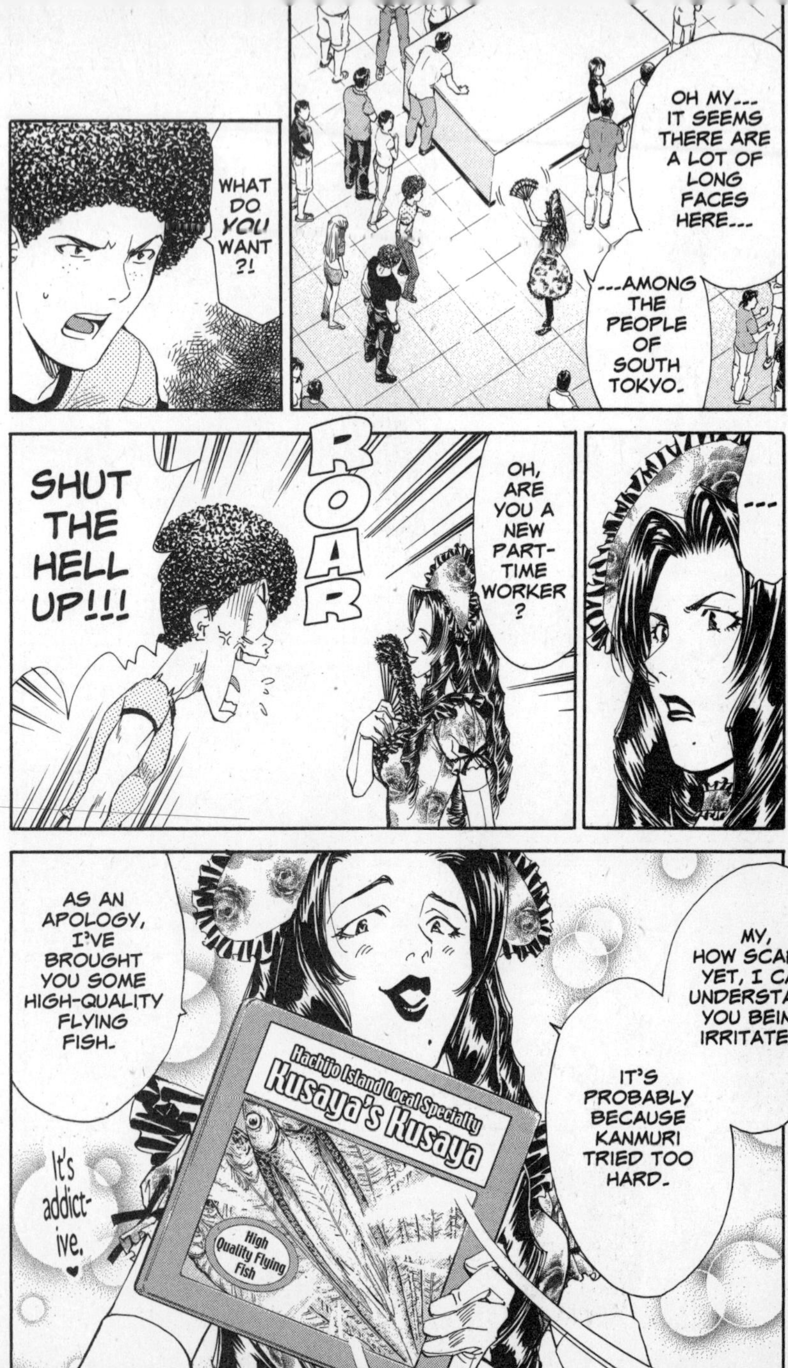

OH MY... IT SEEMS THERE ARE A LOT OF LONG FACES HERE...
...AMONG THE PEOPLE OF SOUTH TOKYO.
WHAT DO *YOU* WANT?!
...
OH, ARE YOU A NEW PART-TIME WORKER?
ROAR
SHUT THE HELL UP!!!
MY, HOW SCARY. YET, I CAN UNDERSTAND YOU BEING IRRITATED.
IT'S PROBABLY BECAUSE KANMURI TRIED TOO HARD.
AS AN APOLOGY, I'VE BROUGHT YOU SOME HIGH-QUALITY FLYING FISH.
Hachijo Island Local Specialty
Kusaya's Kusaya
High Quality Flying Fish
It's addict-ive. ♥

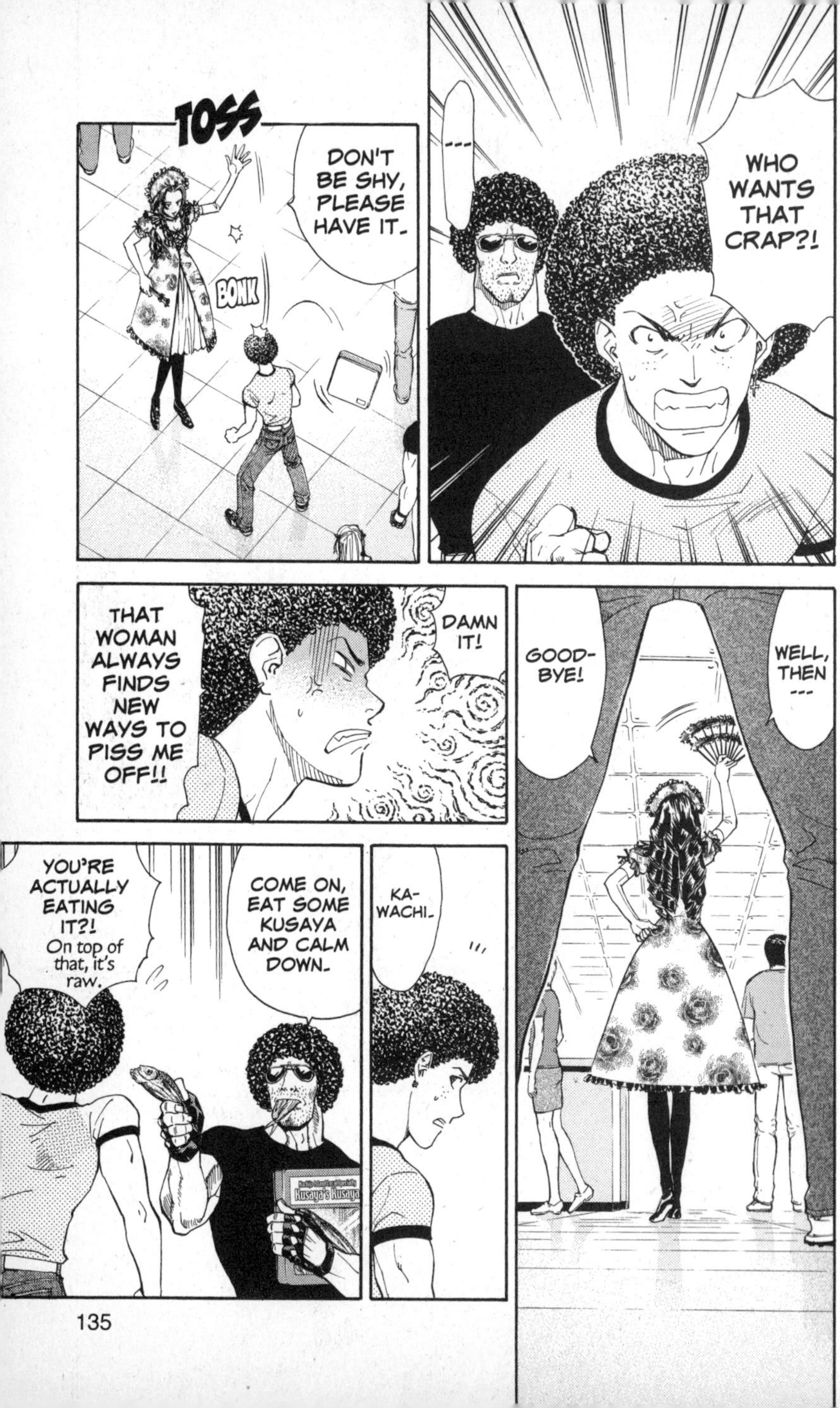
WHO WANTS THAT CRAP?!
...
TOSS
DON'T BE SHY, PLEASE HAVE IT.
BONK
WELL, THEN...
GOOD-BYE!
DAMN IT!
THAT WOMAN ALWAYS FINDS NEW WAYS TO PISS ME OFF!!
KA-WACHI.
COME ON, EAT SOME KUSAYA AND CALM DOWN.
Kusaya's Kusaya
YOU'RE ACTUALLY EATING IT?! On top of that, it's raw.

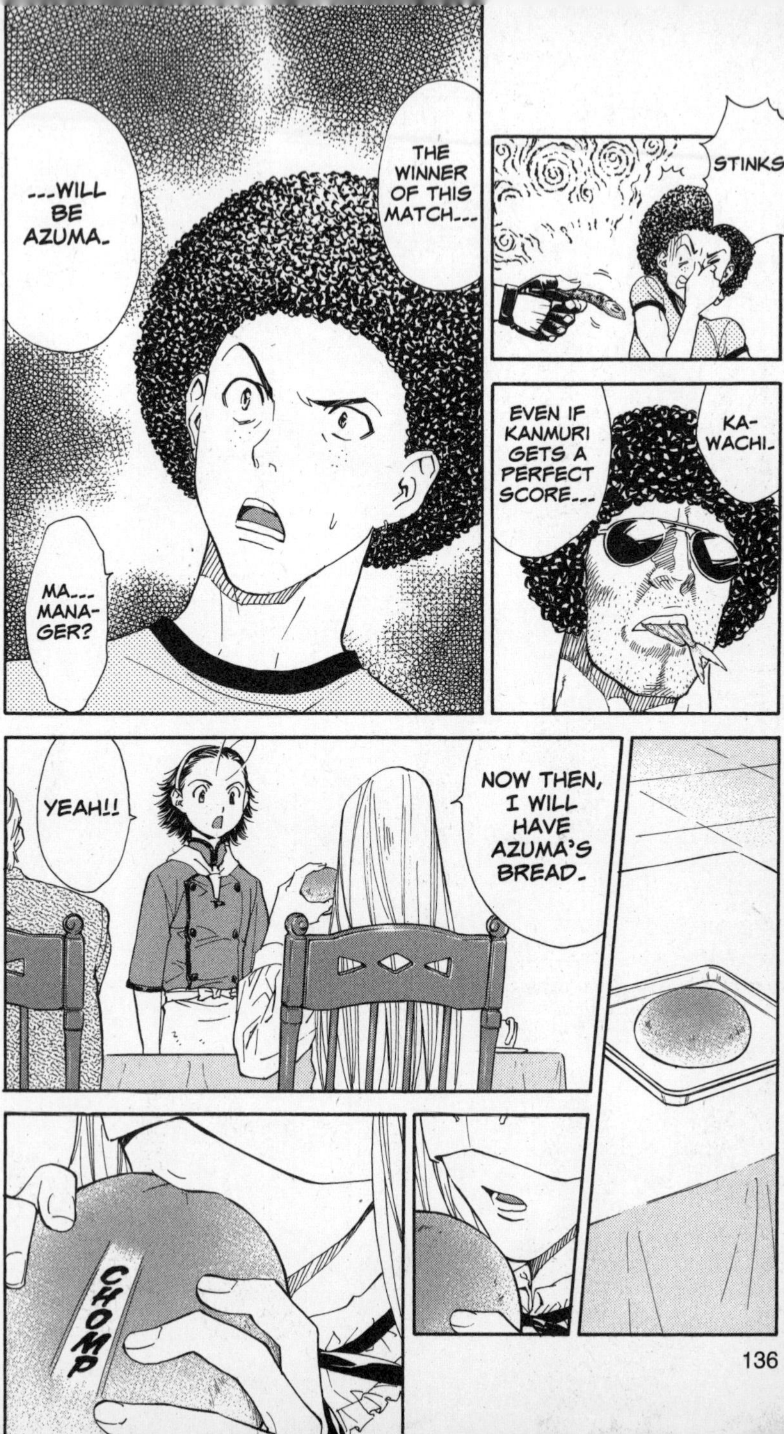
STINKS.
KA-WACHI.
EVEN IF KANMURI GETS A PERFECT SCORE...
THE WINNER OF THIS MATCH...
...WILL BE AZUMA.
MA... MANAGER?
NOW THEN, I WILL HAVE AZUMA'S BREAD.
YEAH!!
CHOMP

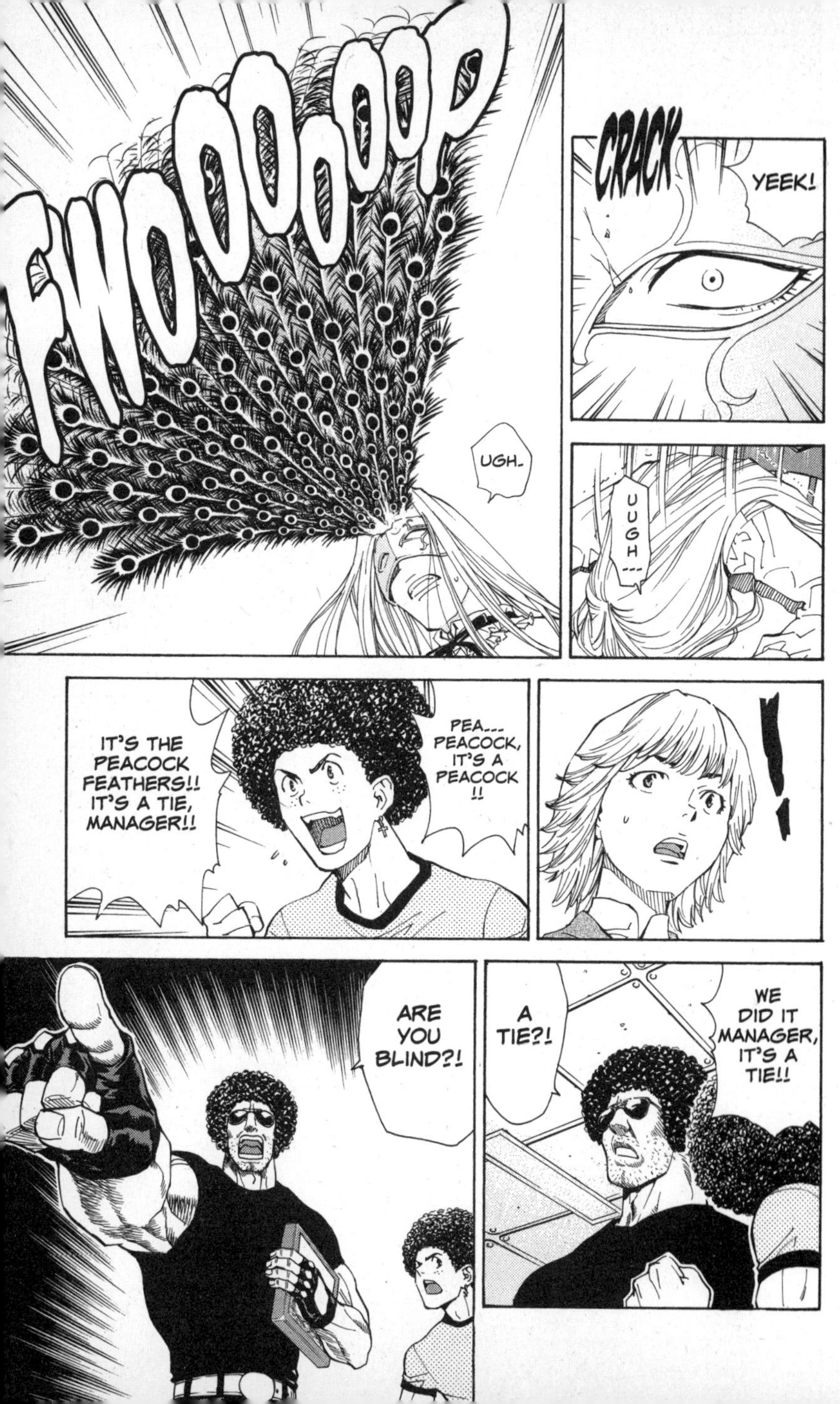
CRACK
YEEK!
UUGH...
FWOOOOOOP
UGH.
PEA... PEACOCK, IT'S A PEACOCK!!
IT'S THE PEACOCK FEATHERS!! IT'S A TIE, MANAGER!!
WE DID IT MANAGER, IT'S A TIE!!
A TIE?!
ARE YOU BLIND?!

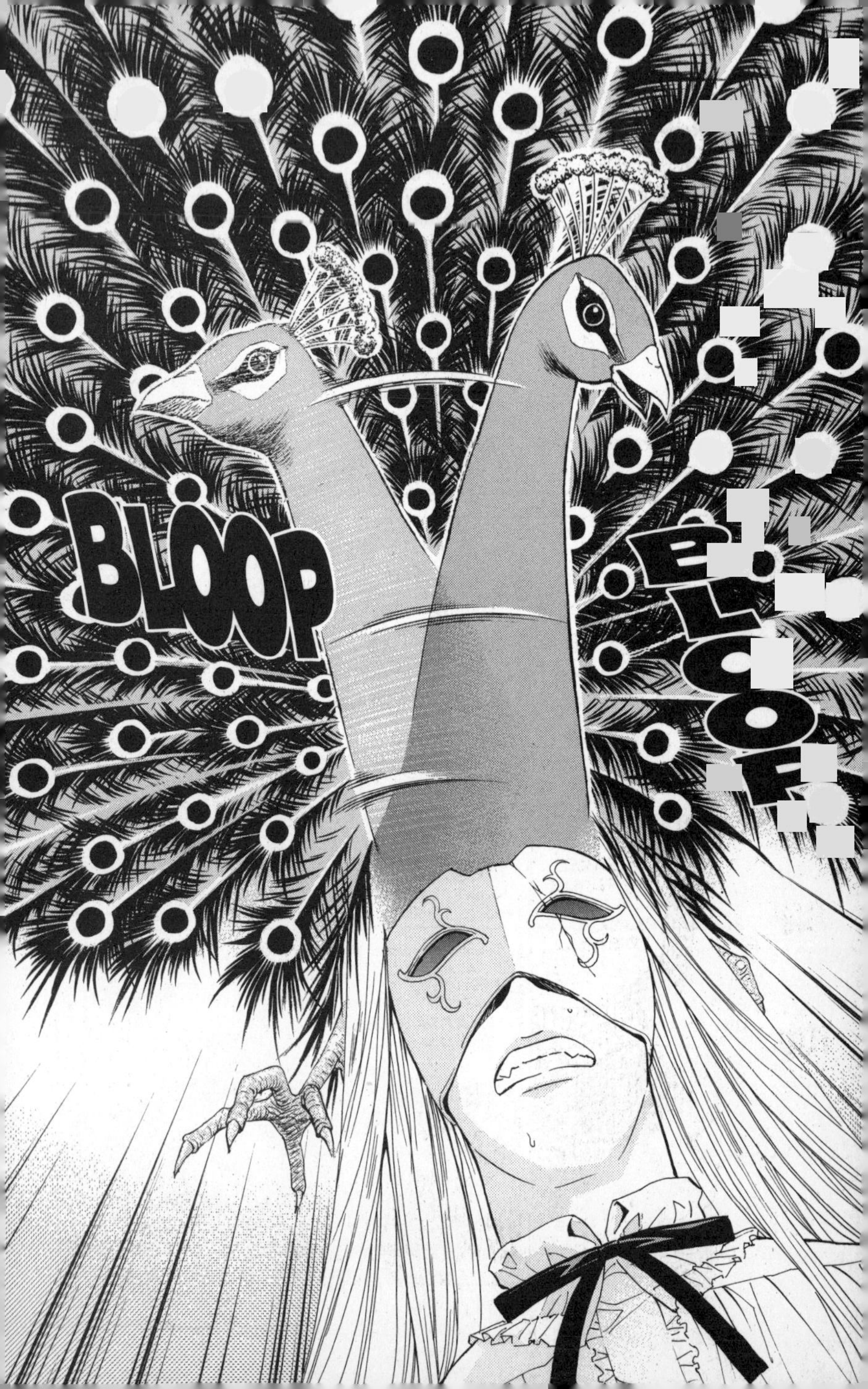
BLOOP
BLOOP

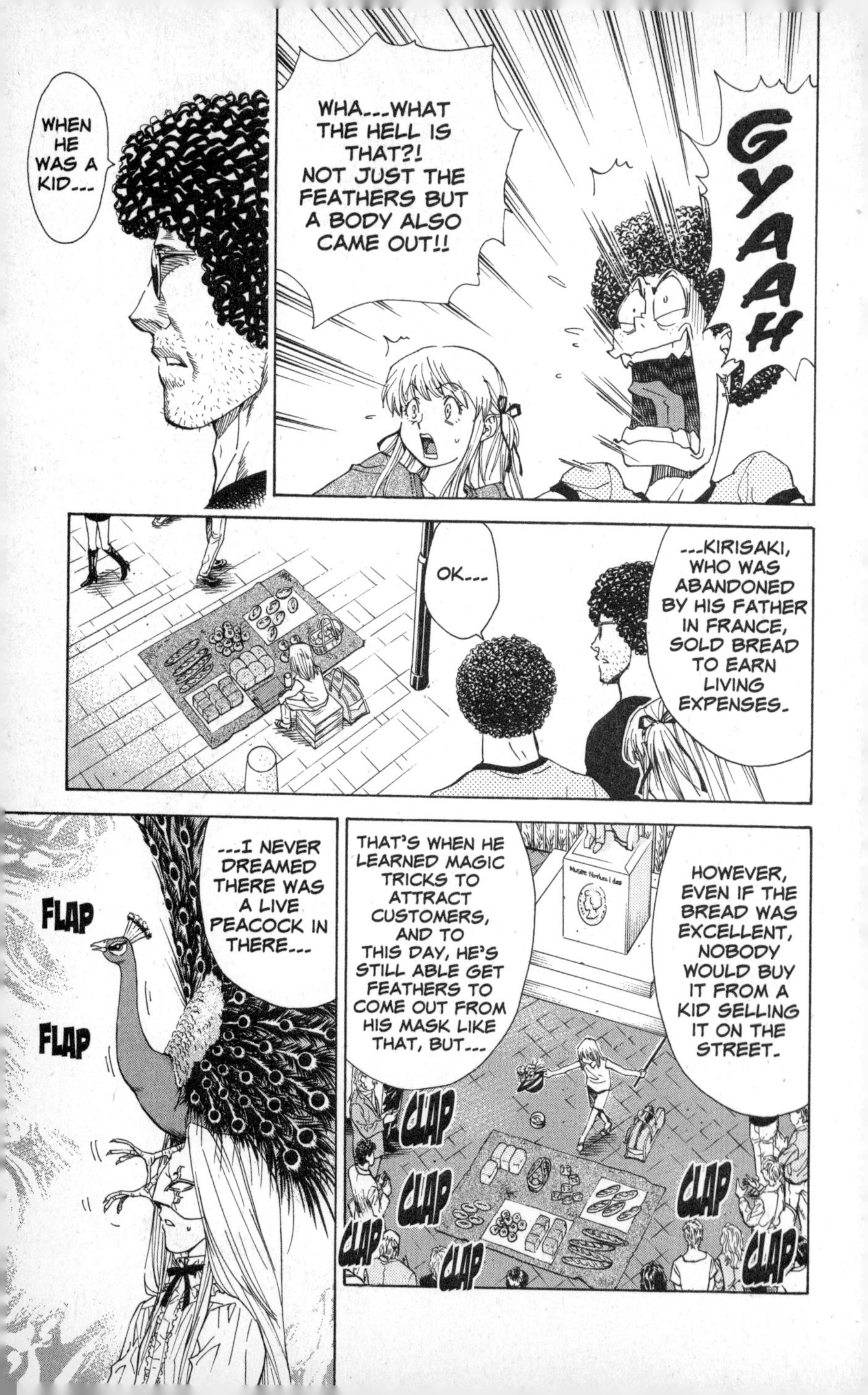
GYAAAH
WHA---WHAT THE HELL IS THAT?! NOT JUST THE FEATHERS BUT A BODY ALSO CAME OUT!!
WHEN HE WAS A KID---
---KIRISAKI, WHO WAS ABANDONED BY HIS FATHER IN FRANCE, SOLD BREAD TO EARN LIVING EXPENSES.
OK---
HOWEVER, EVEN IF THE BREAD WAS EXCELLENT, NOBODY WOULD BUY IT FROM A KID SELLING IT ON THE STREET.
THAT'S WHEN HE LEARNED MAGIC TRICKS TO ATTRACT CUSTOMERS, AND TO THIS DAY, HE'S STILL ABLE GET FEATHERS TO COME OUT FROM HIS MASK LIKE THAT, BUT---
CLAP
CLAP
CLAP
CLAP
CLAP
CLAP
---I NEVER DREAMED THERE WAS A LIVE PEACOCK IN THERE---
FLAP
FLAP

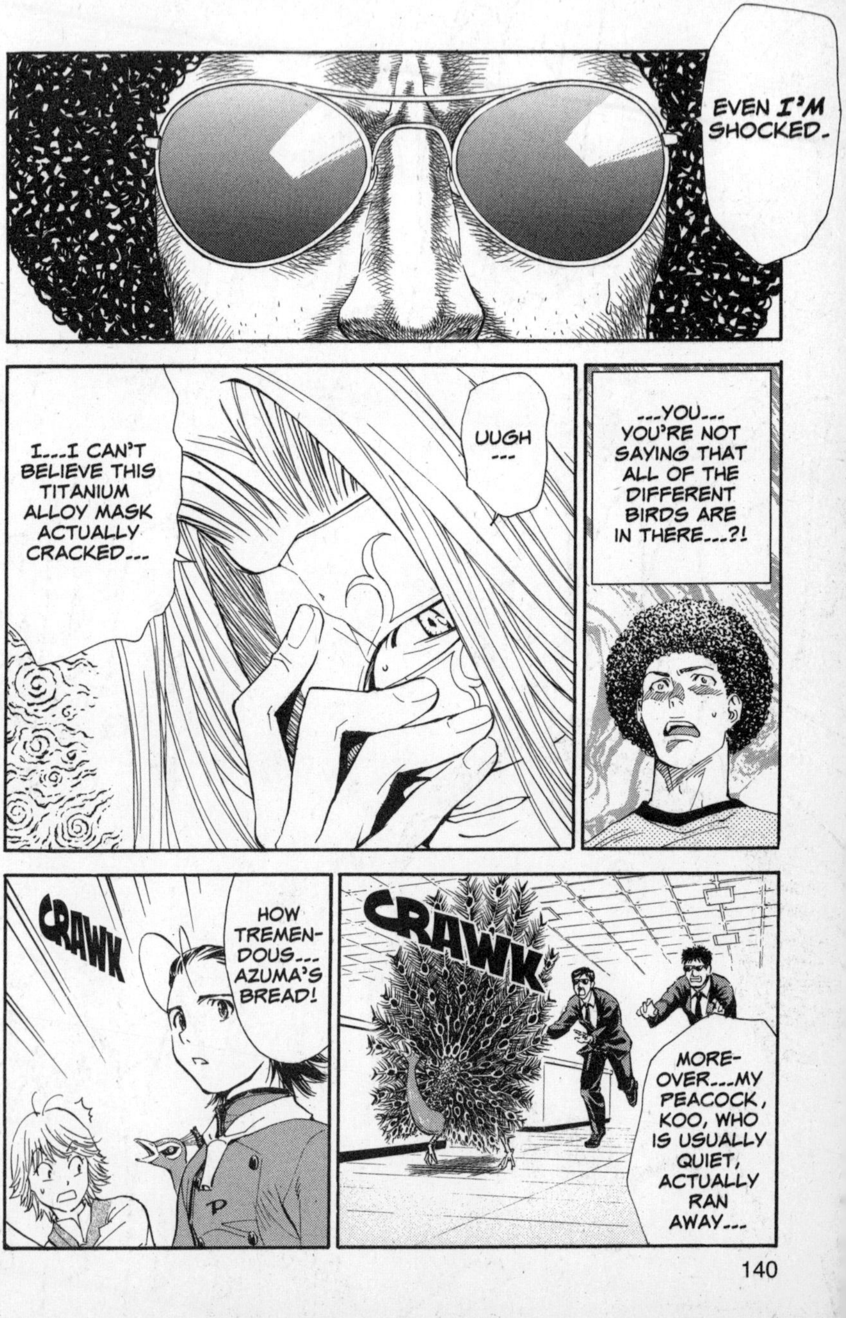
EVEN I'M SHOCKED.
...YOU... YOU'RE NOT SAYING THAT ALL OF THE DIFFERENT BIRDS ARE IN THERE...?!
UUGH...
I...I CAN'T BELIEVE THIS TITANIUM ALLOY MASK ACTUALLY CRACKED...
CRAWK
MOREOVER...MY PEACOCK, KOO, WHO IS USUALLY QUIET, ACTUALLY RAN AWAY...
HOW TREMENDOUS... AZUMA'S BREAD!
CRAWK

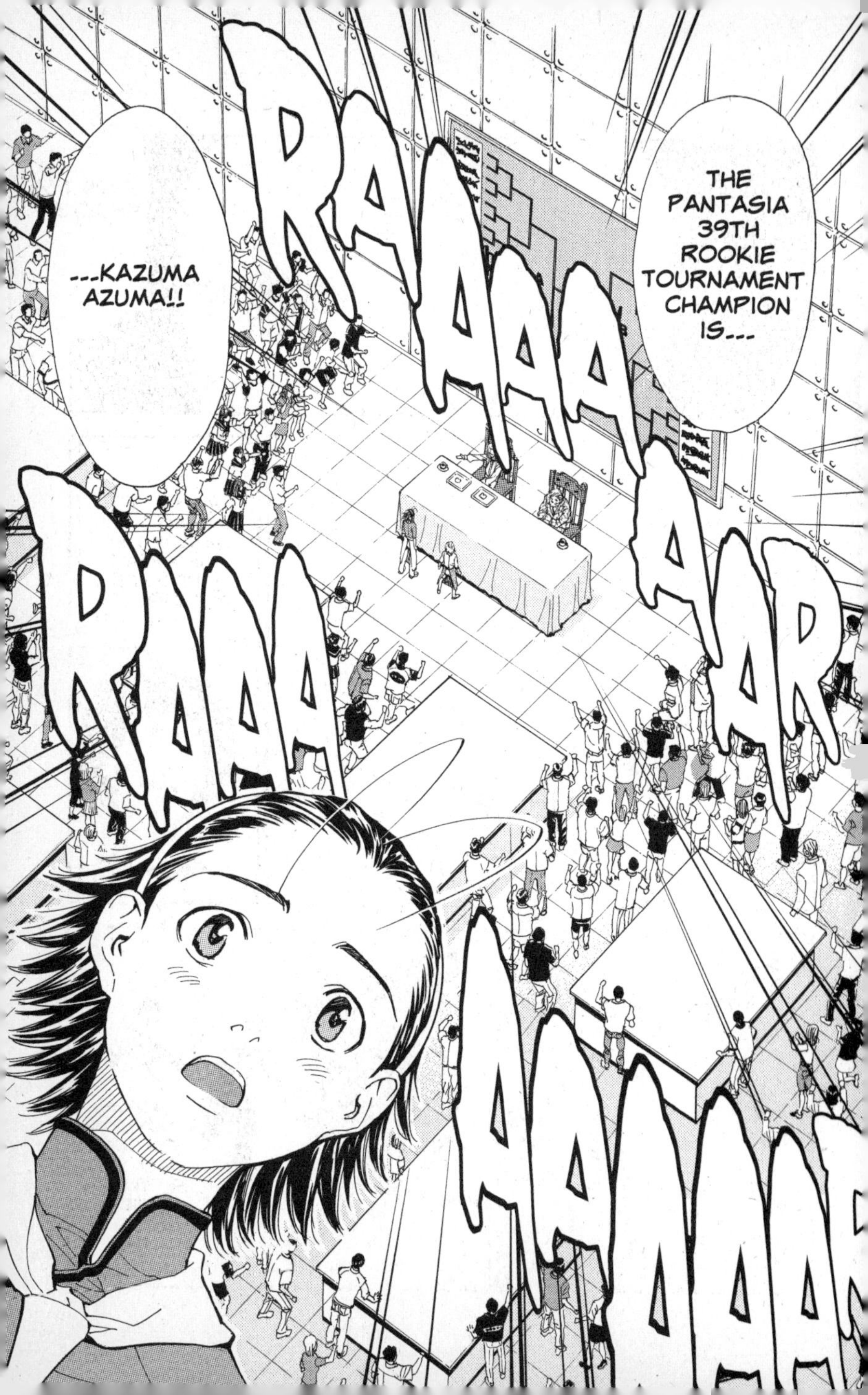
THE PANTASIA 39TH ROOKIE TOURNAMENT CHAMPION IS---
---KAZUMA AZUMA!!

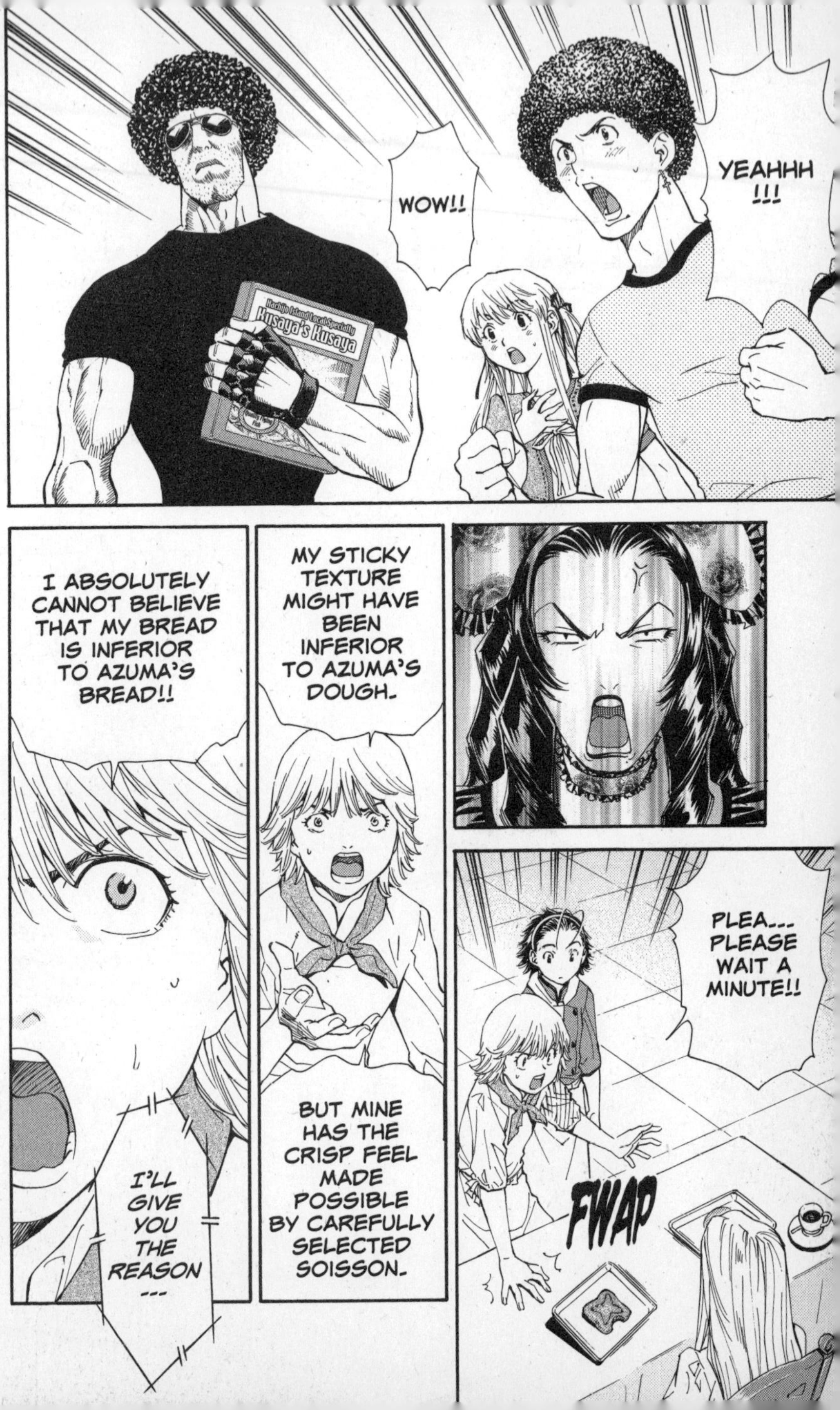
YEAHHH !!!
WOW!!
Hachijo Island Local Specialty
Kusaya's Kusaya
PLEA... PLEASE WAIT A MINUTE!!
FWAP
MY STICKY TEXTURE MIGHT HAVE BEEN INFERIOR TO AZUMA'S DOUGH.
BUT MINE HAS THE CRISP FEEL MADE POSSIBLE BY CAREFULLY SELECTED SOISSON.
I ABSOLUTELY CANNOT BELIEVE THAT MY BREAD IS INFERIOR TO AZUMA'S BREAD!!
I'LL GIVE YOU THE REASON ---

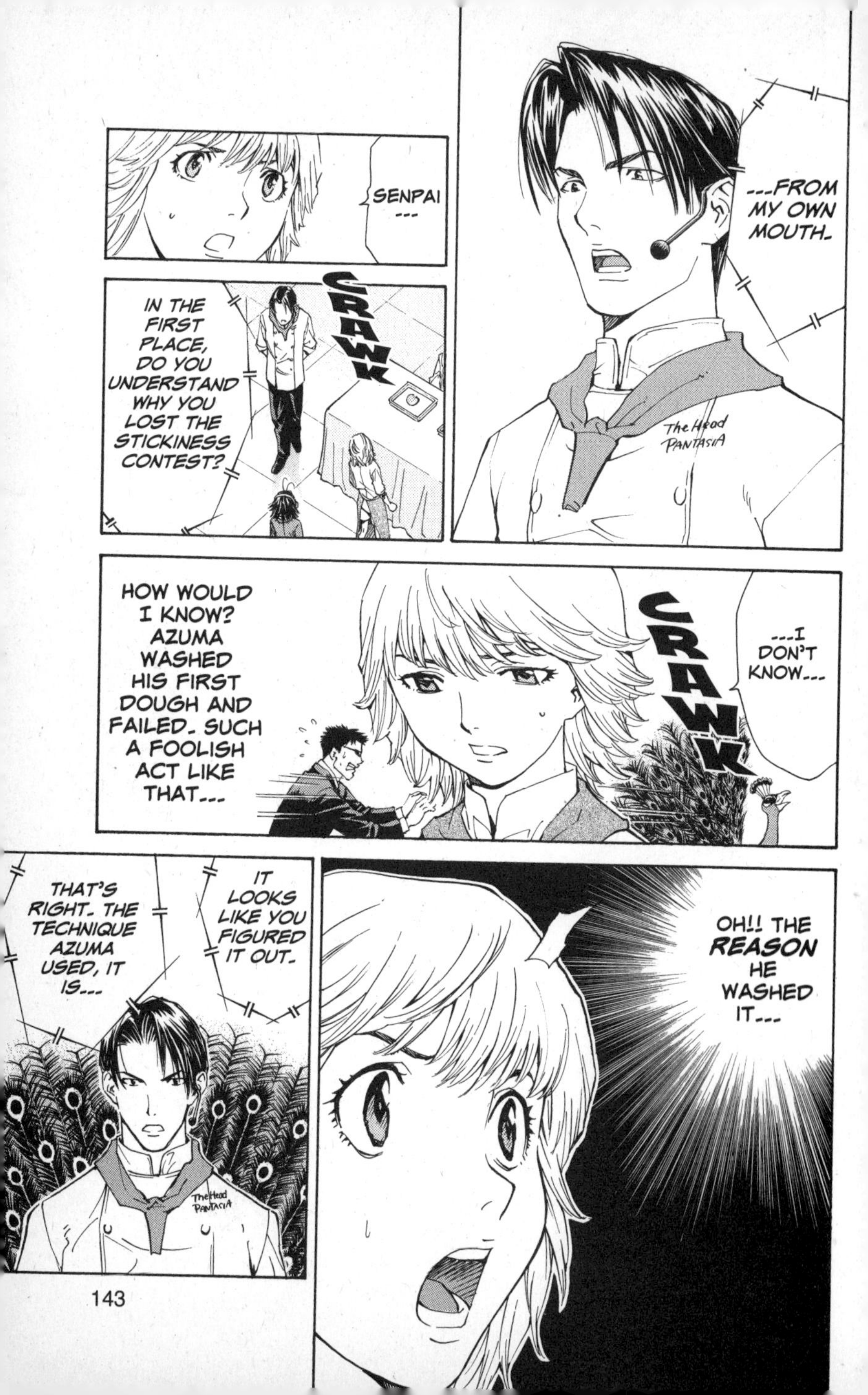
---FROM MY OWN MOUTH.
The Head PANTASIA
SENPAI ---
CRAWK
IN THE FIRST PLACE, DO YOU UNDERSTAND WHY YOU LOST THE STICKINESS CONTEST?
---I DON'T KNOW---
CRAWK
HOW WOULD I KNOW? AZUMA WASHED HIS FIRST DOUGH AND FAILED. SUCH A FOOLISH ACT LIKE THAT---
OH!! THE **REASON** HE WASHED IT---
IT LOOKS LIKE YOU FIGURED IT OUT.
THAT'S RIGHT. THE TECHNIQUE AZUMA USED, IT IS---
The Head PANTASIA

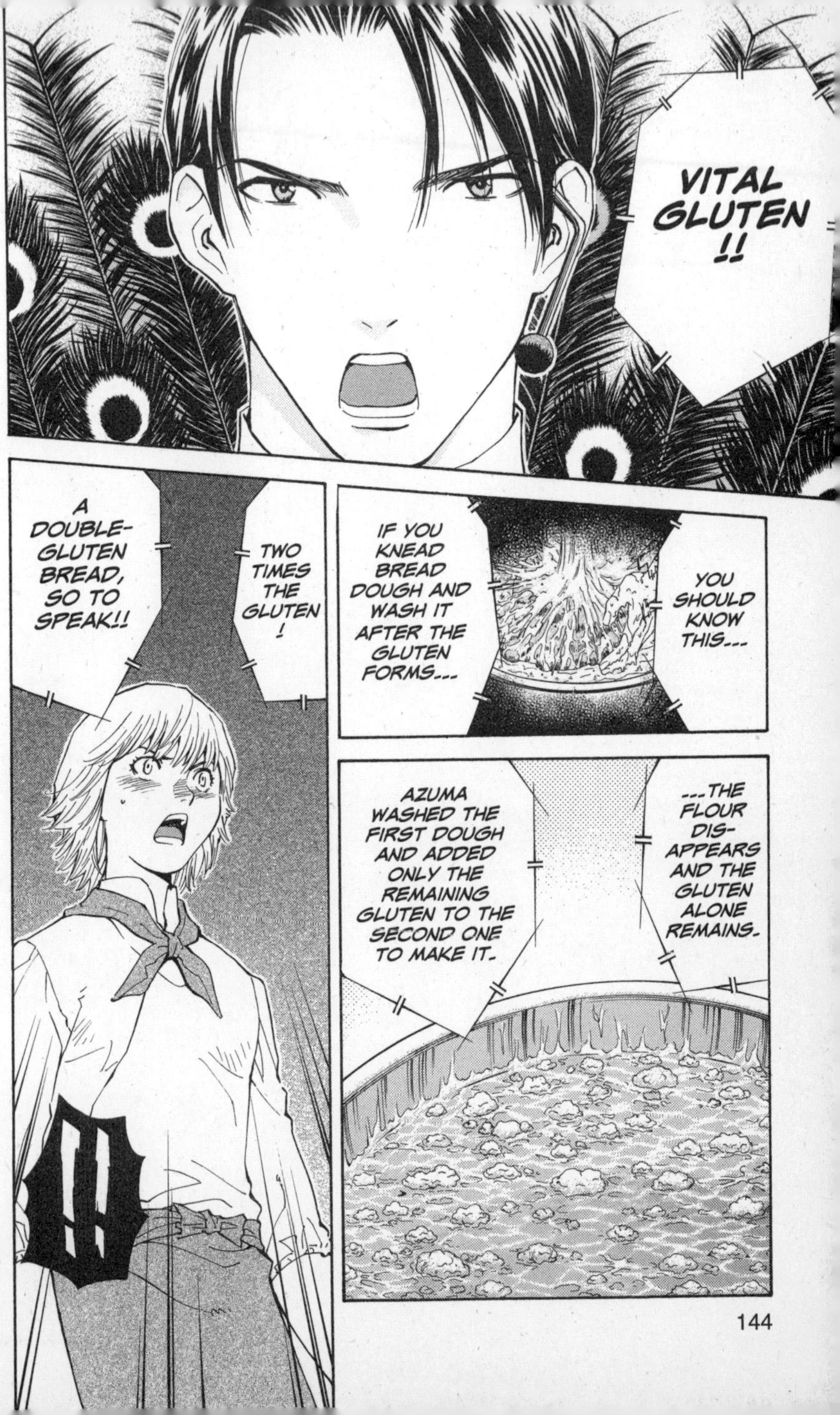

VITAL GLUTEN !!
YOU SHOULD KNOW THIS...
IF YOU KNEAD BREAD DOUGH AND WASH IT AFTER THE GLUTEN FORMS...
...THE FLOUR DIS-APPEARS AND THE GLUTEN ALONE REMAINS.
AZUMA WASHED THE FIRST DOUGH AND ADDED ONLY THE REMAINING GLUTEN TO THE SECOND ONE TO MAKE IT.
TWO TIMES THE GLUTEN !
A DOUBLE-GLUTEN BREAD, SO TO SPEAK!!
!!

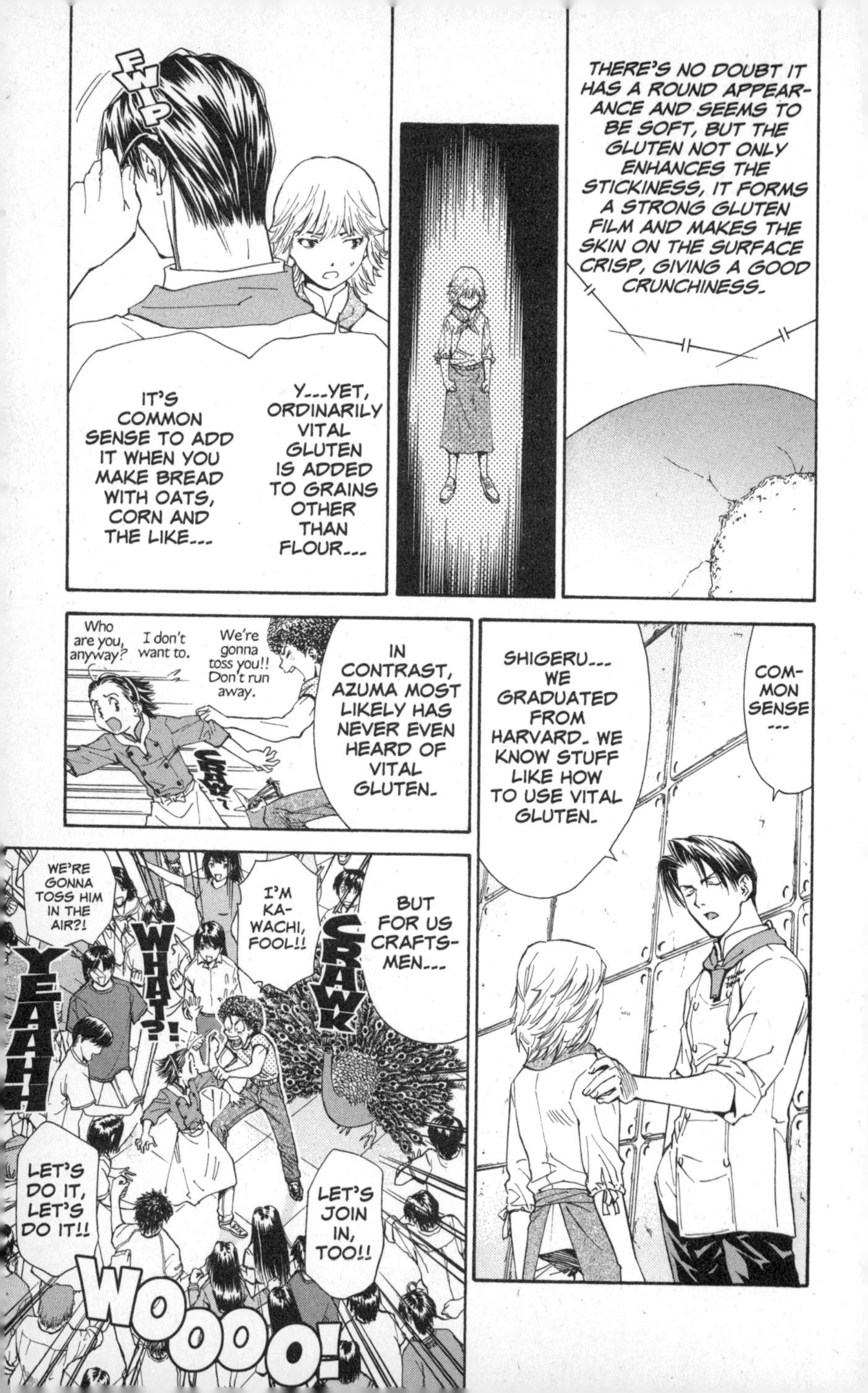
THERE'S NO DOUBT IT HAS A ROUND APPEARANCE AND SEEMS TO BE SOFT, BUT THE GLUTEN NOT ONLY ENHANCES THE STICKINESS, IT FORMS A STRONG GLUTEN FILM AND MAKES THE SKIN ON THE SURFACE CRISP, GIVING A GOOD CRUNCHINESS.
FWIP
Y...YET, ORDINARILY VITAL GLUTEN IS ADDED TO GRAINS OTHER THAN FLOUR...
IT'S COMMON SENSE TO ADD IT WHEN YOU MAKE BREAD WITH OATS, CORN AND THE LIKE...
COMMON SENSE...
SHIGERU... WE GRADUATED FROM HARVARD. WE KNOW STUFF LIKE HOW TO USE VITAL GLUTEN.
IN CONTRAST, AZUMA MOST LIKELY HAS NEVER EVEN HEARD OF VITAL GLUTEN.
We're gonna toss you!! Don't run away.
I don't want to.
Who are you, anyway?
CRAWK
BUT FOR US CRAFTSMEN...
I'M KAWACHI, FOOL!!
CRAWK
WHAT?!
WE'RE GONNA TOSS HIM IN THE AIR?!
YEAH!!
LET'S JOIN IN, TOO!!
LET'S DO IT, LET'S DO IT!!
WOOOO!

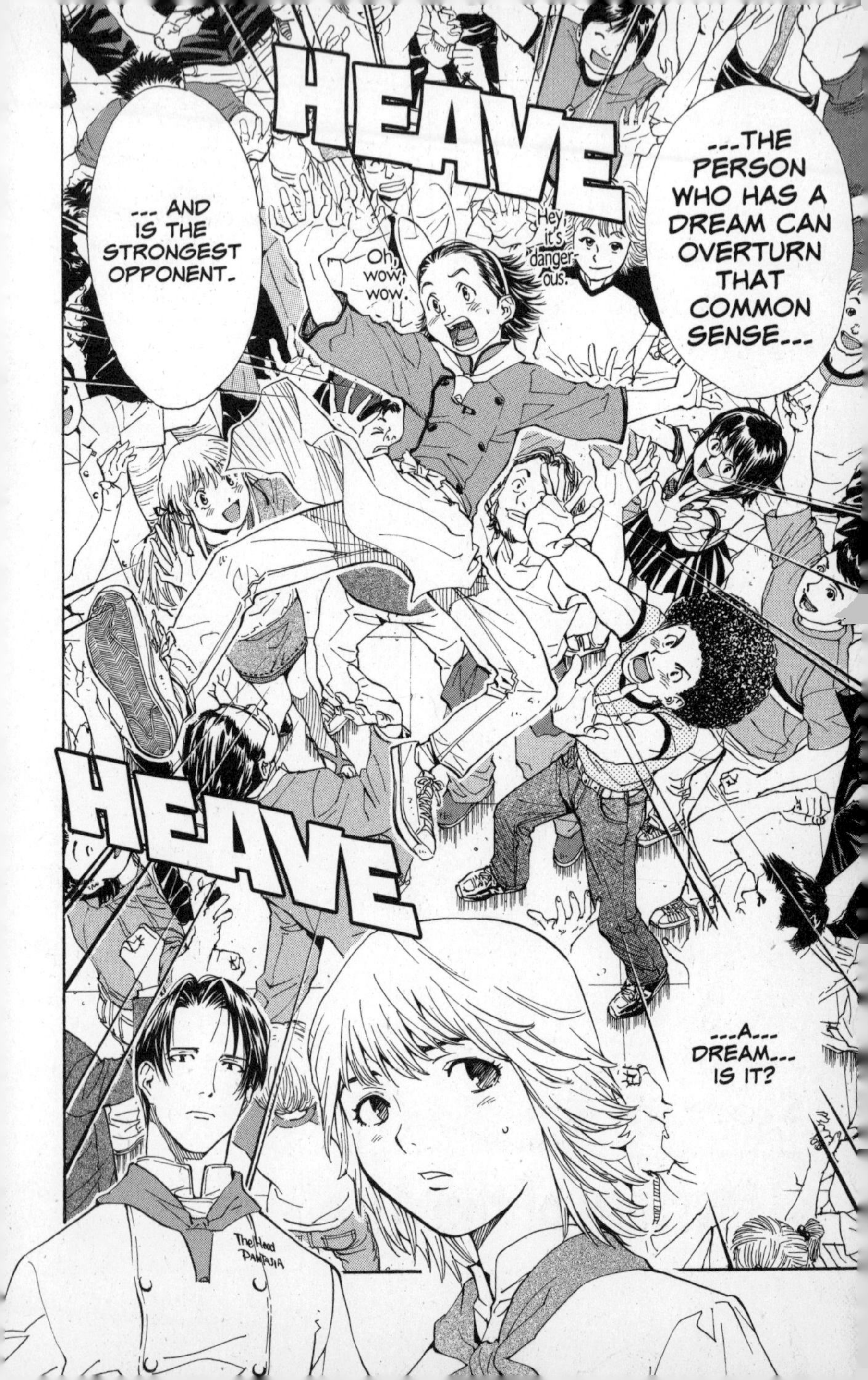
HEAVE
---THE PERSON WHO HAS A DREAM CAN OVERTURN THAT COMMON SENSE---
Hey, it's danger-ous.
Oh, wow, wow.
--- AND IS THE STRONGEST OPPONENT.
HEAVE
---A--- DREAM--- IS IT?
The Head PANTAJIA

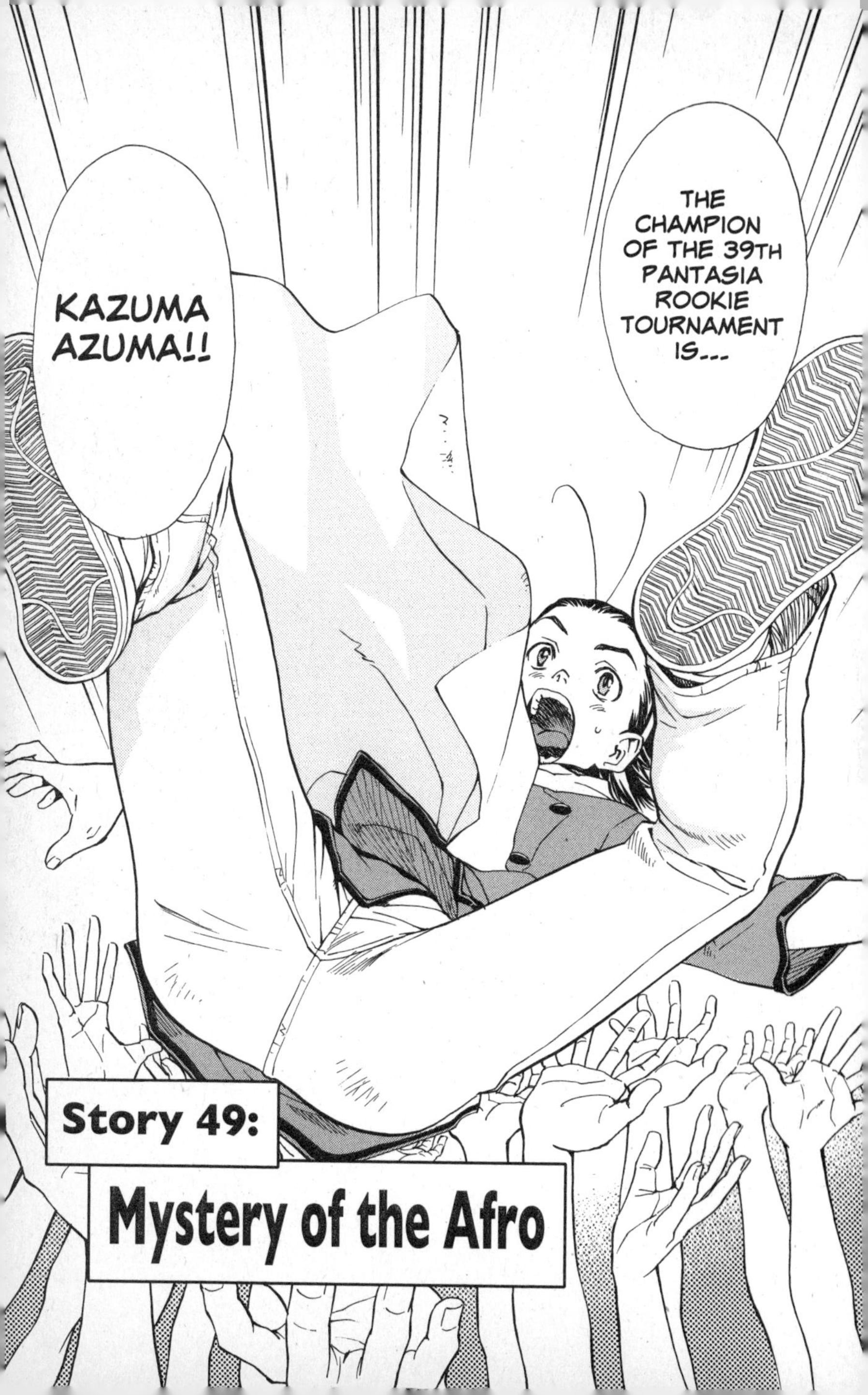
THE CHAMPION OF THE 39TH PANTASIA ROOKIE TOURNAMENT IS...
KAZUMA AZUMA!!
Story 49:
Mystery of the Afro

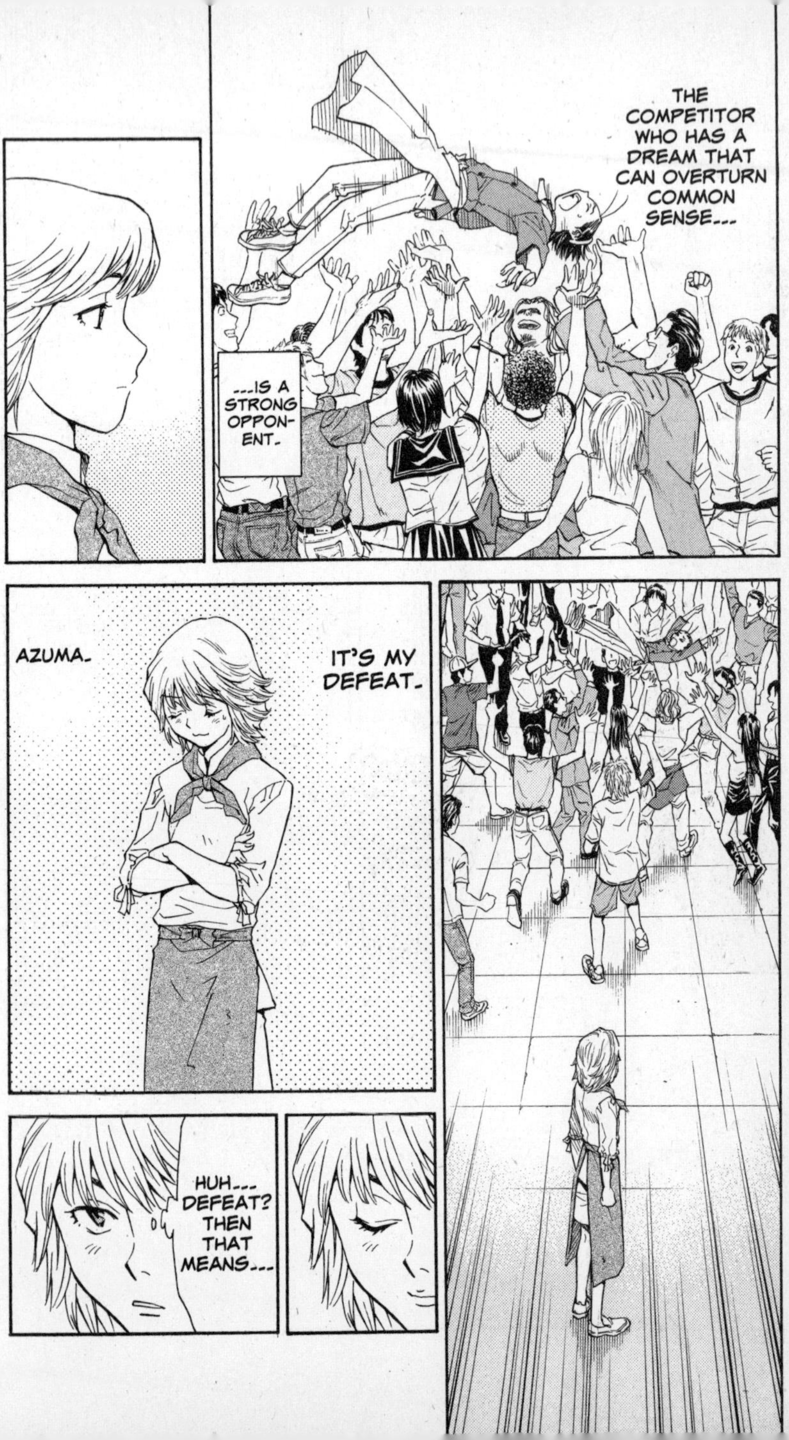
THE COMPETITOR WHO HAS A DREAM THAT CAN OVERTURN COMMON SENSE...
...IS A STRONG OPPONENT.
IT'S MY DEFEAT.
AZUMA.
HUH... DEFEAT? THEN THAT MEANS...

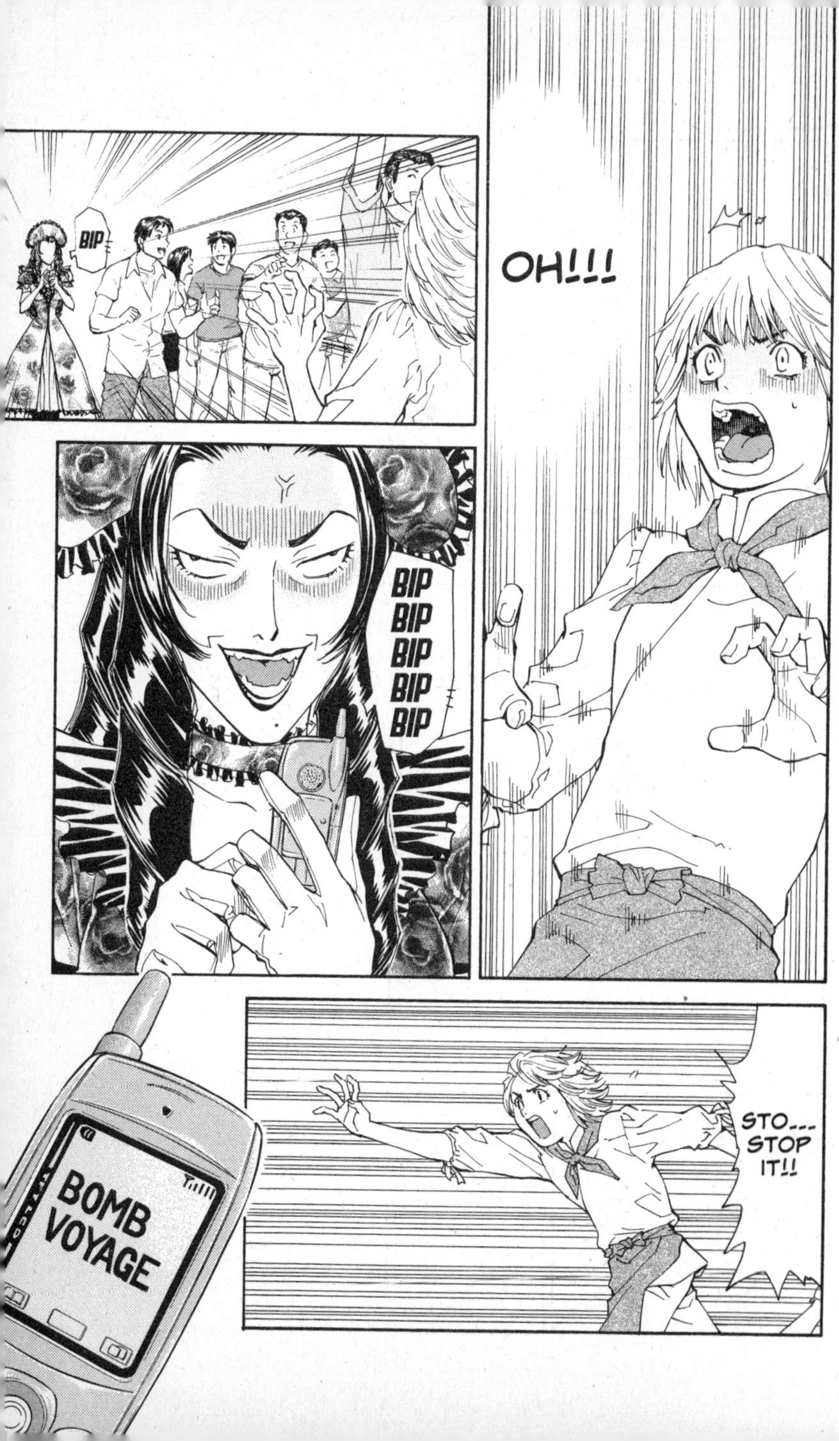
OH!!!
BIP
BIP BIP BIP BIP BIP
STO... STOP IT!!
BOMB VOYAGE

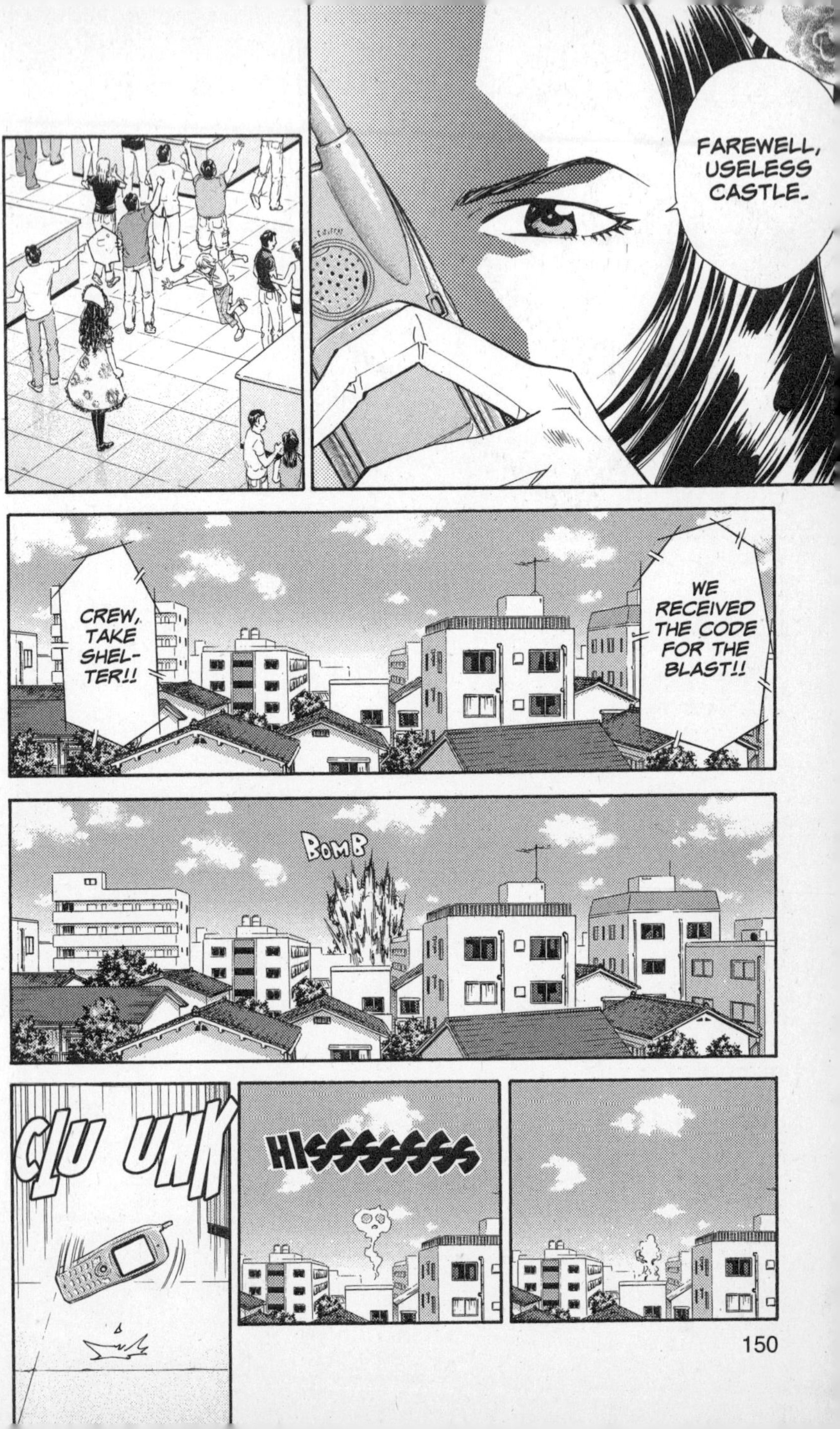
FAREWELL, USELESS CASTLE.
WE RECEIVED THE CODE FOR THE BLAST!!
CREW, TAKE SHEL-TER!!
BOMB
HISSSSSSSS
CLU UNK

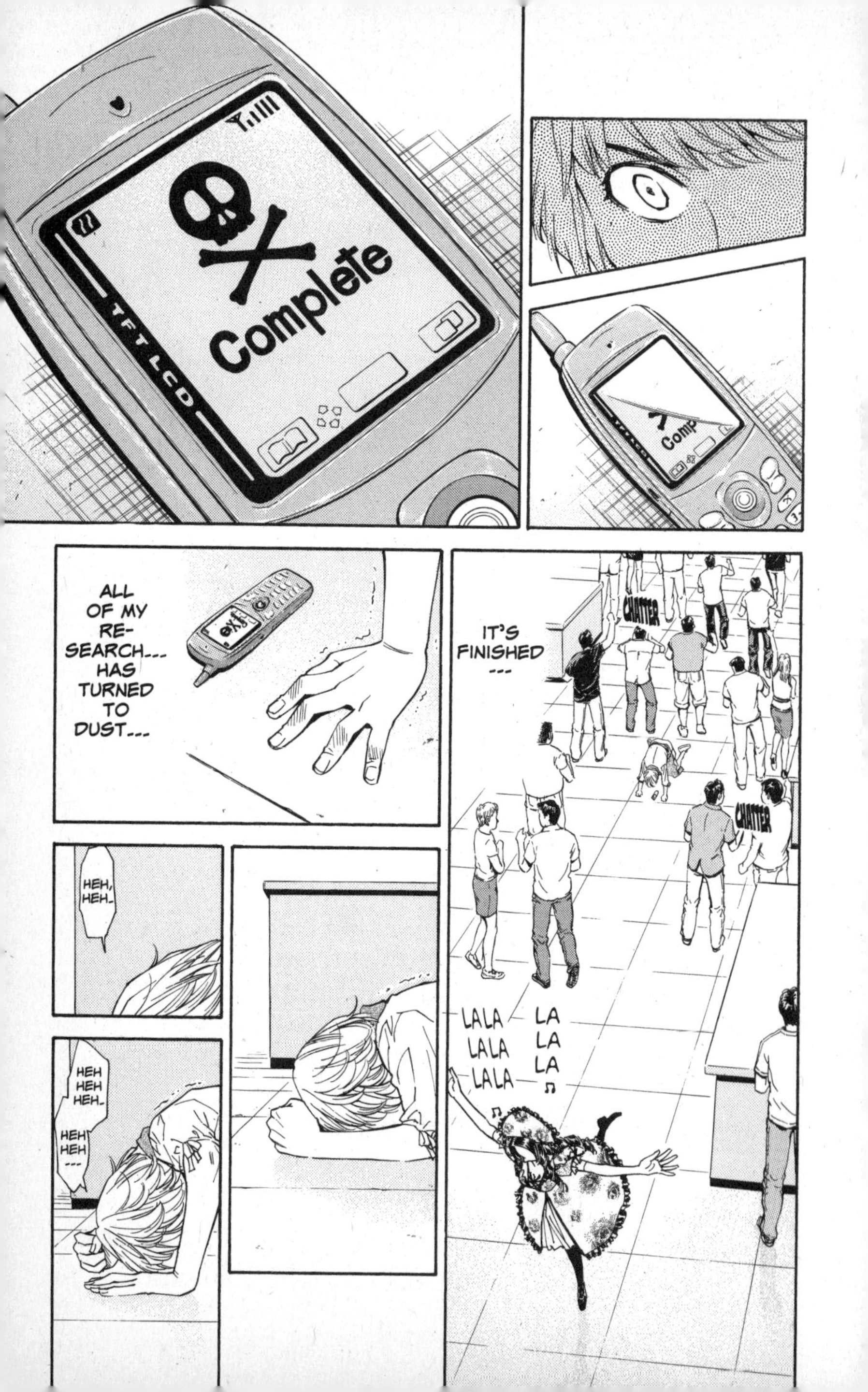
Comp
Complete
TFT LCD
IT'S FINISHED---
CHATTER
CHATTER
LA LA LA
LALA LALA LALA
ALL OF MY RE-SEARCH--- HAS TURNED TO DUST---
HEH, HEH_
HEH HEH HEH_
HEH HEH ---

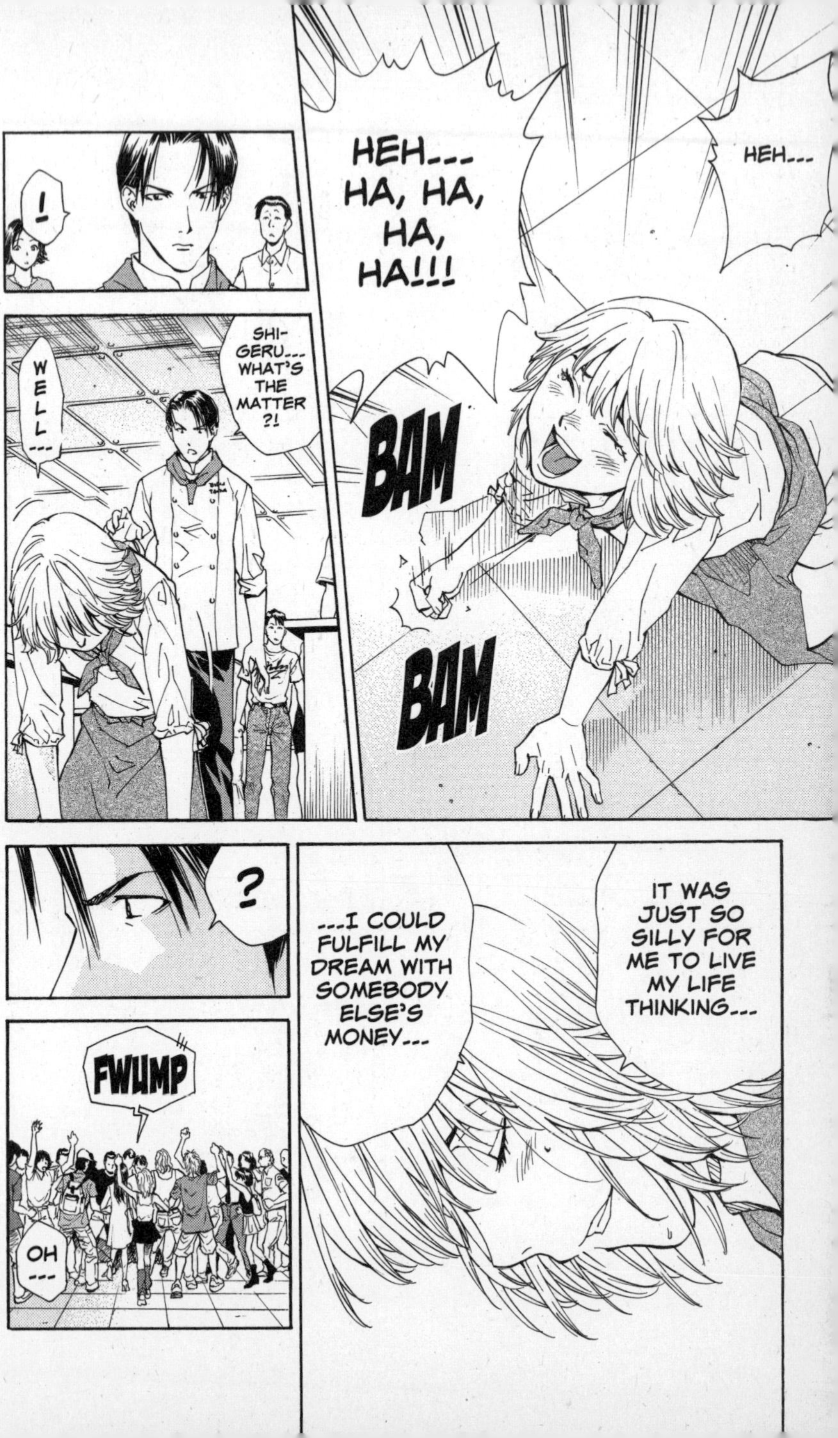
HEH...
HEH... HA, HA, HA, HA!!!
BAM
BAM
!
SHI-GERU... WHAT'S THE MATTER?!
WELL...
IT WAS JUST SO SILLY FOR ME TO LIVE MY LIFE THINKING...
...I COULD FULFILL MY DREAM WITH SOMEBODY ELSE'S MONEY...
?
FWUMP
OH...

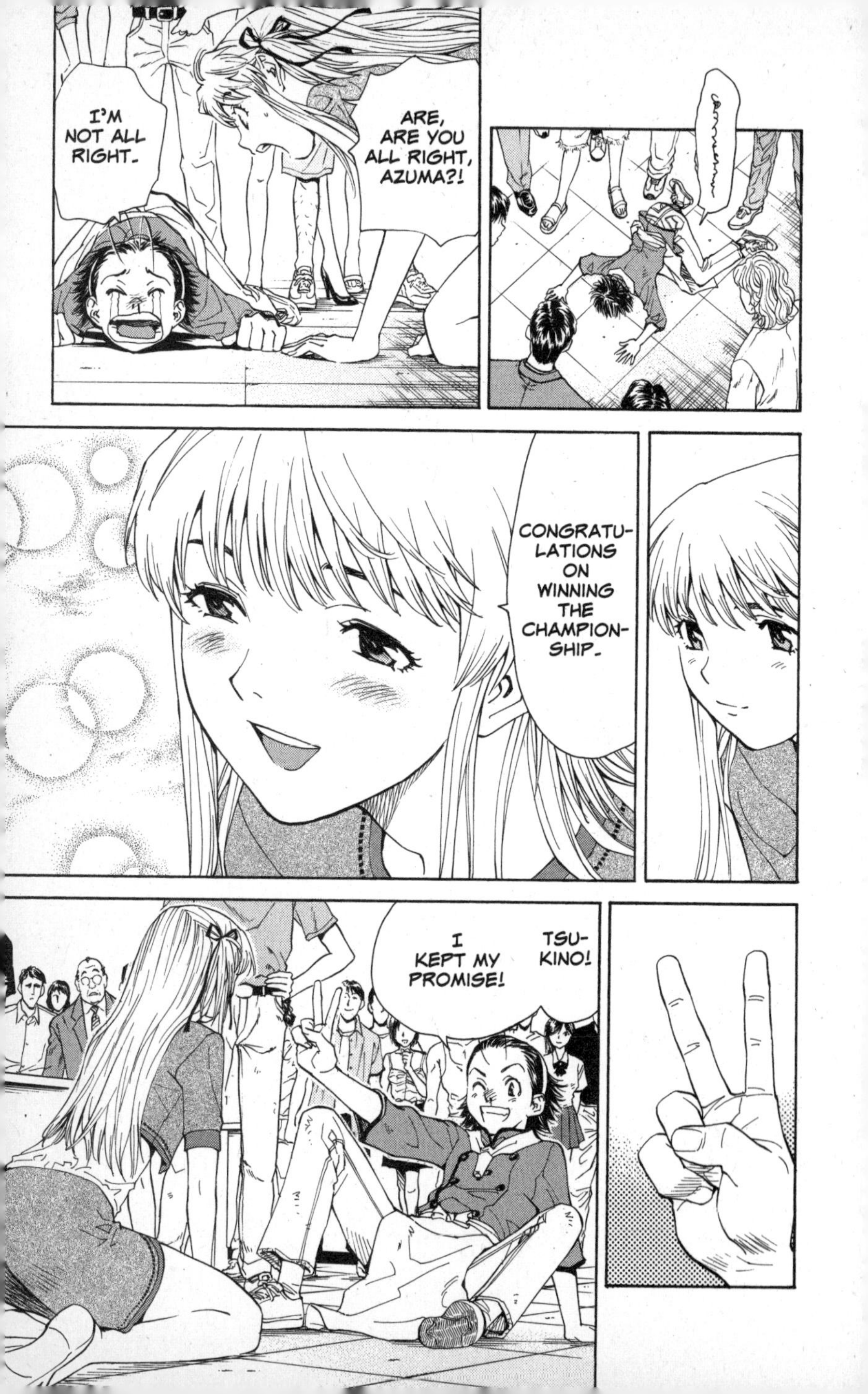
......
ARE, ARE YOU ALL RIGHT, AZUMA?!
I'M NOT ALL RIGHT.
CONGRATULATIONS ON WINNING THE CHAMPIONSHIP.
TSUKINO!
I KEPT MY PROMISE!

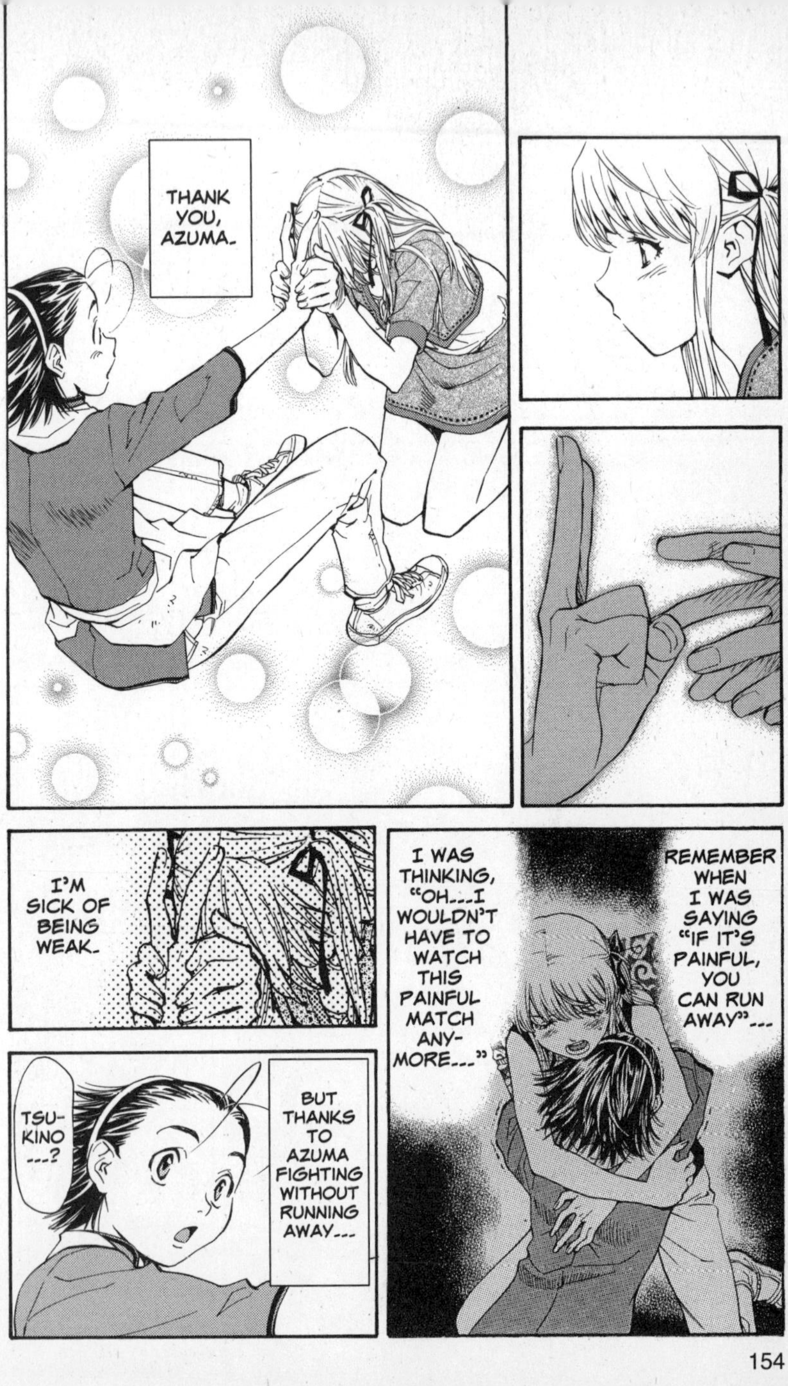
THANK YOU, AZUMA.
REMEMBER WHEN I WAS SAYING "IF IT'S PAINFUL, YOU CAN RUN AWAY"...
I WAS THINKING, "OH...I WOULDN'T HAVE TO WATCH THIS PAINFUL MATCH ANY-MORE..."
I'M SICK OF BEING WEAK.
BUT THANKS TO AZUMA FIGHTING WITHOUT RUNNING AWAY...
TSU-KINO ...?

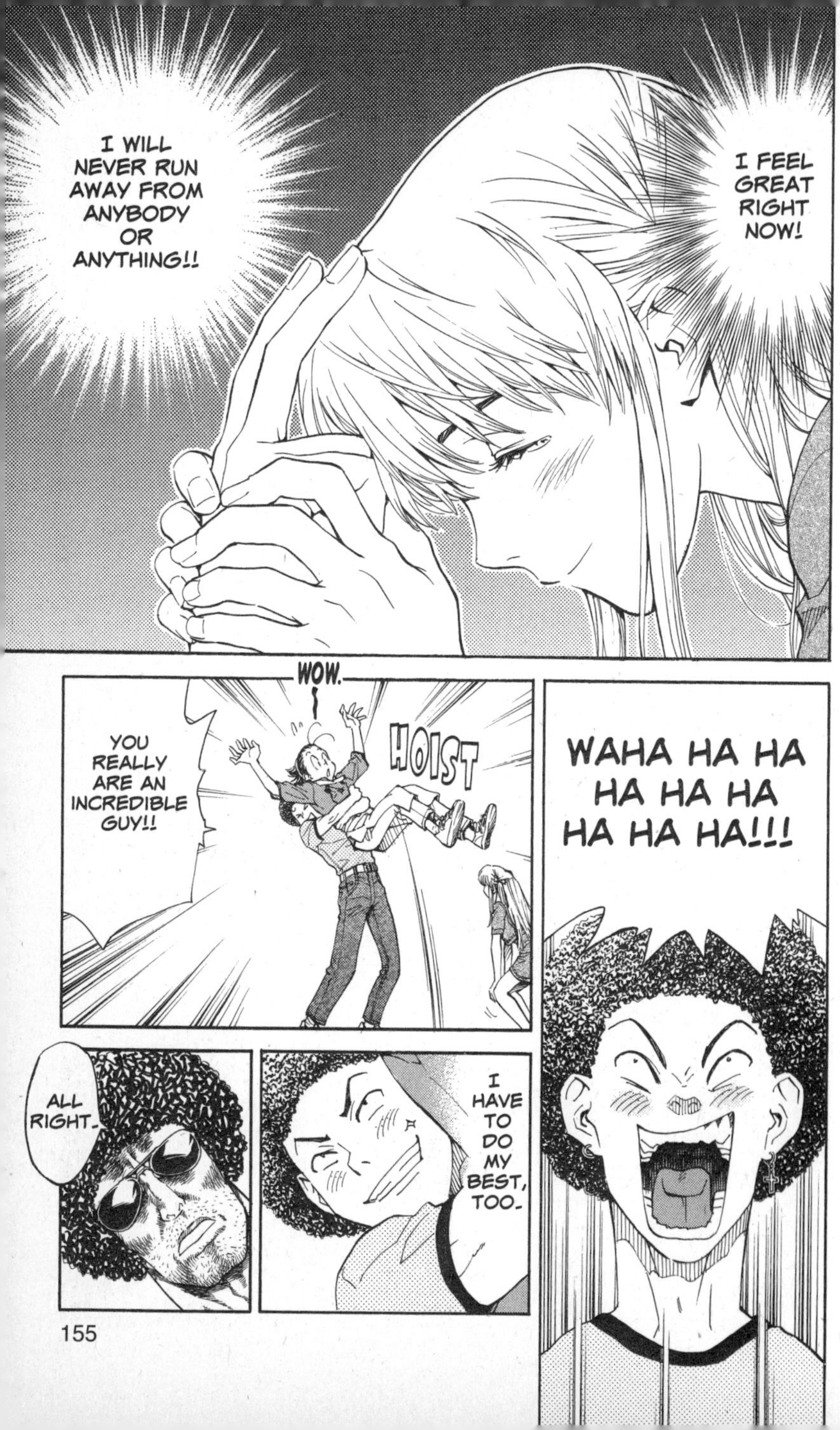
I FEEL GREAT RIGHT NOW!
I WILL NEVER RUN AWAY FROM ANYBODY OR ANYTHING!!
WAHA HA HA HA HA HA HA HA HA!!!
WOW.
HOIST
YOU REALLY ARE AN INCREDIBLE GUY!!
I HAVE TO DO MY BEST, TOO.
ALL RIGHT.

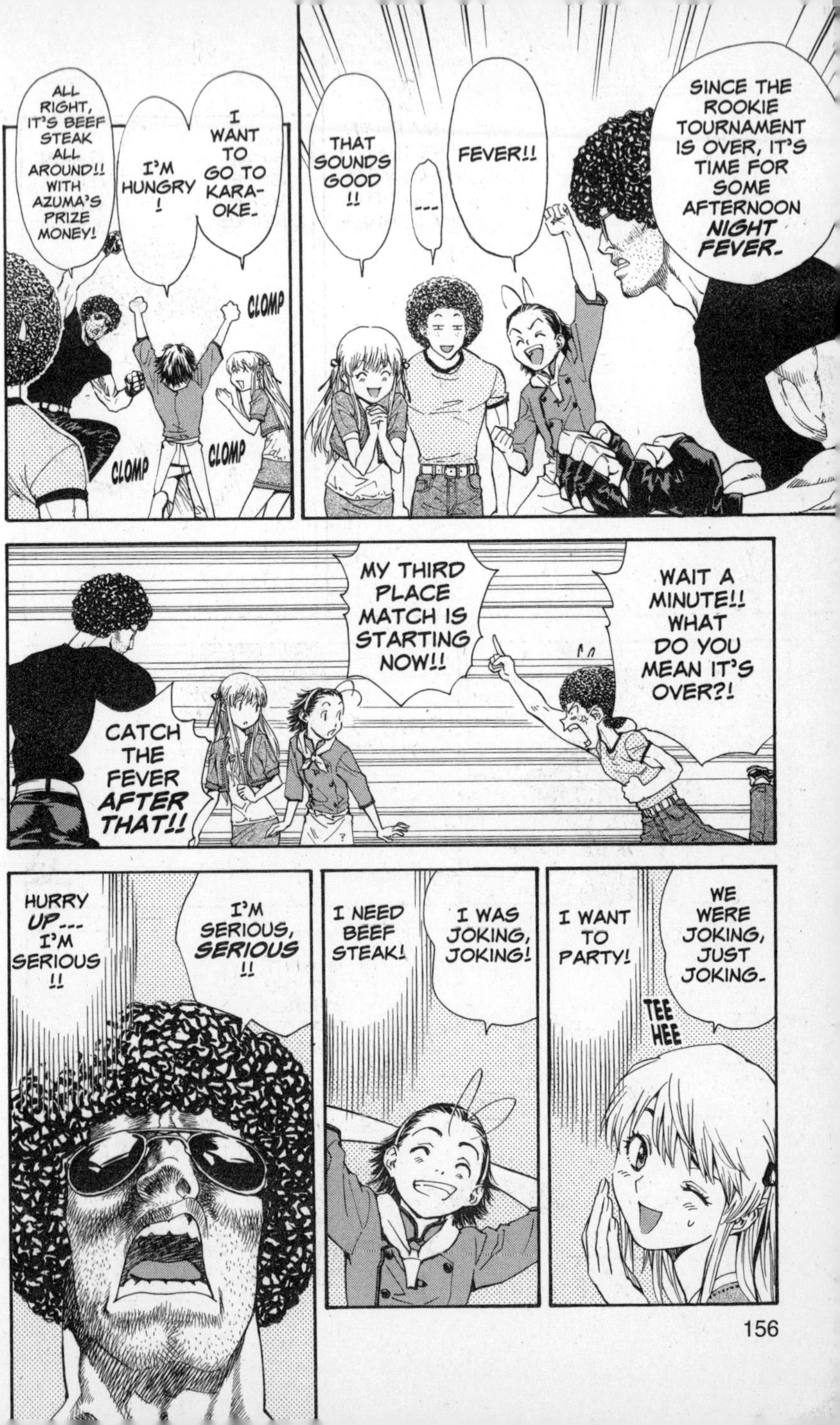

SINCE THE ROOKIE TOURNAMENT IS OVER, IT'S TIME FOR SOME AFTERNOON NIGHT FEVER.
FEVER!!
...
THAT SOUNDS GOOD!!
I WANT TO GO TO KARAOKE.
I'M HUNGRY!
ALL RIGHT, IT'S BEEF STEAK ALL AROUND!! WITH AZUMA'S PRIZE MONEY!
CLOMP
CLOMP
CLOMP
WAIT A MINUTE!! WHAT DO YOU MEAN IT'S OVER?!
MY THIRD PLACE MATCH IS STARTING NOW!!
CATCH THE FEVER AFTER THAT!!
WE WERE JOKING, JUST JOKING.
I WANT TO PARTY!
TEE HEE
I WAS JOKING, JOKING!
I NEED BEEF STEAK!
I'M SERIOUS, SERIOUS!!
HURRY UP... I'M SERIOUS!!

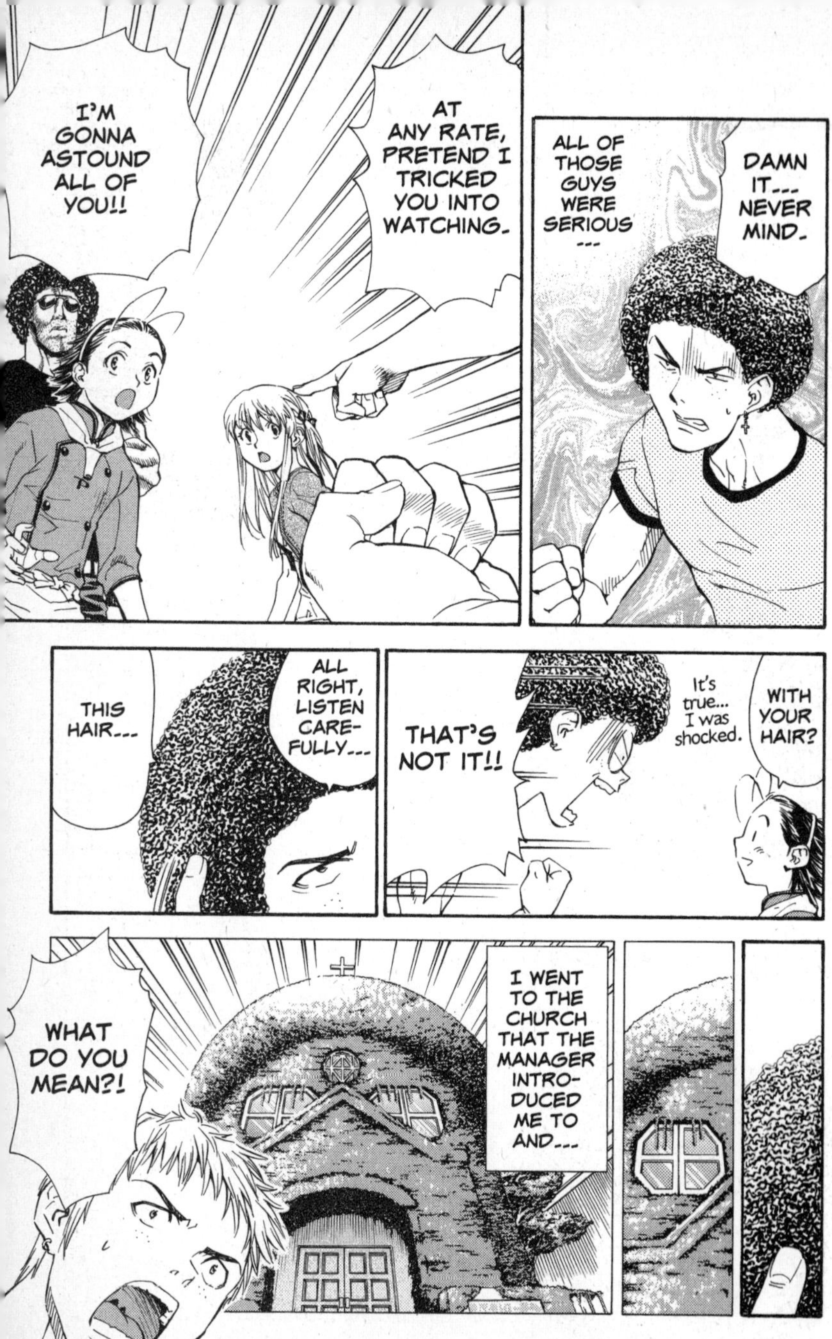
DAMN IT... NEVER MIND.
ALL OF THOSE GUYS WERE SERIOUS...
AT ANY RATE, PRETEND I TRICKED YOU INTO WATCHING.
I'M GONNA ASTOUND ALL OF YOU!!
WITH YOUR HAIR?
It's true... I was shocked.
THAT'S NOT IT!!
ALL RIGHT, LISTEN CAREFULLY...
THIS HAIR...
I WENT TO THE CHURCH THAT THE MANAGER INTRODUCED ME TO AND...
WHAT DO YOU MEAN?!

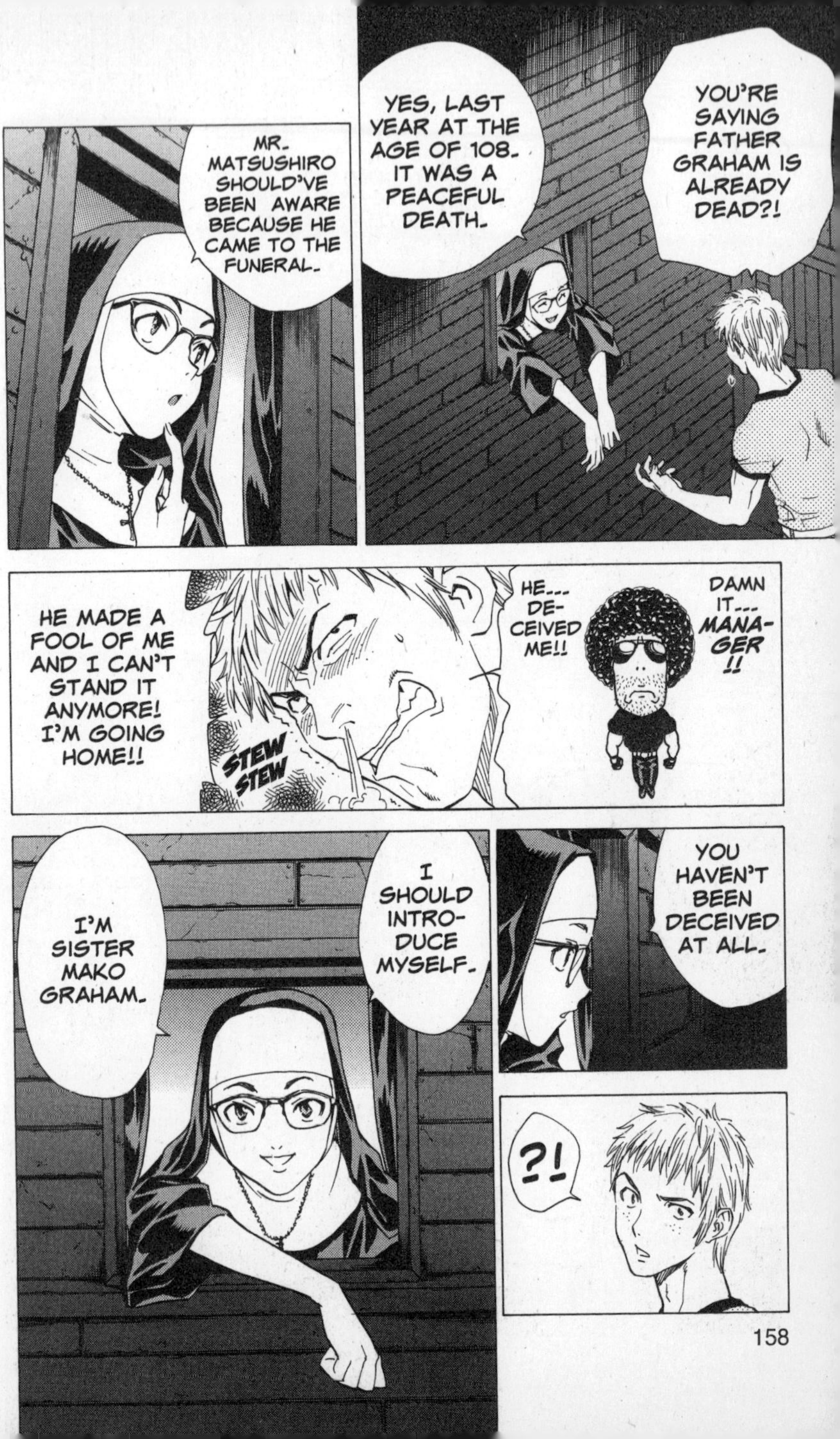
YOU'RE SAYING FATHER GRAHAM IS ALREADY DEAD?!
YES, LAST YEAR AT THE AGE OF 108. IT WAS A PEACEFUL DEATH.
MR. MATSUSHIRO SHOULD'VE BEEN AWARE BECAUSE HE CAME TO THE FUNERAL.
DAMN IT... MANAGER!!
HE... DECEIVED ME!!
HE MADE A FOOL OF ME AND I CAN'T STAND IT ANYMORE! I'M GOING HOME!!
STEW STEW
YOU HAVEN'T BEEN DECEIVED AT ALL.
?!
I SHOULD INTRODUCE MYSELF.
I'M SISTER MAKO GRAHAM.

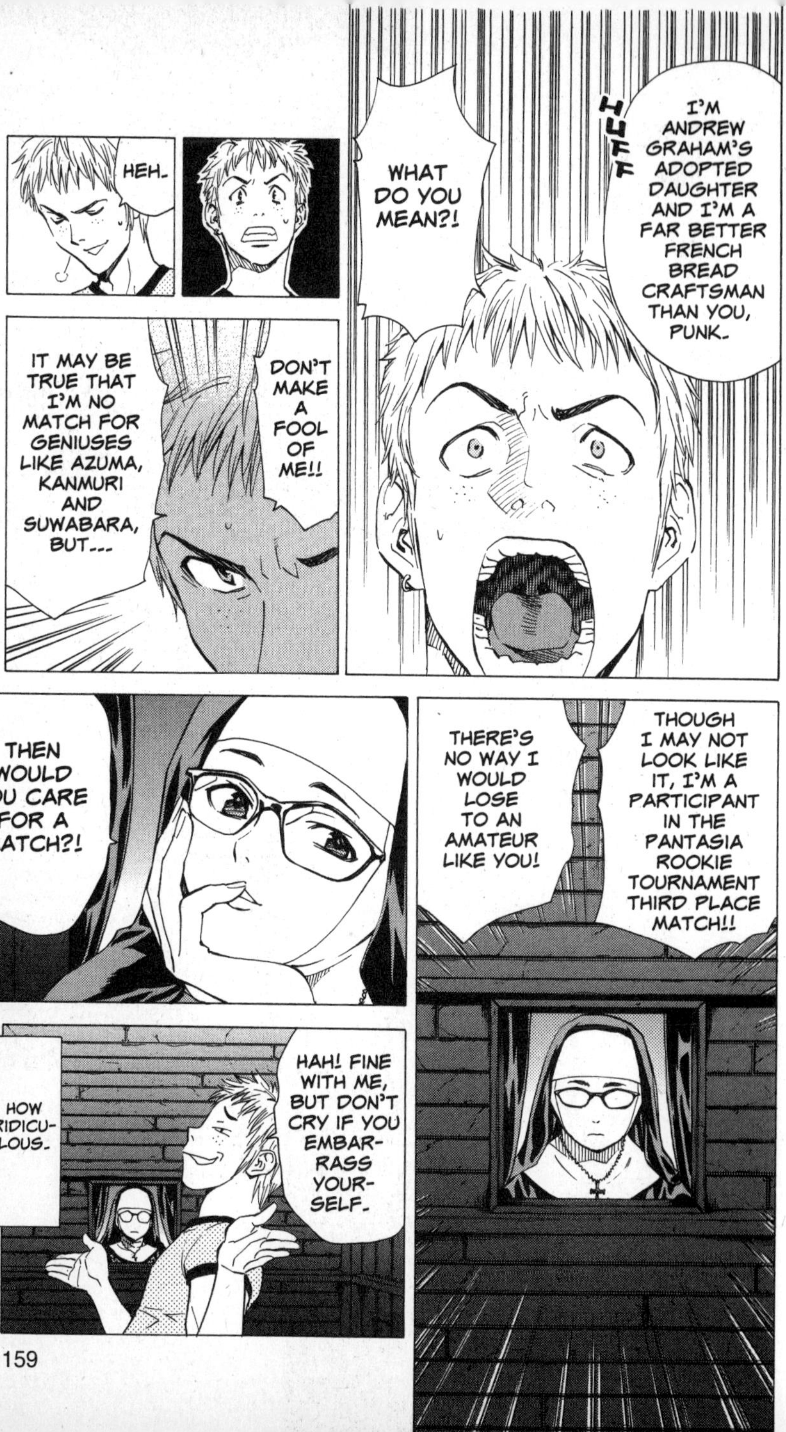
I'M ANDREW GRAHAM'S ADOPTED DAUGHTER AND I'M A FAR BETTER FRENCH BREAD CRAFTSMAN THAN YOU, PUNK.
HUFF
WHAT DO YOU MEAN?!
HEH.
DON'T MAKE A FOOL OF ME!!
IT MAY BE TRUE THAT I'M NO MATCH FOR GENIUSES LIKE AZUMA, KANMURI AND SUWABARA, BUT...
THOUGH I MAY NOT LOOK LIKE IT, I'M A PARTICIPANT IN THE PANTASIA ROOKIE TOURNAMENT THIRD PLACE MATCH!!
THERE'S NO WAY I WOULD LOSE TO AN AMATEUR LIKE YOU!
THEN WOULD YOU CARE FOR A MATCH?!
HAH! FINE WITH ME, BUT DON'T CRY IF YOU EMBARRASS YOURSELF.
HOW RIDICULOUS.

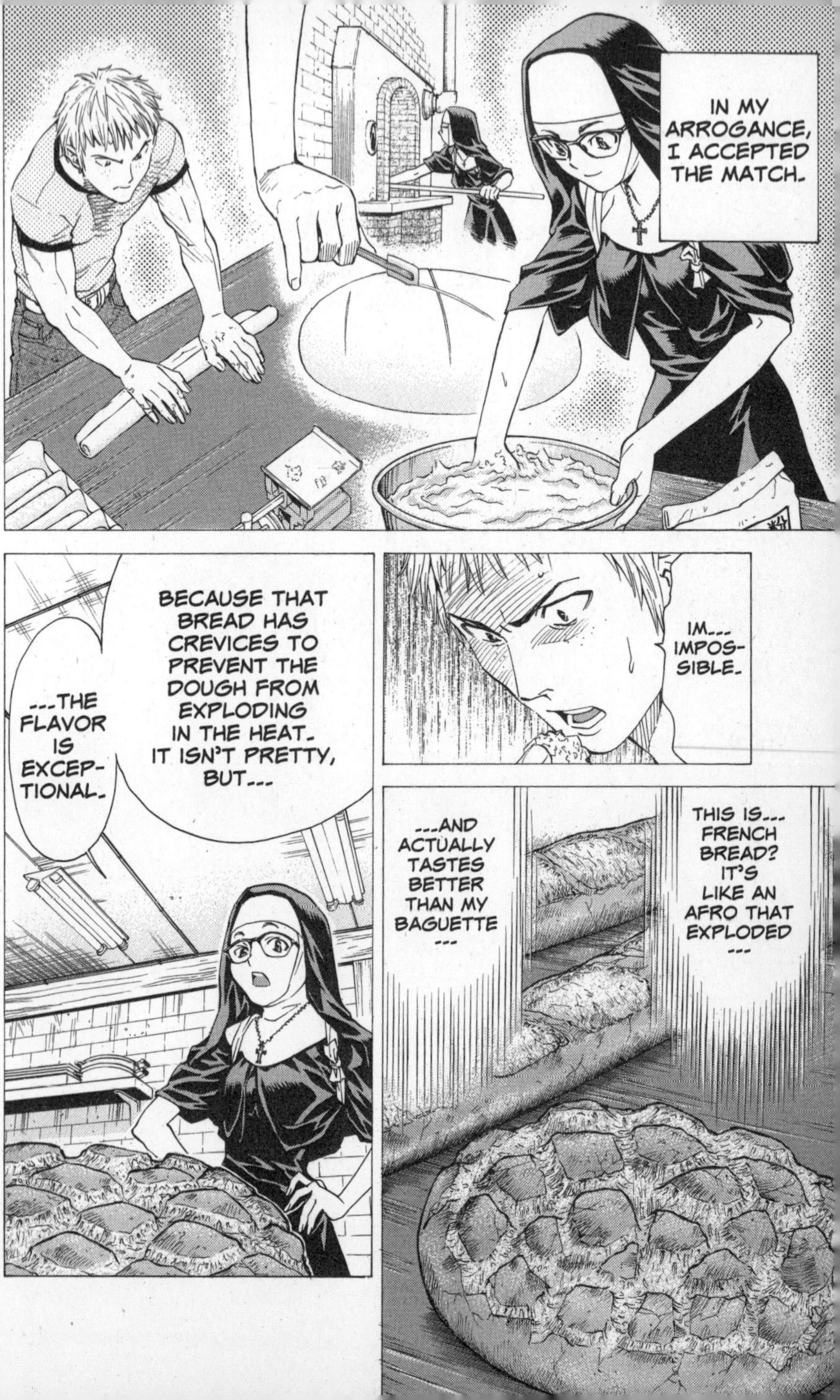
IN MY ARROGANCE, I ACCEPTED THE MATCH.
IM... IMPOSSIBLE.
THIS IS... FRENCH BREAD? IT'S LIKE AN AFRO THAT EXPLODED...
...AND ACTUALLY TASTES BETTER THAN MY BAGUETTE...
BECAUSE THAT BREAD HAS CREVICES TO PREVENT THE DOUGH FROM EXPLODING IN THE HEAT. IT ISN'T PRETTY, BUT...
...THE FLAVOR IS EXCEPTIONAL.

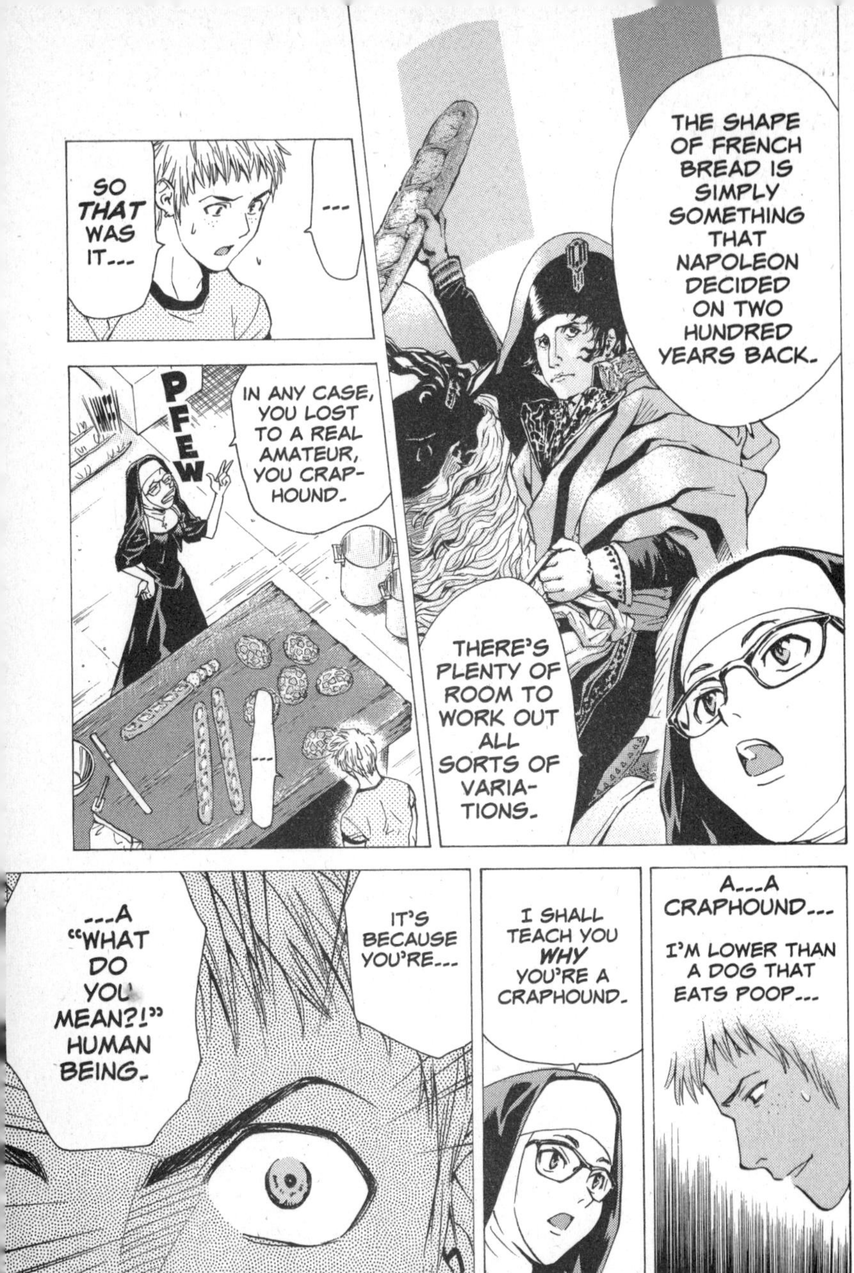
THE SHAPE OF FRENCH BREAD IS SIMPLY SOMETHING THAT NAPOLEON DECIDED ON TWO HUNDRED YEARS BACK.
THERE'S PLENTY OF ROOM TO WORK OUT ALL SORTS OF VARIATIONS.
...
SO THAT WAS IT...
PFEW
IN ANY CASE, YOU LOST TO A REAL AMATEUR, YOU CRAP-HOUND.
...
A...A CRAPHOUND...
I'M LOWER THAN A DOG THAT EATS POOP...
I SHALL TEACH YOU WHY YOU'RE A CRAPHOUND.
IT'S BECAUSE YOU'RE...
...A "WHAT DO YOU MEAN?!" HUMAN BEING.

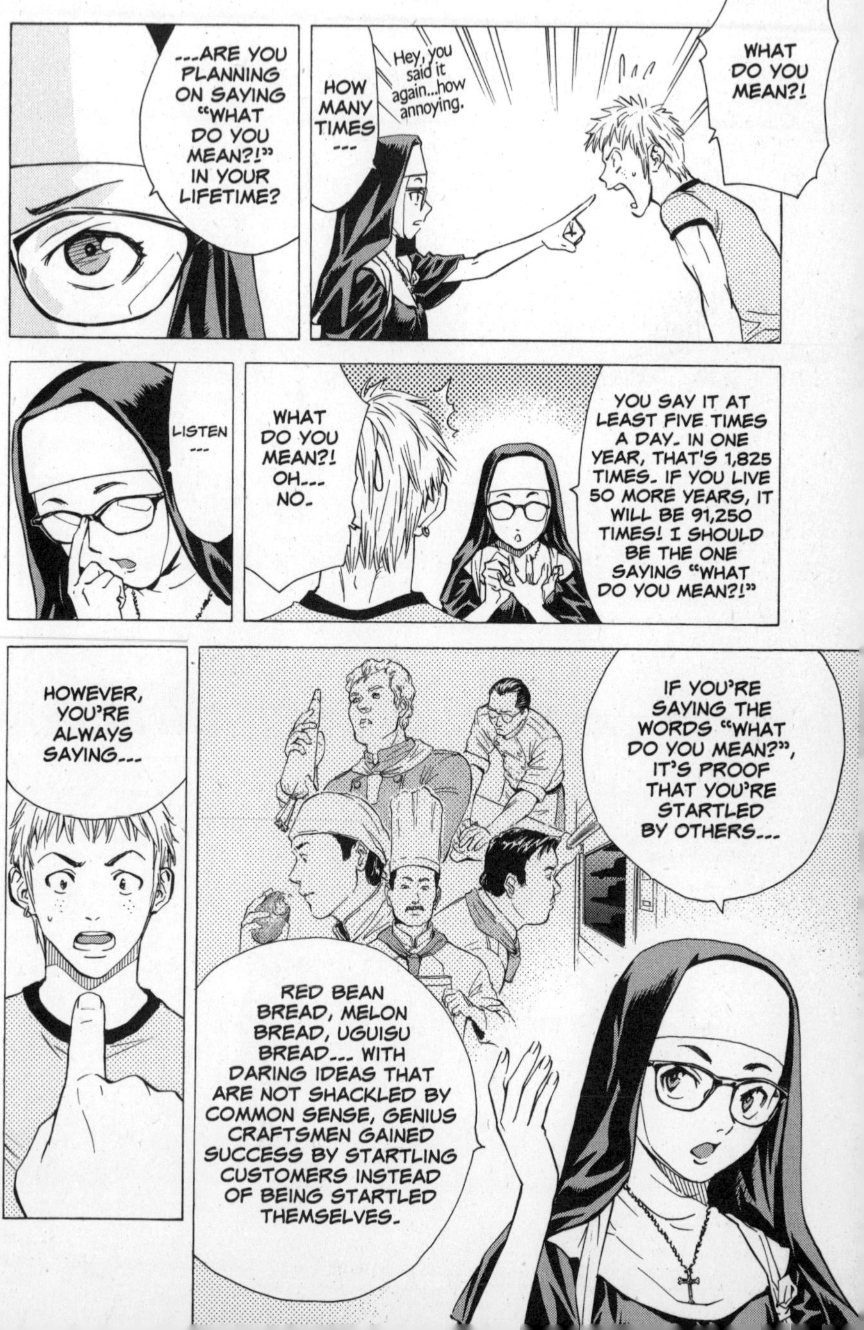
WHAT DO YOU MEAN?!
Hey, you said it again...how annoying.
HOW MANY TIMES ---
---ARE YOU PLANNING ON SAYING "WHAT DO YOU MEAN?!" IN YOUR LIFETIME?
YOU SAY IT AT LEAST FIVE TIMES A DAY. IN ONE YEAR, THAT'S 1,825 TIMES. IF YOU LIVE 50 MORE YEARS, IT WILL BE 91,250 TIMES! I SHOULD BE THE ONE SAYING "WHAT DO YOU MEAN?!"
WHAT DO YOU MEAN?! OH--- NO.
LISTEN ---
IF YOU'RE SAYING THE WORDS "WHAT DO YOU MEAN?", IT'S PROOF THAT YOU'RE STARTLED BY OTHERS---
RED BEAN BREAD, MELON BREAD, UGUISU BREAD--- WITH DARING IDEAS THAT ARE NOT SHACKLED BY COMMON SENSE, GENIUS CRAFTSMEN GAINED SUCCESS BY STARTLING CUSTOMERS INSTEAD OF BEING STARTLED THEMSELVES.
HOWEVER, YOU'RE ALWAYS SAYING---

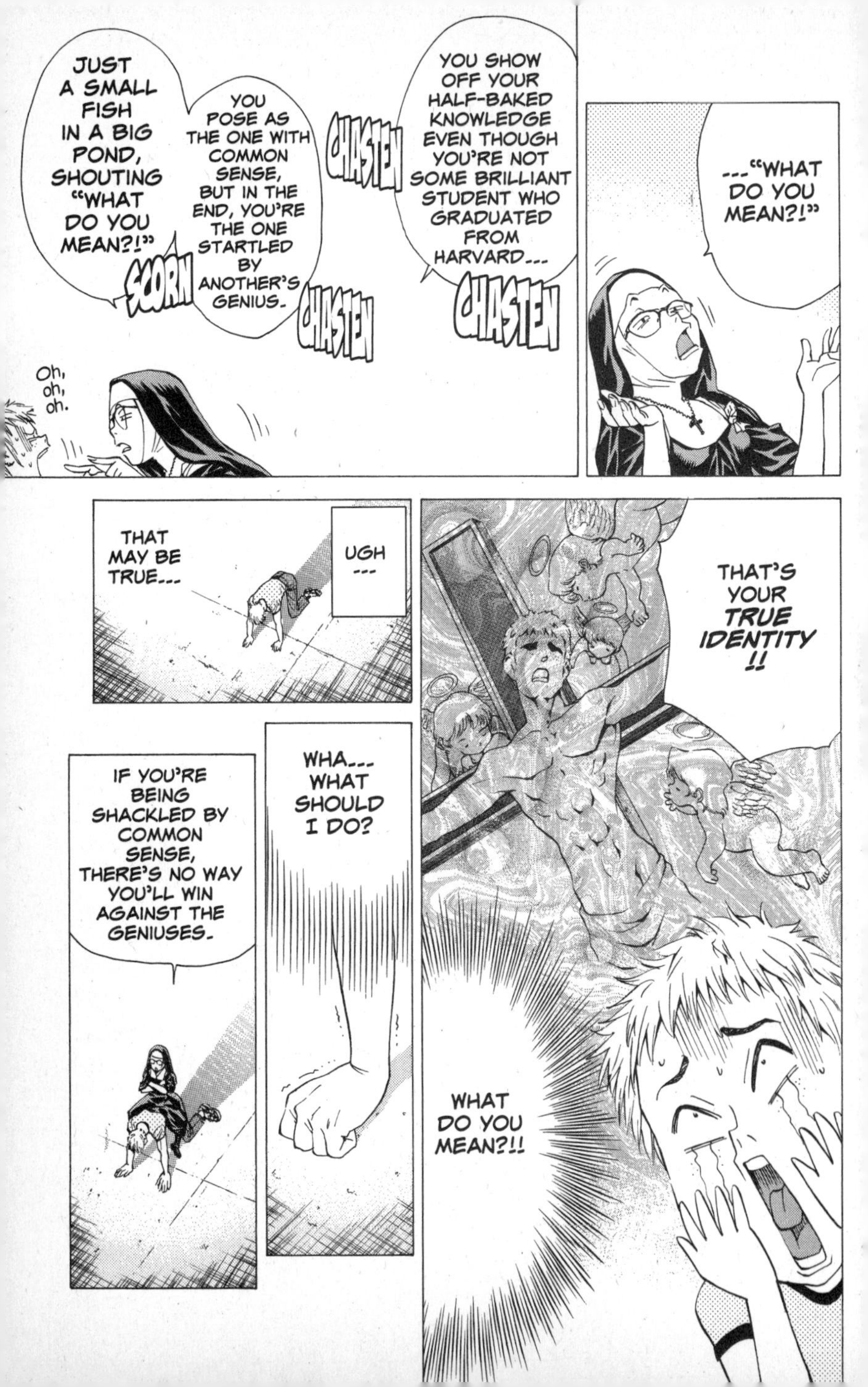
---"WHAT DO YOU MEAN?!"
YOU SHOW OFF YOUR HALF-BAKED KNOWLEDGE EVEN THOUGH YOU'RE NOT SOME BRILLIANT STUDENT WHO GRADUATED FROM HARVARD---
CHASTEN
CHASTEN
YOU POSE AS THE ONE WITH COMMON SENSE, BUT IN THE END, YOU'RE THE ONE STARTLED BY ANOTHER'S GENIUS.
CHASTEN
JUST A SMALL FISH IN A BIG POND, SHOUTING "WHAT DO YOU MEAN?!"
SCORN
Oh, oh, oh.
THAT'S YOUR TRUE IDENTITY!!
WHAT DO YOU MEAN?!!
UGH---
THAT MAY BE TRUE---
WHA--- WHAT SHOULD I DO?
IF YOU'RE BEING SHACKLED BY COMMON SENSE, THERE'S NO WAY YOU'LL WIN AGAINST THE GENIUSES.

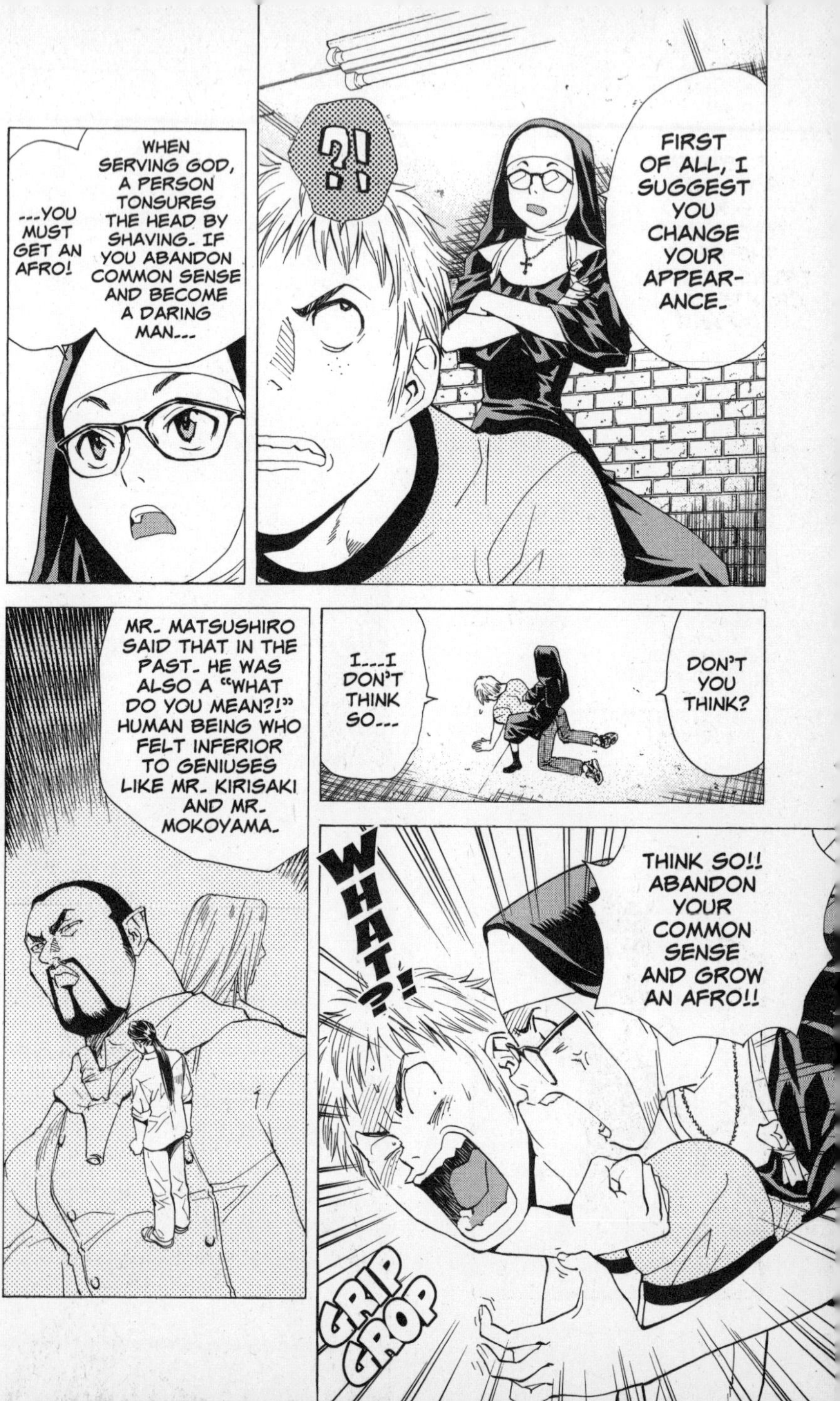
FIRST OF ALL, I SUGGEST YOU CHANGE YOUR APPEAR-ANCE.
?!
WHEN SERVING GOD, A PERSON TONSURES THE HEAD BY SHAVING. IF YOU ABANDON COMMON SENSE AND BECOME A DARING MAN...
...YOU MUST GET AN AFRO!
DON'T YOU THINK?
I...I DON'T THINK SO...
THINK SO!! ABANDON YOUR COMMON SENSE AND GROW AN AFRO!!
WHAT?!
GRIP GROP
MR. MATSUSHIRO SAID THAT IN THE PAST. HE WAS ALSO A "WHAT DO YOU MEAN?!" HUMAN BEING WHO FELT INFERIOR TO GENIUSES LIKE MR. KIRISAKI AND MR. MOKOYAMA.

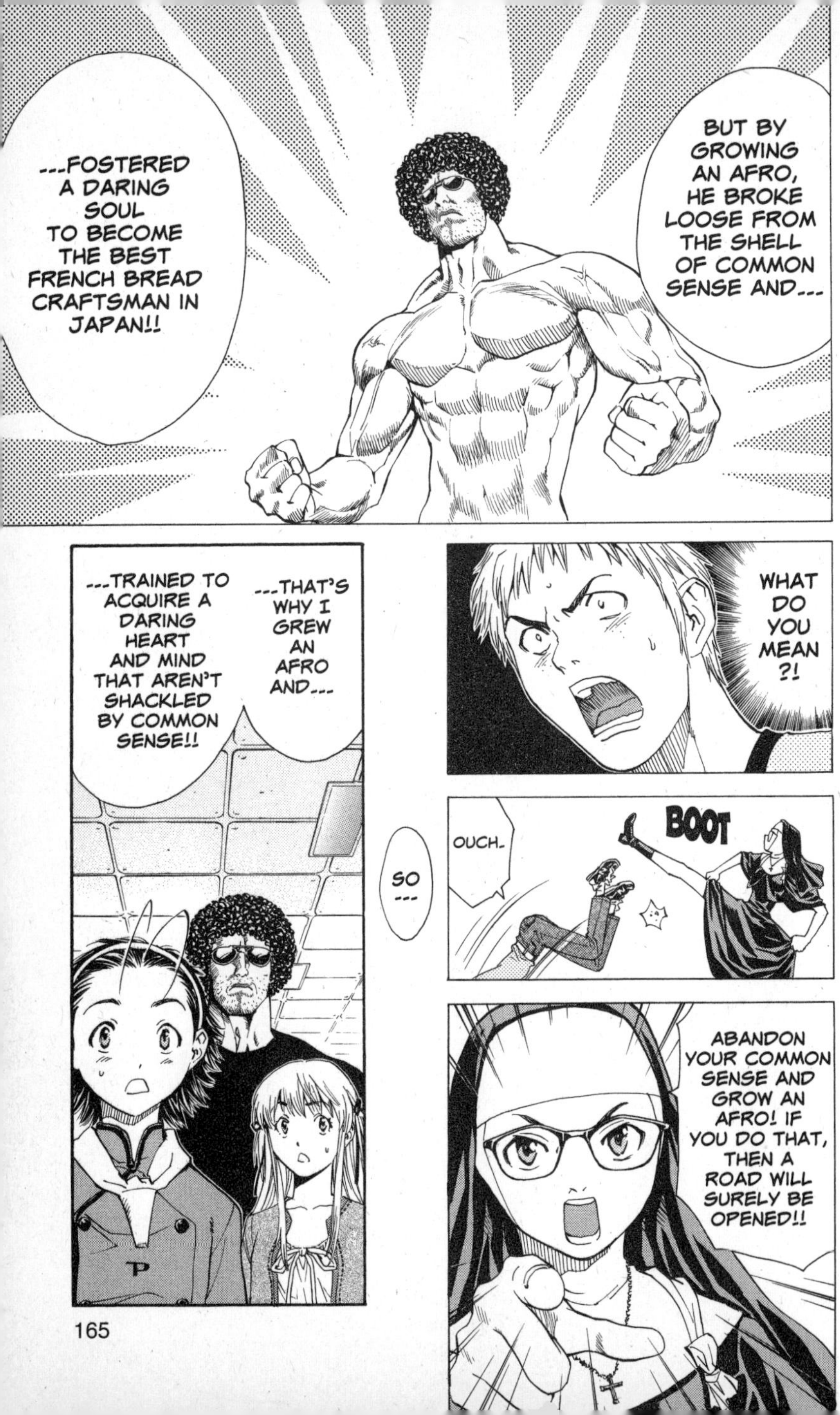
BUT BY GROWING AN AFRO, HE BROKE LOOSE FROM THE SHELL OF COMMON SENSE AND---
---FOSTERED A DARING SOUL TO BECOME THE BEST FRENCH BREAD CRAFTSMAN IN JAPAN!!
WHAT DO YOU MEAN?!
BOOT
OUCH.
SO---
ABANDON YOUR COMMON SENSE AND GROW AN AFRO! IF YOU DO THAT, THEN A ROAD WILL SURELY BE OPENED!!
---THAT'S WHY I GREW AN AFRO AND---
---TRAINED TO ACQUIRE A DARING HEART AND MIND THAT AREN'T SHACKLED BY COMMON SENSE!!

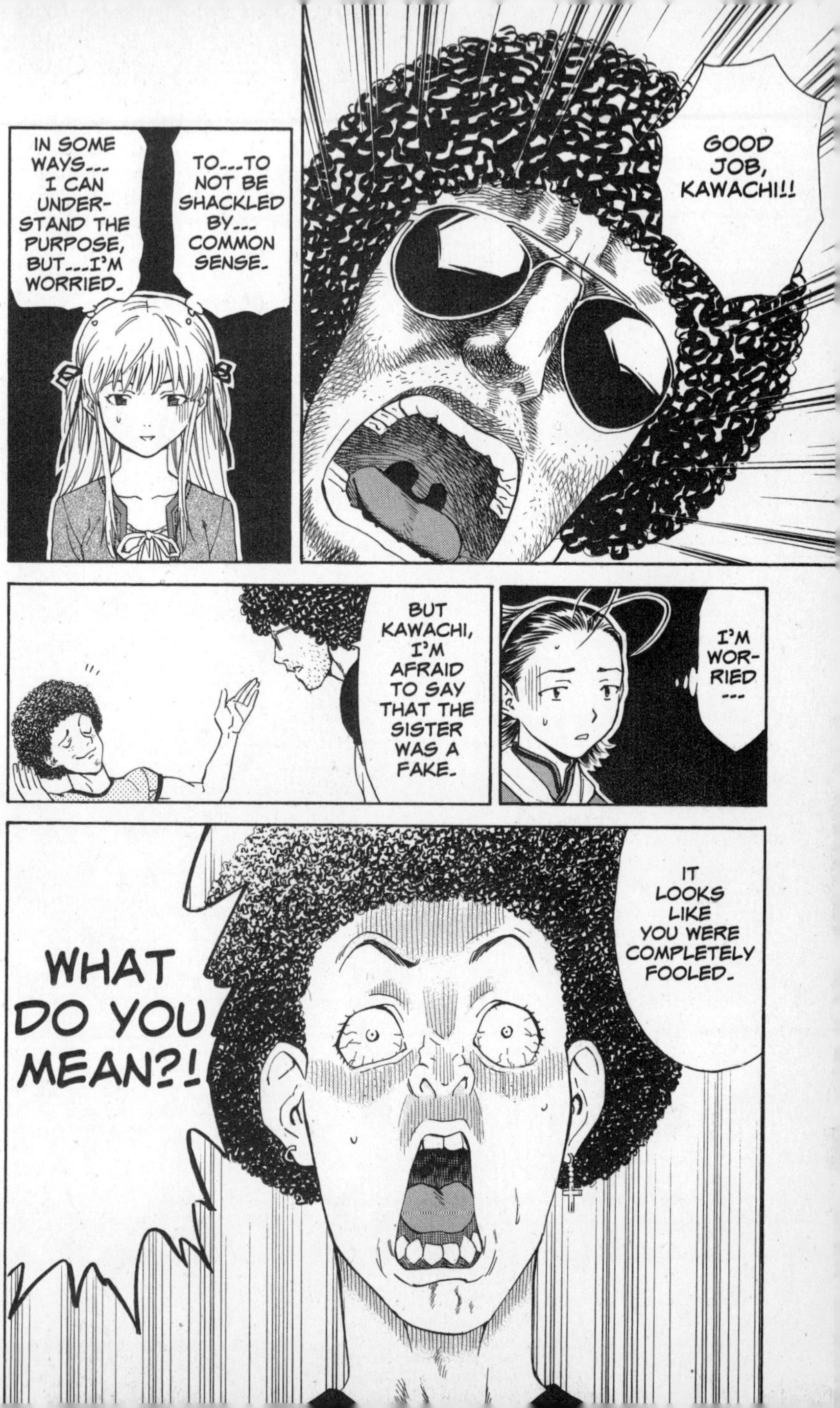
GOOD JOB, KAWACHI!!
TO...TO NOT BE SHACKLED BY... COMMON SENSE.
IN SOME WAYS... I CAN UNDER-STAND THE PURPOSE, BUT...I'M WORRIED.
I'M WOR-RIED...
BUT KAWACHI, I'M AFRAID TO SAY THAT THE SISTER WAS A FAKE.
IT LOOKS LIKE YOU WERE COMPLETELY FOOLED.
WHAT DO YOU MEAN?!

Story 50: No Good.

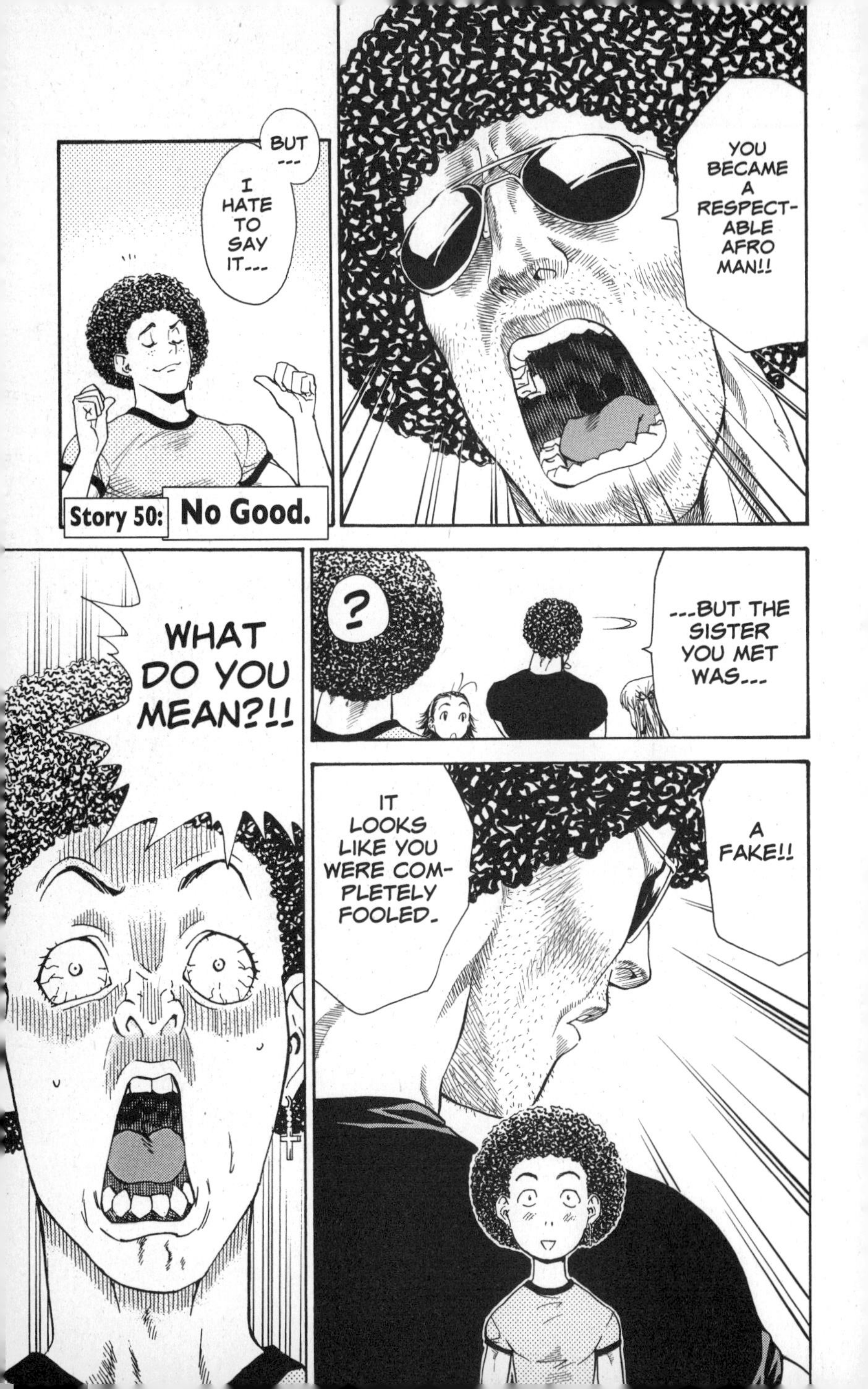
YOU BECAME A RESPECTABLE AFRO MAN!!
BUT ---
I HATE TO SAY IT---
---BUT THE SISTER YOU MET WAS---
?
A FAKE!!
IT LOOKS LIKE YOU WERE COMPLETELY FOOLED.
WHAT DO YOU MEAN?!!

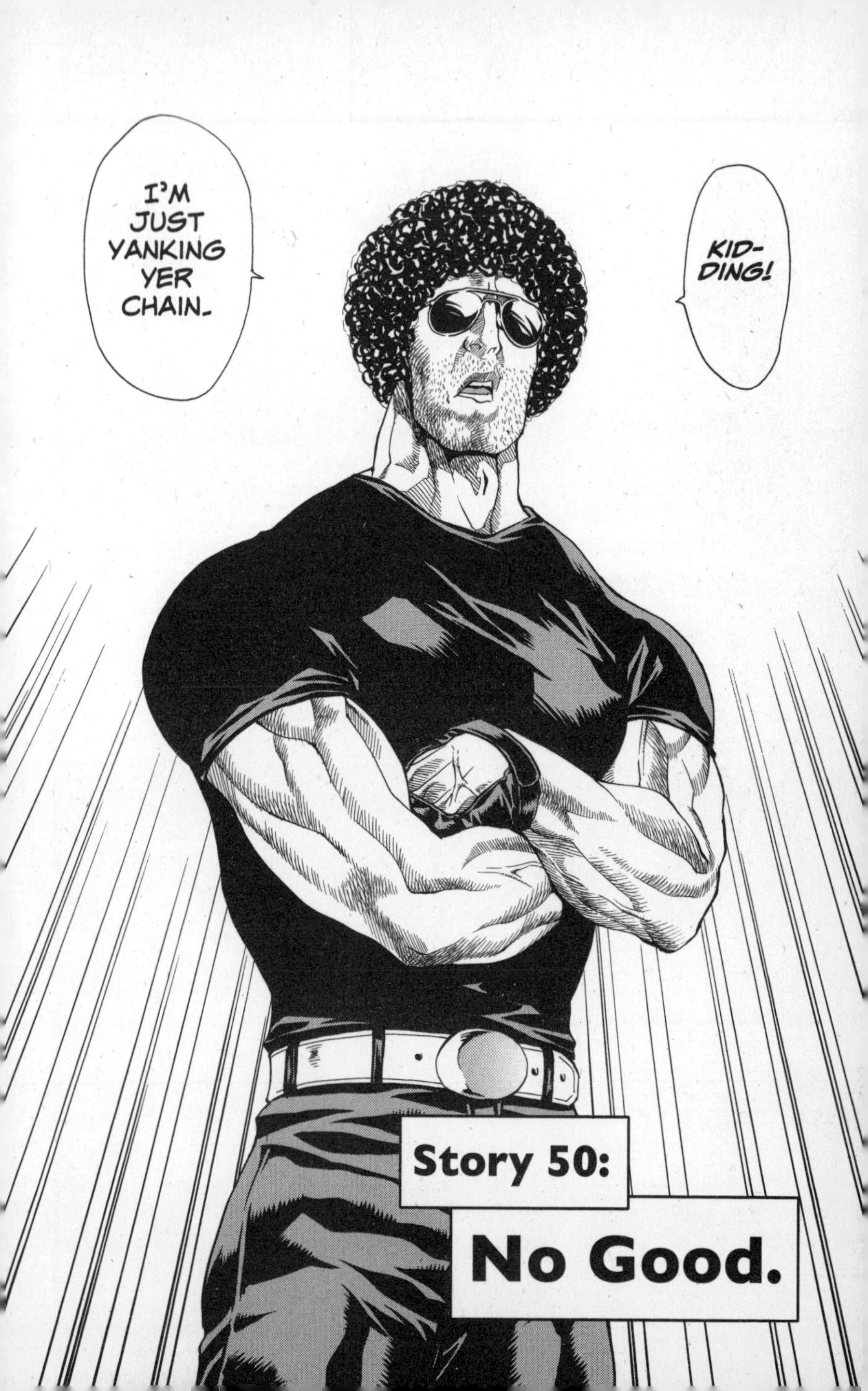
KID-DING!
I'M JUST YANKING YER CHAIN.
Story 50:
No Good.

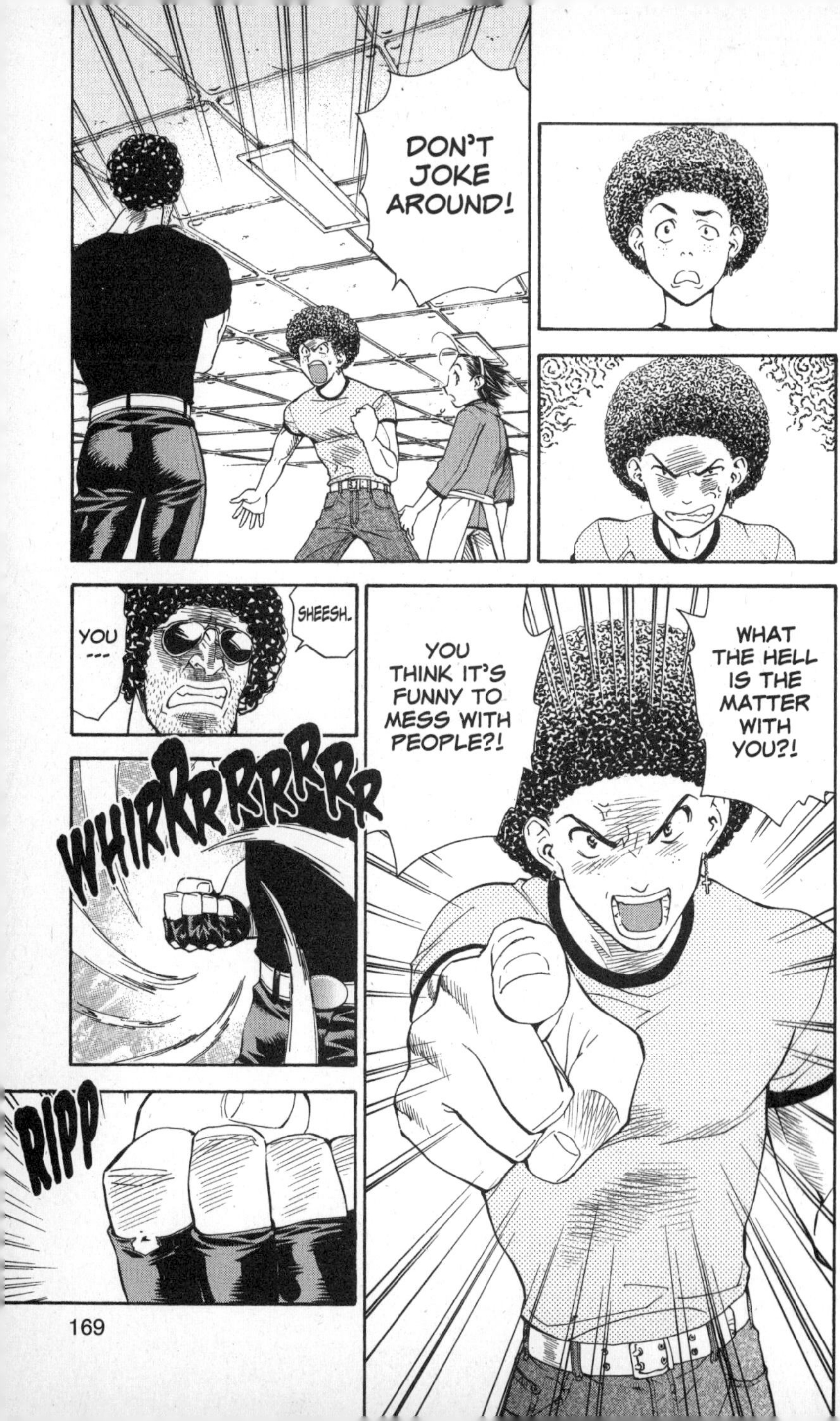
DON'T JOKE AROUND!
WHAT THE HELL IS THE MATTER WITH YOU?!
YOU THINK IT'S FUNNY TO MESS WITH PEOPLE?!
SHEESH.
YOU ---
WHIRRRRRRRR
RIPP

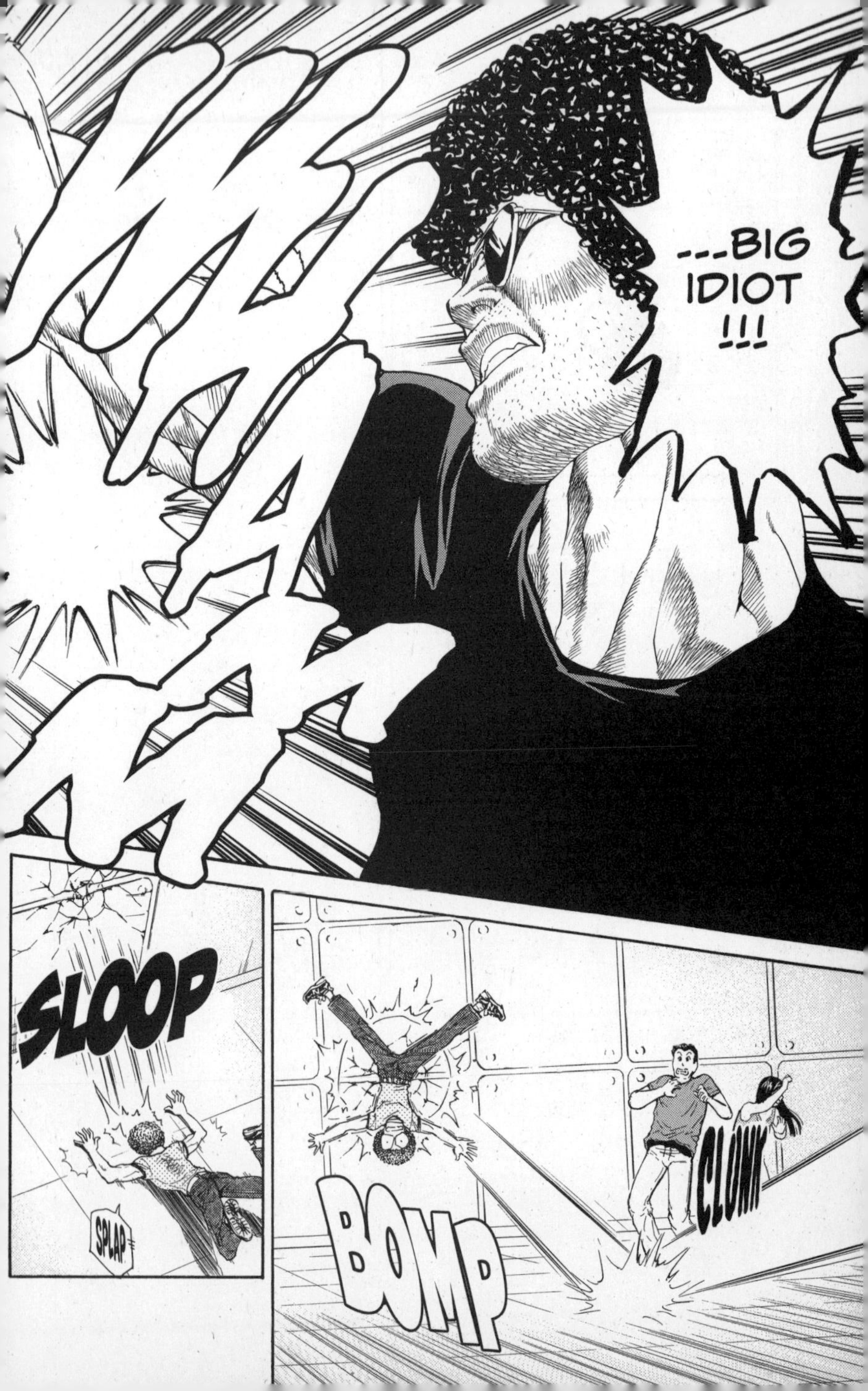
---BIG IDIOT!!!
CLUNK
BOMP
SLOOP
SPLAP

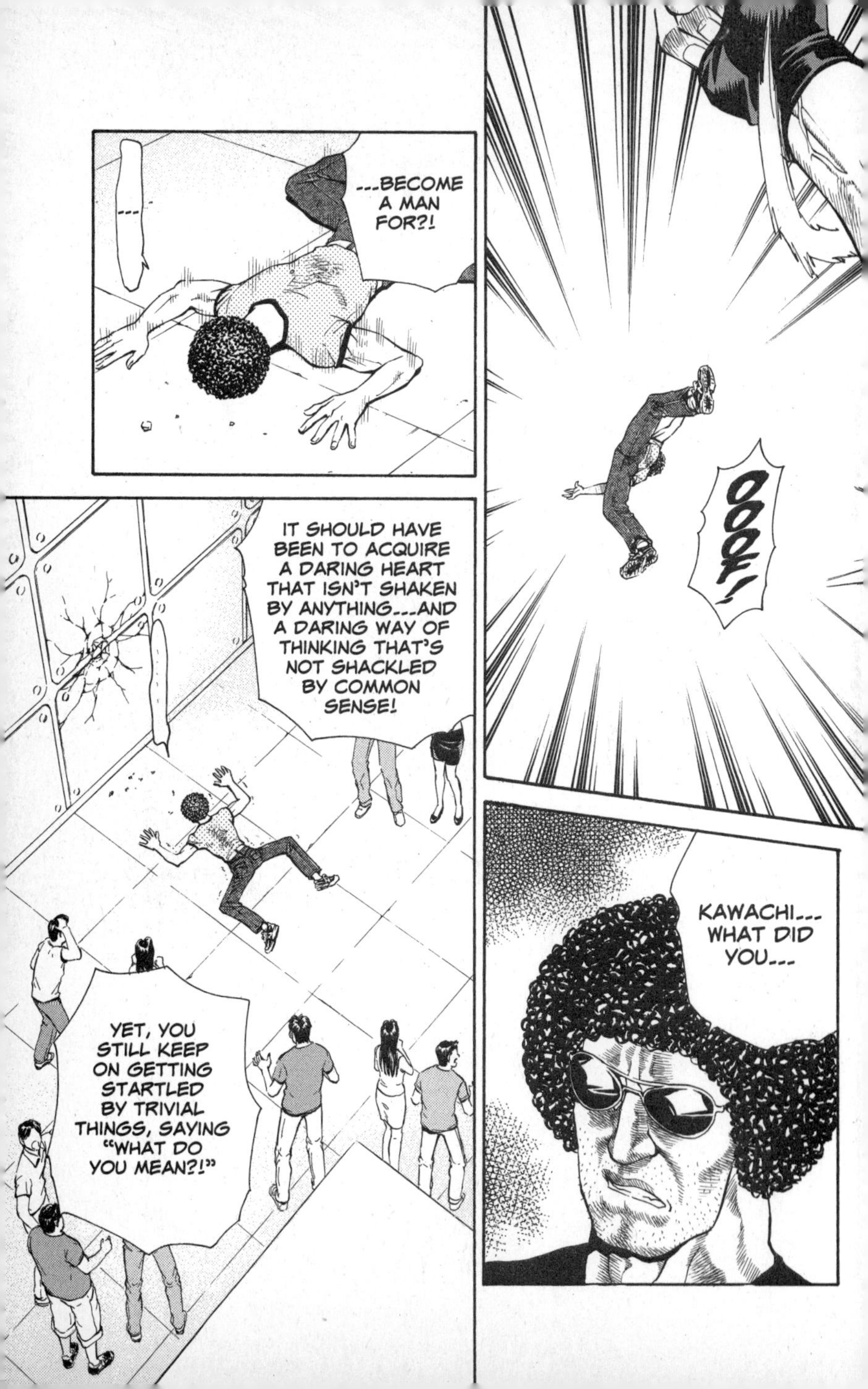
OOOF!
KAWACHI... WHAT DID YOU...
...BECOME A MAN FOR?!
...
IT SHOULD HAVE BEEN TO ACQUIRE A DARING HEART THAT ISN'T SHAKEN BY ANYTHING...AND A DARING WAY OF THINKING THAT'S NOT SHACKLED BY COMMON SENSE!
YET, YOU STILL KEEP ON GETTING STARTLED BY TRIVIAL THINGS, SAYING "WHAT DO YOU MEAN?!"

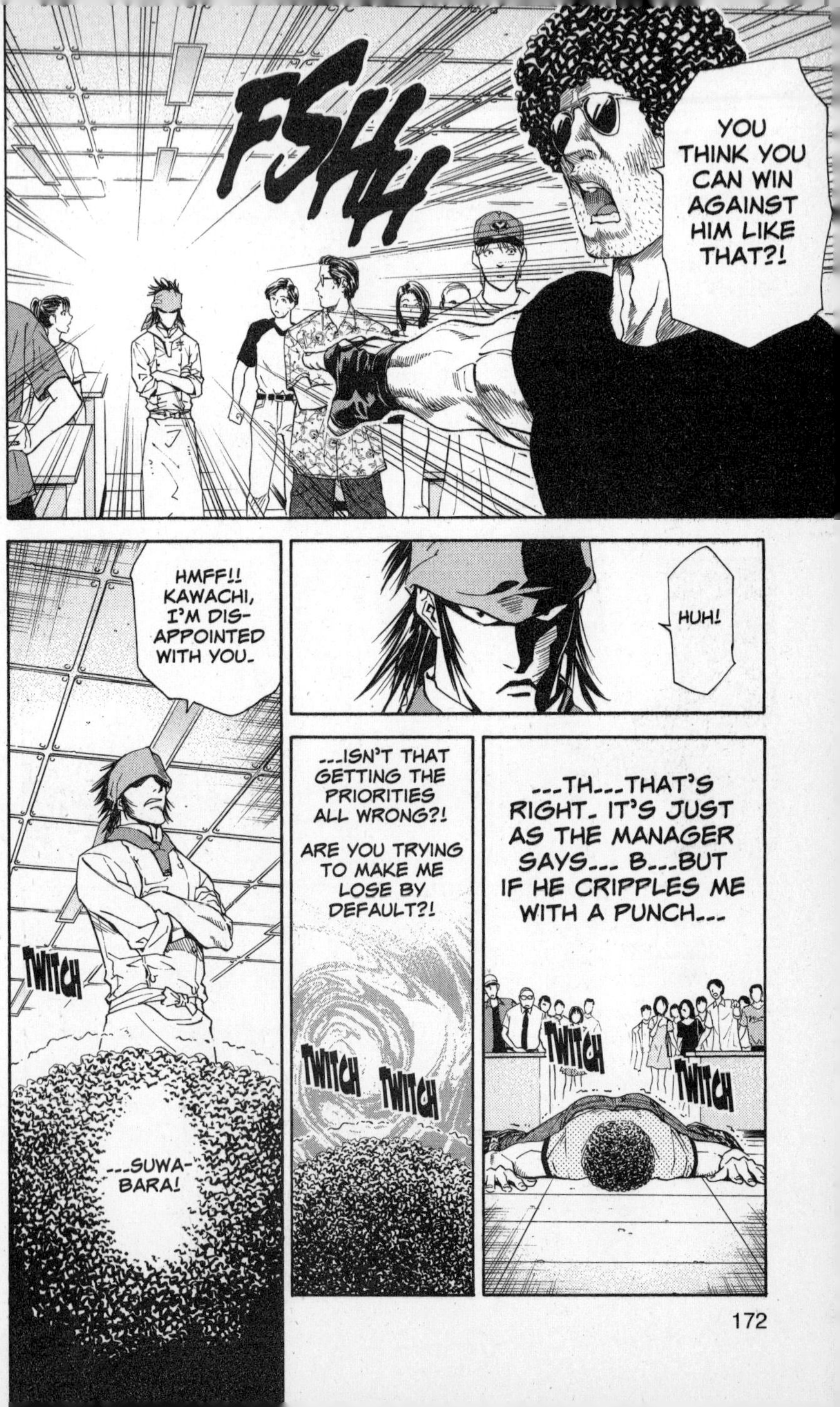
FSHH
YOU THINK YOU CAN WIN AGAINST HIM LIKE THAT?!
HUH!
...TH...THAT'S RIGHT. IT'S JUST AS THE MANAGER SAYS... B...BUT IF HE CRIPPLES ME WITH A PUNCH...
TWITCH
TWITCH
...ISN'T THAT GETTING THE PRIORITIES ALL WRONG?!
ARE YOU TRYING TO MAKE ME LOSE BY DEFAULT?!
TWITCH
TWITCH
HMFF!! KAWACHI, I'M DIS-APPOINTED WITH YOU.
TWITCH
...SUWA-BARA!

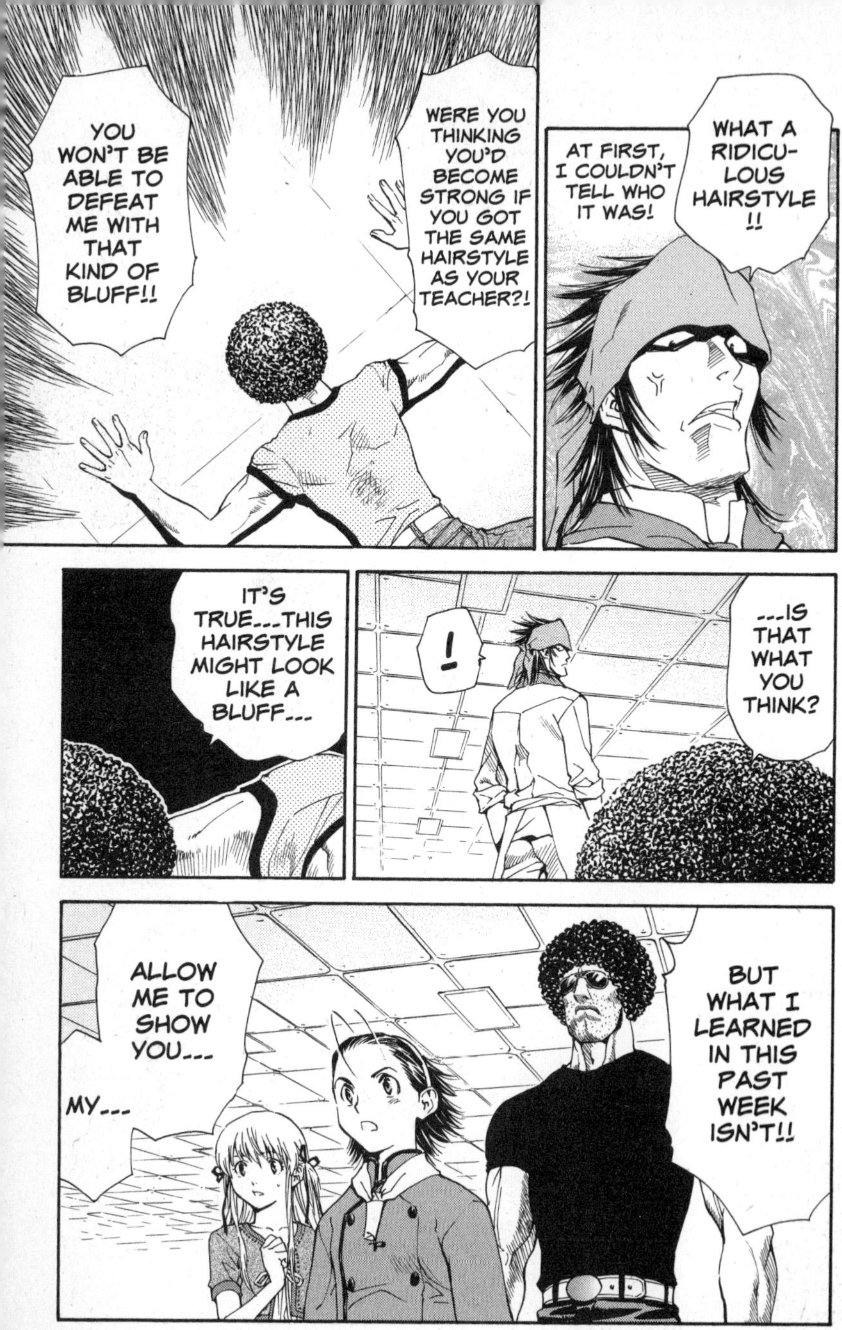
WHAT A RIDICU-LOUS HAIRSTYLE!!
AT FIRST, I COULDN'T TELL WHO IT WAS!
WERE YOU THINKING YOU'D BECOME STRONG IF YOU GOT THE SAME HAIRSTYLE AS YOUR TEACHER?!
YOU WON'T BE ABLE TO DEFEAT ME WITH THAT KIND OF BLUFF!!
...IS THAT WHAT YOU THINK?
!
IT'S TRUE...THIS HAIRSTYLE MIGHT LOOK LIKE A BLUFF...
BUT WHAT I LEARNED IN THIS PAST WEEK ISN'T!!
ALLOW ME TO SHOW YOU...
MY...

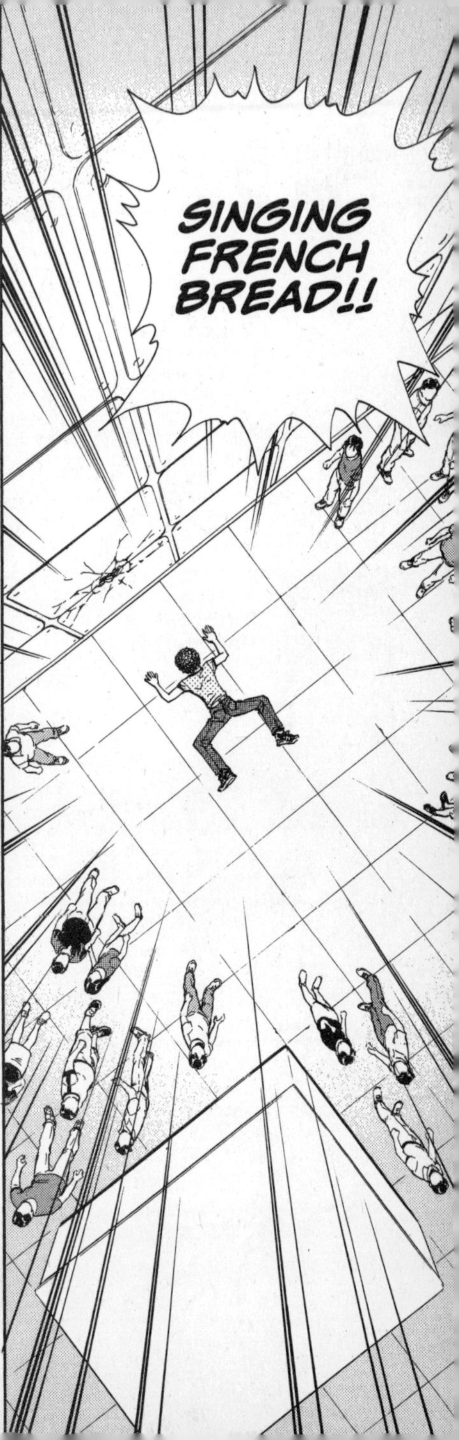
SINGING FRENCH BREAD!!

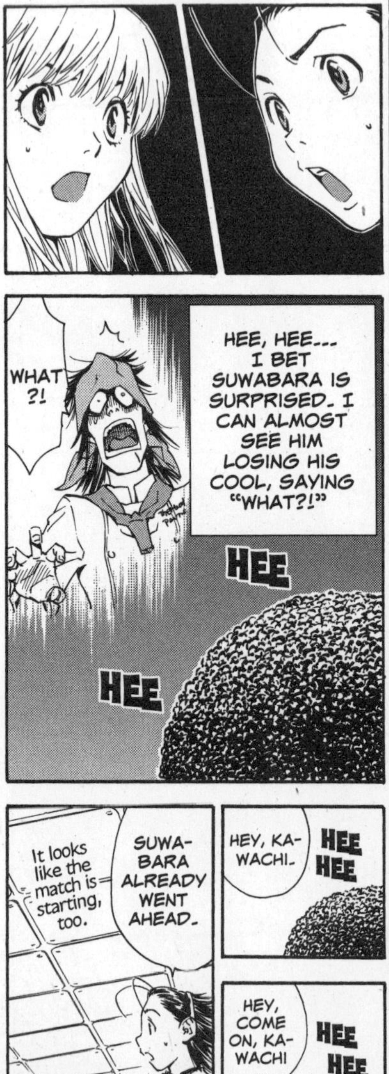
HEE, HEE... I BET SUWABARA IS SURPRISED. I CAN ALMOST SEE HIM LOSING HIS COOL, SAYING "WHAT?!"
WHAT ?!
HEE
HEE
HEY, KA-WACHI.
HEE HEE
HEY, COME ON, KA-WACHI...
HEE HEE
SUWA-BARA ALREADY WENT AHEAD.
It looks like the match is starting, too.

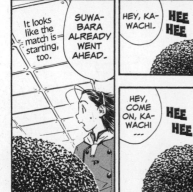

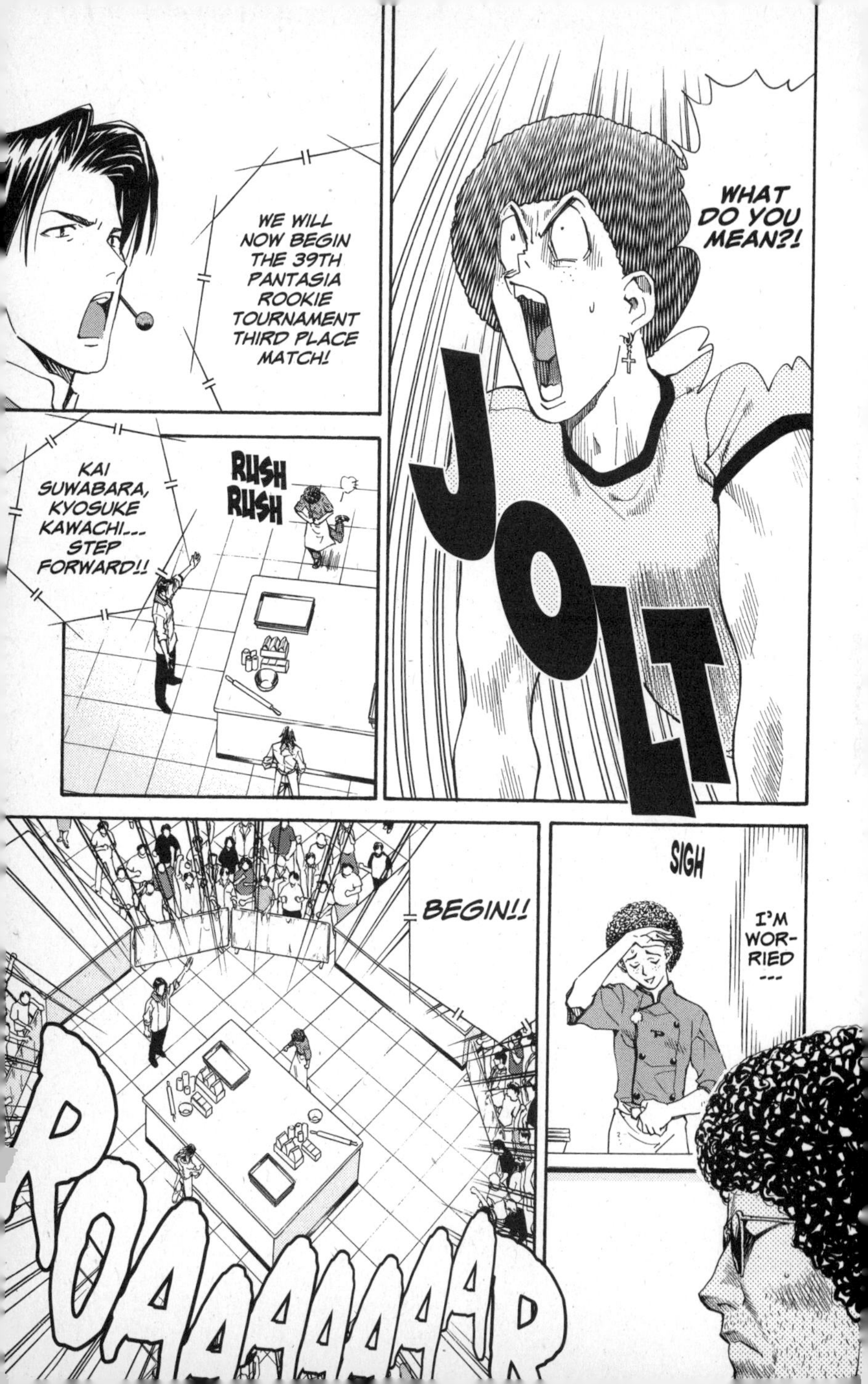
WHAT DO YOU MEAN?!
JOLT
WE WILL NOW BEGIN THE 39TH PANTASIA ROOKIE TOURNAMENT THIRD PLACE MATCH!
RUSH RUSH
KAI SUWABARA, KYOSUKE KAWACHI... STEP FORWARD!!
SIGH
I'M WOR-RIED...
BEGIN!!
ROAAAAAAR

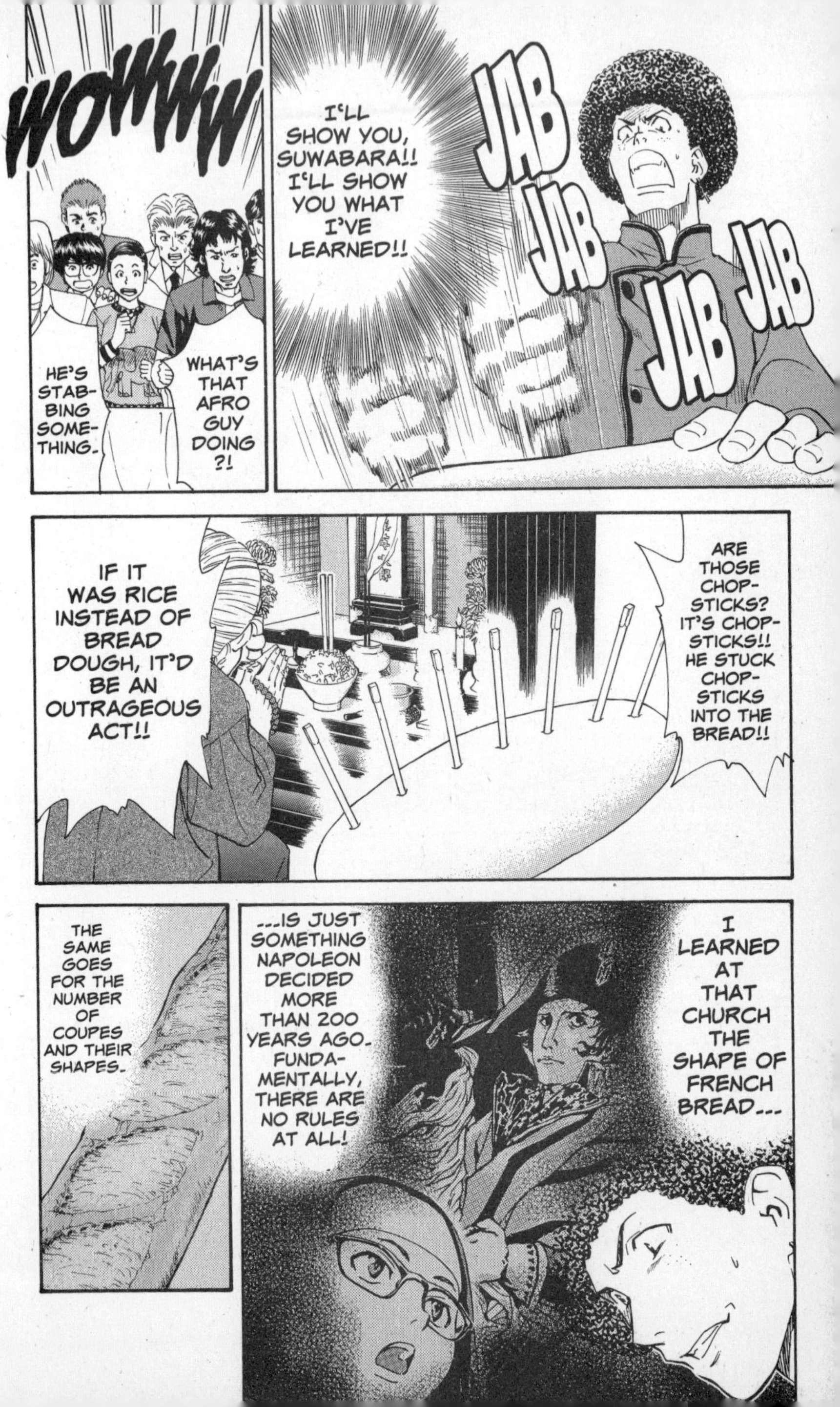
JAB
JAB
JAB JAB
JAB
I'LL SHOW YOU, SUWABARA!! I'LL SHOW YOU WHAT I'VE LEARNED!!
WOWWW
WHAT'S THAT AFRO GUY DOING?!
HE'S STAB-BING SOME-THING.
ARE THOSE CHOP-STICKS? IT'S CHOP-STICKS!! HE STUCK CHOP-STICKS INTO THE BREAD!!
IF IT WAS RICE INSTEAD OF BREAD DOUGH, IT'D BE AN OUTRAGEOUS ACT!!
I LEARNED AT THAT CHURCH THE SHAPE OF FRENCH BREAD...
...IS JUST SOMETHING NAPOLEON DECIDED MORE THAN 200 YEARS AGO. FUNDA-MENTALLY, THERE ARE NO RULES AT ALL!
THE SAME GOES FOR THE NUMBER OF COUPES AND THEIR SHAPES.

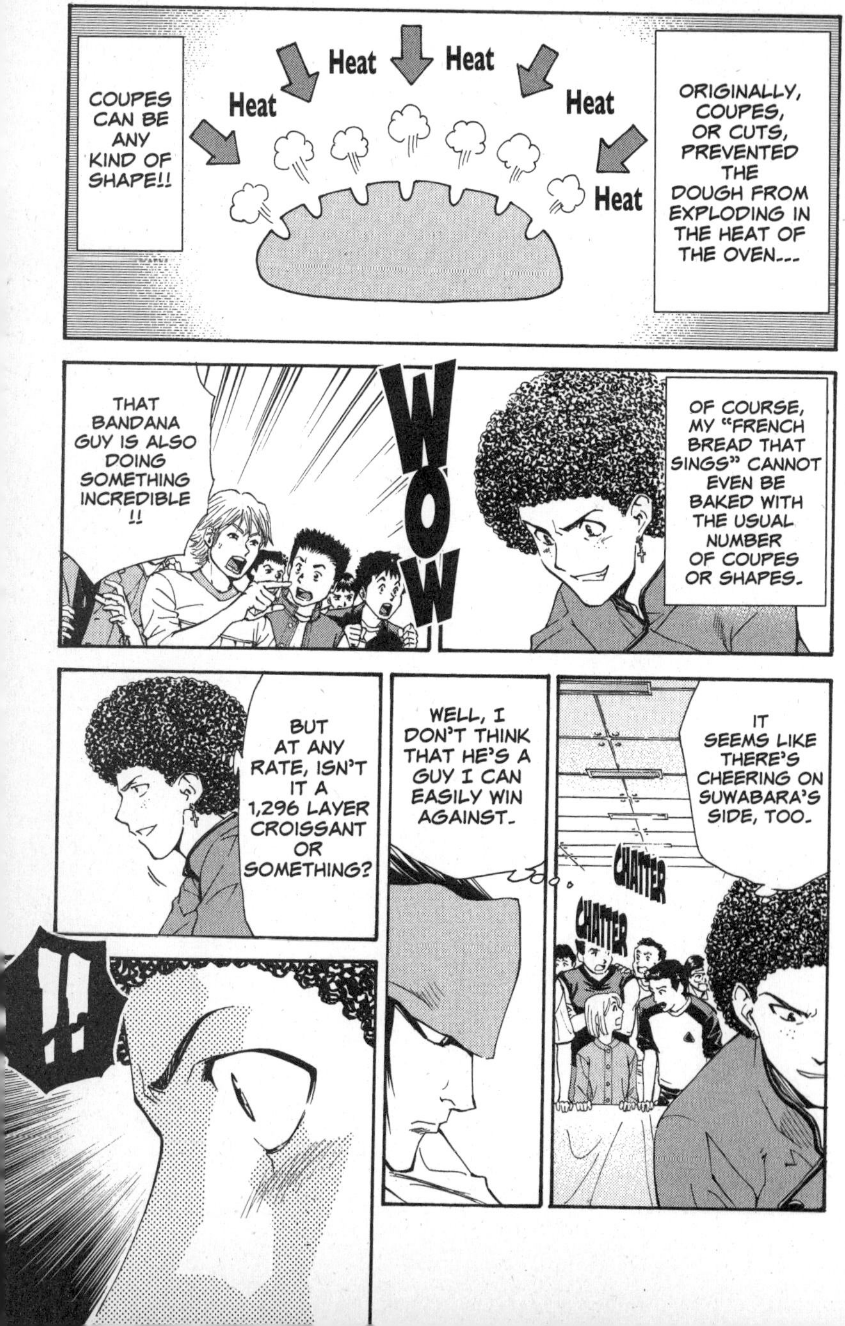
ORIGINALLY, COUPES, OR CUTS, PREVENTED THE DOUGH FROM EXPLODING IN THE HEAT OF THE OVEN...
Heat
Heat
Heat
Heat
Heat
Heat
COUPES CAN BE ANY KIND OF SHAPE!!
OF COURSE, MY "FRENCH BREAD THAT SINGS" CANNOT EVEN BE BAKED WITH THE USUAL NUMBER OF COUPES OR SHAPES.
WOW
THAT BANDANA GUY IS ALSO DOING SOMETHING INCREDIBLE!!
IT SEEMS LIKE THERE'S CHEERING ON SUWABARA'S SIDE, TOO.
CHATTER
CHATTER
WELL, I DON'T THINK THAT HE'S A GUY I CAN EASILY WIN AGAINST.
BUT AT ANY RATE, ISN'T IT A 1,296 LAYER CROISSANT OR SOMETHING?
!!

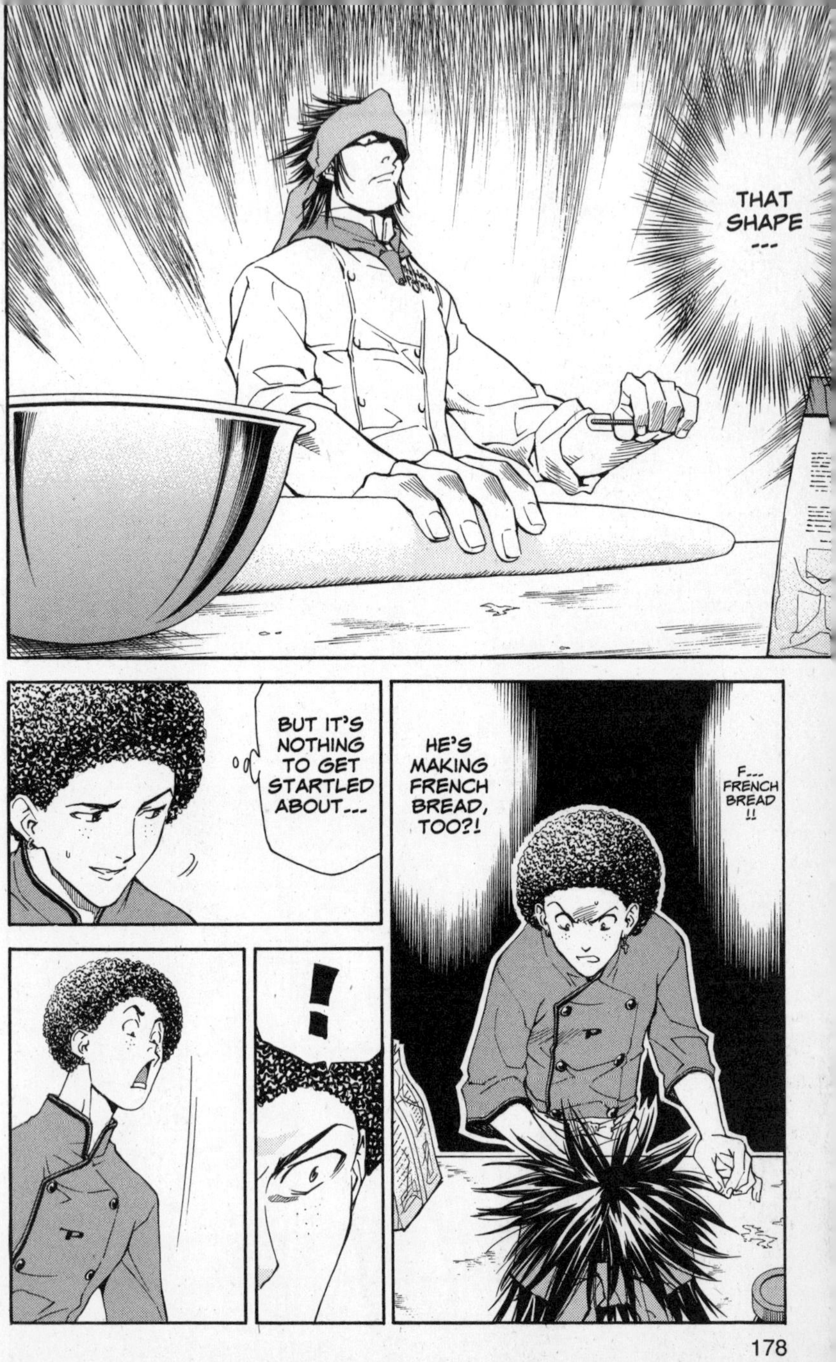
THAT SHAPE ---
F--- FRENCH BREAD !!
HE'S MAKING FRENCH BREAD, TOO?!
BUT IT'S NOTHING TO GET STARTLED ABOUT---
!

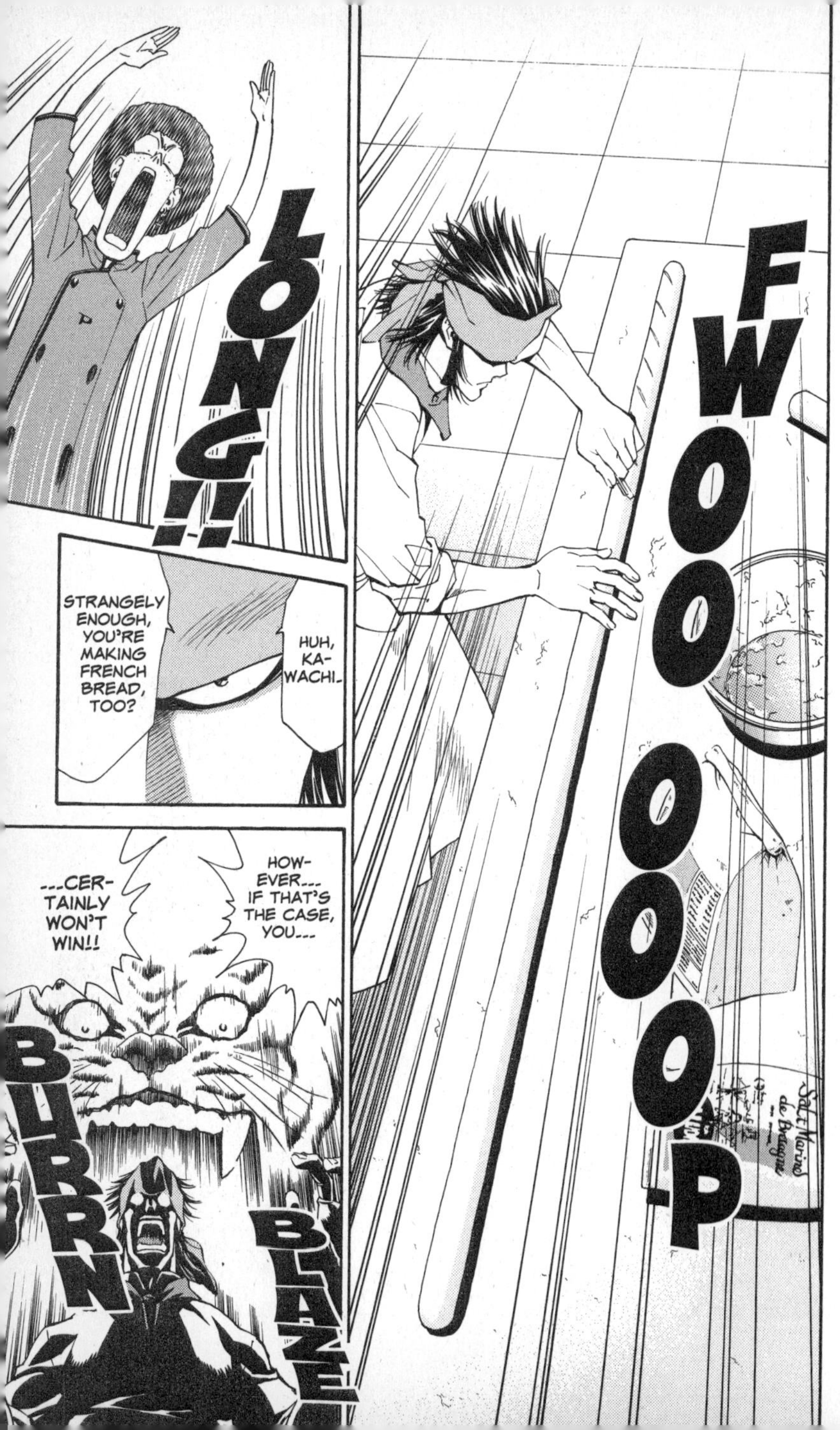
FWOOOOOP
LONG!!
HUH, KA-WACHI...
STRANGELY ENOUGH, YOU'RE MAKING FRENCH BREAD, TOO?
HOW-EVER... IF THAT'S THE CASE, YOU...
...CER-TAINLY WON'T WIN!!
BURN
BLAZE

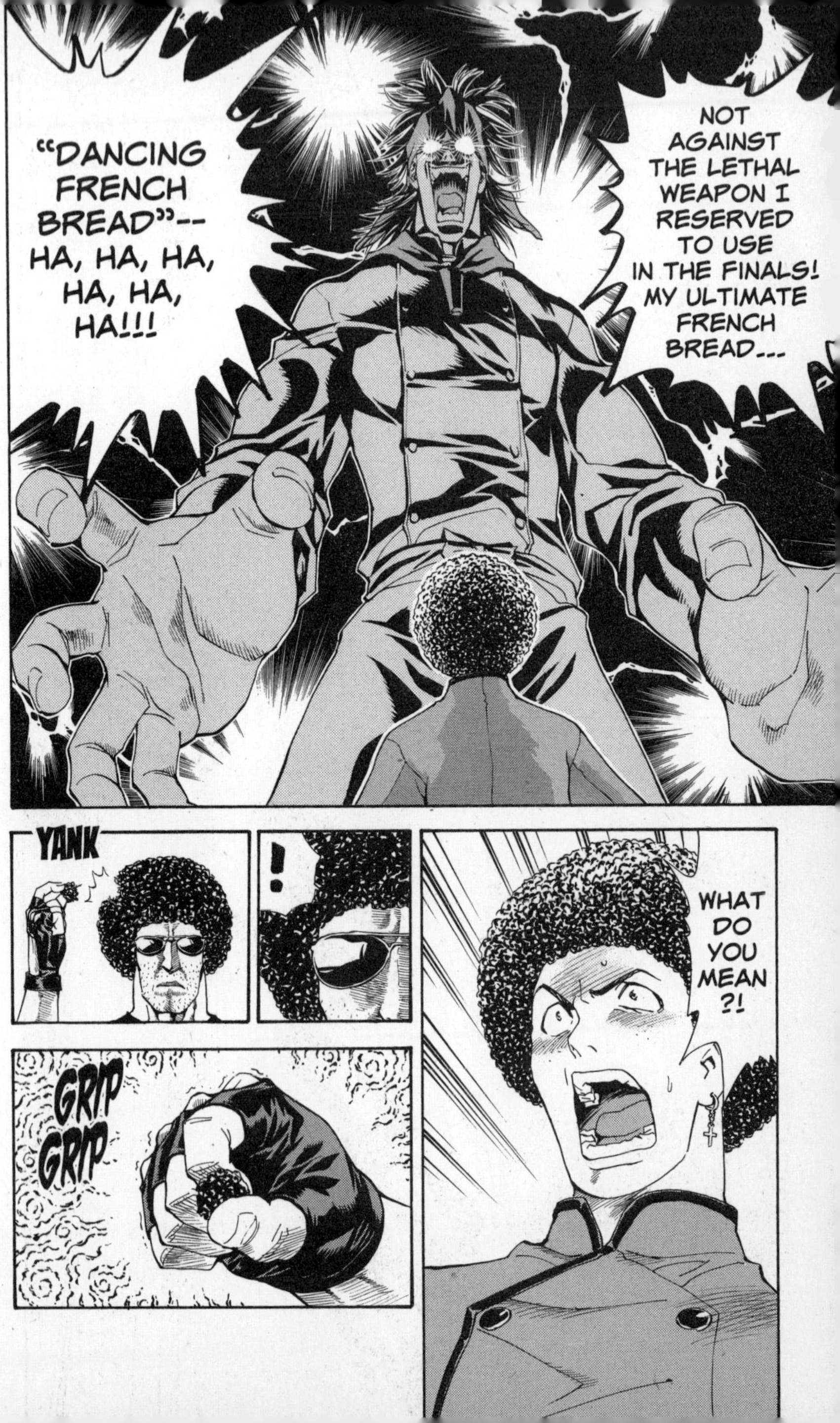
NOT AGAINST THE LETHAL WEAPON I RESERVED TO USE IN THE FINALS! MY ULTIMATE FRENCH BREAD...
"DANCING FRENCH BREAD"-- HA, HA, HA, HA, HA, HA!!!
WHAT DO YOU MEAN?!
!
YANK
GRIP GRIP

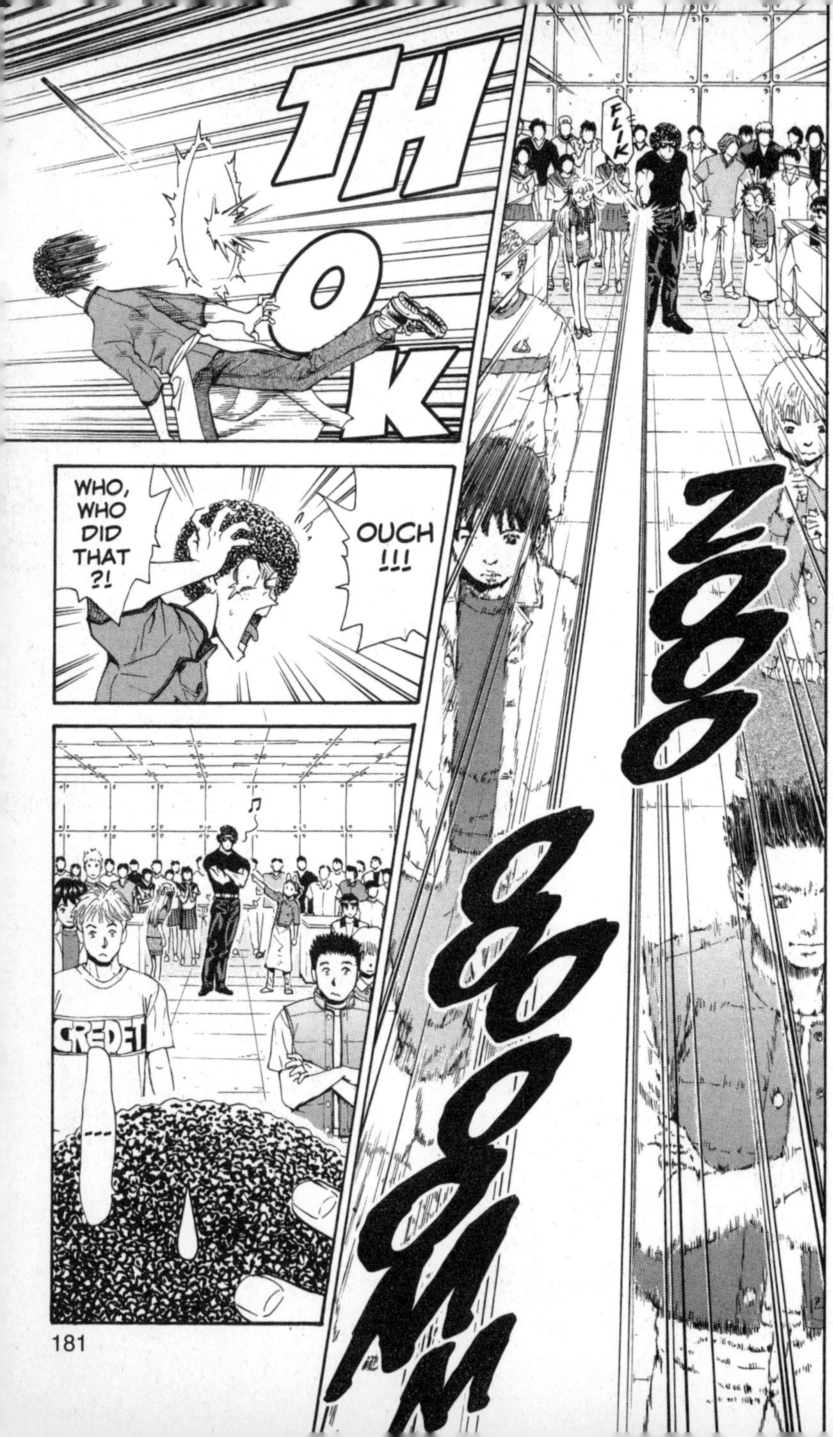
FLIK
ZOOOOOOOOOM
THOK
OUCH !!!
WHO, WHO DID THAT ?!
♪
...
CREDFI

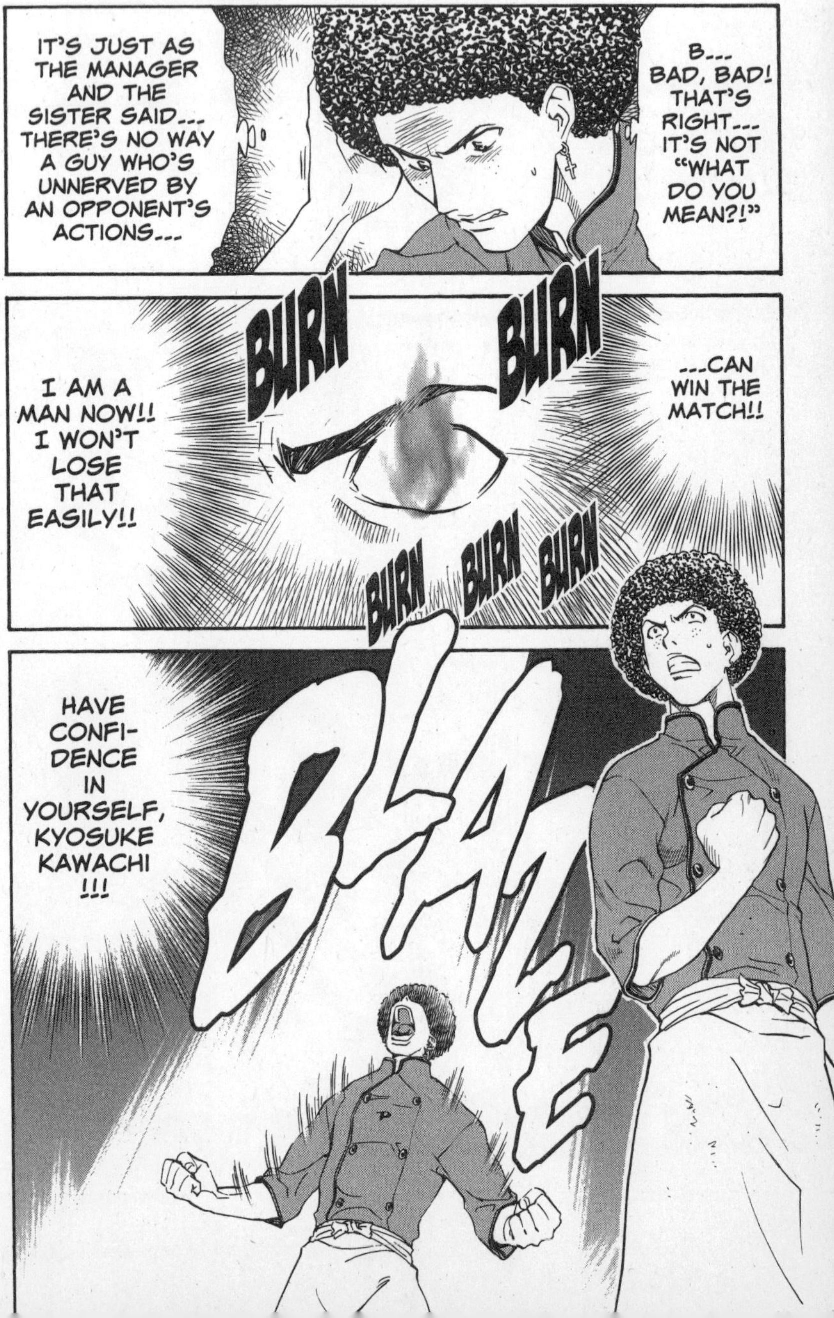
B... BAD, BAD! THAT'S RIGHT... IT'S NOT "WHAT DO YOU MEAN?!"
IT'S JUST AS THE MANAGER AND THE SISTER SAID... THERE'S NO WAY A GUY WHO'S UNNERVED BY AN OPPONENT'S ACTIONS...
BURN
BURN
...CAN WIN THE MATCH!!
I AM A MAN NOW!! I WON'T LOSE THAT EASILY!!
BURN
BURN
BURN
HAVE CONFI-DENCE IN YOURSELF, KYOSUKE KAWACHI !!!
BLAZE

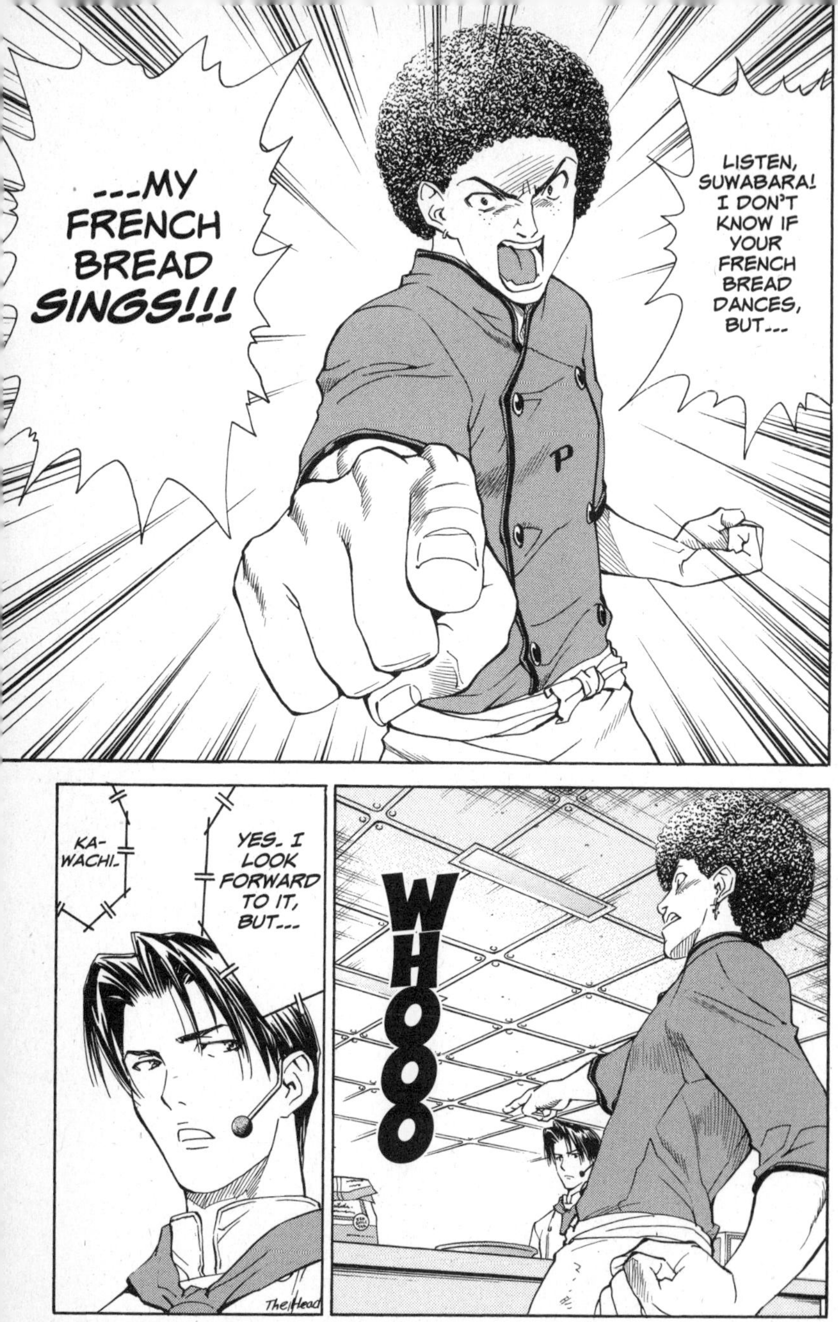
LISTEN, SUWABARA! I DON'T KNOW IF YOUR FRENCH BREAD DANCES, BUT...
...MY FRENCH BREAD SINGS!!!
WHOOO
YES. I LOOK FORWARD TO IT, BUT...
KA-WACHI.
The Head

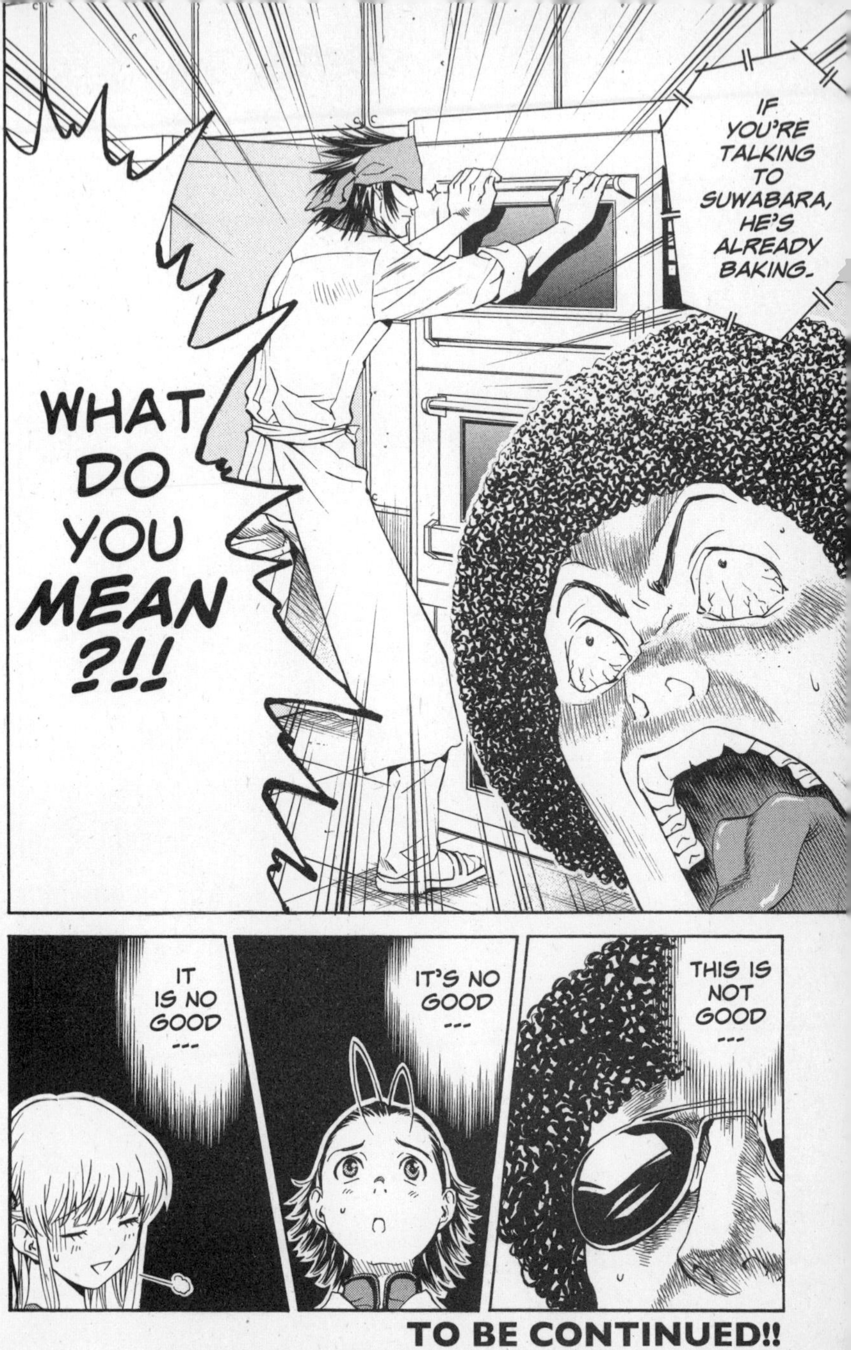
IF YOU'RE TALKING TO SUWABARA, HE'S ALREADY BAKING.
WHAT DO YOU MEAN?!!
THIS IS NOT GOOD ---
IT'S NO GOOD ---
IT IS NO GOOD ---

TO BE CONTINUED!!

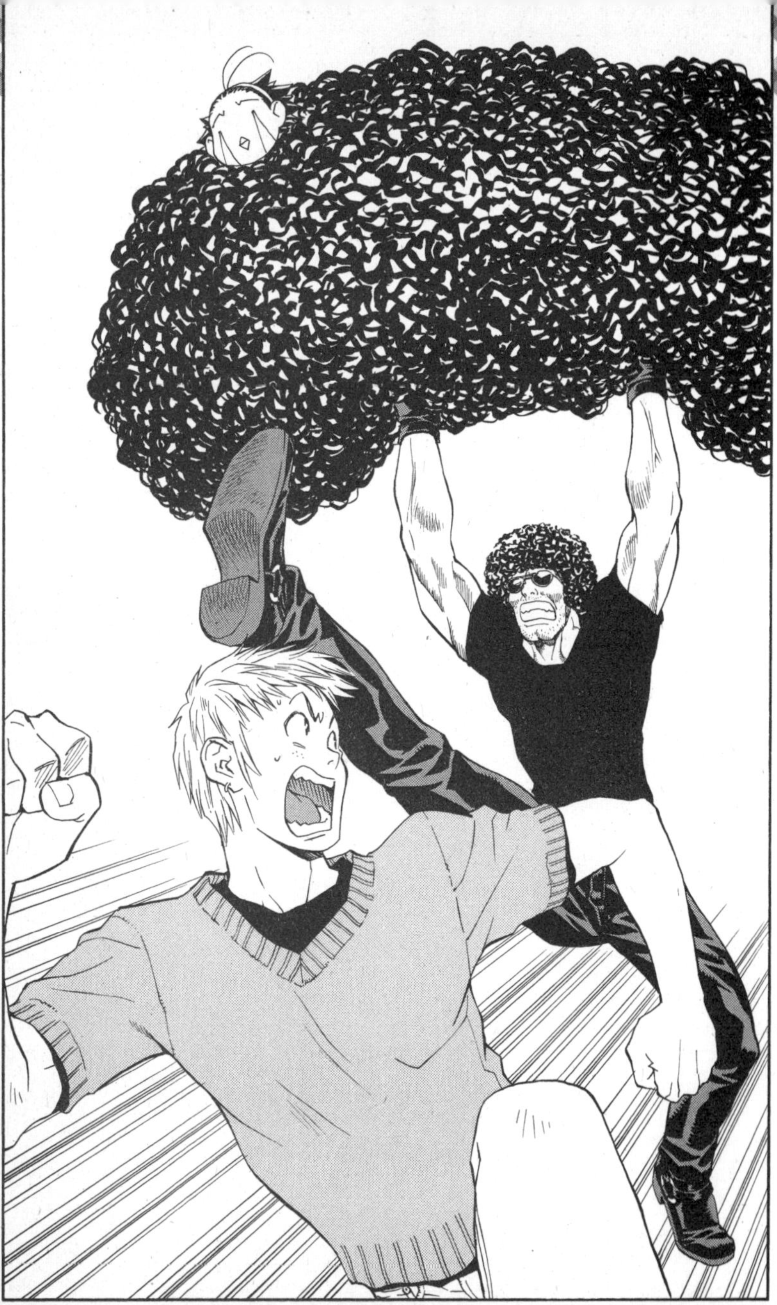

BONUS♥

Public Bathhouse

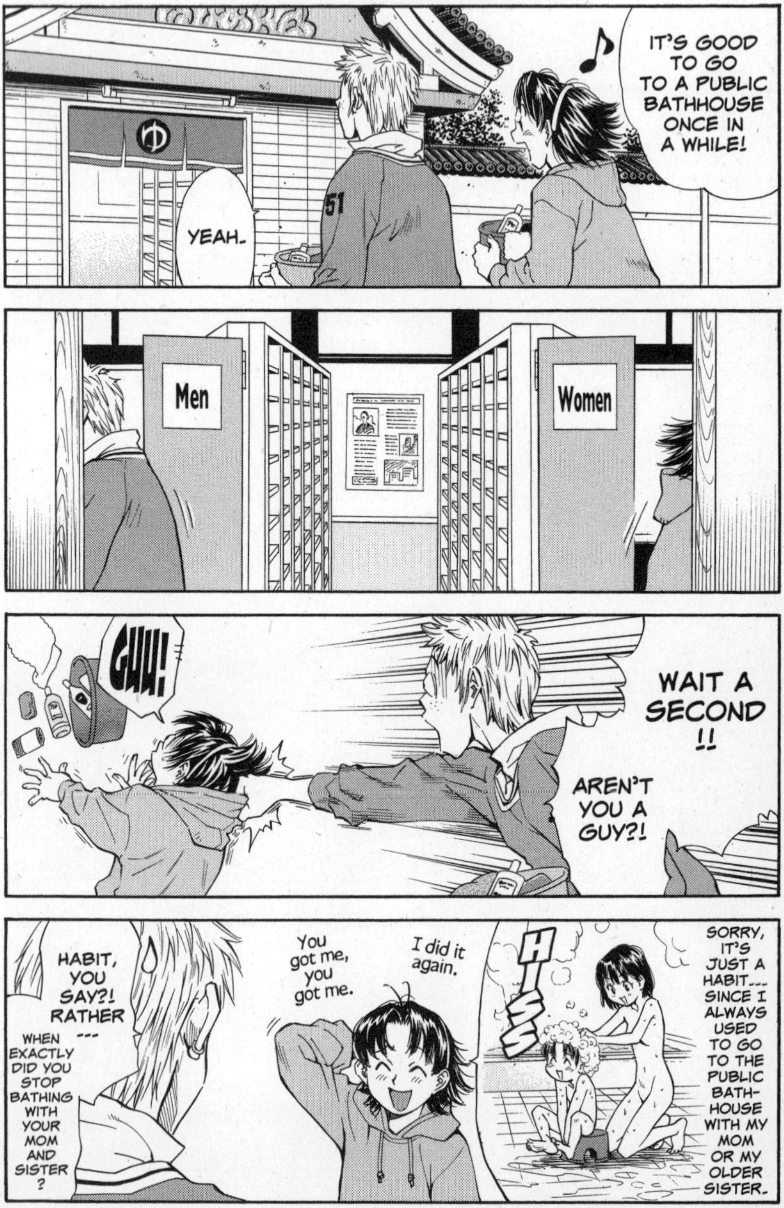
IT'S GOOD TO GO TO A PUBLIC BATHHOUSE ONCE IN A WHILE!
YEAH...
Women
Men
WAIT A SECOND!!
AREN'T YOU A GUY?!
GUU!
SORRY, IT'S JUST A HABIT... SINCE I ALWAYS USED TO GO TO THE PUBLIC BATH-HOUSE WITH MY MOM OR MY OLDER SISTER.
I did it again.
You got me, you got me.
HABIT, YOU SAY?! RATHER---
WHEN EXACTLY DID YOU STOP BATHING WITH YOUR MOM AND SISTER?

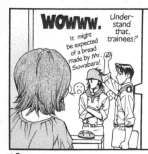

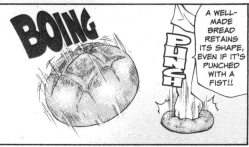

BOING

A WELL-MADE BREAD RETAINS ITS SHAPE, EVEN IF IT'S PUNCHED WITH A FIST!!
PUNCH
BOING
Understand that, trainees?
WOWWW.
It might be expected of a bread made by Mr. Suwabara!
THAT'S AMAZING! MR. SUWABARA'S ROGGENSCHROT!
I'LL BUY TWO!
BOING
BOING
HEY HEY
HEY, KOALA!
DASH
KOALA!!
GRAB
BOIIIING
?

Will we see this in the next episode?!
"Curry Is the House Brand"

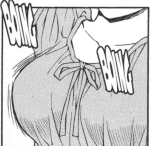

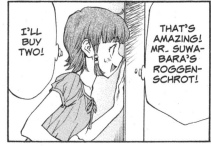

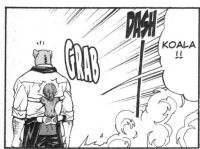

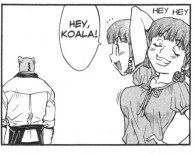

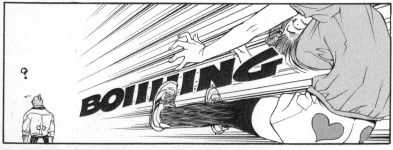

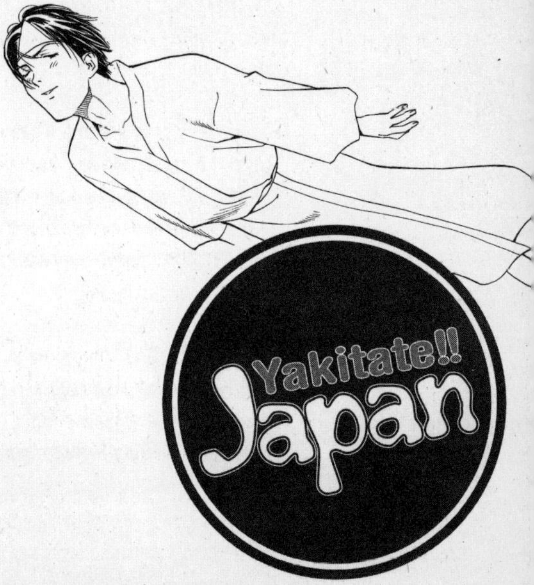

Yakitate!! Japan